Body and Narrative in Contemporary Literatures in German

Herta Müller, Libuše Moníková, and Kerstin Hensel

LYN MARVEN

CLARENDON PRESS · OXFORD

OXFORD
UNIVERSITY PRESS

Great Clarendon Street, Oxford OX2 6DP

Oxford University Press is a department of the University of Oxford.
It furthers the University's objective of excellence in research, scholarship,
and education by publishing worldwide in

Oxford New York

Auckland Cape Town Dar es Salaam Hong Kong Karachi
Kuala Lumpur Madrid Melbourne Mexico City Nairobi
New Delhi Shanghai Taipei Toronto

With offices in

Argentina Austria Brazil Chile Czech Republic France Greece
Guatemala Hungary Italy Japan Poland Portugal Singapore
South Korea Switzerland Thailand Turkey Ukraine Vietnam

Oxford is a registered trade mark of Oxford University Press
in the UK and in certain other countries

Published in the United States
by Oxford University Press Inc., New York

© Lyn Marven 2005

The moral rights of the author have been asserted
Database right Oxford University Press (maker)

First published 2005

All rights reserved. No part of this publication may be reproduced,
stored in a retrieval system, or transmitted, in any form or by any means,
without the prior permission in writing of Oxford University Press,
or as expressly permitted by law, or under terms agreed with the appropriate
reprographics rights organization. Enquiries concerning reproduction
outside the scope of the above should be sent to the Rights Department,
Oxford University Press, at the address above

You must not circulate this book in any other binding or cover
and you must impose the same condition on any acquirer

British Library Cataloguing in Publication Data

Data available

Library of Congress Cataloging in Publication Data

Data available

Typeset by Laserwords Private Limited
Chennai, India

Printed in Great Britain
on acid-free paper by
Biddles Ltd
King's Lynn, Norfolk

ISBN 0-19-927776-1
978-0-19-927776-6

1 3 5 7 9 10 8 6 4 2

**OXFORD MODERN LANGUAGES
AND LITERATURE MONOGRAPHS**

Editorial Committee

C. H. GRIFFIN   E. M. JEFFREYS   A. KAHN
K. M. KOHL   M. L. MCLAUGHLIN
I. W. F. MACLEAN   R. A. G. PEARSON

PREFACE

This book is a revised version of a D.Phil. thesis submitted to the Faculty of Medieval and Modern Languages, Oxford, in 2001. Many thanks are due to colleagues, friends, and family for their help and support then and now. I am indebted to my supervisor, Karen Leeder, for many years of inspiration, ideas, and advice. I am also particularly grateful to Katrin Kohl, Brigid Haines, Ray Ockenden, Jim Reed, Margaret Littler, and Tom Kuhn for reading versions of my work, and for encouragement and feedback; to Jill Hughes at the Taylorian Library; and to Mr Wylie for pointing me in the right direction. Work on my thesis was funded by the AHRB, and I am grateful also to the Modern Languages Faculty for funding for visits to Germany; and to New College, Oxford, and Jesus College, Oxford, for support during my studies and while revising this work. I owe thanks to more friends than I can name here who have helped me in many ways over the years. Finally, I should like to thank my family, for always being there: I dedicate this book to you.

L.M.

CONTENTS

Abbreviations   ix

1. Introduction: 'Daß dies der Osten ist Was im Kopf nicht aufhört'   1
   - Context   11
     - The authors   11
     - Eastern Bloc bodies   16
   - Theory   27
     - Feminist theory and the body   27
     - Feminism   36
     - Trauma, hysteria, and the grotesque   43

2. Herta Müller: 'Das, was von innen kam, angesichts des Äußeren'   53
   - 'Ich hatte das gedruckte schwarze Sprechen in der Haut' (*DT* 76): trauma and the act of writing   54
   - Body   61
     - Dissolution of boundaries   62
     - The alienated body   70
     - State signification   79
   - Narrative   83
     - Textual boundaries   84
     - The fragmentary text   95
     - Collage   103
   - 'Literatur ist doch immer von dort ausgegangen, wo beim Autor die Beschädigung am tiefsten war': conclusion   110

3. Libuše Moníková: 'Ich bin am Ort meines Ursprungs', 'Innen bin ich hohl'   115
   - Hysteria and exile   116
   - Body   122

    'Geringe Anpassung? Ich hinke ja': Francine
       Pallas   123
       Self-representations   129
       Gender/expatriation   143
       Performance   153
       Narrative   156
       Intertextuality   158
       Babel   167
    'Die Literatur ist selbst der Ort, an dem ich mich
    als Schriftstellerin befinde': conclusion   174

4. Kerstin Hensel: 'Wer "draußen" steht, kann
   deutlicher sehen'   180
       The grotesque and irony   181
       Body   188
          Images of the body   189
          Destructive desires: eating and sex   204
          Desire and language   214
       Narrative   217
          Plot: tales of the unexpected   218
          Parody   228
       'Alles, was ich erzähle, ist erfunden': conclusion   240

5. Interchanging Interpretations: Conclusion   244

Bibliography   253

Index   275

ABBREVIATIONS

References to the following texts will be given using the following abbreviated forms. References are to the editions cited; for full publication details see the bibliography. For large groups of citations from a single text, the cipher will be omitted.

HERTA MÜLLER

BF	*Barfüßiger Februar* (Berlin: Rotbuch Taschenbuch, 1990)
DT	*Drückender Tango* (Bucharest: Kriterion, 1984)
FB	*Der Fremde Blick oder Das Leben ist ein Furz in der Laterne* (Göttingen: Wallstein, 1999)
FJ	*Der Fuchs war damals schon der Jäger* (Reinbek bei Hamburg: Rowohlt, 1992)
HD	*Im Haarknoten wohnt eine Dame* (Reinbek bei Hamburg: Rowohlt, 2000)
Ht	*Heute wär ich mir lieber nicht begegnet* (Reinbek bei Hamburg: Rowohlt Taschenbuch [rororo], 1999)
HuS	*Hunger und Seide* (Reinbek bei Hamburg: Rowohlt Taschenbuch [rororo], 1997)
Hz	*Herztier* (Reinbek bei Hamburg: Rowohlt Taschenbuch [rororo], 1996)
IF	*In der Falle* (Göttingen: Wallstein, 1996)
KB	*Eine warme Kartoffel ist ein warmes Bett* (Hamburg: Europäische Verlagsanstalt, 1992)
MFW	*Der Mensch ist ein großer Fasan auf der Welt* (Reinbek bei Hamburg: Rowohlt Taschenbuch [rororo], 1995)
Nd	*Niederungen* (Reinbek bei Hamburg: Rowohlt Taschenbuch [rororo], 1993)
R	*Reisende auf einem Bein* (Berlin: Rotbuch Taschenbuch, 1992)
TS	*Der Teufel sitzt im Spiegel: Wie Wahrnehmung sich erfindet* (Berlin: Rotbuch, 1991)

ABBREVIATIONS

WK   *Der Wächter nimmt seinen Kamm: Vom Weggehen und Ausscheren* (Reinbek bei Hamburg: Rowohlt, 1993)

The Bucharest edition of *Niederungen* (Bucharest: Kriterion, 1982) differs substantially from the Berlin edition; all references to texts from the Bucharest edition will be given in the notes. *Der Wächter nimmt seinen Kamm* is a collection of numbered postcards in a box, and *Im Haarknoten wohnt eine Dame* has no page numbers; references to these two collage texts will be respectively to postcard numbers and first lines.

LIBUŠE MONÍKOVÁ

F   *Die Fassade: M.N.O.P.Q.* (Munich: dtv, 1990)
P   *Pavane für eine verstorbene Infantin* (Munich: dtv, 1988)
PF   *Prager Fenster: Essays* (Munich: Hanser [Edition Akzente], 1994)
S   *Eine Schädigung* (Munich: dtv, 1990)
SAW   *Schloß, Aleph, Wunschtorte: Essays* (Munich: Hanser [Edition Akzente], 1990)
T   *Treibeis* (Munich: dtv, 1997)
Tm   *Der Taumel* (Munich: Hanser, 2000)
VN   *Verklärte Nacht* (Munich: Hanser, 1996)

KERSTIN HENSEL

An   *Angestaut: Aus meinem Sudelbuch* (Halle: Mitteldeutscher Verlag, 1993)
AP   *Auditorium panopticum* (Halle: Mitteldeutscher Verlag, 1991)
G   *Gipshut* (Leipzig: Gustav Kiepenheuer, 1999)
H   *Hallimasch* (Frankfurt am Main: Luchterhand, 1989; Halle: Mitteldeutscher Verlag, 1989)
ImS   *Im Schlauch* (Frankfurt am Main: Suhrkamp, 1993)
Nl   *Neunerlei* (Leipzig: Kiepenheuer, 1997)
TamK   *Tanz am Kanal* (Frankfurt am Main: Suhrkamp Taschenbuch, 1997)
UuK   *Ulriche und Kühleborn* (Stuttgart: Reclam Gutenberg Presse, 1991)

ABBREVIATIONS

Hallimasch was published simultaneously, and in two separate editions, in East and West Germany, by Mitteldeutscher Verlag and Luchterhand respectively. The Mitteldeutscher Verlag edition omits the text 'Hol über, Charon', and contains four texts which do not appear in the Luchterhand version: '1987, wir essen Pizza', 'Der Wasserwalzer', 'Ritter Rosel', and 'Herr Johannes'. The order of the common texts also differs between the two editions. Page references are normally to the Luchterhand edition, except in the case of the four texts which are only in the Mitteldeutscher Verlag edition.

1

INTRODUCTION:
'DASS DIES DER OSTEN IST WAS IM KOPF NICHT AUFHÖRT'

Two substantial developments have affected German literature in the recent past, bringing with them a need to redefine the idea of a national literature in order to recognize the many and varied forms of writing in German and within Germany. The rise to prominence of a multiplicity of 'other' literatures in German has coincided with the demise of the GDR, which was viewed for so long as the source of *the* other German literature. This book considers the relationship between representations of the body and narrative strategies in the work of three women writers from former Eastern Bloc countries who write in German, and whose writing forms part of what one might broadly term 'literatures in German': Herta Müller, born in the Banat, Romania, in 1953; Libuše Moníková (1945–98), born in Prague; and Kerstin Hensel, born 1961 in Karl-Marx-Stadt (Chemnitz), in the GDR. Bringing together these particular three authors highlights their common experience of the repressive socialist regimes of the Eastern Bloc. This is an experience predicated on the state appropriation of the body and its effects inform both the content and the form of the texts I examine.

There is a debate surrounding the definition of literature by migrants and minority speakers of German, with now disputed terms such as 'Gastarbeiterliteratur', 'Ausländerliteratur', and 'MigrantInnenliteratur' betraying the sociological emphasis of many early approaches to the texts.[1] One solution is proposed by Carmine Chiellino with the elastic concept of 'intercultural literature', her preferred term which avoids sociological and West-centric perspectives evident in terms such as 'migrant' or even 'minority literature'. Chiellino includes writers who

---

[1] See Sabine Gross, 'Einleitung: Sprache, Ort, Heimat', *Monatshefte*, 89/4 (1997), 441–51, esp. 442–3; and Carmine Chiellino, in Carmine Chiellino (ed.), *Interkulturelle Literatur: Ein Handbuch* (Stuttgart: J. B. Metzler, 2000), esp. 389–90.

write in languages other than German, or who have returned to their own country, as well as second-generation immigrant writers born in Germany. In this introduction, I refer to literatures in German by immigrant or ethnic German writers, in order to distinguish such writers within Chiellino's much larger grouping.

The emergence and growth in the 1980s and 1990s of other literatures in German has contributed to the need to engage critically with the definition of German literature as well as the way in which it is approached. The fate of literatures by immigrant or ethnic German writers, particularly those from the former Eastern Bloc, is linked to that of GDR literature. Reception of texts by writers from German minorities in other countries (e.g. Romanian-Germans such as Herta Müller) and non-native speakers writing in German (such as Libuše Moníková, whose mother tongue was Czech) has often repeated some of the tendencies which characterized early analyses of GDR literature, whilst also raising specific problems of its own. As was the case with much GDR literature, literary texts by immigrant or ethnic German authors are frequently not analysed primarily as literature.[2] Texts have tended to be viewed as social documents and examined for what they can say about life in another country or, frequently, about the situation of minority German speakers, migrants, or foreigners in Germany. Reception of work by authors from former Eastern Bloc countries, particularly Romanian-German authors, has also been politically motivated, with authors such as Herta Müller taking on the role of a 'politische Instanz' for the West German media.[3]

Reception of Müller's work demonstrates the convergence between perceptions of GDR and literatures by immigrant or ethnic German writers, with her later work being explicitly linked to the GDR. A review in the *Süddeutsche Zeitung* of

---

[2] See Wolfgang Emmerich's criticisms in 'Für eine andere Wahrnehmung der DDR-Literatur: Neue Kontexte, Neue Paradigmen, ein neuer Kanon', in Wolfgang Emmerich, *Die andere deutsche Literatur: Aufsätze zur Literatur der DDR* (Opladen: Westdeutscher Verlag, 1994), 190–207, esp. 193–5; and also the introduction to Wolfgang Emmerich, *Kleine Literaturgeschichte der DDR*, Erweiterte Ausgabe (Leipzig: Kiepenheuer, 1996), esp. 18.

[3] See René Kegelmann, 'An den Grenzen des Nichts, dieser Sprache...': Zur Situation rumäniendeutscher Literatur der achtziger Jahre in der Bundesrepublik Deutschland (Bielefeld: Aisthesis, 1995), 68–9.

Müller's 1989 novel *Reisende auf einem Bein*, which follows a woman from an unnamed land (clearly identifiable as Romania) as she emigrates to West Germany, begins, quoting from the text: ' "Ich habe die Ausreise beantragt. Es ist der letzte Sommer. Ich warte auf den Paß." Ist das ein Absatz aus einem der vielen Zeitungsberichte der vergangenen DDR-Exodus-Monate?'[4] The reference to the more familiar (to the West German audience of both the novel and the review) GDR is symptomatic of a certain trend in the reception of Müller's work. Hannes Krauss gives a critical review of Müller's subsequent novel *Der Fuchs war damals schon der Jäger* (1992), commenting: 'Wenn das Buch trotzdem auf Platz zwei der Südwestfunk-Bestenliste steht, dann liegt das eher am schlechten Gewissen mancher Kritiker, die das prinzipiell Terroristische im Realsozialismus erst nach dessen Ende entdeckt haben.'[5] Critical and popular reception of Müller's work thus both mirrors the earlier tendencies in the reception of GDR literature and also reacts to them. The referential function which literatures in German by immigrant or ethnic German authors perform for Western readers and critics echoes the way in which GDR literature was received for many years: the 'GDR Bonus', the propensity for concentrating on the socio-political aspects of texts to the detriment of their literary aspects and for valuing political views (that is to say, dissidence) above literary worth, appears to have migrated. In this respect, the current rereading and rewriting of GDR literary history to emphasize questions of aesthetic form can point the way in dealing with other literatures in German.

The collapse of the GDR and subsequent German reunification has prompted a reassessment of GDR literature, in the first instance in critical discourse on the subject which had begun before the fall of the Wall and which is now beginning to be reflected in critical practice and literary analysis. Wolfgang Emmerich in 1988 called for an approach to GDR literature and literary historiography which recognized it as

---

[4] Verena Auffermann, 'Gefahr, ins Leere zu stürzen. Westdeutschland, gesehen mit den Umsiedleraugen Herta Müllers', *Süddeutsche Zeitung*, 10 Oct. 1989, Literatur p. v.

[5] Hannes Krauss, 'Jäger-Schnipsel. Herta Müllers Roman *Der Fuchs war damals schon der Jäger*', *Freitag*, 2 Oct. 1992, p. 27.

a 'System widerspruchsvoller, interferierender Bewegungen'.⁶ Recent studies have begun the 'skeptisches, kritisches *rereading*' and rewriting of the literary history of the GDR to this end, examining less well-known authors and proposing methods and objects of analysis which open up new spaces for critical discourse.⁷ This book proposes that this necessary reprivileging of literary devices and form be extended to other literatures in German. It offers a literary approach which combines thematic with formal analysis, examining the relation between representations of the body and narrative strategies in the works of Müller, Moníková, and Hensel through the structures of trauma, hysteria, and the grotesque. This approach is not intended to depoliticize or dehistoricize the texts in question. Instead, I suggest that the focus on the body represents a paradigm which takes account of the specificity of the experience of the repressive Eastern Bloc regimes.

The current meta-discourse on literatures in German by immigrant or ethnic German authors, the critical analysis of reception, and the search for a standpoint from which to read the texts can also inform perspectives on German literatures. Both GDR literature and literatures in German by immigrant or ethnic German writers have been constructed as (West) German literature's other, as exotic and marginal; while this difference may occasionally be viewed positively, the hierarchy underlying the binary opposition is rarely challenged. Leitmotifs in the reception of both Müller and Moníková's work demonstrate negative aspects of the monocultural assumptions of the hegemonic (West) German literature. Reviewers have often alleged incorrect usage of German: their refusal to entertain non-standard forms of German and the desire to erase the marks of a non-native speaker are linked to a desire to exclude difference.⁸

---

⁶ Wolfgang Emmerich, 'Gleichzeitigkeit: Vormoderne, Moderne und Postmoderne in der Literatur der DDR', in Heinz Ludwig Arnold (ed.), *Bestandsaufnahme Gegenwartsliteratur* (Munich: text + kritik, 1988), 193–211, here 194.

⁷ Emmerich, *Kleine Literaturgeschichte der DDR*, 17.

⁸ See, for example, Armin Ayren on *Der Mensch ist ein großer Fasan auf der Welt*, 'Lakonischer Satz, komplexe Welt: Eine Erzählung von Herta Müller', *Stuttgarter Zeitung*, 19 July 1986, p. 50. As these mistakes are only alleged and never cited, it is hard to judge whether they represent incorrect or creative usage. In her acceptance speech for the Chamisso prize, Moníková complains that, were she to repeat some of Arno Schmidt's deliberate grammatical 'mistakes', it would be assumed that

Similarly, an oft-expressed wish on the part of reviewers that both authors would write about Germany (see Müller, *HuS* 30) betrays the attempt to categorize them unambiguously either as German or as non-German writers. However, the acceptance of difference can also reinscribe exclusion. In her introduction to the volume of *Monatshefte* devoted to Müller and Moníková, Sabine Gross argues, for example, that the Chamisso prize (for literature by non-native speakers of German, won in 1991 by Moníková) plays an ambivalent role, functioning as 'Anerkennung verbunden mit Ausgrenzung'.[9] The growing number of collections of literary texts or critical essays dealing solely with other literatures in German, while performing the important function of bringing attention to authors and their work, frequently reproduce exclusion from the norm in a form of critical separatism.

What is needed is a form of recognition of difference (or rather, *différance*) which also contributes to the breaking down and decentring of the hierarchical hegemonic values. The 1996 volume *Schreiben zwischen den Kulturen: Beiträge zur deutschsprachigen Gegenwartsliteratur* represents an important step in this direction; title and subtitle both posit a decentred, non-national, non-ethnocentric literature.[10] Proceeding from a focus on identity within an assumedly multicultural society, the first section consists of essays by a range of authors, who reflect upon their own multiple (or avowedly singular) identities as writers in German. This impulse is countered, however, by a second section of critical analysis, where only 'other' literatures are examined, reducing these to objects once more. The title of Irmgard Ackermann's essay, 'Deutsche ver-fremdet gesehen. Die Darstellung des "Anderen" in der "Ausländerliteratur" ', is emblematic of this implicit ethnocentric perspective, with its hesitant adoption of the term 'other' to designate Germans: the perspective is only apparently decentred. Reading literatures by immigrant or ethnic German writers simply becomes an occasion for self-reflection—an attitude which Emmerich suggests also marked some Western reception of GDR literature.[11]

she simply did not know the language: see 'Ortsbestimmung: Danksagung zum Chamisso-Preis', in *Prager Fenster*, 40–4, esp. 43.

[9] Gross, 'Einleitung', 443.

[10] Paul Michael Lützeler (ed.), *Schreiben zwischen den Kulturen: Beiträge zur deutschsprachigen Gegenwartsliteratur* (Frankfurt am Main: Fischer Taschenbuch, 1996).

[11] See Emmerich, *Kleine Literaturgeschichte der DDR*, 12.

While I have chosen to examine texts by three women writers, I do not consider them primarily as women's writing. Nonetheless, studies of women's writing—and particularly GDR and immigrant or ethnic German woman writers—can provide models of how to approach other literatures in German. Critics dealing with women's writing have been particularly quick to recognize these other literatures, seeing in the position of alterity which they occupy a parallel with women's writing. However, the similarity extends to the fact that women's writing has historically also attracted a great deal of author-based, sociological criticism, and these critics do not always propose new methodologies.[12] Instead, where women's writing is considered as a marginal, or marginalized, aspect of an already marginal literature, these tendencies are sometimes all the more evident.[13] Women's writing has in turn provided a site where GDR and literatures by immigrant or ethnic German writers can be brought together, although when these literatures are viewed as a marginal part of women's writing in general, critics run the risk of privileging the oppression of women over other forms of oppression and at the expense of historical and political specificity. Karen Jankowsky argued in 1993 for a reconfiguration of the canon of GDR women's writing post-reunification, to consider both new authors and different aesthetic forms.[14] One of the questions she proposes as a framework for a new consideration is how work by GDR women writers can offer a way of understanding writers 'whose identities are shaped in moving between different cultures', a function which for

---

[12] See Sigrid Weigel, *Topographien der Geschlechter: Kulturgeschichtliche Studien zur Literatur* (Reinbek: Rowohlt, 1990), 237–40, on the reception of Ingeborg Bachmann, which she sees as emblematic of the treatment of women writers.

[13] For examples of this sociological approach, on GDR literature by women, see Nancy Lukens, 'Der nüchterne Blick: Jüngere DDR-Autorinnen vor und nach der Wende', in Ute Brandes (ed.), *Zwischen gestern und morgen: Schriftstellerinnen der DDR aus amerikanischer Sicht* (Schöneiche bei Berlin: Peter Lang, 1992), 55–68. On minority literature by women, see Irmgard Ackermann, 'German Literature by Foreign Women Writers', in Carol Aisha Blackshine-Belay (ed.), *The Germanic Mosaic: Cultural and Linguistic Diversity in Society* (Westport, Conn.: Greenwood Press, 1994), 243–52.

[14] Karen Jankowsky, 'Canons Crumble Just Like Walls: Discovering the Works of GDR Women Writers', in Friederike Eigler and Peter C. Pfeiffer (eds.), *Cultural Transformations in the New Germany: American and German Perspectives* (Columbia, Mo.: Camden House, 1993), 102–16.

Jankowsky appears to work in one direction only.[15] She gives Müller and Moníková as examples of writers who move between cultures. Despite her introductory remarks, which highlight literary matters, Jankowsky's focus here remains on their presentation of experiences within Germany, that is to say, the sociological content of the texts. (It is perhaps of note that the two texts by Müller and Moníková which Jankowsky references are in fact exceptional in their work for being set in Germany.) She approaches both literatures within a wider context of an international discussion of the position of women in society—a valid issue, but a limited approach where analysis of aesthetic form is concerned.

Feminist theories of embodiment and positionality which inform recent analyses of women's writing are of particular use in analysis of other literatures in German. These theories recognize that the subject is constructed through many different discourses, and reveal the relativity of all subject positions. A later volume edited by Jankowsky with Carla Love, *Other Germanies: Questioning Identity in Women's Literature and Art*, demonstrates this differentiated approach: the volume addresses national identity and history, and also covers West German as well as GDR writers, albeit canonical dissidents with a high profile in the West, Christa Wolf and Monika Maron.[16] The volume acknowledges the non-homogeneous category of women (writers), insisting on 'the intersection of gender politics with issues surrounding ethnicity and constructions of Germanness'.[17] Leslie Adelson's 1993 *Making Bodies, Making History: Feminism and German Identity* provides the most useful model for analysis of writing by women and non-native German speakers based on theories of positionality.[18] Adelson analyses texts by the West German Anne Duden, Iranian-born, naturalized German TORKAN, and Jeanette Lander, an author of Polish-Jewish-American origins (Adelson's hyphens). Adelson's subtle textual analysis focuses on the representation of the body

---

[15] Ibid. 110.
[16] Karen Jankowsky and Carla Love (eds.), *Other Germanies: Questioning Identity in Women's Literature and Art* (Albany, NY: State University of New York Press, 1997).
[17] Ibid. 7.
[18] Leslie Adelson, *Making Bodies, Making History: Feminism and German Identity* (Lincoln: University of Nebraska Press, 1993).

as a site of contested and conflicted identities and examines its construction through and against notions of gender, race, nationality, and history.

This book focuses on representations of the body in texts by writers from the former Eastern Bloc. This combination signals the three authors' common background in countries with similar (although not identical) political systems and therefore also acknowledges the political, social, and cultural specificity of their texts. Furthermore, I posit the concept of trauma as a structure which characterizes the experience and continuing effects of the Eastern Bloc. Chiellino argues that notions of exile, immigration, and expatriation are central to an understanding of intercultural literature;[19] and in an analysis of exile as metaphor and structure in literature, Elisabeth Bronfen describes it as 'das Trauma der Entortung'.[20] Müller recognizes that the collective difference of former Eastern Bloc citizens from West Germans is something that persists in the psyche, despite the collapse of the states themselves:

Ich komme um den Vergleich nicht herum, daß die Leute aus der Ex-DDR im vereinigten Deutschland in einer ähnlichen Situation sind wie ich: Deutsche durch ihre Sprache. Aber auch da keine Westdeutschen. Ausländer in allen anderen Hinsichten der Biographie und Sozialisation. Die Ähnlichkeit mit den Lebensgewohnheiten der Polen, Tschechen, Ungarn, Rumänen ist bei den Menschen aus der Ex-DDR größer als die Ähnlichkeit mit den Lebensgewohnheiten der Westdeutschen. Die Diktaturen in Osteuropa ähnelten sich in den Straßenbildern und Innenräumen. [...] Die Menschen aus der Ex-DDR sind nicht 'Deutsche zweiter Klasse', sondern Westdeutsche an der Oberfläche und innen im Kopf Osteuropäer. (*HuS* 45–6)

This disjunction of outward appearance and internal constructs, between deeds and thoughts, mirrors behaviour under repressive regimes; it is a symptom of trauma. Trauma is a means of conceptualizing the psychological structures which are formed in response to extreme conditions, structures which affect perceptions of the body as well as use of language and the concept of narrative. Structures of trauma are not only represented in

---

[19] See Chiellino, *Interkulturelle Literatur*, 58–60 and 390.
[20] Elisabeth Bronfen, 'Exil in der Literatur: Zwischen Metapher und Realität', *arcadia*, 28/2 (1993), 167–83, here 168.

the imagery and narrative forms employed by Müller, they also underlie the other structures of hysteria and the grotesque employed respectively by Moníková and Hensel. My focus is on images of the body, a motif which has been analysed in studies of both women's writing and other literatures in German. In *Die Stimme der Medusa*, her influential study of women's writing in German first published in 1987, Sigrid Weigel observes that literature has conventionally enforced a dichotomy between women as object and as subject: women's presence has been either as voiceless bodies or as disembodied voices.[21] Whereas the image of the female body is used by male writers as the literary symbol par excellence, women must cast off the marks of their gender—that is, their gendered body—if they themselves are to enter into the literary sphere. The development of women's writing has reacted against this split by linking the delineation of a female subjectivity to the expression of authentic bodily experiences. As Weigel notes, this has led in particular to the representation of the body as suffering: representations of the body as ill or in pain are a reminder of the irreducible physicality of the body which is elided in its use as allegory.[22] While Weigel's analysis is valuable and offers useful theoretical insights, it focuses on writing published in the West, which includes texts by both Moníková and Müller, and largely omits GDR writers, and cannot do justice to the context of the texts from former Eastern Bloc countries. Although the texts I examine are by women writers and do to greater or lesser degrees present the body as suffering, and/or as the locus of female subjectivity, they are by no means exhausted by this definition.

More recently, Leslie Adelson takes a different stance, arguing that bodies in West German literature (not just by women) since the 1970s have functioned less as victims of history or allegories of the nation, but rather as 'heterogeneous sites of contested

---

[21] Sigrid Weigel, *Die Stimme der Medusa*, 2nd edn. (Dülmen-Hiddingsel: tende, 1995), 112.

[22] Weigel also points out that positive representations of the female body are few and far between. One critic who does examine such positive imagery is Beth Linklater, in her study of sexuality in GDR literature, including some texts by Hensel: Beth V. Linklater, *'Und immer zügelloser wird die Lust': Constructions of Sexuality in East German Literatures* (Bern: Peter Lang, 1998).

identities'.[23] Her examination of 'Übergang', a text by Anne Duden which has been taken up by feminist critics, shows how the temptation to universalize the suffering body as an expression of female experience overlooks the historical specificity of the protagonist's multiple identities and, in particular, the more problematic discourse of race. The problems in Duden's text are brought into relief by Adelson's analyses of texts by Iranian-born TORKAN and Polish-Jewish-American Jeanette Lander. Adelson ends her study with a call for analysis of other texts in German which would yield 'insights into the embodied signification of German history'.[24] This book proposes a related analysis, showing how their respective representations of the body situate texts by Müller, Moníková, and Hensel within the cultural discourse and history of the Eastern Bloc countries.

The representation of the body as suffering—as wounded, diseased, or damaged—is, finally, a motif that also characterizes theoretical and literary images of the body in a post-war, and, more pertinently for my work, post-Cold War, historical period of human displacement.[25] The concept of trauma, which structures Müller's texts and is refracted in the figures of hysteria and the grotesque in texts by Moníková and Hensel, highlights representations of the body. Although it is not limited to a post-Cold War context, the idea of trauma places the authors' work within its wider political and historical context. Viewing their texts in this context is not to discount the insights offered by feminist theories of the body, but calls for a continual renegotiation of the relationship between the physical and cultural meanings of the body and the context in which they are represented.

Trauma, hysteria, and the grotesque are all structures which encompass both body and language. Trauma is a response to overwhelming events, and its effects disrupt body images as well as use of language and narrative structures. Hysteria is a psychosomatic disorder, which manifests itself through physical and linguistic mimicry. The grotesque is a literary mode whose force derives from the transgressive body, which also implicates language. Examining texts by Müller, Moníková,

[23] Adelson, *Making Bodies*, 127.   [24] Ibid. 129.
[25] See Karen Remmler, 'Sheltering Battered Bodies in Language: Imprisonment Once More?', in Angelika Bammer (ed.), *Displacements: Cultural Identities in Question* (Bloomington: Indiana University Press, 1994), 216–32, esp. 218–19.

and Hensel through these figures allows me to consider the relation between representations of the body and narrative strategies. The authors are not only concerned with the human body as material reality and discursive construct; they are also explicitly concerned with narrative form. My analysis examines narrative as both 'an account of a series of events, facts, etc., given in order and with the establishing of connections between them' and the 'practice or art of narration or storytelling' (*OED*). I look at linguistic as well as visual elements of the text; plot and the act of storytelling; and intertextuality, quotations, and parody. The narrative strategies that the authors employ subvert and undermine the mode of realism and, in their emphasis on fictionality and textuality, also verge on the postmodern.

In the rest of this Introduction, I introduce the three authors and their works, before offering a reading of the social, political, and cultural context in which they write, focusing on cultural discourses of the body in the Eastern Bloc states. I then set out the theoretical perspectives which provide the framework for this study, beginning with feminist theories of the body and language, and moving on to the individual concepts of trauma, hysteria, and the grotesque and their interrelations.

CONTEXT

The authors

Herta Müller was born in 1953 in Nitzkydorf, a German-speaking village in the Banat, Romania. She studied German and Romanian in Timișoara, and then worked variously as a translator in a factory (until sacked for refusing to collaborate with the *Securitate*, the Romanian secret police) and as a German teacher before being pressured to leave Romania for West Germany, which she did in 1987. Müller's first text, *Niederungen*, a collection of short prose pieces, was published in Romania in 1982, although it had had to be radically modified in order to pass the censors; the manuscript was smuggled to the West and published, under the same title but in different form, by Rotbuch Verlag in 1984. A second publication followed in Romania in 1984 (*Drückender Tango*, which provided some of the material for the 1987 Rotbuch edition, *Barfüßiger Februar*). Müller was forbidden to publish in Romania after 1985. The novel *Der Mensch ist ein großer Fasan auf der Welt*, which Müller wrote while waiting for permission to emigrate, was published in 1986; it shows the gradual decay of a village community as families emigrate to the West. These early works portray the oppressive way of life and values in rural German-speaking communities, frequently from a child's perspective.

The year 1989 saw the publication of *Reisende auf einem Bein*, a novel set in Berlin which is, to date, the closest of all Müller's texts to her own position at the time of writing in time and location. *Reisende* also marks a shift towards 'autofiktional' texts (*IF* 21, Müller's preferred term), with the protagonist Irene resembling Müller herself. The Ceaușescu regime came to a swift and violent end in 1989. Müller's three novels since then—*Der Fuchs war damals schon der Jäger* (1992), *Herztier* (1994), and *Heute wär ich mir lieber nicht begegnet* (1997)—have looked back in time and returned to Romania in increasingly direct depictions of the repression under Ceaușescu and its effects on individuals and their relationships; their protagonists and narrators are particularly close to Müller's experiences.

Aside from her fiction, Müller also produces collages, in the form of a box-set of postcards, *Der Wächter nimmt seinen Kamm: Vom Weggehen und Ausscheren* (1993) and the text *Im Haarknoten wohnt eine Dame* (2000), which take up themes, structures, and images from her prose work. Her substantial oeuvre also encompasses poetological writing (*Der Teufel sitzt im Spiegel: Wie Wahrnehmung sich erfindet*, 1991, which also contains several early collages), essays on literature and dictatorships (the most significant are *In der Falle*, 1996, and *Der Fremde Blick, oder: Das Leben ist ein Furz in der Laterne*, 1999), and journalistic pieces on Romania and victims of other repressive regimes, published in several major German newspapers and in the collections *Eine warme Kartoffel ist ein warmes Bett* (1992), *Hunger und Seide* (1995), and *Der König verneigt sich und tötet* (2003). Müller has won a number of prestigious prizes, one of which, the 1998 Dublin-IMPAC prize for literature in translation (for *The Land of Green Plums*, the English translation of *Herztier*), has brought her to a wider, international audience.

Libuše Moníková was born in Prague in 1945 and died in Berlin in 1998. She studied German and English before emigrating to West Germany, under pressure from the regime, in 1971. She taught at the universities of Bremen and Kassel before turning to writing as a full-time career. Her first text, *Eine Schädigung*, was published in 1981, some time after Moníková had begun writing it: she began the text in Czech, but only completed it after switching to German, the language in which she continued to write. Moníková claimed that a further delay in publication was due to her refusal to adopt a German pseudonym (*PF* 43). Czechoslovakia, and more precisely Prague, are the focus, if not always the setting, for Moníková's texts: *Eine Schädigung*, which deals with the aftermath of a rape, is set in Prague (clearly identifiable, although never named). The novels *Pavane für eine verstorbene Infantin* (1983) and *Treibeis* (1992) feature expatriate Czechs as their protagonists, in the former a university lecturer in Germany, who takes to a wheelchair, in the latter a resistance fighter in the Second World War and a young stuntwoman; both draw on Czech history and historical figures. The narrator of *Verklärte Nacht* (1996), a dancer and choreographer, is also an expatriate, who returns to Prague after a long absence just as the Czech and Slovak nations split. The unfinished, posthumously published *Der Taumel* (2000) portrays an epileptic artist in the period of 'normalization' after the Prague Spring. *Die Fassade* (1987), in many ways atypical of Moníková's work, is set in Czechoslovakia and Russia. This picaresque novel following the adventures of a group of male artists is Moníková's most widely received work, and has been translated into eleven languages.

In addition, Moníková published a collection of parodic plays, *Unter Menschenfressern* (1990), which, as drama, largely fall outside the scope of this study. She also wrote essays on literary topics (especially Kafka and Bores) as well as on historical and political issues, which are published in the collections *Schloß, Aleph, Wunschtorte* (1990) and *Prager Fenster* (1994). Moníková was awarded several literary prizes, most notably the Chamisso prize in 1991, which she accepted with some reservations about this recognition and confirmation of her outsider status as a non-native speaker writing in German (her acceptance speech is published in *Prager Fenster*).

Kerstin Hensel was born in Karl-Marx-Stadt (Chemnitz) in the GDR in 1961, and trained and worked as a nurse while she began to write; and she currently teaches at the Berliner Hochschule für Schauspielkunst. Her first two publications were collections of poetry, and her oeuvre also includes collaborations with graphic artists, works for the stage, opera libretti, radio plays, and film, but in this study I focus on her prose texts. *Hallimasch,* a collection of short stories, was published simultaneously (although in slightly different forms) in East and West Germany in 1989. It portrays eccentric, dispossessed characters in tales ranging in style and historical setting. *Ulriche und Kühleborn* (1990), a limited edition, is a version of the Undine myth, written against Ingeborg Bachmann's 'Undine geht'. *Auditorium panopticum* (1991) is a hyperbolic montage novel set around the time of the *Wende* and featuring a range of literary parodies. Subsequent texts have gradually looked back in time through GDR history: *Im Schlauch* (1993) is a bleak depiction of small-town GDR centring on a runaway teenager. *Tanz am Kanal* (1994), the text which has attracted the most interest, is a two-level narrative dealing with the GDR and post-*Wende* East Germany, told by a homeless writer. Hensel has also published many short texts in newspapers and journals, and a second collection of short stories, *Neunerlei,* in 1997, including some from as early as 1987. The novel *Gipshut* (1999) follows several characters through different eras of the GDR, and the recent *Im Spinnhaus* (2003) is an anecdotal, fictional history of an area of rural Saxony, covering several centuries. Hensel has won several literary prizes, but her work has yet to find a wider, non-German-speaking audience.

There is increasing critical interest in the work of all three authors, consonant with the shift in paradigms in German studies outlined above, which has led to a growing body of work on their texts. This book is the first to bring these three authors together, and the focus on the relation between representations of the body and narrative strategies through the figures of trauma, hysteria, and the grotesque offers new perspectives on their work.

Early articles on Müller, such as those in Norbert Otto Eke's 1991 volume, *Die erfundene Wahrnehmung,* tended toward the apolitical, reading Müller's work in relation to philosophical concepts or literary tropes (such as Claudia Becker's analysis of 'Niederungen' through E. T. A. Hoffmann's 'Serapiontisches Prinzip') which isolate Müller's work from its context.[26] Only recently have individual critics and articles begun to offer a broader perspective, and to consider the relation between the political and the aesthetic in Müller's work in response to the shift in focus evident in the texts published since 1989. This study contends that Müller's early texts must be read in the light of the concerns of more recent texts; to this end, it follows the narrative of trauma which structures, and is increasingly directly articulated in, Müller's work. In this, it takes a lead from Brigid Haines's recent work which demonstrates that traces of trauma are already present in *Reisende*.[27] I show that these structures can be traced back to Müller's first texts. By focusing on the physical aspects of trauma, this work also contributes to a recontextualization of the articles in Eke's volume which begin to analyse the representation of the body in Müller's early work.

Moníková's most widely commented theme is her exploration of Czech history and identity, and this has been linked with her representations of the body: Ulrike Vedder and Helga Braunbeck both emphasize physical embodiment and the body as an image.[28] Although Braunbeck's analysis of the 'body of the nation' raises the possibility of play-acting, she nonetheless insists on the authenticity of the body within Moníková's texts. I argue that the representation of the body in Moníková's work is more complex and less natural, deriving instead from the performative and imitative tendencies of the hysteric. In *Die*

[26] Norbert Otto Eke (ed.), *Die erfundene Wahrnehmung: Annäherung an Herta Müller* (Paderborn: Igel, 1991).
[27] Brigid Haines, 'The Alien Gaze: The Traces of Trauma in Herta Müller's Berlin Novel *Traveling on One Leg*', paper given at EPOCC (Centre for Interdisciplinary Research in European/Post-colonial Cultures) conference on 'Migrations and Minorities', 26 May 2000, Manchester University. Published in revised form as Brigid Haines, '"The Unforgettable Forgotten": The Traces of Trauma in Herta Müller's *Reisende auf einem Bein*', *German Life and Letters*, 55/3 (2002), 266–81.
[28] Ulrike Vedder, 'Die Intensität des Polarsommers: Zu Libuše Moníkovás Roman *Treibeis*', *Frauen in der Literaturwissenschaft Rundbrief*, 41 (1994) ('Osteuropa'), 15–17; '"Mit schiefem Mund auch Heimat"—Heimat und Nation in Libuše Moníkovás Texten', *Monatshefte*, 89/4 (1997), 477–88; '"Ist es überhaupt noch mein Prag?" Sprache der Erinnerung in der Literatur Libuše Moníkovás', in Helga Abret and Ilse Nagelschmidt (eds.), *Zwischen Distanz und Nähe: Eine Autorinnengeneration in den 80er Jahren* (Bern: Peter Lang, 1998), 7–27. Helga G. Braunbeck, 'The Body of the Nation: The Texts of Libuše Moníková', *Monatshefte*, 89/4 (1997), 489–506.

Stimme der Medusa, Sigrid Weigel implicitly links the body images in Moníková's first two texts with a form of 'Körper-Sprache' which is based on Luce Irigaray's analysis of the hysteric.[29] I take up the notion of hysteria, examining it in relation to both imagery and narrative strategies. These strategies in turn open out onto many further aspects of Moníková's work.[30] The emphasis on a lack of authenticity is something this study shares with Antje Mansbrügge's recent monograph, the first on Moníková, which stresses the constructedness and non-essential nature of the idea of the 'author' in relation to Moníková herself as well as her first-person narrators.[31]

Both images of the body and the notion of the grotesque feature independently in criticism of Kerstin Hensel's texts: it is striking how frequently the adjective 'grotesk' is applied to Hensel's work, but critics have not related her texts to the literary tradition of the grotesque, nor to its corporeal manifestations. In *Papierboot*, Birgit Dahlke provides the most substantial analysis of Hensel's texts to date; her analysis offers one paradigm of a relation between representations of the body and narrative strategies, focusing on the way in which each is characterized by the breaking or subverting of conventional gender roles.[32] The shattering of expectations is a key aspect of the grotesque. This study introduces the specific structure of the grotesque, and considers how it links representations of the body and narrative form.

Eastern Bloc bodies

Texts are produced within specific situations, and authors' experiences inevitably determine their writing. The following

[29] Weigel, *Die Stimme der Medusa*, 120–3.
[30] Many of the contributions to Brigid Haines and Lyn Marven (eds.), *Libuše Moníková: In memoriam* (Amsterdam: Rodopi, forthcoming 2005) deal in detail with aspects—especially humour and film—which my study touches upon; as my reading of Moníková's work through hysteria gives a different, though not necessarily incompatible, view of these aspects, I have indicated where they are taken up in this forthcoming volume. As the volume is, at the time of writing, in the stages of editing, it has however not been possible to give full page references to individual articles.
[31] Antje Mansbrügge, *Autorkategorie und Gedächtnis: Lektüren zu Libuše Moníková* (Würzburg: Königshausen & Neumann, 2002).
[32] Birgit Dahlke, *Papierboot: Autorinnen aus der DDR — inoffiziell publiziert* (Würzburg: Königshausen & Neumann, 1997).

section elaborates the status of bodies in Romania, Czechoslovakia, and the GDR as it can be traced in the texts of Müller, Moníková, and Hensel. My aim is not to suggest that literature merely reflects 'reality' nor that these texts represent a form of authentic realism, but neither are literary texts conceived and produced in isolation from their context. I concur with David Bathrick's emphasis on discourse, which means that 'the problems of language and representation force one to rethink the traditional dualisms of text and context, ideology and reality, dominant and subversive works of literature as a network of textual relationships'.[33] In this respect, representations of the body in texts by Müller, Moníková, and Hensel participate in the discourse of the body in the Eastern Bloc states, within which these texts were constructed and which they in turn construct.

Both fictional and non-fiction writings by Herta Müller, Libuše Moníková, and Kerstin Hensel provide evidence of the many ways in which bodies participated and were implicated in political discourse and narratives of the state in the three Eastern Bloc countries, Romania, Czechoslovakia, and the GDR. Although the exact nature of the regimes in the three countries differed, and differed over time within the regimes themselves, they nonetheless resembled each other in controlling the body as an indirect way of controlling the mind of the individual. The struggle for social control over individuals is played out on the body, a literal fact in the totalitarian socialist states of the former Eastern Bloc, where the ideological transition 'vom Ich zum Wir' became the physical incorporation of the individual by the state. Regulation of individuals, their compliance and obedience, was enforced by the regulation of the body, through a whole range of human rights abuses which can be abstracted from the works of the three authors. The regimes considered the individual body to be symbolic of the state and its values; and they relied on physical manipulation of bodies as a means of control and enforcement, which was carried out by the respective secret police forces and also by the state medical authorities. In practice, these two forms of appropriation—symbolic and physical—were never entirely separate; the

---

[33] David Bathrick, *The Powers of Speech: The Politics of Culture in the GDR* (Lincoln: University of Nebraska Press, 1995), 15.

body's physical presence and its semiotic function cannot be isolated the one from the other.

The bodies the authors invoke in their texts are viewed as the property of the state, they are mere physical objects put at its disposal. In its most extreme form, this can be seen in the interrogations and torture which both Müller and Moníková portray, the former increasingly directly in the novels written after 1989, the latter in the opening chapter of *Der Taumel*; Müller also discusses deaths caused by the *Securitate*, the Romanian secret police. Abortion laws (treated by Müller in both literary texts in *Barfüßiger Februar* and journalistic essays in *Hunger und Seide*) and forced medical intervention (the response to Gabriele's rape in Hensel's *Tanz am Kanal*) also testify to the extent to which bodies, and specifically women's bodies, were physically controlled by the state and implicated in upholding its self-image or even its continued existence. The body also participated symbolically in state discourse, as in many other communist regimes, through forms of sport (discussed by all three authors), where the individual body became a sign of the nation.

The body's status as symbolic representation of the nation ultimately also entailed physical manipulation and abuse. Even when an individual defied the state by removing his body from its power and wilfully disposing of it in a symbolic gesture—I am thinking here of Jan Palach's self-immolation, referred to frequently by Moníková, and to which I will return—the state nonetheless reaffirmed its physical control of both body and image. It is in the context of these images of the physical incorporation of the individual into the state that the representations of the body in the work of Müller, Moníková, and Hensel must be seen. The three writers reassert their authority over the body by authoring other representations of the body, ones which lay bare the state's symbolic discourse and which counter, undermine, or subvert it. Images of the body within their texts challenge the body discourse of the hegemonic power—the totalitarian state—by making its effects visible (Müller's representations of trauma), by using the body to act out discontent (Moníková's hysteria), or by representing the body as uncontrollable and disruptive of cultural signification (Hensel's grotesque). In all three cases, the body remains the site on which this conflict is staged. As Ellen Berry points out in the introduction to a study of the body politic in Eastern European countries,

issues of gender and sexuality which have preoccupied Western scholars have, until quite recently, largely been ignored among scholars of state socialist countries both in this country and in the second world, a de-emphasis that replicates the insistent erasure of the body, sexuality, and gender relations as topics of public discourse in these cultures.[34]

The focus on the body in the work of all three authors acts as a protest against the erasure of bodies from the history of the states in question.

The ways in which the body was physically and symbolically appropriated by the state in each of the three countries deserve closer attention, as they form the discursive field in which the texts participate and relate to the wider structures which inform the texts by Müller, Moníková, and Hensel. Müller's work, in both her journalistic essays and her prose writing, details the instrumentalization of the body by the Romanian state apparatus in three main (not unconnected) areas: in the treatment of dissidents, of women, and in sport. Violence and interrogations established the *Securitate* as the ultimate power over the body.[35] Far from attempting to force perceived dissidents to conform, the *Securitate* simply denied, even obliterated their physical presence. 'Accidents' were arranged to get rid of those who spoke out:

Und es gab sie im Land, diese Toten: Streikanführer aus dem Schiltal, denen Ceauşescu persönlich Straffreiheit versprochen hatte, starben bei Verkehrsunfällen.

Und es gab Fensterstürze, Erhängte und Ertrunkene und Vergiftete gab es. Angeblich Suizide. Immer ohne Obduktion schnell ins Grab gelegt. (*HuS* 98)

The suspicious deaths in *Herztier* are among the list here. Even the bodies of those who tried to escape across the border were disposed of (*FJ* 245); the individual was reduced to a body which could be controlled and, potentially, eliminated.

---

[34] *Genders*, 22 (1995) (*Postcommunism and the Body Politic*), 2–3. See also Nanette Funk and Magda Mueller (eds.), *Gender Politics and Post-Communism: Reflections from Eastern Europe and the Former Soviet Union* (New York: Routledge, 1993).
[35] See Dennis Deletant's account of the function of the secret police, Dennis Deletant, *Ceauşescu and the Securitate: Coercion and Dissent in Romania, 1965–1989* (London: C. Hurst & Co., 1995).

Women's bodies were subject to particular objectification, being reduced in law to their ability to bear children. As Müller explains in her essay 'Hunger und Seide: Männer und Frauen im Alltag' (in *Hunger und Seide*), state regulations demanded that all women have five children, and abortions and contraception were outlawed in 1966; compulsory gynaecological examinations were introduced to ensure women did not induce abortions themselves.[36] In 1986, Ceauşescu himself declared the foetus to be the 'socialist property of the whole society', a significant formulation which suggests that the objectification of the individual began even before birth.[37] Childbirth was considered a national industry: in the eyes of the state, women were no better than 'Gebärmaschinen' (*HuS* 78), mere 'raw material in the achievement of some nebulous "national goals"'[38] of sustaining population growth, necessary for the programme of industrialization or, later, of producing orphans which could be sold for hard Western currency (*HuS* 81). Müller's texts also portray the sexual exploitation of women, in enforced prostitution (for passports, in *Fasan*, in the workplace, in *Fuchs*) and in the sexualized forms of coercion employed by the *Securitate* (*Herztier*). State control over the body and its meaning, even in the private sphere and even its interior spaces, was absolute.

The third area in which the Romanian state instrumentalized bodies was in the international arena of sport, which links the Eastern Bloc communist countries. Referring to West German sports personalities, in the essay 'Und noch erschrickt unser Herz', Müller writes,

Es bleibt ein großer Freiraum für sie offen: denn das *Land* drückt sie in keinen Sieg, und kein Verlieren ängstigt sie vor dem *Staat*. Das unterscheidet sie von Sportlern, die aus Diktaturen kommen, die sich, im *pseudopolitischen* Auftrag, und sogar unter *realpolizeilicher* Aufsicht,

---

[36] Cf. Martyn Rady, *Romania in Turmoil: A Contemporary History* (London: IB Tauris & Co., 1992), 44–5. Symptomatic of the repression of bodies (and particularly women's bodies) in history in general, and also of the way in which Western historians consciously or unconsciously reproduce the values of the country they examine, Rady skates over this 'most inhuman' policy in a scant six sentences—only four more than his description of a similar measure of gynaecological examinations for cows (p. 63). See also Doina Pasca Harsanyi, 'Women in Romania', in Funk and Mueller (eds.), *Gender Politics*, 39–52, for a more detailed account.

[37] Quoted by Harsanyi, in Funk and Mueller (eds.), *Gender Politics*, 46.

[38] Ibid.

schinden. Ihre Körper sind verstaatlicht. In ihren Sportlern züchtet jede Diktatur Menschen zum Siegen, Soldaten auf außenpolitischem Feld. So wird jedes Verlieren als ein mißlungener staatlicher Auftrag geschmäht und jeder Sieg als gelungener staatlicher Auftrag gefeiert, also politisch mißbraucht. So war es in Rumänien, so war es in der DDR. (*HuS* 20)

This exploitation of the physical body by the state initially operates on a symbolic level, with the individual body functioning as a metonymic representation of the communist state in a symbolic battle for ideological influence in the world.[39] But it also entails physical and indeed sexual exploitation, as Müller alleges in the case of the world-renowned gymnast Nadja Comăneci: she 'ließ [...] sich vom jüngsten Sohn des Diktators ins Bett ziehen, um draußen in der Welt auf dem Schwebebalken zu stehen. [...] Eine Siegerin wurde sie in den fremden Stadien—doch im eigenen Land blieb sie eine Untertanin' (*HuS* 21). Although Comăneci's discipline required complete control over her own body and its movements, and posits a body-subject, in Romania her status was as a body-object, both as an individual under the regime and, further, as a woman.[40]

The Ceaușescu regime appropriated bodies, making use of their physical capabilities to further real or ideological national aims. At the same time, the body as physical entity was suppressed, through violence or through cultural negation. Enduring peasant values regarding the intrinsic sinfulness of the physical self (in particular, expressions of beauty and female sexuality) combined with communist policy to deny the experience of the body.[41] One such example is the systematic falsification of weather reports, intended to stop people using precious electricity to heat their houses; another the promotion of physically impossible norms for workers. Interestingly, Moníková writes about Romania, commenting on these two political deceptions, that 'die Haut durfte sich nicht erinnern' and 'ihr Körper sollte

---

[39] Cf. James Riordan, 'The Impact of Communism on Sport', in James Riordan and Arnd Krüger (eds.), *The International Politics of Sport in the Twentieth Century* (London: E & FN Spon, 1999), 48–66, esp. 56–7.
[40] For theoretical perspectives on women's problematic position within sport, see Annette Müller, 'Women in Sport and Society', in Riordan and Krüger (eds.), *International Politics of Sport*, 121–49.
[41] See Harsanyi, in Funk and Mueller (eds.), *Gender Politics*, esp. 47–9.

vergessen, wo seine Grenzen liegen', phrases which have considerable resonance for Müller's representations of the body.[42] In such a context, simply conceptualizing the body as independent of the state transforms it into a de facto site of resistance: the voice of the cynical dissident in 'Mein Herz fliegt durch die Wange' declares, '[u]nd meine linke Herzkammer hab ich nicht angemeldet' (*BF* 94). Although this is an act which has no real effect, it represents the level on which resistance can be pursued: it is an individual, notional, private act. Müller's emphasis on the body as a physical presence is a political act; her texts foreground the body and the ineluctable embodiedness of the individual subject. This re-membering of the body is linked to memory. While Müller's texts narrate the traumatically induced distance from the body which the protagonists experience, it is the presence of the body within the texts which provides their impact.

Moníková returns frequently in her writing to two very different subjects which together illustrate a disturbing coupling of the physical and the symbolic in the Czechoslovak state: the Spartakiadas and Jan Palach's self-immolation. The Spartakiadas were festivals of physical culture which aimed at mass participation. Associated with anniversaries of national significance, they combined art and exercise in a display which Vladimir Kostka, one-time chairman of a government committee on sport, described as 'symbolically expressing popular aspirations in physical culture'; the events were 'simultaneously a spontaneous manifestation of the political unity of our nation and peoples'.[43] Clearly intended as a form of national propaganda, the Spartakiadas enacted the subsumption of the individual in the state. In the centrepiece display, individual bodies were incorporated within a larger picture. The narrator of *Verklärte Nacht*, Leonora Marty, gives an account of a Spartakiada, focusing not on the giant pictures produced by the hordes of participants, but on the individual body which is ignored and suppressed by the state. She emphasizes the corporeal and

---

[42] Libuše Moníková, 'Dies habe ich in den Felsen geritzt und jenes in die Mauer', *Der Literatur-Bote*, 6/23 (1991), 10–14, here 13.

[43] Vladimir Kostka in James Riordan (ed.), *Sport under Communism: The USSR, Czechoslovakia, the GDR, China, Cuba* (London: C. Hurst & Co., 1978), 55–66, here 62.

human aspects of the spectacle, bringing to light imperfections and wrong notes in the choreography, invisible to the stadium audience. Descriptions of the physical effects of the exertion on the children involved ('Heulkrämpfe, Durchfall, Sonnenstich, Durst', *VN* 9) and the real dangers of the soldiers' acrobatic programme—'Es starben während des Jahres mehrere beim Training, eine Unzahl wurde verletzt, falsch aufgefangen' (*VN* 13)—reinstate the body. As well as highlighting the elided physical nature of the event, Moníková signals the slippage from symbolic to real expending of bodies for national aims. Leonora's humorous, human account forms a counterpart to the official pictures, rapturously received when shown on Czech television many years later.

The horrific image of Jan Palach's self-immolation in January 1969, following the invasion of Czechoslovakia by Warsaw Pact troops, is a recurring motif in Moníková's work. It is an emblem of the way in which the body's semiotic function is inseparable from its physicality. As Brigid Haines argues, Palach's expending of his own body was intended as a protest at the passivity of the Czechoslovak people as much as at the USSR and the invasion itself.[44] The form of Palach's protest acts out this perceived submission: the self-immolation is shocking because it dramatically stages the body as the willing object (rather than agent) of pain and, ultimately, death. Palach renounces his subjectivity in order to become all body, all object. Moníková emphasizes this paradoxical position in her essay 'die lebenden Fackeln', a formulation which points to the duality of the image—and is echoed in the title, 'lebende Bilder', under which the first chapter of *Verklärte Nacht*, which deals with the Spartakiada, appeared in *Neue deutsche Literatur*.[45] Moníková quotes Palach as declaring 'Ich bin kein Selbstmörder' (*PF* 104), which can be understood not only as a plea to recognize the political motivation behind his act, but also as his having adopted and acted out the position of object. Palach's body functions as a metaphor, but the impact of this metaphor derives from the body's corporeality. Reduced to a physical object—a corpse—the body's

---

[44] Brigid Haines, ' "New Places from Which to Write Histories of Peoples": Power and the Personal in the Novels of Libuše Moníková', *German Life and Letters*, 49/4 (1996), 501–12, here 503.

[45] Libuše Moníková, 'Lebende Bilder', *Neue deutsche Literatur*, 44/3 (1996), 82–7.

signification is no less powerful: the Czechoslovak authorities recognized this fact, and removed Palach's grave, the final physical trace of his body. It later emerged that he had been cremated, further verifying Palach's own statement: in doing so, the authorities identified with, indeed re-enacted, the position of murderer. 'Einen Verbrannten noch einmal zu verbrennen—das Regime konnte sich kaum mehr entblößen' (*PF* 112), Moníková remarks.

Representations of the body in Moníková's fiction derive two tendencies from the images of Palach and the Spartakiada: an emphasis on physicality, the sheer unpredictability of the body, its imperfections and its functions; and a concern with the body's semiotic function. The bodies stage other connections between the symbolic and the physical which operate on different levels of the text, ranging from allegory to choreography. The most insistent of these is the hysteria which structures Moníková's texts, and which is a bodily protest and symbolic expression of discontent.

The GDR is characterized by Hensel as controlling every aspect of the body, albeit in ways which are less immediately violent than in Romania and Czechoslovakia. One striking image of the state's control over the bodies of individuals is to be found in the GDR tale *Tanz am Kanal*, where it is literally inscribed on the body in a form of mutilation. When the young narrator Gabriele reports being raped and slashed with a knife, the police dismiss her account. Instead, they claim that she inflicted the wound herself, denying Gabriele's experience and the physical evidence of the trauma she has suffered; by denying her physicality they also deny her subjectivity. Gabriele's relation to her own body is a political one: her notional crime is at the same time 'Selbstverstümmelung' and 'Staatsverleumdung' (*TamK* 70). Where the body is considered to be a metonymic representation of the state, self-mutilation is an attack on public property. The police force Gabriele's surgeon father to cover the scar with a skin graft—thus undoing the deed and exculpating the state, but also repeating the mutilation it was intended to cover, an act which echoes the Czech authorities' treatment of Palach's body. The state is concerned solely with appearances and surfaces: the charge of rape is entirely suppressed with the removal of the physical evidence, perhaps in a tacit acceptance that rape, too, is an attempt to subordinate the unruly female body. It possesses the power to determine the signification of the body, and can also enforce this signification upon the body.

One of the most frequent images of state appropriation of the body in Hensel's work is sport. Her texts reflect a real emphasis on physical activity and mass participation in sport by the GDR.[46] As a state-regulated leisure activity, sport was intended to foster socialist values within workers and promote a militaristic emphasis on physical ability; on an elite level, it also furthered the struggle for ideological influence in the world. These national aims underlie the physical control which Hensel's texts illustrate. Writing about sport in GDR literature, Marion Brandt argues that sport 'versinnbildlichte [...] die Unterdrückungsmechanismen des DDR-Sozialismus'.[47] Among the many images of sport in Hensel's work, the figure of 'Rollschuhläuferin' Ramona Hufschmid in *Auditorium panopticum* stands out, not least because she is a satirical image of popular, high-profile ice skaters such as Katarina Witt. The character illustrates how symbolic manipulation becomes physical exploitation and, further, the regulation of sexuality and gender. Ramona is considered an envoy of the state, the 'große[s] Glück der Nation' (*AP* 142), although she eventually defects to 'Chinesische Schweiz'. In becoming a national figure, she relinquishes control over her own body, submitting to training, a strict diet, and 'Verbote' (*AP* 142–3).

As a representative of the nation, Ramona's body is public property (seen on television, recognized by all) and is expected to conform to ideological norms which also extend to gender. That Hensel's sporting figures are mostly women is no coincidence. In 'Grus', it is Uschka, who gives birth there, who is the winner in the Sportfest: motherhood is the ultimate sporting achievement for women. Ramona's sexuality is regulated by the 'Verbot, das unter dem Röckchen anfing, des Röckchens

---

[46] See David Childs, a rather dated and partial analysis, which is nonetheless revealing about the state's aims if not about the reality, in Riordan (ed.), *Sport under Communism*, 67–101.

[47] Marion Brandt, 'Turnvater Unser: Zur Sportthematik in ausgewählten literarischen Texten', in Helga Grubitzsch, Eva Kaufmann, and Hannelore Scholz (eds.), *'Ich will meine Trauer nicht leugnen und nicht meine Hoffnung': Veränderungen kultureller Selbstwahrnehmungen von ostdeutschen und osteuropäischen Frauen nach 1989* (Bochum: D. Winckler, 1994), 81–93, here 85.

schändliche Eigenschaft, Kitzel zu erzeugen' (*AP* 143). At the same time, her body is offered up to the masses for their gratification, which in the case of male viewers is unashamedly sexual. Inclusion in society is dependent on putting one's body at the disposal of the state, something which extends to sexual availability (or abstinence) in the case of women, whose bodies are viewed as inherently sexualized. Recent revelations concerning the widespread doping of athletes in the GDR (frequently without their knowledge) confirm the extent to which their bodies were physically appropriated in the name of the state. The doping of GDR female athletes also affected gender: one of the more extreme side effects was the development of male physical attributes; in one case, this led to a sex change.[48]

Sporting prowess entails the appropriation of bodies: for women, this takes a sexual form; for men, the ultimate sporting achievement is the 'Sport fürs Vaterland' (*H* 113): war. Hensel has suggested that football grounds are the last refuge of the 'Nationalismus und Massenfanatismus' associated with fascism.[49] To send people out to war, it is first necessary to stop seeing them as individual human beings; this is the ultimate consequence of the tendency to view bodies as abstract signifying objects. In *Topographien der Geschlechter*, her work on gender-specific uses of the body as metaphor, Sigrid Weigel remarks, 'es [ist] vielmehr notwendig, den Zusammenhang zwischen dem Vernichten realer Leiber (wie im Faschismus) und der verbreiteten Funktionalisierung von Körpern als Zeichen bzw. der Entleibung von Symbolisierungsvorgängen zu untersuchen'.[50] In Hensel's work, the body is portrayed as grotesque, on the one hand as a means of representing the grotesque treatment of the body by the state. On the other hand, her grotesque bodies are out of control: they refuse to conform to symbolic

---

[48] Shot-putter Heidi Krieger underwent a sex-change operation after having been injected with male hormones over a period of years, John Hooper, 'East German Drugs Pushers Escape Jail', *Guardian*, 19 July 2000 (source: **www.guardian.co.uk/international/story/0,3604,344746,00.html**).

[49] Kerstin Hensel in interview with Klaus Hammer, 'Gespräch mit Kerstin Hensel', *Weimarer Beiträge*, 37/1 (1991), 93–110, here 110. See also Kerstin Hensel, 'Kopfball und Verlängerung: Ein Meister aus Deutschland', *Freitag*, 5 July 1996, p. 2, where Hensel invokes Paul Celan's 'Todesfuge' in the phrase 'Fußball ist ein Meister aus Deutschland'.

[50] Weigel, *Topographien der Geschlechter*, 263.

values which determine the signification of the body—such as beauty or strength—and are associated with the breaking of social rules and laws. Moreover, within the text, these grotesque, unrestrained bodies are further implicated in the breaking of laws of narrative. This link is something I address in the following section, which looks at the relation between the body and language, and between representations of the body and narrative strategies.

THEORY

Feminist theory and the body

This study of the relation between representations of the body and narrative strategies in prose texts by Müller, Moníková, and Hensel is situated within the recent increase in interest in the body, in literary criticism as well as in critical theory, which stresses the embodiment of the subject. My analysis of texts by these three authors not only offers new perspectives on their work, but also brings to the wider critical concern with the body new perspectives related to the specific political and social circumstances of former Eastern Bloc countries. This work is undertaken in the belief that literature does not merely illustrate theoretical notions, but is rather, in Judith Butler's words, 'a place where theory takes place'.[51] Literature can enact ideas which are yet to be theorized, and a reading of literature through theory should be at the same time a reading of theory through literature. My readings of the texts are informed by recent feminist theory about the body, which seeks to negotiate the body's position as the locus of both material reality and discursive signification, a position which is reproduced in literature in the relation between images of the body and narrative form. The figures of trauma, hysteria, and the grotesque which I use to examine this relation connect with feminist theory in different ways. Several feminist theorists explicitly invoke the notion of hysteria or the hysteric as a figure which links images of the body and discourse; in the case of

[51] Judith Butler, *Bodies that Matter: On the Discursive Limits of 'Sex'* (New York: Routledge, 1993), 182.

trauma and the grotesque there are implicit, structural links which I take up below.

The body is a complex, contested entity: both materially real and constructed in discourse, it is the site where subjectivity is located and power is inscribed. The body is materialized through entering into discourse; there is no unmarked body prior to its signification in relation to constructs of gender, race, and the viably human. And yet the body is not fully subsumed within discourse; its materiality—its physicality, the embodiment of the subject—exceeds all discourse and language, and thus provides ground for resistance to hegemonic structures. Literature is a site where the complex relationship between materiality and discursive signification of the body can be staged and explored, as this relationship is reproduced in the split between form and content in the text. The marking of the body in discourse and the marking of the body in the literary text are analogous, as Leslie Adelson suggests in her definition of bodies in literature as 'images of real bodies, or, perhaps more precisely, images of bodies imagined to be real'.[52] Literary images of bodies are produced within language, but these bodies are posited as prior to, or outside, the text. As Adelson contends, their meaning, and the meaning of the text, depends on this anteriority. This is the same process whereby bodies are produced in and by discourse, while their materiality is posited as a prediscursive fact. Literary images of the body are just as ineluctably caught up within narrative as real, social bodies are within symbolic discourse; both signal a physical corporeality which cannot fully be contained by either form of discourse.

The following section outlines some of the most important theoretical concepts which inform my analysis. I begin with critic Sigrid Weigel's examination of 'Körper-Sprache' before focusing on Luce Irigaray's understanding of hysteria; I then move on to the notion of gender as performance, developed by Judith Butler. Finally, I consider Butler's discussion of abject, marginalized bodies, which links with Julia Kristeva's theories of language acquisition. These concepts revolve primarily around the question of how the (female) body and language are or can be linked. In addition, the theorists broach the question of

---

[52] Adelson, *Making Bodies*, 2.

how it is possible to resist, subvert, or undermine hegemonic discourse, something which texts by all three of the authors I discuss attempt to do, both in their representations of the body and in the narrative strategies they employ. German literary critic Sigrid Weigel has developed the notion of 'Körper-Sprache' from the feminist theories of Luce Irigaray and Julia Kristeva. Although it draws on their theories of social bodies, and the general relation between the body and discourse, her 'Körper-Sprache' is primarily a literary trope, concerned with the specific relation between images of the body and narrative discourse. Weigel posits it as another way of writing—a way of writing the Other—which can express female alterity:

> Wenn man Literatur von Frauen betrachtet, die auf den Körper Bezug nimmt, bleibt zu fragen, ob es sich um die Darstellung körperlicher Erfahrungen handelt, d.h. um ein Schreiben *über* den Körper, ob die Körper-Sprache als Metapher oder Symbol Bedeutung erhält oder ob es um eine Schreibweise geht, die eine andere Beziehung zwischen Sprache und menschlichem Körper begründet als die der Benennung, indem etwa Sprach-Körper und Körper-Sprache sich berühren.[53]

'Körper-Sprache' is not about the use of the body as literary allegory, which presupposes the absence of the real, physical body. Rather it is a literary mode of expression which seeks to undo, or at least to problematize, the dichotomy of discourse and materiality, where the body is the ultimate referent for language.

As Weigel warns in her 1990 text *Topographien der Geschlechter*, there is a danger that 'Körper-Sprache' is understood simply as a metaphor for body-language in a conventional sense or simply as the use of the body as metaphor.[54] There is also the danger that 'Körper-Sprache' becomes a metaphor for women's writing, or *écriture féminine*, and thus ultimately—as so often happens in theorizations of women's writing—becomes a metaphor for 'woman', reinscribing the patriarchal association of women and the body. Weigel's qualification, showing that Irigaray equates 'Körper-Sprache' with the female body, points

---

[53] Weigel, *Die Stimme der Medusa*, 112.
[54] Weigel, *Topographien der Geschlechter*, 66.

to a problematic tendency towards essentialism in some of the latter's early writing:[55]

> Sieht sie in der Körper-Sprache, genauer in Symptomen und in der Gestik des weiblichen Körpers, Hinweise für eine andere Syntax, eine 'Syntax des Weiblichen', so sagt Irigaray damit nicht, daß diese andere Syntax sich rein äußere oder positiv existent sei, sondern sie reflektiert deren Verhältnis zum herrschenden Diskurs [...].[56]

The conceptualization of an other, feminine syntax as reflecting a relation to power rather than a fixed position, however, offers a more useful paradigm. This is Irigaray's 'parler-femme', in her own words:

> Le problème du 'parler-femme' serait justement de trouver une continuité possible entre cette gestualité ou cette parole du désir—qui, actuellement, ne sont repérables que sous forme de symptômes et de pathologie—et un langage, y compris un langage verbal.[57]

'Parler-femme' exists as the function of continuity between the body's discourse of symptoms and language. Understood in this sense, 'Körper-Sprache' can be seen as a purely contingent, ideal construct; it does not exist as such, but can function as a tool by which to examine writing about, on, or of the body.

The problem of 'Körper-Sprache' is a central one for my approach, which also posits a relation between narrative discourse and the body. As an idea, 'Körper-Sprache' represents a way of conceptualizing the priority of the body which can help negotiate this complex relationship. I suggest, and have argued elsewhere, that the hysteria which is both thematized in, and structures, Moníková's texts can be regarded as a form of 'Körper-Sprache'.[58] Aspects of the trauma which I examine here in Müller's texts also approach 'Körper-Sprache', although her texts do not foreground a female or feminine subjectivity. Images of the body and narrative strategies in both their texts derive from figures (trauma and hysteria) which are predicated on the body, and the figure is an expression or

---

[55] See Toril Moi's criticisms of Irigaray in Toril Moi, *Sexual Textual Politics* (London: Routledge, 1985), esp. 137–47.

[56] Weigel, *Die Stimme der Medusa*, 116.

[57] Luce Irigaray, *Ce sexe qui n'en est pas un* (Paris: Minuit, 1977), 134–5.

[58] On one text only, see Lyn Marven, 'Women in Wheelchairs: Space, Performance and Hysteria in Libuše Moníková's *Pavane für eine verstorbene Infantin* and Ines Eck's *Steppenwolfidyllen*', *German Life and Letters*, 53/4 (2000), 511–28.

reflection of subjectivity. The grotesque, on the other hand, is located in an object (or person) to whom the subject reacts. Although it is a structure which links both body and language, as 'Körper-Sprache' does, these do not express subjectivity; instead, the grotesque stages their disjunction. Nonetheless, I argue that linguistic or narrative grotesque is also predicated on the grotesque body.

The notion of 'Körper-Sprache' is derived from Irigaray's theory of hysteria. According to Irigaray, the hysteric represents woman caught ineluctably within patriarchal discourse, denied subjectivity within, and unable to speak from a position outside, as there is no outside to hegemonic discourse. This leaves the hysteric with two possible strategies, mimicry and mutism:

> L'hystérie, *ça parle* sur le mode d'une gestualité paralysée, d'une parole impossible et aussi interdite... Ça parle comme *symptômes* d'un 'ça ne peut ni se parler ni se dire'... Et le drame de l'hystérie, c'est qu'elle est schizée entre cette gestualité, ce désir paralysés et enfermés dans son corps, et un langage qu'elle a appris en famille, a l'école, dans la société, qui ne fait absolument pas continuité, ni, bien sûr, métaphore, avec les 'mouvements' de son désir. Il lui reste donc, á la fois, le mutisme et le mimétisme. Elle se tait et, en même temps, elle mime. Et—comment pourrait-il en être autrement?—mimant-reproduisant un langage qui n'est pas le sien, le langage masculin, elle le caricature, le déforme: elle 'ment', elle 'trompe', ce qui est toujours attribué aux femmes.[59]

The hysteric (woman as mimic) stages her own exclusion from patriarchal discourse in her language of physical symptoms and mimicry of verbal language. She deforms language as she deforms her body. Enacting the 'specular logic of patriarchy' allows women to salvage some remnant of their own desires.[60] Irigaray proposes that women deliberately assume the position which they have traditionally been assigned, miming this mimicry and overdoing it, in order to undo it. Irigaray similarly reclaims deception and lying as necessary and valid strategies for woman, the invalid within patriarchy. The hysteric also has a silent, gestural language; her voice is to be heard in the blank spaces between words, in the gaps of a text.

---

[59] Irigaray, *Ce sexe*, 134.   [60] Moi, *Sexual Textual Politics*, 135.

Irigaray's concept of an 'other syntax', elaborated in *Ce sexe qui n'en est pas un*, provides a model for the subversion of hegemonic discourse. For Irigaray, syntax does not simply refer to grammar, but to the very structures of society: 'cette syntaxe du discours, de la logique discursive, plus généralement aussi cette syntaxe de l'organisation de la société, cette syntaxe "politique".'[61] A feminine syntax would perforce be visible in literature which, as Irigaray notes, both is constructed in and constructs social discourses; it therefore both reflects and enacts a 'parler-femme'.[62] This 'other syntax' derives from the language of the body, and is visible

> dans la gestualité du corps des femmes. Mais, comme cette gestualité est souvent paralysée, ou entrée dans la mascarade, effectivement, c'est parfois difficile á 'lire'. Sinon dans ce qui résiste ou subsiste 'au-delà'. Dans la souffrance, mais aussi dans le rire des femmes.[63]

Irigaray invokes the figure of the hysteric here, whose gestures are both paralysed and faked, who both suffers and laughs. In doing so, she posits a second possible strategy for expressing female subjectivity other than suffering: laughter. Laughter represents the potential to resist, subvert, and undermine, which is in part due to its being rooted in the body. Laughter is manifested by the body as physical gestures which distort its shape, bringing 'das Heterogene, Zwieschlächtige und Unreine ins Spiel; das Materielle, Körperliche, das dem Wissen widersteht'.[64] It represents a form of opposition which cannot be pinned down in binary structures. In literature, laughter is further linked to mimicry through parody, a mode which plays an important role in the work of Moníková and Hensel.

Irigaray's characterization of women's gestures under patriarchal discourse as 'entrée dans la mascarade' is taken up by Judith Butler in her notion of performative gender, developed in *Gender Trouble* (1990).[65] Butler contends that all gender is a

---

[61] Irigaray, *Ce sexe*, 130.   [62] Ibid. 129.   [63] Ibid. 132.
[64] Marianne Schuller, 'Wenn's im Feminismus lachte...', in Inge Stephan, Sigrid Weigel, and Kerstin Wilhelms (eds.), *'Wen kümmert's, wer spricht': Zur Literatur und Kulturgeschichte von Frauen aus Ost und West* (Cologne: Böhlau, 1991), 63–72, here 71.
[65] Judith Butler, *Gender Trouble: Feminism and the Subversion of Identity*, 10th Anniversary edn. (New York: Routledge, 1999), see particularly ch. 3, 'Subversive Bodily Acts', 101–80.

masquerade: gender is not the expression of an inner essence, but is rather the effect of repeated gestures and acts, which produce the identity they purport to express. She analyses drag as well as lesbian 'butch' and 'femme' identities as acts which intentionally suggest dissonance between gender identity and performance and reveal 'the imitative structure of gender itself—as well as its contingency'.[66] Butler suggests further that 'gender parody reveals that the original identity after which gender fashions itself is an imitation without origin'.[67] This is true of gender as a concept (or rather, in Butler's terms, a strategy) as well as its manifestation in, or on, the individual body. As she explains, gender is not a natural or universal category, but rather the product of a process of sedimentation of norms over time as well as the effect of the iterative performance by the individual. Gender is performed on the surface of the body and in an exterior space; it posits a prior, 'interior' signification of an essence, concealing its own performance. The possibility of apprehending the performance of gender, and thus, more significantly, transforming notions of gender, is located in the fact of the 'occasional *dis*continuity' of the repeated acts.[68]

While it is true, as Elaine Showalter suggests, that there can be 'no expression of the body which is unmediated by linguistic, social and literary structures', recent feminist theory also takes the inverse to be true: that there are no linguistic, social, and literary structures which are unmediated by the body.[69] In both *Gender Trouble* and *Bodies that Matter*, Butler analyses 'unthinkable' physical forms, abject bodies which fall 'outside' gendered, racialized norms of physical appearance as well as sexuality (which she contends is produced and regulated in relation to gender) and whose refusal to conform to these norms calls into question constructs of gender and race. The transgression of norms of the body is regarded as a threat to the very structure of society as the regulation of the body and its meanings is precisely the basis for the regulation of the social. Butler quotes Mary Douglas's remark that 'the body is a model that can stand for any bounded system. Its boundaries can

---

[66] Ibid. 137.   [67] Ibid. 175.   [68] Ibid. 179.
[69] Elaine Showalter, 'Feminist Criticism in the Wilderness', in Elaine Showalter (ed.), *The New Feminist Criticism: Essays on Women, Literature and Theory* (London: Virago Press, 1986), 243–70, here 252.

represent any boundaries which are threatened or precarious.'[70] The body's role as model for the social is not simply based on metaphor or analogy, but synecdoche: the body is the part which not only represents the whole, but upon which the whole is based. The boundaries of the body have particular significance in this respect.

In Butler's analysis, the boundaries of the body are also the limits of the social, but these boundaries are in fact always permeable. The distinction inscribed on the body between the 'inner' and 'outer' enforces the taboos of society: those who breach the boundaries of the body in unregulated ways also represent the threat to society from outside. This 'outside' is, however, not fully outside discourse:

> The bisexuality which is said to be 'outside' the Symbolic and that serves as the locus of subversion is, in fact, a construction within the terms of that constitutive discourse, the construction of an 'outside' that is nevertheless fully 'inside', not a possibility beyond culture, but a concrete possibility that is refused and redescribed as impossible. What remains 'unthinkable' and 'unsayable' within the terms of an existing cultural form is not necessarily what is excluded from the matrix of intelligibility within that form; on the contrary, it is the marginalized, not the excluded [...]. [71]

Bisexuality as Butler discusses it here is representative of all forms of sex and sexuality which exceed the norm. What is marginalized is still part of that discourse, without representation (in both senses) but not outside it.[72] Butler proposes that resistance to fixed structures is therefore to be achieved 'not from a "position", but from the discursive possibilities opened up by the constitutive outside of hegemonic positions'.[73]

The margins of the body ultimately represent—and can therefore guarantee or unsettle—the limits of intelligibility of language. Julia Kristeva suggests that the permeable margins of the body, and particularly liminal bodily fluids, pose a threat to the stability of the self.[74] Body image is implicated in the psychological development of the subject and its entry into language.

---

[70] Butler, *Gender Trouble*, 168.   [71] Ibid. 98.
[72] Adelson makes this useful distinction, *Making Bodies*, 59.
[73] Butler, *Bodies that Matter*, 12.
[74] See Julia Kristeva, *Pouvoirs de l'horreur* (Paris: Seuil, 1980), esp. the essay 'De la saleté à la souillure', 69–105.

In order to create a unified identity, the boundaries of the body must be established and the Other delineated and expelled. This process of abjection is a key stage in the formation of the subject; where it is not fully accomplished (as it never can be), the acquisition and mastery of language is threatened. Trauma reverses this process, destabilizing the subject's body image as well as their use of language. Bodily fluids are the abject, that which is both a part of the self and other; they are a permanent threat to the stability of the body. Their liminal status represents 'une menace venue des interdits qui instaurent les frontiéres internes et externes dans lesquelles et par lesquelles se constitue l'être parlant—frontiéres que déterminent aussi les différences phonologiques et sémantiques articulant la syntaxe de la langue'.[75] On a wider level, the process of abjection also characterizes the creation of the 'other' in society. Bodily fluids and the abject bodies Butler invokes are key images of the grotesque, which confronts us with that which breaks society's norms and boundaries.

The problematization of the boundaries of the body and consequent discussion of the constructions of inner/outer in the body, the social system, and its discourses and language by Butler and Kristeva underpins this study. All three writers explore and challenge notions of inner and outer, in relation to the body, discourse, and society, and their respective margins. The titles of the three following chapters all refer to a structural opposition between 'inner' and 'outer', which is constructed in different ways and which derives respectively from the figures of trauma, hysteria, and the grotesque. Chapter 2, on Müller, is titled 'Das, was von innen kam, angesichts des Äußeren': this quotation from Müller's poetological writing in *Der Teufel sitzt im Spiegel* characterizes the effects of trauma. It suggests a relation between the self and the world which is based on reflection and duality, a relation which in the course of Müller's work moves through symbiosis to the disintegration of the boundaries between inside and outside. Chapter 3, on Moníková, carries two quotations, 'Ich bin am Ort meines Ursprungs' and 'Innen bin ich hohl', respectively by the narrators of *Pavane für eine verstorbene Infantin* and *Verklärte Nacht*. The development from

---

[75] Ibid. 85.

one to the other in Moníková's work reflects hysteria's refusal of authenticity. Neither an inner self nor the interiority of the body is a guarantor of an intact and original identity; instead, there is only performance and simulation. Finally, the title of Chapter 4, on Hensel, 'Wer "draußen" steht, kann deutlicher sehen', signals her critical viewpoint and the distance inherent in the mode of the grotesque. It demonstrates her understanding of the possibility of subversion of prevailing discourses from the constitutive outside (the 'draußen' which is already defined within discourse, hence Hensel's use of quotation marks).

Feminism

My analysis draws on feminist theory, particularly as it engages with the signification of the body, and this study is located within a wider project, which has engaged feminist theorists and critics, of refiguring the body. While my own approach is a consciously feminist one, the authors themselves profess unwillingness to be labelled 'feminist'. Of course, this stance arguably says more about their different definitions of feminism than their work itself, which has variously been the subject of feminist criticism. However, in my examination of their texts, I suggest that the three authors challenge and subvert hegemonic structures, and patriarchy is one facet of these structures. Moreover, problems identified by feminist critics in the work of the three authors turn out to be crucial ones which bear intrinsically on their wider aesthetics.

Like many women from the Eastern Bloc, Müller, Moníková, and Hensel are wary of Western feminism, whose agenda and priorities do not always coincide with those of women from former socialist states.[76] Asked in an interview whether *Fasan* is a 'bewußt feministischer Roman', for example, Müller declares, 'Ich bin keine Feministin. Ich bin vielleicht eine Individualistin und ich bin eine Frau.'[77] She rejects a homogenized conception of women as victims, pointing out that women—she gives Elena

[76] See the introduction and essays in Funk and Mueller (eds.), *Gender Politics*.

[77] Müller, in interview with Brigid Haines and Margaret Littler, 'Gespräch mit Herta Müller', in Brigid Haines (ed.), *Herta Müller* (Cardiff: University of Wales Press, 1998), 14–24, here 19.

INTRODUCTION 37

Ceaușescu as an example—are also complicit in oppression.[78] Such a generalized view of women as the universally oppressed has also been rejected by recent feminist theories of positionality, which recognize the multiple discourses in and through which the subject is constructed and constructs itself; these more differentiated theories acknowledge that neither 'woman' nor 'gender' is a unified, discrete category.[79] Müller's refusal to align herself with feminism also stems from her distrust of totalizing theories. She admits an interest in 'das Verhältnis zwischen Sexualität und Macht', however, and her writing contains clearly critical accounts of the exploitation of women.[80] Müller's texts portray an inherently patriarchal society; gender roles in the rural Banat community in particular are fixed and are rooted in old-fashioned peasant values.[81] The sexual exploitation of women pervades all aspects of life, from the prostitution which guarantees a passport in *Fasan*, to the sexualized interrogation methods employed by Hauptmann Pjele in *Herztier*.

While Müller portrays the complicity of women in perpetuating repressive traditions (Amalie's mother in *Fasan*, for example), she herself has been accused of colluding in misogynistic views. Karin Bauer's analysis of the objectification of women in *Der Mensch ist ein großer Fasan auf der Welt* concludes that the narrative perspective merges with the male perspective represented by Windisch, the main protagonist, and that as a result the marginalization of women within the society portrayed is reproduced on the level of the text.[82] Although it is true that the narrative voice offers no overt criticism of Windisch, I do not agree that it thereby fails to challenge his exaggeratedly misogynistic views. The juxtaposition of Windisch's views on his wife's prostitution during the war with a chapter detailing

---

[78] See Haines, ' "Leben wir im Detail": Herta Müller's Micro-Politics of Resistance', in Haines (ed.), *Herta Müller*, 109–25, here 124 n. 24.
[79] See Adelson, *Making Bodies*, esp. 57–70, and also Chris Weedon, *Feminist Practice and Poststructuralist Theory* (Oxford: Basil Blackwell, 1987).
[80] Herta Müller, in interview with Verena Auffermann, 'Gerechtigkeit ist ein Unwort. Ein Gespräch mit der Schriftstellerin Herta Müller über die Staatssicherheit, die Sprache und die Macht', *Süddeutsche Zeitung*, 14/15/16 Aug. 1992, Feuilleton p. 15.
[81] See Müller in interview with Haines and Littler, in Haines (ed.), *Herta Müller*, 19; and also Harsanyi, in Funk and Mueller (eds.), *Gender Politics*, 39–52.
[82] Karin Bauer, 'Zur Objektwerdung der Frau in Herta Müllers *Der Mensch ist ein großer Fasan auf der Welt*', *seminar*, 32/2 (1996), 143–54, here 153–4.

Katharina's own experiences, for example, makes it clear that Windisch distorts the truth. And it seems unlikely that Müller would expect the reader to view uncritically characters who make such hyperbolic, superstitious, and clearly bigoted statements as 'die Juden verderben die Welt. Die Juden und die Weiber' (*MFW* 77). Here, as in other places in this text, Müller verges uncharacteristically on irony.

However, Bauer's article touches on the key question for Müller's work as a whole, namely whether her narrative strategy 'mimetisch aufbricht oder nur vervielfältigt' the patriarchal, oppressive structures of society.[83] I contend that the making visible of these structures is an end in and of itself; the very fact that they can be perceived signals that they are not all-encompassing. Müller's focus on the traumatic effects of repression and her insistence on making these legible is, ultimately, a step towards countering them.

Much remains to be analysed in Müller's portrayal of gendered subjects and bodies. With the exception of *Fasan*, Müller's narrators or main protagonists are all female: what is the significance of using female bodies as the locus of criticism? In her work, as in Moníková's and Hensel's texts, women's bodies become a focus for resistance precisely because they are doubly excluded by the patriarchal socialist regimes. The interpersonal relationships Müller examines similarly tend to be between women: problematic mother–daughter relationships or female friendships, such as the quasi-love affair between the narrator and Tereza in *Herztier*, might be an interesting focus for feminist criticism. Finally, the figures of Amalie, Lola, and Lilli in *Heute*, all three of whom are sexually exploited or turn to a form of prostitution out of necessity (it is hard to distinguish between the two), are evidence that Müller is interested in female sexuality and femininity.

Of the three authors, Moníková is the most concerned to depict the oppressive patriarchal structures operating within society; one reason she gives for leaving Czechoslovakia is the widespread sexual inequality (*PF* 20–2). Her texts portray the marginalization of women in different cultures, and feature (not

---

[83] Bauer, 'Zur Objektwerdung der frau', 153.

unproblematic) utopian women's communities; even her male protagonists often possess a feminist consciousness (Prantl in *Treibeis*) or are inducted into radical, separatist women's groups (Orten in *Die Fassade*). However, Moníková is critical of the excesses of some forms of feminism. In *Pavane* she satirizes the victim-culture of early women's movements, as well as revealing the privileges of rich, white Western feminists such as Virginia Woolf who claim the position of the universal, oppressed subject of feminism. Moníková recognizes that other constructs such as class, nationality, or ethnicity, whose meanings are historically and socially contingent, characterize positionality in relation to power.

Moníková's first two texts attracted particular attention from feminist critics due to their focus on the female body and 'Körper-Sprache'. Other aspects of Moníková's narrative have proved more problematic for feminist critics. Regula Venske calls the change in style from *Pavane* to *Die Fassade* an 'Anpassung an die Männerliteratur', arguing that the text fails to deconstruct the perspective of the male as norm.[84] The shift from single female protagonists in the first two texts to the multiple male protagonists of *Die Fassade* does also coincide with a shift in narrative style, as Venske notes, away from the body towards intertextuality and a postmodern playfulness. (One wonders which of these factors accounts for *Die Fassade* being Moníková's best-known text.) However, Moníková's subsequent texts go some way to countering her argument. *Treibeis* (1992) continues the postmodern emphasis on the inauthentic—which I argue is already apparent in *Pavane*—but the change in narrative perspective in the final chapter from third person to a first-person, female narrator (Karla) undermines the focus on the male protagonist at the beginning of the text. Interestingly, Moníková's final, unfinished novel *Der Taumel* cuts across the dichotomy of the first three texts, moving towards a kind of 'Körper-Sprache' in the male protagonist's epilepsy.[85]

---

[84] Regula Venske, *Das Verschwinden des Mannes in der weiblichen Schreibmaschine: Männerbilder in der Literatur von Frauen* (Hamburg: Luchterhand, 1991), 89.
[85] According to editor Michael Krüger in the epilogue to the novel, '*Der Taumel* sollte neben *der Fassade* (1987) das zweite Hauptwerk im Werk von Libuše Moníková werden'; Moníková's enthusiasm for the earlier novel was, he says, only matched by that for the later one, *Tm* 191.

Moníková explicitly situates her writing in relation to male writers, something which both Venske and Maria Kublitz-Kramer problematize. Kublitz-Kramer sees the figures of Kafka and Arno Schmidt in *Pavane* as a 'väterliche Genealogie', a counterpoint to images of 'Schwesterlichkeit' and female mythology in the text.[86] Just as Jana in *Eine Schädigung* fights back, but does so using her attacker's weapon—hence she remains caught up in the same structures of violence and power—Venske argues that in *Pavane* Moníková also enters into, rather than challenges, patriarchal discourse: 'auch hier erfolgt die "Entmannung", wenn man so will, im vorgegebenen Medium, wenn nämlich die Ich-Erzählerin Kafkas *Schloß* weiterschreibt.'[87] I maintain that Moníková's mimicry can in fact be seen as Irigaray's hysterical mimicry, a subversive rather than respectful imitation, and a potentially useful feminist strategy. Francine and Moníková's revision of Kafka in order to change the fates of Olga and Amalia does not simply continue where Kafka left off, but does so in a parodic, even humorous mode, something made clear in the 'Vier Versuche, die Familie Barnabas zu rehabilitieren' in *Schloß, Aleph, Wunschtorte*. Moreover, Moníková does not only tackle male writers: *Pavane* is also written against Ingeborg Bachmann's *Der Fall Franza* and references to Bachmann recur in other texts, especially *Verklärte Nacht*.[88]

Hensel, like Müller, refuses to call herself a feminist, associating feminism with separatism and 'Fraulichkeit'. Dismissing the importance of feminism in her work in an interview, Hensel explains, 'Ich wehre mich strikt dagegen, als fraulich beurteilt zu werden.'[89] Hensel uses the term 'fraulich' rather than the

---

[86] Maria Kublitz-Kramer, *Frauen auf Straßen: Topographie des Begehrens in Erzähltexten von Gegenwartsautorinnen* (Munich: Fink, 1995), 188.

[87] Venske, *Das Verschwinden*, 89. Delius also describes the versions as written 'in Kafkas Auftrag in Kafkas Stil', Friedrich Christian Delius, 'Rede auf die Fürstin Libuše: Zum Tode von Libuše Moníková', *Deutsche Akademie für Sprache und Dichtung* (Jahrbuch 1998), 183–8, here 185, although he does not criticize Moníková for it.

[88] Moníková also writes about Bachmann's celebrated poem 'Böhmen am Meer' in an article of the same title, in *Prager Fenster*, 56–62. Dana Pfeiferová outlines the influence of Bachmann in *Die Fassade*, in Dana Pfeiferová, '"Das Reich der Kunst erschaffen": Ingeborg Bachmann im Werk Libuše Moníkovás', *Literaturmagazin*, 44 (1999) (*Prag-Berlin: Libuše Moníková*), 78–84.

[89] Kerstin Hensel, in interview with Karl Deiritz and Rolf Stefaniak, '"Ich teste meine Grenzen aus"': Gespräch mit Kerstin Hensel', *Deutsche Volkszeitung*, 3 Nov. 1989, p. 11.

more obvious 'weiblich', drawing a clear distinction between gender (cultural designation) and sex (biological fact). Her rejection of feminism is in fact a rejection of prescriptive definitions of femininity, and in her texts she shows the consequences for both sexes of fixed, prescriptive notions of gender identity. Both sexes are constricted by cultural norms and the processes of socialization; both sexes transgress conventional body images. For every woman who does not measure up to cultural standards of beauty, there is a man who cannot live up to ideals of physical ability.[90]

However, these social constrictions affect the sexes differently and unequally: the women almost always come off worst. Ritter Rosel, independent-minded, sexually uninhibited, and facially disfigured, is an outsider in a way that her husband Harald, with his child's voice and unable to fulfil knightly ideals of courage, is not. She is outside society, perceived as 'wild', whereas he is merely an outsider within society. A similarly unequal situation arises in representations of sex. The uncontrollable appetites of Magd Konstanze or Ingrid Tabea and the inadequacy of the men in 'Herr Johannes' or Siegfried Kulisch in *Im Schlauch* are all subject to irony. However, the women in 'Herr Johannes' suffer more than the men, and the 'battle of the sexes' reveals that, ultimately, the battlefield is woman's body: women are both fought and conquered. Representations of women as 'Wildnis' or allegorical 'Schlachtfeld' are two strategies of patriarchal discourse which Sigrid Weigel analyses in *Topographien der Geschlechter*. As this would suggest, Hensel's texts reflect feminist concerns, whether consciously or unconsciously. Hensel engages with mythical figures which have been taken up by feminist theorists, such as Lilith and Undine, and with figures ripe for feminist deconstruction, such as Don Juan. Finally, Hensel also engages with recognized feminist women writers in German, such as Bachmann and Irmtraud Morgner, although she distances her own writing from their texts through parody and irony.

Hensel refuses to be classed as a woman writer, using for herself the masculine term 'Dichter', and deliberately distancing herself from the writing of affect and authenticity which is

---

[90] See Birgit Dahlke, 'Weibliche Männer, männliche Weiber? Gender in Transit', in Birgit Dahlke and Beth Linklater (eds.), *Kerstin Hensel* (Cardiff: University of Wales Press, 2002), 67–77.

usually labelled as 'women's writing'. Questions about her experiences as a woman are rebuffed: 'Einen Mann fragt niemand, ob er sich beim Schreiben als Mann fühlt.'[91] While her stance here is understandable—the insistence on the author as instance and on biographical detail slips very easily, in the case of women writers, into a sociological, essentialist perspective—it avoids many valid questions about gender, not least whether it is something which can simply be thought away from writing. In *Papierboot*, her survey of young women writers published unofficially in the GDR, Birgit Dahlke begins the section on Hensel with two questions which point to both the problems and the potential that Hensel's narrative style represents in relation to women's writing: 'Wie steht es um die Souveränität der Autorin, wenn sie die autobiographische Schreibweise ganz bewußt meidet? Ist die ästhetische Problematik nur mit der Ich-Perspektive verbunden, läßt sie sich umgehen, wenn diese gemieden wird?' Dahlke asks.[92] On the one hand, a move away from autobiography and first-person narrative avoids the emphasis on the authenticity of woman's voice, which tends to essentialize 'woman'. On the other hand, though, as Dahlke makes clear, the purportedly gender-neutral or androgynous, distanced narrator is itself a male construct.[93] Women writers adopting this form of narration run the risk of being complicit in power structures. It is significant that both Müller and Moníková come up against criticism from feminists when they depart from their typical first-person narratives or narratives with female protagonists and focalizers, which are in both cases based on the authors' own experiences. Conversely, Hensel's most widely received text is *Tanz am Kanal*, a first-person narrative which purports to be authentic. Hensel's use of the grotesque necessitates a distanced, superior, and anonymous narrator—but this does not make the text objective. I argue that the irony which is a part of the grotesque and which has become the dominant mode of Hensel's texts entails judgement, and where gender images are concerned, this judgement can be considered feminist.

---

[91] Hensel, in interview with Dahlke, *Papierboot*, 276.
[92] Ibid. 152.
[93] Ibid. 158–60. Cf. Gisela Ecker, 'Der Kritiker, die Autorin und das "allgemeine Subjekt": Ein Dreiecksverhältnis mit Folgen', in Stephan, Weigel, and Wilhelms (eds.), *'Wen kümmert's, wer spricht'*, 43–56.

Trauma, hysteria, and the grotesque

The relationship between body and language, and between representations of the body and narrative strategies in the texts of Müller, Moníková, and Hensel, is staged respectively through the figures of trauma, hysteria, and the grotesque. I use the terms trauma and hysteria within a literary framework; I am concerned with their literary inflections rather than strict scientific usage. Considering trauma, hysteria, and the grotesque on a structural level highlights the ways in which they can be reflected within narrative. The three tropes operate on different levels of the text: they manifest themselves in images of the body and in the text, through syntax and narrative syntax or plot. They can be recognized in strategies such as parody, intertextuality, and the use of other languages, or in the visual aspects of the text. Finally, they even operate on a supratextual level, characterizing the development of the oeuvres of the three authors. Trauma, hysteria, and the grotesque also relate to each other and thus facilitate comparisons between all three authors and their texts; this means that, although in each case the figure I examine is the dominant mode of the author's work, it is not exclusive of the others.

While the individual chapters each begin with a discussion of the relevant figure, I outline all three in turn below in order to highlight how they relate to each other. Trauma is the pivotal concept: hysteria is a reaction to it, the grotesque a form of resistance of its effects. By portraying the effects of trauma—directly, or as refracted in hysteria and the grotesque—texts by all three authors testify to the lasting effects of the experience of the Eastern Bloc; they illustrate the fact 'Daß dies der Osten ist Was im Kopf nicht aufhört' (*WK* 4).

Trauma is defined by Cathy Caruth, whose writing on the subject is central to literary critical interest in it, as 'a response, sometimes delayed, to an overwhelming event or events'.[94] Trauma characterizes the structure of an experience: it is located in the fact of being overwhelmed and in surviving, rather than the event itself. Frequently, it is the result of a confrontation with death, but other extreme experiences, such as torture, exile, or

---

[94] Cathy Caruth, in Cathy Caruth (ed. and introds.), *Trauma: Explorations in Memory* (Baltimore: Johns Hopkins University Press, 1995), 4.

rape, can also induce trauma. Texts by all three authors include such events. It is notable that these key causes centre on the body, invoking physical violence or displacement. The effects of trauma take two main, interrelated forms: trauma disrupts the structures of memory and it creates a distorted body image.

Trauma is defined primarily by the fact that it cannot be integrated into a narrative memory and exists only as gap or blank spot; it therefore cannot be articulated. Although the memory of the traumatic event is unavailable to conscious recall and linguistic formulation, it remains as a foreign body in the psyche and returns in the form of flashbacks, hallucinations, or dreams, which are notable for being surprisingly literal. The experience of trauma is thus one of simultaneity, of living in two worlds (past and present) at the same time, and of continually re-experiencing the event. A traumatic event or image comes to possess the individual; it is characterized by latency and belatedness, taking effect after the event. Trauma's inaccessibility to memory is defined by theorists in almost literary terms: 'It is not transformed into a story, placed in time, with a beginning, a middle and an end (which is characteristic for narrative memory). If it can be retold, it is still a (re)experience.'[95] It is not only narrativity which implicates literature in the representation of trauma, but also its particular use of language: as Caruth explains, the question of

> what it means to transmit and to theorise around a crisis that is marked, not by a simple knowledge, but by the ways it simultaneously defies and demands our witness [...] can never be asked in a straightforward way, but must, indeed, also be spoken in a language that is always somehow literary: a language that defies, even as it claims, our understanding.[96]

The possibility of overcoming trauma lies in working it into a narrative. However, the political imperative to communicate, to put the experience into words in order to bear witness to it, runs the risk of diluting its very force. Literary representations of trauma can reproduce its effects, for example in the use of parataxis to signal gaps in the syntax of memory or different

---

[95] Bessel A. van der Kolk and Onno von der Hart, 'The Intrusive Past: The Flexibility of Memory and the Engraving of Trauma', in Caruth (ed.), *Trauma: Explorations in Memory*, 158–82, here 177.

[96] Cathy Caruth, *Unclaimed Experience: Trauma, Narrative, and History* (Baltimore: Johns Hopkins University Press, 1996), 5.

tenses to signal the intrusion of the past into the present. In this way, the experience can be communicated, while its effects—the evidence of having been damaged and thus the source of criticism—are preserved.

Trauma affects the individual's sense of identity, as well as their perception of their body. Trauma is often characterized by a feeling of numbness or dislocation; it leads to dissociation, the experience of the self as other, and the splitting of the self into two (or more) elements or identities, symptoms which have an equivalent in corporeal experience. Therapists Jean Goodwin and Reina Attias offer four typologies of traumatic distortions of the body image, namely 'the body in many pieces, the death of the core self, the alien and disruptive body and the body whose interior spaces have been poisoned or ruined'.[97] Trauma disrupts the delimitation of the body and its separation from the world: 'I don't know what it is to have a boundary, to feel all the way out to the edges', claims one patient quoted by Goodwin and Attias.[98] These feelings—that the body is not delimited, or not whole, or alien—all correspond to stages in the psychological development of the infant and its coming to language; by staging a form of regression, trauma ultimately disrupts the use of language. Goodwin and Attias additionally draw a connection with 'Körper-Sprache' and hysteria, suggesting that the body tells about itself in stories, creating a narrative through its symptoms.

Trauma is currently attracting growing interest in cultural and literary studies as 'a vantage point from which to define the modern predicament of mutually entangled histories, communities and writings'.[99] Caruth suggests one reason for its influence:

In a catastrophic age, that is, trauma itself may provide the very link between cultures: not as a simple understanding of others but rather, within the traumas of contemporary history, as our ability to listen through the departures we have all taken from ourselves.[100]

---

[97] Reina Attias and Jean Goodwin, in Reina Attias and Jean Goodwin (eds.), *Splintered Reflections: Images of the Body in Trauma* (New York: Basic Books, 1999), 287.
[98] Ibid. 129.
[99] Mary Jacobus, in preface to *Diacritics*, 28/4 (1998) (*Trauma and Psychoanalysis*), 3.
[100] Caruth, in Caruth (ed.), *Trauma: Explorations in Memory*, 11.

Trauma further connects what are often seen as postmodern literary images and strategies—of fragmentation, alienation, and disruption—with a political reality and ethical dimension. It emphasizes the culturally, politically, and historically specific context within which the text is produced.

Hysteria develops in response to a trauma which cannot be abreacted, as Elisabeth Bronfen has argued persuasively in her recent work *The Knotted Subject: Hysteria and its Discontents*.[101] Hysteria is a psychosomatic disorder which is characterized by the imitation of other illnesses. The hysteric converts the psychic gap left by trauma into somatic symptoms, which constitute a form of body language:

This original trauma, which is to be conceived structurally, is then semantically encoded in a series of representations of traumatic impact; it occurs belatedly in the language of the symptom, both in the unconscious and the conscious register.[102]

Hysteric symptoms are an expression of psychic, not organic, damage. They are façades, protective fantasies constructed after the event which both encode and screen memories of traumatic impact. These fictions are acted out on the body and stand in for articulation of the trauma. These bodily scenarios are not constant, however: as the analyst unravels the symptoms and transforms them into a narrative, the hysteric's symptoms mutate, staging the impossibility of ever accessing the original trauma. Hysteria engenders an ever-changing performance of self-representations which project 'die Versehrtheit der Identität, das heißt die Ungewißheit von *gender*, oder—möglicherweise sogar hauptsächlich—die Verletzbarkeit des wandelbaren, sterblichen Körpers'.[103] The hysteric's mimicry reveals that both cultural significations of the body and its materiality are vulnerable and incomplete. In a wider sense, as Bronfen suggests, these simulations enact Butler's idea that

---

[101] Elisabeth Bronfen, *The Knotted Subject: Hysteria and its Discontents* (Princeton: Princeton University Press, 1998).
[102] Ibid. 37.
[103] Elisabeth Bronfen, 'Mourning becomes Hysteria: Zum Verhältnis von Trauerarbeit zur Sprache der Hysterie', in Gisela Ecker with Maria Kublitz-Kramer (eds.), *Trauer tragen — Trauer zeigen: Inszenierungen der Geschlechter* (Munich: Fink, 1999), 31–55, here 36.

subjectivity is a performance, an imitation without an original.[104] Hysteria represents the structuring of the subject, the construction of the self, through the body, as a representation over and about nothing.

Typical physical manifestations resemble some of the effects of trauma, particularly in the dissociation of the body: the hysteric's state is 'a psychic state in which their own body functions, psychological functions, character traits are experienced and appear as an (apparently) *other*, a quasi-altered, self-representation'.[105] The typical hysterical fit is a form of disjunction between consciousness and body; hysterical paralysis similarly enacts the alienation of the body's parts. Just as traumatic flashbacks are strikingly literal, so too do hysterical symptoms constitute a very literal acting out of psychic disturbance. There is, however, no precise definition of hysteria or its symptoms. As a syndrome, it both constitutes and screens a gap in medical knowledge; it is the 'other' which is excluded from medical classification, and yet which completes it.[106] This is echoed in the ambiguous position of the hysteric in relation to hegemonic discourse: she reveals its fallibility, but ultimately upholds it. The hysteric performs her symptoms for an interpellator, the analyst, whose power to interpret them she sustains, even while challenging it. This ambiguity, which Bronfen emphasizes, is in contrast to the purely subversive mimicry which Irigaray posits.[107]

Hysteria also implies a relation to society, culture, and history: typical symptoms alter to reflect the concerns of any given social, cultural, and historical context and reflect cultural discontent. The hysteric is frequently to be found among the marginalized and powerless in society (women and the lower classes in particular). One reason for this may lie in the circumscription of trauma by the dominant discourse so that the experiences of these marginalized groups are denied. Arguing from a feminist perspective in Caruth's anthology, Laura S. Brown explains that

'Real' trauma is often only that form of trauma in which the dominant group can participate as a victim rather than as the perpetrator

---

[104] Bronfen, *The Knotted Subject*, 41.
[105] Ibid. 40. [106] Ibid. 102.
[107] Toril Moi's criticisms of Irigaray centre on this point, suggesting that Irigaray's own writing in fact perpetuates rather than undoes patriarchal discourse in mimicking it, Moi, *Sexual Textual Politics*, 141–3.

or etiologist of the trauma. The private, secret, insidious traumas to which a feminist analysis draws attention are more often than not those events in which the dominant culture and its forms and institutions are expressed and perpetuated.[108]

Brown argues that incest and rape, for example, are dismissed on the one hand due to their relative frequency, so that they fall within the range of normal experience for some groups of society, and on the other because the experience of these groups is not taken to constitute the norm. The hysteric reproduces the repression of trauma from hegemonic discourse in the repression of its verbal articulation, which instead returns through the language of the body. Hysteria thus stages the denial of the trauma of the marginalized and of being marginalized, while also insisting on that trauma.

The grotesque is the result of an encounter with something which threatens our perceptions of the world; as in trauma, it is the structure of this experience which constitutes the grotesque, not the object encountered. Psychoanalytic critic Carl Pietzcker defines it as 'die Struktur eines Bewußtseinsvorganges, in dem die Erwartung sinnvoller Einordnung von etwas, das sich ihr widersetzt, enttäuscht wird'.[109] But this is not the total destruction of order and expectations, rather a perpetual dialectic of setting up and destroying expectations. The grotesque is characterized primarily by the ambivalent reaction this dichotomous structure provokes: between fear and laughter, fascination and horror or disgust. As Pietzcker explains, 'Das Lachen kommt aus der Freude an der Vernichtung verhaßter Vorstellungen; es braucht nicht laut zu sein und kann in Grauen und Ekel beinahe ersticken', while 'das Grauen' belongs to the grotesque, 'weil es dem Ich die Möglichkeit nimmt, etwas, was es für wirklich hält, durch bestimmte Vorstellungen zu beherrschen'.[110] As Wolfgang Kayser suggests in his early and influential study, these 'Vorstellungen' must be fundamental to our understanding of the world: the grotesque renders 'die Kategorien unserer

---

[108] Laura S. Brown, 'Not Outside the Range: One Feminist Perspective on Psychic Trauma', in Caruth (ed.), *Trauma: Explorations in Memory*, 100–12, here 102.

[109] Carl Pietzcker, 'Das Groteske', *Deutsche Vierteljahrsschrift*, 45 (1971), 197–211, here 203.

[110] Ibid. 208 and 209 respectively.

Weltorientierung' unstable.[111] Like hysteria, then, the grotesque makes visible the values of its contemporary context and in doing so, indicates that they are not absolute. Bakhtin sees the grotesque as a historical phenomenon which precedes the collapse of social or political structures.[112] And also like hysteria, the grotesque is ambiguous: it disrupts, but also confirms the strength of, social norms and cultural signification.

The human body is central to the force of the literary mode of the grotesque, as reactions to it make clear: laughter implicates the body; and 'Ekel' is a visceral, instinctive bodily reaction, closely linked to the abject.[113] This focus on the human body provides a means of comparison with trauma and hysteria. Key manifestations of the grotesque are metamorphosed, distorted, or unstable human bodies; the grotesque body transgresses its limits, calling into question the stability of the body's borders and its proportions. Arnold Heidsieck sees as the modern form of the grotesque, 'der Körper eines Menschen, ja dieser Mensch selbst und seine leere Hülle, eine bloße Sache'.[114] This image can help to outline the difference between the grotesque and trauma, which lies in the structure of the experience. The image of a person as an object is grotesque as it disrupts our expectations that being human involves being a thinking subject; at the same time, the alienation of the body from consciousness is an effect of trauma. This is the point where the grotesque and trauma intersect: the grotesque is the external counterpart to trauma's internal disorder; it is acted out on the body as trauma acts on the psyche. Put another way, what is imagined in trauma is represented visibly and literally in the grotesque. Similarly, the 'Verfremdung im Ich', which Kayser identifies, is an effect of trauma when experienced by the individual; witnessed by another, it is grotesque.[115]

---

[111] Wolfgang Kayser, *Das Groteske: Seine Gestaltung in Malerei und Dichtung* (Oldenburg: Gerhard Stalling, 1957), 199.
[112] Mikhail Bakhtin, *Rabelais and his World*, trans. Hélène Iswolsky (Bloomington: Indiana University Press, 1984), 41.
[113] For more detailed analysis of 'Ekel', see Lyn Marven, '"Wie ein Festmahl nach langer Hungerszeit": Don Juan and Desire in "Herr Johannes"', in Dahlke and Linklater (eds.), *Kerstin Hensel*, 35–50.
[114] Arnold Heidsieck, *Das Groteske und das Absurde im modernen Drama* (Stuttgart: Kohlhammer, 1969), 116.
[115] Kayser, *Das Groteske*, 156.

Unlike trauma and hysteria, which represent psychological disorders in the individual, the grotesque is attributed not to the person who experiences it (and whose ambivalent reaction defines it) but to the object experienced. In the works of the three authors, this distinction sheds light on the preference for first-person narratives which both Müller and Moníková show, and Hensel's tendency to employ third-person narration. Even Müller and Moníková's third-person texts evince a kind of complicity between narrator and protagonist which enables the narrative and textual strategies to function as a projection of the protagonists' psyches. The ironic third-person narrative perspective Hensel employs with only one exception, on the other hand, enforces distance from the protagonists. This distance can be seen as a defence against, or a refusal of, trauma and traumatization. Hensel herself admits,

wir [haben], was an steter Groteske oben wie unten im Staate ablief, bereits Anfang der achtziger Jahre glasklar gesehen, gesagt und geschrieben [...] und, statt in Zähren zu zerfließen oder den Gashahn aufzudrehen, weiter gelacht, gespottet und getrunken [...]. Ja, es war manchem nicht zu helfen gewesen; und natürlich kann man Gelächter auch als Verdrängung sehen.[116]

What is repressed continually threatens to return: the grotesque represents this threat and negotiates it. Conversely, the grotesque's dichotomous structure means that it is also a first admission of trauma: Müller's earliest texts in fact draw on features of the grotesque, which segues into the later, more dominant mode of trauma. The grotesque relies on the reader being affected: the reader's experience is intrinsic to the grotesque, whereas she is only called on to witness the trauma of Müller's work, or interpret and sustain the hysteric's performance in Moníková's texts. While all three modes imply criticism of the society they portray, the grotesque relies on this being the reader's society, hence its political implications.

The three chapters of my thesis trace out a narrative of trauma, from its direct representation in Müller's work, through its refraction into hysteria in Moníková's, to the refusal of trauma in Hensel's use of the grotesque. One key image and cause of

---

[116] Hensel, 'Über dem Jammertal', *Neue deutsche Literatur*, 1 (1993), 77–83, here 81.

trauma which unites all three authors is exile. All three authors have found themselves outside their country of origin as the result of political and historical circumstances, a fact which is reflected in, and informs, the trajectory of their work in different ways; all three demonstrate the belatedness of traumatic impact. Müller was compelled to leave Romania, a final act of psychic splitting enforced by the state; although she emigrated to a country where her mother tongue was spoken, this too became a mark of difference rather than assimilation. She has only begun to write about the Ceauşescu regime since it collapsed, suggesting that physical distance alone was not sufficient to enable her to articulate her experiences. Moníková similarly felt pressured to leave Czechoslovakia at the beginning of the period of 'normalization' which followed the Prague Spring, and exile and hysteria are closely linked in her work. The Velvet Revolution in 1989, and, four years later, the splitting of the state of Czechoslovakia into its component parts (depicted in *Verklärte Nacht*), are turning points in her work: only after this final radical separation did Moníková return to the blind spot of Czech history, the most repressive period of 'normalization', in the fragments of *Der Taumel*. Finally, the collapse of the GDR and reunification forced a whole population into a form of exile. Although Hensel's work before the *Wende* contains allegorical references to the GDR, her work since then has become ever more concerned with portraying everyday life in the GDR, moving gradually back in time from the 1970s and 1980s (*Im Schlauch*, *Tanz am Kanal*) to the 1950s (*Gipshut*). Hensel sees the task of writing post-unification as 'die Schmerzpunkte nicht nur berühren, sondern die Wunden offenhalten; gegen Nostalgie sein und gegen Vergessen'.[117] Acknowledging the trauma and traumatization is the issue here.

In the following three chapters, I trace the way in which the figures of trauma, hysteria, and the grotesque act as the nexus of the relationship between representations of the body and narrative strategies respectively in prose texts by Herta Müller, Libuše Moníková, and Kerstin Hensel. Chapter 2 focuses on Müller's corporeal images of trauma, which centre on two forms: the dissolution of the boundaries between the body and the world,

---

[117] Ibid. 83.

and the fragmentation of the body. I demonstrate how these structures are reflected in narrative, in the problematic merging of different levels of the text and in parataxis. Müller's collages are shown to be the culmination of both her representations of the body and these narrative techniques. Chapter 3 examines representations of hysteria in Moníková's texts, which engenders the self-representations by individual characters as well as the constantly reworked performances of Moníková's texts. I suggest that the mimicry of the hysteric can be seen in the quotations, intertextual allusions, and the use of foreign languages (which here include German). Chapter 4 analyses Hensel's texts in relation to the grotesque. Representations of the body in her work draw on characteristic images of the grotesque, while the ambivalent reaction which defines the mode is achieved through irony, which highlights the act of narration. I show how Hensel's plots are based on the grotesque's structure of expectation and disruption, exhibiting a form of narrative excess that reflects the grotesque body which exceeds its boundaries.

2

HERTA MÜLLER:
'DAS, WAS VON INNEN KAM, ANGESICHTS DES ÄUSSEREN'

The structure underlying Herta Müller's work is the notion of trauma, which unites the representation of the body with language and narrative strategies. In her work, the body remains the predominant and primary concern. Traumatic events evident in Müller's texts are caused by, and rooted in, physical experience: torture and interrogation, threat of violence, and, ultimately, death. The body also acts as the impetus to writing for Müller, as her poetological essays make clear, describing this impulse in terms which recall the effects of trauma. Representations of the body dominate the early texts as an expression of trauma; only gradually are these corporeal representations linked to external, political strategies. In later texts, as the representation of the repression in Ceauşescu's Romania becomes more direct, trauma is articulated increasingly through aesthetic strategies, through narrative techniques and the use of collage. These strategies derive from specific forms and structures visible in the representation of the body.

Two recent articles have begun to consider Müller's writing in relation to trauma theory: Beverley Driver Eddy examines the function of testimony and trauma narratives in *Herztier*, linking the personal stories of the narrator and her friends to the wider narrative of Romania's recent history.[1] Brigid Haines traces patterns of trauma in *Reisende auf einem Bein* and its effect on Irene's sense of identity, in order to demonstrate that the novel prefigures the more direct representations of repression in the later texts.[2] Neither of these critics focuses on images of the body, however, which are particularly prominent in Müller's early work, and which I propose to consider as already

[1] Beverley Driver Eddy, 'Testimony and Trauma in Herta Müller's *Herztier*', *German Life and Letters*, 53/1 (2000), 56–72.
[2] Haines, 'The Alien Gaze'.

representing the trauma which can only emerge belatedly as narrative—belatedly, that is, in terms of the chronology of Müller's work, and also, significantly, after the sudden fall of the Ceauşescu regime in 1989.

The first half of this chapter deals with images of the body, focusing on three structures which represent the effects of trauma: first, the collapse of boundaries between the self and the world; secondly, the representation of the self as alienated, other, or double; and finally, fragmentation, the experience of the body in parts. These structures underpin the narrative strategies which I examine in the second half of the chapter. I consider the collapse of distinction between 'discours' and 'histoire' in the text, which mirrors the collapse of the boundaries of the body;[3] and parataxis and gaps in the text which reflect the fragmentation of the body. These narrative techniques emphasize the physicality of the text, and culminate in the collages which I analyse both as a motif in *Reisende auf einem Bein* and in Müller's two collections of collages, *Der Wächter nimmt seinen Kamm* and *Im Haarknoten wohnt eine Dame*. I begin by looking at the figure of trauma in more detail, outlining its relevance to Müller's work and relating it to images of the writing process in her poetological essays.

'Ich hatte das gedruckte schwarze Sprechen in der Haut' (DT 76): trauma and the act of writing

In her most recent essay, *Der Fremde Blick*, Müller is at pains to stress that this alien/outsider gaze identified in her work by critics is not merely her foreigner's view of Germany, and much less a literary viewpoint: it rather derives from her experiences of interrogation and surveillance in Romania. The gaze is a response to repressive conditions, embodying and reproducing the alienation from her surroundings that Müller experienced when these were continually tampered with and controlled by the *Securitate*. This alien/outsider gaze enacts the paradox of trauma: 'that the most direct seeing of a violent event may occur

---

[3] The terms 'discours' and 'histoire' are taken from Gérard Genette, 'Frontières du récit', in Gérard Genette, *Figures II* (Paris: Seuil, 1969), 49–69, here 62 and *passim*. See below for detailed definition of the terms.

as an absolute inability to know it.'[4] It is a form of everyday perception common to all victims of terror, and not the mark of the writer. But not all victims of terror are writers, and nor is literature the unmediated transcription of trauma. The gaze is an effect of trauma, but it is also the source of the writing process; and Müller reproduces the effects of trauma through literary techniques and forms.

Although it results from undeniably, painfully real experiences, the nature of trauma is such that these are translated into entirely unreal conceptions of the body and self as nondelimited, split, or fragmented. These conceptions can only be represented through literary imagery. Elaine Scarry's influential 1985 text *The Body in Pain: The Making and Unmaking of the World* explores the relation between body and language by looking at the special case of torture.[5] Torture is an extreme example of a traumatizing event, and Scarry's analysis of the torture process explains how trauma can affect both body image and language. Torture is based around pain, which 'has no referential content. It is not *of* or *for* anything. It is precisely because it takes no object that it, more than any other phenomenon, resists objectification in language.'[6] Scarry's position is predicated on a conception of language as referential, an understanding which is necessary for the communication of pain, the political aim which is at the heart of her project. Scarry's statement also implicitly signals another form of language, one which also resists referentiality and which may therefore be able to express this pain, albeit indirectly—the poetic. Trauma is not only represented in images of the body in Müller's work, but also through narrative strategies which have a 'poetic' rather than referential function, in Roman Jakobson's terms, and which disrupt the realism which is often imputed to her texts.[7]

Representations of the body in Müller's work demonstrate the close links between the effects of trauma and the process of psychological development, in which body image is implicated in

---

[4] Caruth, *Unclaimed Experience*, 91–2.
[5] Elaine Scarry, *The Body in Pain: The Making and Unmaking of the World* (New York: Oxford University Press, 1985).
[6] Ibid. 5.
[7] Roman Jakobson, 'Linguistics and Poetics' (1960), discussed by Christine Brooke-Rose, *A Rhetoric of the Unreal: Studies in Narrative & Structure, Especially of the Fantastic* (Cambridge: Cambridge University Press, 1981), see esp. 22.

the acquisition of language. Torture enforces a form of regression in its victim: as Scarry explains, it 'graphically objectifies the step-by-step backward movement along the path by which language comes into being and which is here reversed or uncreated or deconstructed'.[8] Torturers aim to reduce the victim to a physical state where 'the body and its pain are overwhelmingly present and voice, world and self are absent'.[9] The end result is that the victim experiences self and world as undifferentiated; this is 'experienced spatially as either the contraction of the universe down to the immediate vicinity of the body or as the body swelling to fill the entire universe'.[10] Cathy Caruth similarly suggests that in trauma 'the outside has gone inside without any mediation'.[11] The child in 'Niederungen' epitomizes this merging of self and world, which is a result of the repression of both the Banat village and Ceauşescu's state, the two concentric dictatorships. Müller's narrative focus on individual objects is linked to this contraction of the universe, as objects constitute the immediate outside world but also, as personal belongings, provide a bridge between body and world, just as the body is the bridge between self and world.[12]

The experience of the body as fragmented results from this regression, and can be plotted against Lacan's understanding of infant development.[13] Having been separated from its mother, the child perceives its body in parts, which only coalesce into a unitary body image through seeing the whole in a mirror. This 'mirror stage' represents the body as fundamentally alienated from the self: it is whole, but perceived as other; the stage is characterized by dual relationships. Inauguration into the Symbolic order, and thus into language, results from the intervention of a third element (the father) into this dualism. Images of the body as other, or in parts—psychic splitting and fragmentation—reflect these two stages. In Müller's texts, splitting is often represented precisely through mirror images, as well as in the projection of a child self (most notably in *Herztier*) and in the particular relation of narrator and protagonist in *Reisende*

---

[8] Scarry, *The Body in Pain*, 20.   [9] Ibid. 45.
[10] Ibid. 35.   [11] Caruth, *Unclaimed Experience*, 59.
[12] Haines takes up this concern with detail in "Leben wir im Detail".
[13] Moi provides a useful, succinct summary of Lacan's theories, *Sexual Textual Politics*, 99–101.

which reflects the dissociation of body and voice. The autobiographical elements of Müller's work can also be understood as a form of splitting, where Müller creates an alter ego—the self as other—within her texts. The doubling of female characters where one is complicit in the activities of the state—the pairs of friends Irene and Dana, Adina and Clara, the 'ich' of *Herztier* and Tereza—compounds this tendency and, furthermore, represents another related phenomenon, 'the survivor's identification with the opposite pole in the victim–oppressor polarization, the most difficult wound to heal'.[14]

Individual aspects of the self or even emotions may also be designated 'not-I' and experienced as exterior.[15] Mirroring this externalization is the feeling of alien objects within the body, as observed by Goodwin and Attias.[16] Müller's depiction of emotion, most notably fear, reflects both of these patterns; fear exists as an independent entity which disregards the boundaries of self and body. The projection of fear onto discrete, external objects converges on images of 'Der Diktator' (Ceaușescu) and, more specifically, his eye; the metonymic representation is the image which possesses the victim of trauma. Müller's focus on fragmentation and on radically alienated body parts (evident from *Barfüßiger Februar* onwards) shows the slow return to language which necessarily precedes the attempt to turn trauma into narrative. In the later novels, these phenomena are identified in the strategies of the state, in the terror and the interrogations depicted in the texts. Recognizing their external status, separating agent from effect, is a further step towards re-establishing the boundaries of the body.

Many of the poetic effects of Herta Müller's texts represent traumatic symptoms. Moreover, for Müller, trauma is constitutive of the act of writing itself. In her earlier poetological essays, the act and process of writing itself, indeed her inspiration to write, resembles structures of trauma, particularly in its

---

[14] Henry Krystal, 'Trauma and Aging: A Thirty-Year Follow-Up', in Caruth (ed.), *Trauma: Explorations in Memory*, 76–99, here 94. Müller herself was betrayed by a close friend, who informed on her and wrote to her after she had left Romania; see Müller in interview with Irene Etzersdorfer, '"Warum sind Sie enttäuscht, Herta Müller?" Ein Gespräch mit der rumäniendeutschen Autorin über ihr Land nach dem Umsturz', *Die Presse*, 24 Oct. 1992, p. vii.

[15] Krystal, 'Trauma and Aging', 85.

[16] Attias and Goodwin (eds.), *Splintered Reflections*, 134.

incorporation of the body. The body is, for Müller, inseparable from the act of writing, which is both corporeal and spatial in origin: 'Das Biologische des Körpers ist im Schreiben auch genauso drin, wie es in allen anderen Dingen drin ist.'[17] Both the body and language are marked by a 'Riß', a figure for the splitting which results from psychic trauma and, further, the trauma which constitutes subjectivity:

> Gerade durch den Riß, dadurch, daß wir geteilt sind, gehören unsere beiden Hälften zusammen.
> Seltsam sind die Körperteile, die wir nur einmal haben: die Zunge, der Kehlkopf, der Nabel. Ach ja, und das Herz, von dem man spricht, als wäre es außen, über der Haut. [...]
> Züge, Bissen, Worte, Griffe, Schritte: in allem ist der Riß. (*TS* 76–7)

Language is marked by the 'Riß', which is also a cipher for the *différance* which enables language to function. This also suggests a more general understanding of trauma as part of the subject's coming to language, which may account for the apparently incompatible readings of Müller's work as a representation both of trauma narrative and of postmodern subjectivity.

The impetus to writing is the interpenetration of inner and outer worlds, something Müller describes in the present tense and in strikingly physical terms:

> Das Schreiben ist jedesmal das Letzte, was ich (immer noch) tun kann, ja muß, wenn ich nichts mehr anderes tun kann. Es ist immer, wenn ich schreibe, der Punkt erreicht, wo ich mit mir selber (und das heißt auch mit dem, was mich umgibt) nicht mehr umgehen kann. Ich ertrage meine Sinne nicht mehr. Ich ertrage mein Nachdenken nicht mehr. Es ist alles so verstrickt geworden, daß ich nicht mehr weiß, wo die äußeren Dinge anfangen und aufhören. Ob sie in mir sind, oder ich in ihnen. Es brechen Stücke Welt heraus, als hätte ich alles geschluckt, was ich nicht tragen kann.
> So kommt es, daß ich das Schreiben als das Gegenteil von Leben, und als das Gegenteil von Denken empfinde. Ein großer Rückzug, ich weiß nicht wohin, und ich weiß nicht worauf. An keinen Ort und nicht auf mich selbst. Es ist die lückenlose Unwirklichkeit [...].
> Tagelang, wochenlang schaue ich auf die äußeren Dinge um mich und auf mich selbst. Ob ich mich darin zerlege, oder sie in mir, bis der Punkt kommt, an dem ich den Rückzug ins lückenlos Unwirkliche mach, ich weiß es nicht. (*TS* 33–5)

---

[17] Müller, in interview with Haines and Littler, 'Gespräch mit Herta Müller', 17.

The point where external and internal are indistinguishable from one another cannot be located; it is a blind spot beyond conscious thought (both 'Denken' and 'Nachdenken'). It is characterized by alienation from the self and the senses, the body's means of interaction with the world, and by fragmentation ('zerlegen'). This is the fragmentation perpetrated by the gaze: 'genaues Hinsehen [heißt] zerstören [...]. Wenn man Menschen, auch wenn sie einem nahestehen, ansieht, wird man schonungslos. Man zerlegt sie. Das Detail wird größer als das Ganze' (*TS* 25–6). It is reproduced in Müller's narrative perspective, which focuses on individual details which become overwhelming. Although the effect remains the same, it is now turned back on the outside world, recreating and reproducing there what had originally been imposed from outside in the form of trauma. Literature gains the power to affect reality through this interaction of self and world:

Nicht nur aus den eigenen Texten gehen die Sätze hinaus, in die Dinge. [...] Und meist stellt sich dieses Bild der konkreten Wahrnehmung als Kopie der gelesenen, erfundenen Wahrnehmung im Kopf dar. [...] Nicht die Bilder im Kopf werden wie der Ort, sondern der Ort wird wie die Bilder im Kopf. (*TS* 53)

This phenomenon leads to a conception of the relation between literature and reality which is the exact opposite of that which informs realism: reality reflects literature, and not vice versa.

Müller terms her literary perspective 'die erfundene Wahrnehmung' (*TS* 13 and *passim*), acknowledging its hybrid origins, as well as its autonomy and refusal of boundaries: 'Die Wahrnehmung, die sich erfindet, steht nicht still. Sie überschreitet ihre Grenzen' (*TS* 19). It has its basis in Müller's childhood perceptions, where the workings of the imagination were experienced as uncontrollable and independent of the conscious mind:

Ich merke an mir, daß nicht das am stärksten im Gedächtnis bleibt, was außen war, was man Fakten nennt. Stärker, weil wieder erlebbar im Gedächtnis, ist das, was von innen kam, angesichts des Äußeren, der Fakten.
  Denn das, was von innen kam, hat unter den Rippen gedrückt, hat die Kehle geschnürt, hat den Puls gehetzt. Es ist seine Wege gegangen. Es hat seine Spuren gelassen. (*TS* 10)

The startling physicality of this scenario echoes several elements of trauma: it is the structure of the reaction to an event—'das, was von innen kam, angesichts des Äußeren'—which determines its effect, and this effect consists in it being 'wieder erlebbar', that is, not integrated into memory but recurring, as a very literal re-experience. This possession by the image is mirrored in the physical possession and invasion of the body, which, significantly, blocks the throat, the channel of the voice.

Müller's texts are structured by the coordination of syntactic and semantic gaps, which combine to create '[das] lückenlos Unwirkliche' (*TS* 35): the text's blank spaces enable an uninterrupted unreality to be projected. The text is a balancing act between the 'geschriebenen' and the 'verschwiegenen Satz':

> Der geschriebene Satz ist ein nachweisbarer Satz zwischen vielen verschwiegenen Sätzen. Nur seine Nachweisbarkeit unterscheidet ihn von den verschwiegenen Sätzen. [...] Und er ist auch nur nachweisbar, weil er die verschwiegenen Sätze in sich enthält, indem er sie vorwegnimmt und hinterherträgt. (*TS* 36)

It is precisely this repressed, unwritten content which Müller notices in other texts:

> Ich merke es an den Texten anderer Autoren, ich fühle es aus den Büchern. Das, was mich einkreist, seine Wege geht, beim Lesen, ist das, was zwischen den Sätzen fällt und aufschlägt, oder kein Geräusch macht. Es ist das Ausgelassene. (*TS* 19)

Like 'das, was von innen kam', 'das Ausgelassene' is autonomous and a concrete physical presence. Semantic gaps in Müller's work indicate in the first instance the unassimilated traumatic event, drawing attention to unseen violence and threat; syntactic gaps emphasize stasis, freezing a moment of perception in time. These gaps are linked to structures of memory, as well as to narrative, as Müller notes: 'das Auslassen ist ein Mittel, ohne das man überhaupt nichts erinnern kann'.[18]

The act of writing, or at least the spur to it, appears to reproduce the moment of trauma; insofar as it leads to creativity, however, this can be seen as potentially liberating. In Scarry's

---

[18] Müller, in Beverley Driver Eddy, '"Die Schule der Angst"—Gespräch mit Herta Müller, den 14. April 1998', *German Quarterly*, 72/4 (1999), 329–39, here 334.

account, torture and interrogation produce their effects by a 'mime of uncreating', which Müller appears to reverse here.[19] 'Die erfundene Wahrnehmung' can be seen in this light as a literary correlative of the necessary reworking of the traumatic event into a perception which is available to conscious recall and integrated into a narrative.

I turn now to images of the body in Müller's work, which represent trauma in three forms: through the dissolution of the boundaries between self and the world; the experience of the self or body as double or split; and fragmentation. These images can be both negative and positive, depending on their context; they are both effect of trauma and literary effect. I end the section by considering the strategies of the state which mimic and enforce the structures of trauma.

BODY

Images of the body in Müller's work represent three effects of trauma, namely the dissolution of the boundaries between inside and outside; dissociation, the experience or observation of the self as other; and the fragmentation of the body. These particular figures resemble conventional literary tropes and have indeed been compared to them by critics. Claudia Becker relates *Niederungen* to E. T. A. Hoffmann's 'Serapiontisches Prinzip', implying a Romantic, potentially liberating view of the merging of self and world.[20] Margaret Littler analyses the dislocation and the diffusion of identity in *Reisende auf einem Bein* as an example of the postmodern nomadic subjectivity theorized by Rosi Braidotti, which is characterized by a non-fixed identity propelled only by desire.[21] While these two interpretations offer illuminating ways of approaching these as individual texts—and Littler gives the caveat that *Reisende* is exceptional

[19] Scarry, *The Body in Pain*, 20.
[20] Claudia Becker, ' "Serapiontisches Prinzip in politischer Manier"—Wirklichkeits- und Sprachbilder in *Niederungen*', in Eke (ed.), *Die erfundene Wahrnehmung*, 32–41.
[21] Margaret Littler, 'Beyond Alienation: The City in the Novels of Herta Müller and Libuše Moníková', in Haines (ed.), *Herta Müller*, 36–56; Rosi Braidotti, *Nomadic Subjects: Embodiment and Sexual Difference in Contemporary Feminist Theory* (New York: Columbia University Press, 1994).

among Müller's texts in being open to such a postmodern reading, due to its setting in a pluralist society[22] — it is my concern here to show how these figures belong to a wider narrative of trauma visible in Müller's texts. *Reisende* is a pivotal text in Müller's oeuvre: it portrays the effects of trauma but at a remove from Romania, and thus prefigures and facilitates the representation of the Ceauşescu regime in subsequent texts. Images and experiences of the body are a key to this narrative of trauma.

Dissolution of boundaries

The dissolution of the boundaries of the self is enacted in Müller's texts as the collapse of the distinction between the body and the world. In early texts this is depicted using sexual imagery. 'Der Wolf im Berg', in the Bucharest-published *Drückender Tango*, presents the interaction of the individual and surrounding nature as unproblematic, emphasizing transitory intercourse rather than a loss of self:

In den Wiesen wächst die schwarze Frau, den Fuß im Sand, den Kopf im Astgewirr. Der Wind treibt sie den Berg hinauf zu den Steinen. So ist ihr Schritt der Halm mit spröder Gicht, die Distel ist er, in den Adern schwer behängt mit violetten Igeln. [...]

Die rote Katze sieht durchs Holz, wie die schwarze Frau unter dem Rand des Kopftuchs, hinter dem Knoten, der am Kehlkopf drückt, ins Dickicht geht, wie sie die Röcke hebt und den Wolf zur Quelle lockt mit ihrem nabelfremden Bauch, wie sie sich im Wasserspiegel ihm von unten zeigt, wie sie die Augen schließt, die Lippen öffnet, bis das Wasser stöhnt [...]. (*DT* 16)

The woman here is a part of the meadow, and her intercourse encompasses both animal and the element, water. Imagined intercourse in 'Das Fenster' also implies a fluid relation between the female narrator and nature: 'Die Brücke ist hohl und stöhnt, und das Echo fällt mir in den Mund' (*Nd* 110). In both 'Damals im Mai' (*Niederungen*, Bucharest) and 'Heide' (*Drückender Tango*), the first-person narrator observes, and is drawn into, intercourse within nature, again, interestingly, centring on water. Water functions like the mirrors which are a

---

[22] Littler, 'Beyond Alienation', 52. I do not entirely agree with Littler on this point, which I take up below.

recurrent motif in Müller's texts and which I analyse below. Both surface and depth, located in/on the ground but reflecting the sky, water is a symbol of the fluid boundary between the elements, and thus of the collapse of binary distinctions.

More frequently, however, the dissolution of boundaries between self and world is associated with violence and the suppression of identity. In 'Niederungen', the child protagonist identifies with threatened animals (sparrows, a calf), in a displacement of the fact that she also feels threatened by her parents' aggression. The symbiosis is negative, as the child is vicariously exposed to danger, as is the case when the pig is slaughtered:

Ich hörte das Schwein. Es stöhnte. [...]
    Ich lag im Bett. Ich fühlte das Messer an meiner Kehle.
    Es tat mir weh, der Schnitt ging immer tiefer, mein Fleisch wurde heiß, es begann zu kochen in meinem Hals.
    Der Schnitt wurde weit größer als ich, er wuchs übers ganze Bett, er brannte unter der Decke, er stöhnte sich ins Zimmer.
    Die zerrissenen Eingeweide rollten über den Teppich hin, sie dampften und rochen nach halbverdautem Mais.
    Ein maisvoller Magen hing über dem Bett an einem Darm, der immer dünner wurde und zuckte.
    Als der Darm abreißen wollte, zündete ich das Licht an. (*Nd* 31)

The passage shows the transgression of several boundaries. Initially the child and the pig are discrete entities, expressed in the sentence structure (subject–object); then the child identifies with the pig and experiences the slaughter; finally, the child's imagination projects the horrors onto the outside world, in a fictional form of reality. There is a difference between the empathetic, although unreal, experience of the child feeling the knife and the wholly imagined scenario of intestines over the bed. The latter is an effect of trauma, an intrusive, all-too-literal image recalled in *Reisende*, in Irene's shocking description of Christmas decorations: 'Es war, wie wenn man Eingeweide über Tannen hängt' (*R* 35).

The symbiosis of child and nature finds its apotheosis in the following scene, reflecting the child's need for unconditional love which is not fulfilled by her mother:

Der Sommer wälzte seinen schweren Blumenduft aus dem hohen Gras über mich. Die wilden Grasblumen krochen mir unter die Haut. Ich ging an den Fluß und goß mir Wasser über die Arme. Es wuchsen hohe Stauden aus meiner Haut. Ich war eine schöne sumpfige Landschaft.

Ich legte mich ins hohe Gras und ließ mich in die Erde rinnen. Ich wartete, daß die großen Weiden zu mir über den Fluß kommen, daß sie ihre Zweige in mich schlagen und ihre Blätter in mich streuen. Ich wartete, daß sie sagen: Du bist der schönste Sumpf der Welt, wir kommen alle zu dir. [...]

Ich wollte weit werden, damit die Wasservögel mit ihren großen Flügeln Platz in mir haben, Platz zum Fliegen. Ich wollte die schönsten Dotterblumen tragen, denn auch sie sind schwer und leuchtend. (*Nd* 78)

The passage is written as statements of fact rather imagined experience. Mutual interpenetration is emphasized in the symmetrical constructions, in the oppositions of 'aus'/'in', 'über'/'unter', the contrast of the heavy flowers with the light birds, and the suggestion of simultaneous movement towards and away from the child. The harmony of child and nature is fragile; here the child's identity is intact: although she becomes part of nature, it is as a distinct and discrete entity (the marsh) and the passage is narrated as the experience of an 'ich', a desiring subject. In other passages, however, the child is subsumed into nature:

Am Dorfrand liegt das alte Geschirr. [...] Aus einer Waschschüssel ohne Boden wächst Gras mit leuchtendgelben Blütenständen.

Der Wurm frißt im bitteren Fleisch der Schlehen und treibt einen farblosen Saft durch die blaue verhauchte Fruchtschale.

Im Inneren des Strauches sind die Blätter am Ersticken. Die Zweige stoßen sich aus dem Graben, sie wachsen in langen spitzen Stacheln zu Ende und verformen sich auf der Suche nach Licht. [...]

Unter der Brücke ist im Winter Schnee und im Sommer Schatten. Wasser ist nie darunter. Der Fluß kümmert sich nicht um sie, er fließt an ihr vorbei. [...]

Die Brennesseln peitschen ihre bewegten Schatten ins Dorf. Sie kriechen mit ihrem Feuer in die Hände und lassen rote geschwollene Bisse zurück, deren Zungen am Blut lecken und in den Adersträngen der Hände schmerzen. (*Nd* 35)

A description of a slowly decaying, stifling nature is given a further dimension by the final metaphor of the nettles, which act on the body. The extraordinarily dense poetic imagery draws attention to the narrative instance as its source—the consciousness which draws the elements of the metaphor together, and whose hands are 'bitten'. The faint pathetic fallacy of the previous few lines is transformed in retrospect into a projection of the specific situation of the child onto its surroundings by the resignalling of the narrative instance. It is the child who is 'am Ersticken', who 'verformt sich auf der Suche nach Licht' (or perhaps love), who is ignored by its surroundings (human and organic). The absence of an experiencing 'ich' indicates that the child's consciousness is not just projected but entirely displaced onto its surroundings.

The displacement of consciousness—in 'Niederungen', a consciousness of neglect and violence—onto the outside world resembles the conventional literary devices of pathetic fallacy and anthropomorphism. Several early texts published in Romania have nature as their ostensible subject, but are in fact concerned with the human. In 'Pferdeköpfe and 'Das kalte Lied', in *Drückender Tango*, trees have human features.[23] Images of sunset invoke violence: 'Sonne dreht sich leer im Abend, öffnet sich die Adern. Himmel ist voll mit Frost und dick mit Blut' (*DT* 5); 'das Meer wurde ruhig und blutig. Es war voller Wasser und voller Blut'.[24] In these texts, the projection of violence onto nature also functions as a veiled reference to the political repression which cannot be depicted directly. Just as descriptions of the rural Banat also function as a microcosm of the repressive political situation, Müller's consciousness of the violence of the Ceauşescu regime is displaced onto seemingly unpolitical, pastoral scenes.

Whereas in these earlier texts the merging of self and world is represented as the projection of the 'ich' onto nature, in later texts the reverse occurs: nature, in the form of the landscape of the country, impresses upon the 'ich', the flipside of the same experience. In the 1991 prose piece 'Das Land am Nebentisch', Avram, who escapes Romania, expresses this oscillation between positions: 'Ob Avram das Äussere schluckte oder ins Äussere geschluckt wurde, das konnte er nie unterscheiden. Avram

[23] In art therapy, drawings of trees function as expressions of body image: see Barry M. Cohen and Anne Mills, 'Skin/Paper/Bark: Body Image, Trauma and the Diagnostic Drawing Series', in Attias and Goodwin (eds.), *Splintered Reflections*, 203–21, here 216.
[24] Herta Müller, 'Damals im Mai', *Niederungen* (Bucharest: Kriterion, 1982), here 112. Cf. also 'Der Mann mit der Zündholzschachtel' (*Nd* 113–15), which literalizes the metaphor of sunset as the sky on fire.

empfand es als gegenseitig, weil er es anders nicht ertragen konnte.'[25] The notion of belonging to a country (not a state), never a politically innocent conception, is expressed in this merging of body and landscape, which points to the destructive force of the external environment. In *Herztier*, Lola, who came to the city from the countryside, writes in her diary, 'was man aus der Gegend hinausträgt, trägt man hinein in sein Gesicht' (*Hz* 10). Her face bears the traces of her origins:

> Lola kam aus dem Süden des Landes, und man sah ihr eine armgebliebene Gegend an. Ich weiß nicht wo, vielleicht an den Knochen der Wangen, oder um den Mund, oder mitten in den Augen. Sowas ist schwer zu sagen, von einer Gegend so schwer wie von einem Gesicht. Jede Gegend im Land war arm geblieben, auch in jedem Gesicht. Doch Lolas Gegend, und wie man sie an den Knochen der Wangen, oder um den Mund, oder mitten in den Augen sah, war vielleicht ärmer. (*Hz* 9)

The inseparability of face and country, emphasized by the repetition in the passage, means that Romanians abroad are immediately recognizable to each other. Müller identifies a Romanian man in a station café in Vienna: 'ein ganzes Land hing an einem Menschen. Ein ganzes, mir bekanntes Land, saß am Nebentisch. Ich hatte es sofort wiedererkannt' (*TS* 122). In less poetic terms, their faces express their experiences: both the trauma of repression and the trauma of leaving. This almost superstitious conception of the physical relation between land and self is elaborated in 'Zwischen den Augen zwischen den Rippen', in *Eine warme Kartoffel ist ein warmes Bett*:

> Die Beziehung zwischen einem Land und einer Person, die darin lebt, ist die, daß das Land über die Person hinwegrollt. Das ist ein Gewicht, das man annimmt, auch wenn man es nicht erträgt. Man trägt dieses Land: an den Fußsohlen, an den Fingerspitzen, im Nacken und an der Kehle. (*KB* 17)

Notable here once more is the physicality of the expression. The experience of belonging to a land, and particularly to Romania, further effects the reduction of the body to contiguous parts. The lack of differentiation between self and world

---

[25] Herta Müller, 'Das Land am Nebentisch', *Neue Zürcher Zeitung*, 6 Dec. 1991, pp. 41–2, here 41.

thus prefigures the fragmentation of the body, which I return to below.

In its most extreme form, the merging of body and land equals death, symbolically and literally. People who tried to cross the Romanian border to escape over land or across the Danube were frequently shot, and their bodies left to decompose in the fields and rivers. The motif recurs in the later texts, at its most stark in *Der Wächter nimmt seinen Kamm* (1993): 'Donau | Landschaft im Rücken', 'die Männer Wasser im Mund', and 'Flußbett aus dem Haar' (postcard 14), or 'eine verrückte Pappel um den Hals in der Erde' (postcard 76). After the turning point of *Reisende*, Müller's novel *Der Fuchs war damals schon der Jäger* (1992) is the first of her texts to address the Ceaușescu regime directly. In the text, Adina and Paul contemplate trying to cross the border:

> Sollen wir hinters Feld an die Donau, fragte Adina, sollen wir flüchten, willst du Schüsse hören und dir ausrechnen, daß wir es sind. Wir bräuchten keine halbe Stunde und würden da drüben im Weizen liegen, bis im Sommer der Mähdrescher kommt. Paul zog Adina an der Schulter zurück, und sie sagte in sein Gesicht, der Buchhalter wird die steigenden Eiweißprozente im Mehl erklären. Paul hielt mit der Hand ihren Mund zu. Sie stieß seine Hand weg und sah die Kartoffel verschwimmen. Manchmal, sagte sie, wird euch beim Essen ein Haar in den Zähnen hängen, eines, das nicht dem Bäcker in den Teig gefallen ist. (*FJ* 261)

Adina's scenario invokes the grotesque idea of the human as edible; a certain black humour comes from the incongruous detail of the 'steigende Eiweißprozente' and the political overtones of the state-regulated industry. Far from being a poetic expression of subjective experience, Adina's understanding is all too lucid and direct, marking the change in the articulation of trauma in Müller's work.

Reisende auf einem Bein (1989) is the only one of Müller's texts to be set outside Romania, and it reconfigures the relationship between self and surroundings as mutual and positive rather than destructive. The text opens with a description of the boundaries of Romania, the coast:

> An den Treppen der Steilküste, wo Erde bröckelte, sah Irene wie in all den anderen Sommern die Warntafel stehen: 'Erdrutschgefahr'.
> Die Warnung hatte in diesem losgelösten Sommer zum ersten Mal wenig mit der Küste und viel mit Irene zu tun. (*R* 7)

The link between the crumbling coast, the 'losgelöst' summer, and Irene's unstable identity is made self-consciously, moving beyond the metaphorical equivalence implied in other texts. Irene refuses to identify with 'das andere Land' (Romania) which she has left, situating herself instead in relation to a city, Berlin, a move which, as Margaret Littler suggests, represents 'a more positive reconceptualization of the city as "habitat", an extension of the bodily experience of space'.[26] It is also a more positive reconceptualization of the dissolution of boundaries between the self and the world evident in earlier texts. Littler explains Irene's identification with Berlin with reference to Donna Mazzoleni, who views city life as 'a point at which the most elementary distinction of space—the distinction between "inside" and "outside", which is the very distinction between "I" and "the world"—grows weaker'.[27]

The differences between Irene's situation and that of the child in 'Niederungen' lie in the setting—the pluralist, mutable city as opposed to the conservative, inflexible village. The liberating potential of the images in *Reisende* derives from the sole fact of their having been removed from a violent context; their existence, however, originates in precisely that violent context. The structures of experiences remain the same, for example, in this reversal of agency and movement: 'Irene trug den Koffer durchs Stiegenhaus hoch. Dann ging ein Flur durch sie hindurch. Dann eine Küche. Dann ein Bad. Dann ein Zimmer' (*R* 38). Instead of Irene moving through the rooms, the outside acts upon her, rendering her temporarily insubstantial. The child in 'Niederungen' experiences a similar reversal of agency, although this time the child remains solid and the effect is damaging: 'Ich fühle, wie schwer der Hof mir auf den Zehen liegt, der Hof lastet mir auf den Füßen, der Hof schlägt mir beim Gehen in die Knie' (*Nd* 87). Moreover, Irene's relationship with the city is not fixed, but variable and mutually pursued:

Stadt und Schädel war die Abwechslung von Stillstand und Bewegung.
    Wenn der Schädel stillstand, wuchs der Asphalt. Wenn der Asphalt stillstand, wuchs die Leere im Schädel.

---

[26] Littler, 'Beyond Alienation', 47.
[27] Donna Mazzoleni, 'The City and the Imaginary', *New Formations*, 11 (1990), 91–104, here 101.

Mal fiel die Stadt über Irenes Gedanken her. Mal Irenes Gedanken über die Stadt. (*R* 62-3)

The self is depicted in physical terms, metonymically as the 'Schädel', as is the relation between self and city, as 'herfallen'. Irene chooses to identify with Berlin, because of the similarities between her dislocated, contingent sense of self and the situation of the radically divided city:

> Es war ein Kommen und Gehen der besetzten und geräumten Orte. [...] Das war ein Zusammenhang zwischen Irene und der Stadt.
> Doch, er war mühsam, der Zusammenhang, oft zwischen Stadt und Schädel so verstreut, daß Irene ihn erfinden mußte. (*R* 143)

The other protagonists have no such choice about belonging to Romania, and the dissociation which propels Irene is imposed on them from outside.

Irene explores the city through her immediate surroundings, in preference to gaining an overview of the city and its topography, seeing it as a series of individual places and objects (bridges, for example). Irene's connection with her flat marks a different form of projection of the psyche into the outside world; she perceives her rooms as an extension of her body. Rooms represent both an enlargement of the body and civilization in miniature.[28] Self and world converge symbolically in the room: 'Ich wohne von Kopf bis Fuß' (*DT* 61), declares Inge in 'Möbelstücke'. Reinforcing boundaries, walls prevent 'undifferentiated contact with the world' of the type evident in Müller's texts.[29] Irene experiences her room simultaneously as a body in its own right and as a continuation of her body:

> Irene dreht das Gesicht zur Wand.
> An der Wand grenzte sich deutlich ein Viereck ab. Das war weißer als der Rest der Wand. [...] Es war weiß wie Haut. Es war ein Rücken.
> Irene sah die Rippen durch die Haut. Der Rücken atmete. [...]
> Irene spürte die Wärme des Rückens, die Wärme des Betts, die Wärme der Kleider und die Wärme der Haut.
> Jede Wärme war anders.
> Der Rand der Decke lag um den Hals. Irene fühlte sich wie begraben.
> Ihre Lider wurden länger. Reichten für das ganze Gesicht. Für das ganze Zimmer reichten Irenes Lider. (*R* 42)

---

[28] See Scarry, *The Body in Pain*, 38-9, and Mazzoleni, 'The City', 97.
[29] Scarry, *The Body in Pain*, 38.

Initially, the room is a separate, living entity; Irene internalizes it by closing her eyes.

On an even smaller scale, Irene relates to specific objects around her, as a means of making contact with the outside world. In the repressive climate of Romania, personal possessions offered a stability denied the individual, and the reassurance of familiarity:

> Wie überrascht war ich manchmal am Morgen, wie fühlte ich mich gerettet, wenn ich die Augen öffnete und sah, daß da, wo die Haut zu Ende war, das Bett, das Zimmer begann. [...] Immer mehr Gegenstände. Und ich konnte atmen, konnte weg von der Haut: Überall Gegenstände, wo die Haut zu Ende war. (*TS* 91)

Familiar objects allow the individual to transcend the confines of the body; they represent the self within the outside world. Precisely because of their liminal status, however, the relationship moves between investment and horror. Müller has strong reactions to objects, as she explains to Beverley Driver Eddy: 'Das Fremdeln hab ich ja dort vor Gegenständen. [...] Ein Gegenstand ist ein fremder Stoff, der sich einschleicht und das Faszinosum entsteht ja auch erst durch die Fremdheit.'[30] Müller's choice of the term 'fremdeln', usually used of strangers, is telling: personal objects were often tampered with by the *Securitate* (see *FB* 9–11). The relationship has its origins in the effects of trauma, evident in the text 'Das Haar auf der Schulter', where Müller describes the scene of an interrogation: 'Ich wollte keine Angst vor ihm haben, ein Gegenstand werden, den es schon gab in diesem Raum: mich in das Holz des kleinen Tisches schleichen, in den Fußboden, ins zerknüllte Papier neben meiner Hand.'[31] Even while it represents the effects of trauma, dispersing oneself into surrounding objects is reinterpreted as a strategy for survival. It is a strategy recreated in Müller's focus on detail and immediate perceptions within her texts.

The alienated body

At its most extreme, the disembodiment of the self and its disintegration leads to the perception of the body, or its parts,

---

[30] Driver Eddy, "Die Schule der Angst", 330.
[31] Herta Müller, 'Das Haar auf der Schulter: Fünf Texte zur Messe in C-Dur von Franz Schubert', *Frankfurter Rundschau*, 25 May 1996, p. ZB3.

as independent, separate entities. Victims of physical threat or violence often conceive of their body as split from their self in response to the horrors they experience. In Müller's texts, alienation of the body and fragmentation are both explicitly linked to physical threat, specifically to the 'Verhör'. The more acute the physical terror, the more fragmented the body becomes; emotions are externalized and detached, and the body is reduced to its component parts.

The recurring motif of clothes without a body—the representation of the absence of a person—provides a link between the relationship with objects and psychic splitting. Clothes are at once personal objects and an image of the self. Adina's fear, induced by the *Securitate* entering her room while she is out, manifests itself in her perception of her own clothes: 'Adina sieht den Mantel auf dem Bett, er liegt, als wäre ein Arm drin, als greife eine Hand unter die Decke' (*FJ* 167). The narrator of *Herztier* similarly projects the horror of a friend's death and the fear of her own onto a vision of a dress: 'Das Kleid auf dem Stuhl verwandelte sich in eine ertrunkene Frau. Ich mußte es wegräumen. Die Strumpfhose hing wie abgeschnittene Beine von der Stuhllehne' (*Hz* 235). Consonant with their traumatic origin, both images explicitly refer to physical threats and death.[32] At times of stress, the protagonists experience themselves as absent in their own clothes: 'Adina zieht die Strumpfhose an, ihre Beine sind nicht in der Strumpfhose. Sie zieht den Mantel an, ihre Hände sind nicht im Mantel' (*FJ* 197). For Inge, the vulnerable character who figures frequently in Müller's early work, a phantom presence also indicates her own absence, or death: 'Die Person, die Inge in all ihren Kleidern sieht, hat ein fremdes Gesicht. Die Person, die Inge in ihren Kleidern sieht, hat ein totes Gesicht, hat ein Leichengesicht' (*DT* 61). The disjunction of clothes and wearer signals here dissociation and the experience of the self as totally other.

---

[32] In this light, Irene's metonymic description of women walking seems disconcerting: 'Mit leicht verrutschten Nähten gingen Frauenstrümpfe den Rinnstein entlang, auf Straßenenden zu, als hätten die Frauen nur Beine. Beine für Männer. Beine mit Schlingen. Sie fingen Blicke ein' (*R* 75). Stockings are a particularly suitable garment for this eerie effect: they act as a form of second skin, and retain the body's shape after being removed. A typically feminine object and a rare commodity in Romania, they are also associated with Lola and her death in *Herztier*: see esp. *Hz* 30.

Psychic splitting results from trauma: the self is divided into both subject and object, where the 'subject-me' is frequently located outside the body and observes it.[33] The protagonist of *Heute wär ich mir lieber nicht begegnet* observes herself eating, after the shock of finding an amputated human finger: 'Ich war ja gesund, und den Kuchen aß eine Hinfällige, sie glaubte, essen zu müssen und aß um ihr Leben' (*Ht* 160). *Barfüßiger Februar*, a text which deals with distance, from one's homeland and within it, contains many examples of the body as alienated other. In 'Der Tau auf dem Depots', the state policy of outlawing abortion underlies the women's distanced relation to their own bodies: 'Frauen wollten nicht die lauten Mäuler in den Bäuchen' (*BF* 75). Reflexive pronouns show the self as grammatical object: 'Hab mich nicht weggeschmissen. Hab mich nie gekannt. Hab mich am Morgen nur geschminkt. Lidschatten wie Staub und Glas. Hab mich nicht angeschaut' (*BF* 76). The act of putting on make-up is synonymous with the objectification of one's own face: 'Wir denken uns weg von unserem Augenlid und schminken es. Da wird das Auge uns unter der Hand zum Gegenstand' (*TS* 99). Other outsider positions lead to similar experiences of splitting. The neglected child Mathias in 'Viele Räume sind unter der Haut' experiences the world as radically divided: the hairdresser's hunchback becomes 'der Buckel, der Heimliche, den der Friseur bei sich trägt' (*BF* 64); in his mother's face 'war sie und eine andere Person' (68).

Irene experiences splitting at several points in *Reisende*, most notably when looking at a passport photo of herself, where she sees,

> Eine bekannte Person, doch nicht wie sie selbst. Und da, worauf es ankam, worauf es Irene ankam, an den Augen, am Mund, und da, an der Rinne zwischen Nase und Mund, war eine fremde Person gewesen. Eine fremde Person hatte sich eingeschlichen in Irenes Gesicht.
>
> Das Fremde an Irenes Gesicht war die andere Irene gewesen. (*R* 18)

The verb 'einschleichen' (used by Müller in remarks to Eddy, above) also relates this experience to the phenomenon of alien objects. The 'other Irene' takes on external, concrete form as another woman whom Irene sees in a restaurant; a customer looks at them both and asks, 'Wer von euch beiden ist denn

---

[33] Adelson, *Making Bodies*, 21.

die Attrappe' (*R* 156). At the same time, Irene sees Thomas and Franz—her two lovers—take on each other's features; her doubling is mirrored in theirs. One thinks also of the setting of the text, Berlin, in 1989 still split in two: surely the reason why Irene feels such affinity for the city. If, as Brigid Haines suggests, Irene's identity is more clearly defined by the structures of trauma than has previously been acknowledged, then it is also the case that the city she inhabits is not as unproblematically postmodern and pluralist as Littler posits: frequent references to 'die Mauer' signal the radical division of Berlin, a sign of Germany's post-war trauma writ large in the city.

More than this, though, the split is also enacted in the relationship between Irene and the narrator, which stages the split between observing (narrating) consciousness and the experiencing body. Haines has suggested that the third-person narrative demonstrates 'a very blurred boundary between the narrator's voice and the protagonist's thoughts', something which would have a precedent in the blurred boundaries of the body.[34] I would characterize the relationship not as one between two different (albeit close) figures, however, but rather as one between and within the divided figure of Irene.[35] The narrator is an 'other Irene', or, put differently, Irene herself becomes the other in the narrative; the narrator functions as Irene's voice and thoughts, representing them in the third person, while Irene herself stands for the body which is absent from, or which exceeds, the text. The prose of *Reisende* is a form of disembodied language, devoid of gesture, such as the description of conventional body language: the 'telegrammatic' conversation between Irene and an Italian immigrant (*R* 61), for example, is entirely lacking in the 'Gestik und Mimik' which would normally make it comprehensible.[36] Textual gestures are similarly absent: typically for

---

[34] Haines, 'The Alien Gaze'.
[35] Interestingly, Müller remarks about *Reisende*, 'Ich wollte mit der Person Irene von mir selber weggehen', in 'Die Weigerung sich verfügbar zu machen. Herta Müller und Richard Wagner im Gespräch', *Zitty*, 26 (1989), 68, cited by Grazziella Predoiu, *Faszination und Provokation bei Herta Müller* (Frankfurt am Main: Peter Lang, 2001), 148. Müller's statement displays another grammatical split (between 'ich' and 'mir'), for which the figure of Irene is a cipher.
[36] Stephan Düppe, 'Geschicke der Schrift als Strategie subjektiver Ohnmacht. Zu Herta Müllers poetologischen Vorlesungen *Der Teufel sitzt im Spiegel*', in

Müller's work, the text contains no quotation, question, or exclamation marks. The narrative also rejects movement: Irene is portrayed solely in individual places, in unrelated episodes; there is no defined plot. On a syntactic level, movement is also rejected in the use of parataxis, the suppression of causal links between sentences, which is characteristic of Müller's narrative style and taken to extremes in *Reisende*. The disjunction between mind and body finally also inheres in Irene's preferred method of communication, the postcard, a means of impersonal, that is, not embodied, speech; it prefigures the postcard collages Müller herself creates in *Der Wächter nimmt seinen Kamm*.

A form of splitting can be seen in the concretization of emotions. Emotion is translated into a physical feeling or an object which has a separate existence within the body or in the outside world. The consequent sense of unreality conveys the uncontrollable, all-pervasive fear which existed in Romania, a fear which exceeded itself, creating, as René Kegelmann says, 'eine Atmosphäre, die weit über die reale Bedrohung für eine Person hinausgeht'.[37] The figure of the father in *Herztier* attempts to suppress feelings by objectifying them: instead of acknowledging his experiences in the Second World War, he 'steckt sein schlechtes Gewissen in die dümmsten Pflanzen und hackt sie ab' and physically suppresses his memories of killing:

> Er hatte Friedhöfe gemacht [...]. Die Friedhöfe hält der Vater unten im Hals, wo zwischen Hemdkragen und Kinn der Kehlkopf steht. Der Kehlkopf ist spitz und verriegelt. So können die Friedhöfe nie hinauf über seine Lippen gehen. (*Hz* 21)

The similarly unemotional Windisch has two moments where his feelings are expressed as physical sensations: his anger at his daughter's sexual exploitation by the Milizmann forms a 'brennende Kugel' in his throat; and his disgust at the thought of his daughter's sexuality in itself leads to him vomiting, expelling his disgust from his body (*MFW* 85 and 86 respectively). It

---

Ralph Köhnen (ed.), *Der Druck der Erfahrung treibt die Sprache in die Dichtung: Bildlichkeit in Texten Herta Müllers* (Frankfurt am Main: Peter Lang, 1997), 155–69, here 164.

[37] Kegelmann, 'An den Grenzen des Nichts, dieser Sprache...', 126.

is significant that these concrete emotions are located in the throat: they signal the inability to articulate emotion.[38]

Emotions can be expelled from the body, as an animate object; or they can invade or act on the body as separate physical entities. In *Der Fuchs war damals schon der Jäger*, fear is independent of the body:

> Wenn man lange im Café sitzt, legt sich die Angst und wartet. Und wenn man morgen wiederkommt, liegt sie schon da, wo man sich hinsetzt. Sie ist eine Blattlaus im Kopf, sie kriecht nicht weg. Wenn man zu lange sitzen bleibt, stellt sie sich tot. (*FJ* 47)

The metaphor of the greenfly does not motivate the concretization but locates it within the physical environment and, in particular, associates it with the poplar trees which symbolize an unspecified threat (see below). In *Herztier*, the narrator explains the process which leads to externalization:

> Doch Angst schert aus. Wenn man sein Gesicht beherrscht, schlüpft sie in die Stimme. Wenn es gelingt, Gesicht und Stimme wie ein abgestorbenes Stück im Griff zu halten, verläßt sie sogar die Finger. Sie legt sich außerhalb der Haut hin. Sie liegt frei herum, man sieht sie auf den Gegenständen, die in der Nähe sind. (*Hz* 83)

The shift to the present tense here marks a generalization: this is a universal condition. Portraying fear as independent of the person who experiences it mimics the lack of control the dissidents had over their own lives. As Claudia Becker says, though, 'Wer über seine Angst spricht, spricht sich zugleich gegen bestehende Ordnungen und Verhältnisse aus', precisely because fear is a recognition that social conditions are wrong.[39] The proliferation of examples in the later, more overtly political novels suggests that this is a response to an extreme political

---

[38] In *Herztier* the child's inability to voice its fears aloud is described in similar, physical fashion: 'Das Kind redet weiter. Beim Reden bleibt etwas auf der Zunge liegen. Das Kind denkt sich, es kann nur die Wahrheit sein, die sich auf die Zunge legt wie ein Kirschkern, der nicht in den Hals fallen will. Solange die Stimme beim Reden ins Ohr steigt, wartet sie auf die Wahrheit. Aber gleich nach dem Schweigen, denkt sich das Kind, ist alles gelogen, weil die Wahrheit in den Hals gefallen ist. Weil der Mund das Wort *gegessen* nicht gesagt hat. | Das Wort geht dem Kind nicht über die Lippen' (*Hz* 15).

[39] Becker, '"Serapiontisches Prinzip"', 40. See also Norbert Otto Eke, '"Sein Leben machen | ist nicht, | sein Glück machen | mein Herr": Zum Verhältnis von Ästhetik und Politik in Herta Müllers Nachrichten aus Rumänien', *Jahrbuch der deutschen Schillergesellschaft*, 41 (1997), 481–509, here 498.

situation. Where the friends are unable to overcome their fear, Müller's texts use poetic devices in order to stage this fear and to distance it; moved into the unreal and fictional, it can be controlled, although never dissipated.

Splitting within the self and the alienation of aspects of identity leads inexorably towards the body's separation into individual parts. Hands and fingers are one of the most frequent and insistent of motifs in Müller's texts; they figure in traumatic flashbacks and are specifically implicated in violence and political oppression. In 'Viele Räume unter der Haut', Mathias's alienation from his body is focused on his hands:

> Mathias knipst das Licht öfter an und aus. Als könne er das Zimmer und sich selbst mit der Fingerspitze mit einem Daumendruck erfinden und verschwinden machen.
> Mathias knipst sich an und aus. [...]
> Mathias schaute seinen Händen zu. Er weiß nicht, was sie tun. Für wen. (*BF* 73)

In *Herztier*, the narrator experiences her body as alien as a result of her treatment by the secret police: 'Ich sah bei jedem Handgriff meine Finger, kannte die Wahrheit meiner eigenen Hand aber nicht besser als die Finger meiner Mutter oder Terezas Finger' (*Hz* 141). Fingers are a point of contact with the world;[40] in *Reisende*, they symbolize knowledge just out of reach of Irene's consciousness: 'Der Sinn der Reise war wie kalte Fingerspitzen, war da, wo der Körper aufhörte. Irene spürte ihn nicht' (*R* 137).[41] While the limbs clearly function as a metonymic representation of the individual, this prefigures the representation of hands or fingers as entirely separate from the body. This arises in part because hands and fingers are often taken control of by others, as in the traumatic nail-cutting scene in *Herztier*. The child's fear that the mother will cut off its fingers, instead of cutting its nails, is sublimated in a grotesque fantasy that the mother secretly eats the child's severed fingers. In 'Meine Finger' the child narrator's mother binds her hands because

---

[40] Margaret Littler also sees feet as a privileged point of contact, Littler, 'Beyond Alienation', 49; cf. also Ralph Köhnen, 'Über Gänge. Kinästhetische Bilder in Texten Herta Müllers', in Köhnen (ed.), *Der Druck der Erfahrung*, 123–38.

[41] Fingers are also implicated in stealing, an act of defiance: Müller reports shoplifting in 'Das Ticken der Norm', saying 'Ich stahl nicht, weil ich diese Dinge brauchte, sondern weil ich zehn spitze Finger an den Händen trug, die vor der Bedrohung des Staats so oft gezittert hatten' (*HuS* 93).

she insists on walking on them. Once the child has surrendered to convention, her disembodied fingers are implicated in violence exactly like the mother's: 'Und meine Zeigefinger sind Schlagfinger. Und meine Mittelfinger sind Zerrfinger. Und meine Ringfinger sind Reißfinger. Und meine kleinen Finger sind Ziehfinger. | Was soll aus meinen Fingern werden, die mir aus dem Fleisch der Hände stehen' (*BF* 79).

Severed fingers also represent an unarticulated threat. In an interview with an immigration official—a situation which evokes her experiences with the *Securitate* in Romania—Irene sees a finger in the official's mouth, and the protagonist of *Heute* finds an amputated finger in a matchbox. Even more abstract, but no less traumatic, is Irene's observation: 'Seit drei Tagen sah Irene überall, auf den Straßen, Leute, denen der rechte oder linke Zeigefinger fehlte. Irene fühlte seit heute, dem dritten Tag, daß ihre Zeigefinger gefährdet waren. Sie vermied es, sie zu benutzen' (*R* 159).[42] For Müller, fingernails are emblematic of the removable body part, which is an alien object even when still attached to the body:

Wo die Haut aufhört, ist alles an uns selbst, an unserem Körper schon Gegenstand. Alles, was nicht weh tut, wenn wir es, und wenn es noch so sehr zu uns gehört, entfernen, ist schon Gegenstand. Wir schneiden uns die Fingernägel, wir schneiden uns das Haar. (*TS* 99)

Both hair and fingernails continue to grow after death, a fact alluded to in *Herztier*, which accounts for their independent existence. Both objects are, significantly, invoked by the dissidents in *Herztier* as part of their secret code: they put hairs in letters to see if they are opened and write 'Ein Satz mit Nagelschere für Verhör' (*Hz* 90).

The most extreme effect of dissociation is fragmentation, which appears increasingly in the later texts. In 'Das Land am Nebentisch', and its companion piece in *Der Teufel sitzt im Spiegel*, a man is identified as Romanian by the fragmentary composition of his appearance:

Der Mann war so fremd, so ähnlich, daß Avram ihn kannte. Nicht den Scheitel, nicht den Knopf, nicht den Absatz am Schuh. Nur wie sich

---

[42] Cf. also Müller's memory of the same in *Der Fremde Blick*, 29, where it is an expression of impending madness, and where the imputed link with the *Securitate* is much stronger.

der Scheitel auf den Knopf bezog und der Knopf auf den Absatz des Schuhs.[43]

Here it is the radical contiguity of the man's appearance (like the effect of a collage) which betrays his origin. Fragmentation—particularly evident in 'Das Land am Nebentisch', or *Der Fuchs war damals schon der Jäger* and *Herztier*—is directly linked to the oppression of the Romanian state. When Adina realizes the danger that her friend Clara's relationship with one of the *Securitate*, Pavel, has put her in, she experiences her body as autonomous parts: 'ich will dich nicht mehr sehen, schreit Adina, nie wieder. Ihre Hände schlagen um sich, ihre Auge sind aufgerissen, ihr Blick ist der Jäger, springt aus den Augen und trifft. Was der nasse Mund schreit, ist Glut auf der Zunge' (*FJ* 223). Adina's body similarly appears to act independently as a reaction to the intrusion by the secret police into her flat; it is not Adina herself who touches the mutilated fox fur, rather 'Adinas Schuhspitze zieht das linke Hinterbein weg' (*FJ* 199). Adina's body mirrors the fox fur: as she checks for its severed limbs (the sign that the *Securitate* have been in the flat), her body too is divided into parts.

In an interrogation scene in *Der Fuchs war damals schon der Jäger*, fragmentation is reflected back on the outside world. Abi's confusion and the threat of violence are reflected in the increasingly fragmented, disembodied features of the interrogator and Pavel (which features belong to whom becomes less and less clear):

Schreib, sagt die Stimme. Die Augen in der Stirn sind hellbraun. Sie drehen sich und werden dunkel. [...] Unter der Stimme in der Kinnfalte steht eine kleine Schnittwunde. Sie ist ein paar Tage alt. [...]

Abi sieht ein Muttermal zwischen Hemdkragen und Ohr [...]. Gesicht ohne Gesicht [line from a banned poem—LM], also hat er sein Gesicht verloren, sagt die Schnittwunde, hebt die Hand an die Stirn. [...] Das Muttermal sitzt neben der Schnittwunde und sieht hinaus durch die Scheibe. [...]

[D]ie hellbraunen Augen sind groß geöffnet und hart. Sie glänzen und sehen Abi an. Die hellbraunen Augen sind auf seinen Wangen, die ihnen nicht gehören, in Abis Fingerspitzen, in seinem Gesicht [...].

Das Muttermal lacht und das Telefon läutet. Die Schnittwunde drückt den Hörer an die Wange und sagt: nein, ja, was, na wie.

[43] 'Das Land am Nebentisch', 42. Cf. *TS* 122.

Gut. Der Mund flüstert dem Muttermal ins Ohr, und im Gesicht des Muttermals steht nur das helle Licht und keine Regung. (*FJ* 146-9)

Metonymy—the substitution of the part for the whole—is taken to destructive extremes; the whole disintegrates into parts. On a wider level, 'der Diktator' exists only as metonymy: his presence is as official portraits, of which only the 'Auge' and the 'Stirnlocke' are mentioned in Müller's work. There is no doubt that these metonymic images, frequent motifs within *Fuchs*, are intended to be threatening. However, they also allow the threat to be pinned down, even while intensifying it, as happens when a friend of Müller's cuts the eye from a portrait of Ceauşescu:

Wir haben gelacht, schallend gelacht, weil uns das Auge jetzt noch mehr bedrohte. Er hatte die Überwachung durch das ausgeschnittene Auge auf die Überwachung selbst gestoßen. Es war greifbar und nicht größer als ein Fingernagel, das, was wir täglich spürten. (*TS* 27-8)

Likewise, when the narrator of *Herztier* reduces her body to a list of parts during an interrogation, it is as an attempt at resistance:

1 Jacke, 1 Bluse, 1 Hose, 1 Strumpfhose, 1 Höschen, 1 Paar Schuhe, 1 Paar Ohrgehänge, 1 Armbanduhr. Ich war ganz nackt, sagte ich. [...]
Alles war aufgeschrieben in Rubriken auf einem Blatt. Mich selber schrieb der Hauptmann Pjele nicht auf. Er wird mich einsperren. Es wird auf keiner Liste stehen, daß ich 1 Stirn, 2 Augen, 2 Ohren, 1 Nase, 2 Lippen, 1 Hals hatte, als ich hierherkam. [...] Ich wollte im Kopf die Liste meines Körpers machen gegen seine Liste. (*Hz* 144-5)

Although here the narrator reduces her body to its component parts, she nonetheless attempts to hold the sum of them in her head, a move which counteracts the split between mind and body. Her itemization can only reproduce the same effect of fragmentation, but this act still allows her to regain a sense of agency, if not identity.

State signification

Structures of trauma which become increasingly visible in Müller's texts are also increasingly identified as strategies of the state: the narrator of *Herztier*'s list of body parts mimics Hauptmann Pjele's list. Both the repressive state and the oppressive rural communities force the internalization of their values—Müller talks of the 'Zeigefinger im Kopf' (another severed limb) which perpetuates these norms.[44] Scarry notes that it is the aim of the torturer to force the victim to experience the body as the agent of his or her pain, rather than recognizing it as the product of physical torture.[45] Acknowledging such structures as external, situating them beyond the body, is, therefore, a step towards countering them. The strategies of the state are portrayed in the first instance as sexual manipulation in *Fasan*; more acute forms of physical violence and intimidation emerge in *Fuchs* and *Herztier* and more recently in the essay *Der Fremde Blick*. These strategies are frequently contradictory: far from requiring the dissidents to conform, the state instead forces them to transgress.

This double-edged policy can be seen in the function of the boundaries of Romania: 'illegal crossing of the frontier' (that is, without a passport, notoriously difficult to obtain) was punishable by imprisonment; nonetheless, the policies of the state directly contributed to the many escape attempts.[46] Müller herself was in effect forced into emigrating to West Germany through being dismissed from her job and through the type of pressure exerted on the dissidents in *Herztier*. Where the citizens of the state are not allowed to cross boundaries, the *Securitate* specialize in transgressions. *Securitate* men enter Adina's flat, touch her possessions, and change them; they leave small signs of their presence, cigarette butts and sunflower seed husks in the toilet bowl. Metaphorically, then, they also interfere with her body; tellingly, when Adina flees to the country to avoid being detained, her face is described as 'verstellt, ihre Wangen sind eingebrochen' (*FJ* 248).

The *Securitate* also force others to cross boundaries, as Georg's death shows: 'Georg lag sechs Wochen nach der Ausreise am frühen Morgen in Frankfurt auf dem Pflaster. Im fünften Stock des Übergangsheims stand ein Fenster offen' (*Hz* 234). This is the work of the *Securitate*, who attempt to manipulate the meaning of his death.[47] The causal link between the open

---

[44] See esp. the essays 'Wie Wahrnehmung sich erfindet' and 'Der ganz andere Diskurs des Alleinseins' in *Der Teufel sitzt im Spiegel*.

[45] Scarry, *The Body in Pain*, 47.   [46] Deletant, *Ceauşescu*, 95.

[47] Although the facts initially pose the question of whether Georg jumped or was pushed—suicide or murder—it is also possible that he was already dead before he was deposited on the pavement and that in fact the whole scenario was staged.

window and Georg lying dead on the pavement is only implied, paradoxically by parataxis. The scenario illustrates the corporeal prohibition of crossing boundaries: Georg's transition from life to death is mirrored in his fall, in a staged defenestration which shows the room to be fatally permeable. His death is orchestrated by the agents of the *Securitate* working beyond the borders of Romania, and is linked to Georg's emigration; eerily fittingly, it occurs in an 'Übergangsheim'. The narrator of *Herztier* finds a word to fit Georg's death: 'Überendlich' (*Hz* 248), a paradoxical formulation which sums up its transgressive, transcendent nature.

Within the texts, the state promotes particular structures based on stable, unitary identity in a person, and the identity of words and objects, while employing techniques which enforce fragmentation, as the narrator of *Herztier* experiences. In *Der Fuchs war damals schon der Jäger*, Abi's identity is over-determined by the secret police:

Schreib, hat er gesagt. Ich habe den Kugelschreiber angefaßt, und er hat durchs Fenster in den Fabrikhof geschaut und diktiert, ICH, und ich habe gefragt, ICH oder SIE, und er hat gesagt, schreibe ICH und deinen Namen. Mein Name reicht doch, habe ich gesagt, das bin doch ICH. Er hat geschrien, schreib, was ich dir sag, und dann hat er gemerkt, daß er schreit, hat sein Kinn angefaßt und seinen Mundwinkel zwischen Daumen und Zeigefinger zusammengedrückt und leise gesagt, schreibe ICH und deinen Namen. Ich habe es geschrieben [...]. (*FJ* 214)

As Adelson makes clear, interrogators do not entirely deny the identity of the victim: 'torturers *accord* their prisoners no agency, while *ascribing* certain forms of agency to them.'[48] The *Securitate* also make use of handwriting as a sign of identity, dictating to the person interrogated, in effect putting words into their mouth. Hauptmann Pjele dictates a lewd version of the friends' poem to the narrator of *Herztier*:

Der Hauptmann Pjele fragte: Wer hat das geschrieben. Ich sagte: Niemand, es ist ein Volkslied. Dann ist es Volkseigentum, sagte der Hauptmann Pjele, also darf das Volk weiterdichten. Ja, sagte ich. Dann dichte mal, sagte der Hauptmann Pjele. Ich kann nicht dichten, sagte

---

[48] Adelson, *Making Bodies*, 20.

ich. Aber ich, sagte der Hauptmann Pjele. Ich dichte, und du schreibst, was ich dichte, damit wir uns beide vergnügen [...].

Der Hauptmann Pjele nahm das Blatt und sagte: Schön hast du gedichtet, deine Freunde werden sich freuen. Ich sagte: Das haben Sie gedichtet. Na, na, sagte der Hauptmann Pjele, das ist doch deine Schrift. (*Hz* 104, 106)

The assumption is that surface appearance is all and, thus manipulated, the appearance becomes reality: if the narrator of *Herztier* writes what is dictated, it becomes her own invention.

The *Securitate* insist on meaning as such, the correspondence of words and objects, rejecting the possibility of word-play—of poetry, in short. They are readers, of lyrics and of letters (literally, as they open all correspondence), and also leave signs for others to read, traces which reveal their presence and intentions, such as Adina's fox-fur rug, whose tail and legs are cut off one by one while she is out. It is a message to Adina, that the secret police could kill her whenever they wanted; the fox fur is a countdown: 'Noch ein Fuß, sagt [Paul], und dann' (*FJ* 202). The suspicious unsolved deaths of characters in *Herztier* can be read as emblematic of their emphasis on the materiality of the signifier, here, the body itself, and thus also on the materiality of language. The respective deaths of Lola, Kurt, Georg, and the narrator's grandmother appear to be suicide or simply accidental—or rather, they are intended to appear as such. The *Securitate* attempt to determine absolutely the signification of the body by staging murder as something else; language and the body converge in a narrative of death. The narrator's suspicion about the deaths enacts a form of rewriting, changing the ending of their lives, as it were, in order to make visible the *Securitate*'s manipulation of signs. But both texts—the narrator's version of the deaths and *Herztier* itself—must ultimately remain ambiguous, reflecting the nature of trauma: as Scarry remarks, 'In physical pain, then, suicide and murder converge, for one feels acted upon, annihilated, by inside and outside alike [...] inside and outside and the two forms of agency ultimately give way to and merge with one another' (one thinks here also of Jan Palach's suicide as described by Moníková).[49] When the narrator considers suicide by drowning, she rejects the idea because

---

[49] Scarry, *The Body in Pain*, 53.

she does not wish to comply with the signification of her body determined by the *Securitate*; she does not want to be complicit in her own murder. She does not want to make her interrogator's words come true: 'Dich stecken wir ins Wasser gelingt dem Hauptmann Pjele nicht' (*Hz* 112), she remarks defiantly.

Writing and the possibilities of fiction are linked, in Müller's work, with the political context of the Ceauşescu regime. The following section looks at narrative strategies in more depth, focusing on techniques which reflect the structures I have already examined in the representation of the body, namely the dissolution of boundaries, dissociation, and fragmentation.

NARRATIVE

Müller uses several different narrative strategies which mimic the effects of trauma. The splitting of *Herztier* into two time levels, with the past (the narrator's childhood) narrated in the present, and the related splitting of the narrator into a first and third person ('das Kind'), correspond respectively to trauma's disruption of chronology and its dissociation. Past and present collapse in *Fasan*, and *Heute* consists of a series of flashbacks which the narrator experiences while travelling to an interrogation. Other literary devices represent the overwhelming perception which characterizes trauma: the use of anaphora points to simultaneity and the inability to subsume individual images into a linear narrative; shorter pieces in *Niederungen*, such as 'Der Überlandbus' with its recording of direct speech, privilege sensory perceptions over reflection, with the result that the text is no more than the impression of the world—in a strong sense—upon a (largely absent) narrator.

What I concentrate on here are those textual structures which manifest, first, the dissolution of boundaries and, secondly, the fragmentation foregrounded by Müller's representation of the body. The dissolution of boundaries between self and world is further reflected in the slippage between the 'discours' and 'histoire' in the text. By 'discours', I refer to the text as narration, to those elements which draw attention to the wording or to the narrative instance, in short, the poetic function; 'histoire' denotes the content of the text, the events which happen within the world to which it refers.⁵⁰ Slippage between the two levels is marked by instances of the unreal, which focus attention on the fictionality of the text. Fragmentation is represented on a narrative level as parataxis and the occurrence of gaps in the text; this concern with form highlights the physicality of the text and its status as artefact.

Textual boundaries

In a tale in the Bucharest edition of *Niederungen*, Inge returns from an interrogation and sees herself reflected in the television screen: 'Inge sah Inge auf dem Bildschirm kopfstehen'.⁵¹ Inge has literally been turned upside down by her experiences; she is split, something realized grammatically, as she occupies both subject and object positions. Moreover, Inge's reflection appears to act of its own accord, in an image of dissociation. Significantly, this shift from real to unreal is occasioned by the confusion of images: Inge does not watch broadcast images which give the illusion of depth and reality, but rather her own reflection on the surface of the television screen. Reflective surfaces—mirrors, windows, and liquid—are frequent motifs in Müller's texts; they are a cipher for the slippage between surface and depth which is repeated on a textual level. Müller's texts blur the distinction between the content of the text, the 'histoire'—the ostensibly real images and actions, like those broadcast on Inge's television—and the surface of the text, the 'discours'—the words, which themselves become the focus and the interest of the text.

The 'Verbot vor dem Spiegel' (*TS* 22) in the rural Banat is the literal manifestation of the refusal to allow reflection upon the community's values. It also enforces alienation from one's own body:

Und wenn sie an die Schränke gehen, schauen sie hinauf zur Zimmerdecke, um sich nicht nackt zu sehen, denn in jedem Zimmer

⁵⁰ In *Figures* Genette uses the terms 'récit (histoire)' to refer to passages where there is no need to question who is speaking, or where nothing suggests the presence of a speaker. The term 'récit' properly refers to this type of realist narration, rather than the events themselves; its English translation, 'narrative', is ambiguous. I therefore prefer the terms 'histoire' and 'discours', and will retain the original French, as the accepted English translations ('story' and 'discourse' respectively) have more general usage.

⁵¹ Herta Müller, 'Inge', *Niederungen* (Bucharest), 116–20, here 120.

des Hauses kann irgend etwas geschehen, was man Schande oder unkeusch nennt. Man muß bloß nackt in den Spiegel schauen oder beim Strümpfehochrollen daran denken, daß man seine Haut berührt. In Kleidern ist man ein Mensch, und ohne Kleider ist man keiner. Die ganze große Fläche Haut ist eine Schande, die Nacktheit ist ein Ekel, ein Verbot, eine Sünde.[52]

In *Der Mensch ist ein großer Fasan auf der Welt*, a lack of self-reflection is represented in the confusion of reality and reflected image. The text is structured as a series of reflections: the present-day narrative is reflected in the tales from the village during the Second World War. The reader is forced to make connections between past and present, unreal scenarios and reality, and thus cannot escape doing what Windisch avoids, namely reflecting on the values of the village. Before her visit to the Milizmann (where she is to offer sex in return for emigration visas), Amalie stands in front of a mirror while her mother helps her to get dressed. The distinction between the bodies reflected in the mirror and the real bodies is blurred:

Im Spiegel stehn die Augen von Windischs Frau. [...] Windischs Frau greift in den Spiegel. Sie zupft mit welken Fingern auf Amalies Schulter die Träger ihres Unterkleids zurecht. [...]
    Amalie hält das Gesicht ganz nahe vor den Spiegel. Ihr Augenaufschlag ist aus Glas. (*MFW* 81–2)

Here the narrative perspective fuses image and reality; written as statements, it suggests that it is Amalie's mother who confuses the two, reaching into the mirror to adjust her daughter's underwear. The confusion reflects the mother's bad faith, her suppression of the knowledge that she is helping her daughter prostitute herself, just as she had to prostitute herself in order to survive after the war.[53]

A second mirror image represents Windisch's bad faith concerning the same knowledge. Windisch looks in the mirror and sees the Milizmann, who represents Windisch's collusion in this exploitation:

---

[52] *Niederungen* (Bucharest), 45: this version is more explicit than the Berlin edition (cf. *Nd* 60).
[53] Cf. a similar scene in 'Das Fenster', in *Niederungen*, where the mother helps the daughter to put on the cumbersome traditional nine-skirted costume, inducting her into similarly constrictive values.

Die Mütze des Milizmanns dreht sich um den Spiegelrand. Seine Schulterklappen blinken. Die Knöpfe seines blauen Rocks wachsen in die Spiegelmitte. Über dem Rock des Milizmanns steht Windischs Gesicht.
　Windischs Gesicht steht einmal groß und überlegen überm Rock. Zweimal lehnt Windischs Gesicht klein und versagt über den Schulterklappen. Der Milizmann lacht zwischen Windischs Wangen in Windischs großem, überlegenem Gesicht. Er sagt mit nassen Lippen: 'Mit deinem Mehl kommst du nicht weit'.
　Windisch hebt die Fäuste. Der Rock des Milizmanns zersplittert. Windischs großes, überlegenes Gesicht hat einen Blutfleck. Windisch schlägt die beiden kleinen, verzagten Gesichter über den Schulterklappen tot. (*MFW* 85)

The Milizmann represents Windisch as other: the two are intertwined in the mirror image, with Windisch's face superimposed on the Milizmann's body, and with the Milizmann's features appearing in Windisch's face. They are indeed the same: Windisch is complicit in his daughter's prostitution—alluded to by the reference to the sacks of flour, which were Windisch's first bribe (*MFW* 16). His aggression at the sight of the figure in the mirror represents his unwillingness to acknowledge this. Windisch does not just resemble the Milizmann in his misogynistic views of women; as Karin Bauer demonstrates, Windisch is aware that Amalie is in effect prostituting herself for him.[54] Tellingly, Windisch joins in a vulgar song he overhears, which puts him grammatically in the place of the Milizmann: 'Sollst mir dein Tochter schicken, ich will sie einmal ficken' (*MFW* 39). The mirror enacts this changing of places visually.

Mirrors act as the locus of the unreal as textual effect. The short prose text 'Die große schwarze Achse' opens with the statement 'Der Brunnen ist kein Fenster und kein Spiegel' (*BF* 6). Yet it functions as both throughout the text, alternating between reflective surface and transparent view. The tale begins with the following passage:

Großvaters Gesicht wuchs wie von unten neben meines hin. Zwischen seinen Lippen stand das Wasser. [...]
　Großvaters Gesicht war grün und schwer. [...]
　Der Brunnenrand war wie ein Schlauch aus grünen Mäusen. Großvater seufzte leis. In seine Wange sprang ein Frosch. Und seine Schläfe sprang in dünnen Kreisen über mein Gesicht, und nahm sein

---

[54] Bauer, 'Zur Objektwerdung der Frau', 148.

Haar, und seine Stirn, und seine Lippen mit dem Seufzen mit. Und nahm auch mein Gesicht mit an den Rand. (*BF* 6)

Whereas the mirrors in *Fasan* are depicted as unreal—the mother reaches into one, Windisch's reflection shows someone else—here the way the reflection is described creates an unreal image within the text. The narrator refers to the image of her face simply as 'mein Gesicht'; as a result, the literal, surface reading of the text is at odds with the 'real' picture.

The tale concerns the young narrator's search to see 'die große schwarze Achse[, die] unterm Dorf die Jahre dreht' (ibid.), which is to be seen 'durch den Brunnen' (ibid.): the reflective surface of the fountain must function as a window. Stefan Gross examines the 'Bilderketten' which run through the text and concludes that the narrator does in fact see the 'große schwarze Achse', an allegory of death, three times.[55] In two of these chains, reflections are key images: in the first, the image is in the 'Teich' which 'war klein und hielt den Spiegel hin. Er konnte soviel Kot und soviel Nacht nicht wiederspiegeln' (*BF* 22), hence in a mirror which does not reflect. In the second chain of images, the figure of Leni is a link: she appears '[h]interm Fensterglas wie unterm Wasserspiegel' (*BF* 7); and then 'Leni ging und eine Wolke stand im Fensterspiegel' (*BF* 10). Again it is the confusion of opacity, reflection, and transparency which enables the transference of signification. Gross concludes, 'So wird der Blick in den Brunnen zugleich Initiation in die erfundene Wahrnehmung'.[56] Literary perception is the result of this confusion of reflection and transparency. Significantly, the chains are generated by a slippage between levels of the text, between 'histoire' and 'discours': it is contiguity within the 'histoire' which prompts the transference of symbolic signification.

The notion of the mirror which one can look through is (as in *Alice through the Looking Glass*) a step into fiction, into the unreal; it is an image of literature, which reflects reality in order to make its workings transparent. Müller's alter ego, the narrator of *Herztier*, experiences the ambiguity of reflection and

---

[55] Stefan Gross, 'Dem Schmied ist Glut ins Aug gespritzt. Von realen und erfundenen Teufeln. Zur Erzählung "Die große schwarze Achse"', in Eke (ed.), *Die erfundene Wahrnehmung*, 60–73.
[56] Ibid. 70.

transparency when looking at her own opposite, Lola, in the hostel window:

> Aber ich weiß noch, daß mir an diesem frühen Abend schwindlig war, als ich lange zum Fenster sah. In der Scheibe baumelte das Zimmer. Ich sah uns alle sehr klein um Lolas Bett stehen. Und über unsere Köpfe hinweg sah ich Lola sehr groß durch die Luft und das geschlossene Fenster in den struppigen Park gehen. [...]
> Das grindige Pendel schlug damals, als Lola keuchte und nicht bei sich war, in meinem Kopf.
> Nur einen von Lolas Männer hatte ich im Spiegelbild der Fensterscheibe nicht gesehen. (*Hz* 26–7)

The vision is a premonition of Lola's death and an image of dissociation, but it is also a signal of the narrator's status as a writer. Müller's narrative functions in a similar way: it focuses on the surface of the text, which is normally transparent; her texts reject realism as a window on the world.

The focus on the surface of the text manifests itself in an emphasis on the narrative instance. In 'Niederungen', the overlap of the 'discours' and the 'histoire' implied in the first-person perspective leads to instances of the unreal, which express the child's projections or perceptions of the world:

> der Teig, den sie kneten, bläst sich auf wie ein Ungeheuer und kriecht, irr und besoffen von der Hefe, durch das Haus. (*Nd* 33)
>
> Zwischen uns und den Nachbarn ist der Garten voller Himbeeren. Sie sind so reif, daß man sich die Finger daran blutig pflückt. Vor ein paar Jahren hatten wir keine Himbeeren, nur der Nachbar hatte ein paar Stauden in seinem Garten. Jetzt sind sie herübergekommen in unseren Garten, und bei ihm steht keine einzige Ranke mehr. Sie wandern. [...] In ein paar Jahren werden auch wir keine mehr haben, sie werden weitergewandert sein. Iß dich jetzt satt, denn das Dorf ist klein, und sie wandern zum Dorf hinaus. (*Nd* 92–3)

The creeping dough and the wandering raspberries are clearly part of the child's fantasy, rather than any objective reality—the dough is an 'Ungeheuer', a fantasy monster. In the second example, the foreshortening of time necessary to apprehend the raspberry plants' fantastic movement signals the narrative perspective. Such effects are not restricted to the first-person narratives, however; elements of 'discours' intruding into a 'récit', in Genette's terms, also invoke the unreal. The following set of images is from *Der Fuchs war damals schon der Jäger*:

Die Fenster sahen in den Innenhof. (*FJ* 14)
   Die stillen Straßen der Macht, wo der Wind, wenn er anstößt, Angst hat. Und wenn er fliegt, nicht wirbelt. Und wenn er poltert, lieber seine Rippen bricht, als einen Ast. (31)
   Die Sonne steht hoch, sie steht auf der Stadt. Die Ruten werfen Schatten, der Nachmittag lehnt auf den Schatten der Angelruten. Wenn er kippt, denkt Adina, wenn der Tag abrutscht, wird er in die Felder um den Stadtrand tiefe Gräben schneiden, der Mais wird brechen. (39)
   Die weißen Stühle aus Eisen sind weggeräumt, der Winter braucht keinen Stuhl, er sitzt nicht, er geht um den Fluß, hängt unter den Brücken. (193)
   Es ist ein Winter in der Stadt, ein langsamer, vergreister, der seine Kälte in die Menschen steckt. [...] Ein Winter geht da um den Fluß, wo statt des Wassers nur das Lachen friert. (218)

Descriptions of windows, wind, sun, and winter properly belong to a 'récit', but in these passages, there is a transition from metaphorical use of verbs of movement or action (e.g. 'Die Fenster sahen') to an unreal situation where this movement is taken literally. Personification is achieved through the repeated use of pronouns, which allows for the suggestion of human attributes. This effect also represents the reality of life under Ceauşescu, where representatives of the *Securitate* were everywhere and saw everything. Undercurrents of the unreal are to be found beneath the surface of all Müller's work, as she herself notes, 'Surrealität [ist] nicht etwas anderes als Realität, sondern eine tiefere Realität.'[57]

The unreal in Müller's texts marks the disruption not only of the laws of the world, which moves the texts out of the realms of realism, but also of the conventions of the text. Poetic devices of metaphor or personification on the level of the 'discours' are exaggerated and become part of the 'histoire'. The culmination of the interaction between these two levels of the text is the generation of the narrative by associative links on the level of the 'discours'. The 'Wahrnehmung, die sich erfindet' (*TS* 15) is reflected in the text by a self-generating narrative based on associations: 'wenn der geschriebene Satz seine Wahrheit hält [...] kann er den nächsten Satz erfinden' (*TS* 36). Progress by associations structures the episodic narrative of *Der Mensch ist*

---

[57] Müller, in interview with Haines and Littler, 'Gespräch mit Herta Müller', 18.

ein großer Fasan auf der Welt. Associations developed from poetic devices enable the transition of the narrative from one 'scene' to the next. The images of eating in 'Ein Stein im Kalk öffnet das Maul. Der Apfelbaum zittert. [...] Der Apfelbaum tränkt seine grünen Äpfel', prompts the tale of 'ein Apfelbaum, der seine Äpfel selber fraß' (both *MFW* 32). 'Niederungen' is similarly structured around associations; in one passage, the narrative is structured and generated by the poetic image of fear manifested as snakes. These snakes inhabit the imagination, dreams, and the stories told to the narrator by her grandmother:

> die Angst ringelt sich durch das weiße umherschwebende Gefieder der verblühten Butterblumen. Jedes Blatt, jeder Stengel wird eine Schlange. Das Gezücht wimmelt im Klee, es sammelt und knäult sich im Hals und im Bauch.
> Nachts kommt der Traum durch den Hinterhof ins Bett.
> Da steht der Strohschober mit seinen regenfaulen Halmen wie Schlamm. Lange schwarze Schlangen kriechen darüber und wühlen sich in ihn hinein. [...] Ich bin aufgewacht [...]. Die Schlangen kriechen zurück in die Zacken der Butterblumen.
> Und dann bringt Großmutter eines Tages die Schlangen wieder her. Sie kriechen aus dem Sattel ihrer Bluse, aus ihren Stimmbändern, aus einem Gespräch, das wie immer mit 'früher' beginnt. [...] Früher gab es viele Schlangen im Dorf. (*Nd* 37–8)

The snakes slip between the different levels of the text, inspired by the metaphor 'die Angst ringelt sich', appearing in the dream, in the grandmother's tale, and seemingly 'real' when mentioned in the main narrative. Tenses in 'Niederungen' are similarly unstable, and the narrative appears to move fluidly from one to another. The introduction of a child's fairy tale, for example, appears to transpose the main narrative into the past:

> Ich stelle mich in den Hinterhof und esse die Kerne zusammen mit den Hühnern. Dabei denke ich an das Märchen, in dem ein Mädchen immer zuerst ihre Tiere fütterte und dann erst selber aß. Und das Mädchen wurde später eine Prinzessin [...]. Und sie waren das glücklichste Paar weit und breit.
> Die Hühner hatten alle Kerne aufgepickt und schauten mit geneigten Köpfen in die Sonne. Die Sonnenblume war leer. Ich zerbrach sie. (*Nd* 21)

It seems that the introduction of the imperfect tense in the fairy tale also leaks into the actual narrative. Reliving the past—an effect of trauma—is transformed into a more distanced perspective through the introduction of a framed, staged fiction and narration.

The unreal is a textual effect, arising from the representation of real events, or through the independent play of the 'discours' itself, where it is an example of the 'Wahrnehmung, die ihre Grenzen überschreitet'. Instances of the unreal demonstrate 'das Eindringen der Wörter in die Realität, der Kampf der Wörter, der Sprichwörter, der Sätze, der Metaphern, der Bilder, die Wörter sind, der Wörter, die Bilder sind, untereinander, um die Realität, um die Herrschaft über die Realität'.[58] In this, then, they represent within the text the role of literature itself, and its power to make 'der Ort [...] wie die Bilder im Kopf'. Müller's use of the unreal offers a third possibility besides the two resolutions of the fantastic posited by Todorov: occurrences in her texts are neither natural, nor supernatural, but fictional.[59] According to Todorov, the fantastic is a liminal mode, which depends on absolute and sustained ambiguity between a natural and supernatural explanation of some unexplained event; it exists only as a 'frontière' between these possibilities, both of which pertain to the 'histoire'.[60] Müller's unreal occurrences exist, on the other hand, on the boundary between 'discours' and 'histoire'.

Der Mensch ist ein großer Fasan auf der Welt demonstrates this effect:

Vor der Stirn des Schneiders flattert ein Kohlweißling. Die Wangen des Schneiders sind bleich. Sind wie ein Vorhang unter seinen Augen.
Der Kohlweißling fliegt durch die Wange des Schneiders. Der Schneider senkt den Kopf. Der Kohlweißling fliegt weiß und nicht zerknittert aus dem Hinterkopf des Schneiders hinaus. Die dürre Wilma flattert mit dem Taschentuch. Der Kohlweißling fliegt durch ihre Schläfe in ihren Kopf hinein. (*MFW* 111)

This is no hallucination—there is no one watching and both the tailor and Wilma seem unaware of the butterfly. The butterfly appears from out of nowhere; its flight through the tailor's head seems to be the result of the simile of his cheeks being 'wie ein

---
[58] Gross, 'Dem Schmied ist Glut ins Aug gespritzt', 72–3.
[59] Tzvetan Todorov, *Introduction à la littérature fantastique* (Paris: Seuil, 1970).
[60] Ibid. 49.

Vorhang', and the visual similarities between the handkerchief and the butterfly allow it passage through Wilma's head. Elements of the 'discours' thus generate an action on the level of the 'histoire'. Again, the association is death, the ultimate punishment for transgression of boundaries: an earlier incarnation of a similar butterfly (in a chapter entitled 'Der Kohlweißling') walks across Amalie's reflection in a mirror, and is squashed by her mother; textually associated with death, the butterfly comes to the village folk, who are the reflection of Windisch and his family, who have since emigrated. The butterfly indicates decay and collapse in the village.

The refiguring and condensation of images (inspired by the 'histoire') into symbols (part of the 'discours') is common in Müller's work.[61] In 'Viele Räume sind unter der Haut', the unreal image of an ash-grey hen is at some remove from its original explanation: 'Das Kind, das allein geht, dreht den näheren größeren Schuh. Er ist bleich. Im Bierschaum schwimmt ein aschgraues Huhn. In den Hals der Soldaten' (*BF* 61). The source of this imagery is some six pages back:

Der Hahn steigt auf ein aschgraues Huhn. Drückt ihm den kleineren hochroten Kamm in den Sand. Schiebt ihm den Kopf hinauf in den Hals. Unter den schmäleren bleicheren Schnabel.

Vater, komm, er macht es tot, hat das Kind, das allein geht, in den Hof geschrien. Der Mann mit dem Hut hat die Augen geschlossen. [...] Er liebt es, hat er gesagt. [...] Im Augenweiß des Kindes, das allein geht, ist ein aschgraues Huhn in den Sommer geflogen. Hinauf in den Himmel gestürzt. (*BF* 55)

The ash-grey hen is a symbol of violent sexuality, entirely appropriate to the soldiers in the text, and evoked by the same 'bleich' colouring. Its reappearance is unreal, as the hen is transposed from the real into the figurative.

The repetition and development of images on the level of the 'discours' imbues them with symbolic significance. In *Der Fuchs war damals schon der Jäger*, the image of the poplar trees as knives is repeated frequently after its initial exposition:

---

[61] The condensation of images to form a kind of surreal shorthand is also the process by which dreams function; see *TS* 62–5 for Müller's understanding of dreams and their similarity to her narrative—they are a 'Fiktion der Wahrheit der erfundenen Wahrnehmung' (*TS* 64). Many of Müller's texts feature dreams.

um das Dach stehen Pappeln. Sie sind höher als alle Dächer der Stadt, sind grünbehängt, sie tragen keine einzelnen Blätter, nur Laub. Sie rascheln nicht, sie rauschen. Das Laub steht senkrecht an den Pappeln wie die Äste, man sieht das Holz nicht. Und wo nichts mehr hinreicht, zerschneiden die Pappeln die heiße Luft. Die Pappeln sind grüne Messer. (*FJ* 9)

The image is condensed into the two nouns 'Pappel' and 'Messer'. Visual similarities inspire the metaphorical phrasing of 'zerschneiden die heiße Luft', whence comes the statement '[d]ie Pappel *sind* grüne Messer' (my italics). However, the image is taken further: 'Wenn Adina die Pappeln zu lange ansieht, drehen sie die Messer von einer Seite zur anderen im Hals. Dann wird ihr Hals schwindlig' (ibid.). Later in the text the metaphor is further condensed to 'die Messer der Pappeln' (*FJ* 21). This genitive formulation is frequent in Müller's work ('das Blut der Melonen', *FJ* 77; or 'das Proletariat der Blechschafe und Holzmelonen', *Hz* 37) and becomes a form of surreal shorthand. The process becomes a poetic form of 'bisociation', the pairing or associating of incompatible elements observed in the art of trauma victims.[62] The meaning of these phrases is entirely contingent, giving rise to symbols which are peculiar to the texts.

In *Herztier*, this condensation of images is ultimately a political strategy, linked to the creation of a space within language allowing for private expression, or freedom within the repressive state for dissidents. The characters attempt to communicate with each other despite the dangers and the lack of privacy (all letters are opened by the secret police) by using a code:

Beim Schreiben das Datum nicht vergessen, und immer ein Haar in den Brief legen, sagte Edgar. Wenn keines mehr drin ist, weiß man, daß der Brief geöffnet worden ist. [...] Ein Satz mit Nagelschere für Verhör, sagte Kurt, für Durchsuchung einen Satz mit Schuhe, für Beschattung einen mit erkältet. Hinter die Anrede immer ein Ausrufezeichen, bei Todesdrohung nur ein Komma. (*Hz* 90)

Ultimately the utopian space within language which the dissidents sought cannot overcome the conventional meanings, or even coexist with them: it collapses as soon as it becomes codified. What is needed is a purely contingent and contextual

---

[62] Cohen and Mills, 'Skin/Paper/Bark', 204.

set of meanings, whose presence can only be suggested, rather than represented within language: poetry, in other words.

A process of codifying experience is apparent in the structures of *Herztier*. Fleeting references are condensed: images of dependency and sexual exploitation come together in the phrase 'ich [bin] der Strohhalm mit offenen Beinen und geschlossenen Augen' (*Hz* 211)—talking of her frequently absent lover, the narrator had declared, 'Von Liebe sprach er nie. Er dachte an Wasser und sagte, ich sei ein Strohhalm für ihn. Wenn ich ein Strohhalm war, dann aber einer auf dem Boden. Dort lagen wir jeden Mittwoch nach der Arbeit im Wald' (*Hz* 170). Moreover, this process is also reversed: *Herztier* begins with a short, unsignalled preface, eventually revealed as the displaced conclusion to the text; the text itself is a 'Sack mit Wörtern' (*Hz* 7). Gradually the significance of the ominous list, 'einen Gürtel, ein Fenster, eine Nuß und einen Strick' (*Hz* 7), is revealed: the respective ambiguous deaths of Lola (by hanging), Georg (falls from a window), Tereza (the nut is cancer), and Kurt (another hanging). By reading the text, the reader is initiated into the circle of intimates; the individual words stand for events which the text can only outline. The contradictory movements of images (from metaphor to simile or vice versa) are in part due to the non-linear chronology of the novel. Tereza's cancer is intimated as 'die Nuß' on page 156—'noch unsichtbar von außen, [war] die Nuß unter Terezas Arm immer dabei. Sie ließ sich Zeit und wurde dick. | Die Nuß wuchs gegen uns. Gegen alle Liebe'. Only later is the metaphor deconstructed—'Terezas Armhöhle war nackt. Ich sah darin einen Knoten so dick wie eine Nuß' (176)—just as Tereza's death from the cancer is related before scenes in which she still features. Referring to this movement, Müller remarks, 'ich [habe] diese Metapher gezwungen, strikte Realität zu werden'.[63] The text gradually both unravels itself, revealing meanings, and creates new symbols based on the 'Schnur der Zufälle' (*Hz* 204), sustaining a thread through recurring and intertwined metaphors.

It is this set of metaphors, one created entirely on the level of the 'discours' by the narrator, rather than the references or code which the characters share, which potentially transcends the

---

[63] Müller, in interview with Haines and Littler, 'Gespräch mit Herta Müller', 18.

events of the 'histoire'. However, Ricarda Schmidt suggests that the condensation of metaphors resembles the totalizing structures of the state; analysing the metaphor of the 'Proletariat der Blechschafe und Holzmelonen' in particular, she notes, 'doch beruht der komische Effekt auf der gleichen homogenisierenden, universalisierenden Geste, die der Roman an anderen Stellen als totalitaristisch charakterisiert'.[64] While Müller cannot escape such structures entirely—such is the nature of the traumatic effect—she does at times manage to exceed them: in the contingency of the metaphors of death in the text, and the ambiguity of formulations such as the 'Herztier' itself, as well as by reversing the process of abstraction, which makes that very process visible. Over and above individual, soluble phrases, the process of inventing poetic language is entirely politicized; like the code invented by the dissidents, it seeks a private space within language. The text of *Herztier* sustains poetic and symbolic language in the face of political repression and is itself, in its occasionally ambiguous poetic language, a political statement.

The fragmentary text

Experiencing the body in fragments is a response to extreme physical danger; the dissolution of the self which it entails is further represented as a fragmentary narrative. This fragmentation of the psyche is a precondition of narrative itself, and manifests itself in the first instance in staged disjunction and disrupted syntax. Gaps in the text, evident in both the linguistic and narrative structures of Müller's texts, force the reader to (re)construct links between sentences or episodes; frequently, these gaps highlight acts of violence. As this technique has attracted particular interest from critics of Müller's work, I concentrate on tracing how it forms a link between images of the body and representations of trauma, and the collage work which is of increasing importance in Müller's oeuvre. In addition, exaggerated, literal instances of gaps, in the blank spaces in the text, and the manipulation of typography, demonstrate a move towards an understanding of the text as a visual artefact, something which finally also links with Müller's production of collages.

[64] Ricarda Schmidt, 'Metapher, Metonymie und Moral. Herta Müllers *Herztier*', in Haines (ed.), *Herta Müller*, 57–74, here 68.

The structure of Müller's texts works on principles of contiguity, simultaneity, and omission. These are expressed by parataxis, on the level of syntax and in the narrative structure of the texts themselves. Linear progress of the narrative is disrupted by the episodic structure of the tales and by frequent unexpected or unassimilable shifts in narrative chronology. In her poetological essays, Müller describes the process of writing in these programmatic terms:

> Die Unruhe ist in der Stille der Wahrnehmung ein Überfall. Versucht man den Überfall der Unruhe beim Schreiben zu treffen, die Drehung, durch die der Sprung ins Unberechenbare einsetzt, muß man in kurzen Takten seine Sätze schreiben, die von allen Seiten offen sind, für die Verschiebung. Es sind Sprünge durch den Raum. [...] Das Übereinanderherfallen von Schnitten zwischen den absichtlich schiefgestellten, Rücken an Rücken oder Kopf an Kopf gezwungenen Sequenzen einer Passage, die ja ein Vorgang werden soll. (*TS* 19–20)

Müller's view of literature is based on a spatial, physical understanding of writing which translates into specific literary structures, highlighting simultaneity ('das Übereinanderherfallen') and the suppression of connections ('absichtlich schiefgestellten [...] Sequenzen'). Her conception of the poetic is also based on the interruption of the normal flow of language: 'was ist Poesie anderes, als daß sich in einem Moment, durch etwas, was wir gar nicht genau begründen können, alles umstülpt.'[65] The fragmented sentence or narrative performs this function, as it is 'durchbrochen von dem maßlosen anderen' (*TS* 20). It is possible to see, too, in this conception of poetry, that the incomprehensible and unpredictable workings of the totalitarian state would lend themselves to a poetic representation.

Paratactic structures within texts distance the narrative and give poetic weight to Müller's prose. Parataxis, with its lack of subordinating conjunctions and relative clauses, suppresses causality: 'Clara sieht die Fliege nicht, die Sonne ist ein glühender Kürbis, sie blendet' (*FJ* 7). Here, the logical, semantic progression of ideas is disrupted, by the startling metaphor, and the order of the clauses (it would be more logical to write

---

[65] Herta Müller, in interview with Wolfgang Müller, '"Poesie ist ja nichts Angenehmes": Gespräch mit Herta Müller', *Monatshefte*, 89/4 (1997), 468–76, here 470.

'die Sonne blendet, sie ist ein glühender Kürbis'), as well as by the suppressed 'because': Clara does not see the fly *because* she is blinded by the sun. The ambiguous nature of Lola's death is reflected in syntactic parataxis. The repeated 'und' which introduces her death suggests both an unforeseeable, random event, and also its inexorability: 'Und neben Lolas Bett, wo die Broschüren fehlten, stand ein kahler, dunkler Fleck. Und Lola hing an meinem Gürtel im Schrank' (*Hz* 30). Tellingly, the blurb on the rororo paperback edition echoes this parataxis: 'Lola kam aus dem armen Süden Rumäniens, wollte dem Elend mit Hilfe eines erfolgreichen Mannes entfliehen und hing eines Tages am Strick.' The staged lack of causality in turn suggests inexorable chains of events, revealing a more profound and more political causality which eludes expression. As Ricarda Schmidt argues, Lola and the other characters in *Herztier* are indeed ultimately killed by the state, even if they are not murdered by the *Securitate*; however, the causal relationship between the oppression and deprivation of life in Romania and these putative suicides is left for the reader to reconstruct.[66] On a wider level, both *Fuchs* and *Herztier*, like the earlier texts, are episodic, with individual chapters or incidents only loosely connected. Only *Heute* is a narrative, in the sense of an account of connected events: it is structured around the narrator's tram journey to an interrogation, which gives the narrative its driving force.

The paratactic structure lends significance to otherwise unimportant descriptions, by emphasizing individual elements, and is reflected in the impressionistic sequences of images which constitute whole passages of narrative and which occasionally collapse into absurdity. Narrative continuity is disrupted by focusing on specific moments, and descriptions disintegrate into series of images as the detail becomes overwhelming:

So sind die schönen blauen Augen meiner Puppe.
   Eisblumen spinnen ihr Dickicht über die Fenster. Ich fühle einen schönen Schauder auf der Haut. Mutter schneidet mir die Nägel so kurz, daß mir die Fingerspitzen wehtun. Ich fühle mit den frischgeschnittenen Fingernägeln, daß ich nicht richtig gehen kann.

[66] Schmidt, 'Metapher', 64.

> Ich gehe immerzu auf den Händen. Ich fühle auch, daß ich mit diesen kurzen Nägeln nicht richtig reden und nicht richtig denken kann. [...]
> Die Eisblumen verschlingen ihre eigenen Blätter, sie haben das Gesicht milchiger blinder Augen.
> Auf dem Tisch dampft die heiße Nudelsuppe. Mutter sagt: wir gehen essen, und wenn ich nach der ersten Aufforderung nicht da bin, dicht am Tischrand stehe, zeichnen die Spuren ihrer harten Hand meine Wange. (*Nd* 43)

There is no attempt to link these separate images either syntactically or chronologically. The images do not come together to produce a whole picture, instead the perception of reality is of a series of individual and discrete images, compounded by the use of the present tense (is this a single event or a repeated sequence?). Here the narrative structure enacts the process of the 'zerstörerischer Blick'. Underlying this structural parataxis are thematic (often symbolic) associations which operate in place of an explicit syntactic or narrative link. Maternal violence is one thread which connects the fingernails to the soup in the passage, the incestuous destruction echoed in the ice flowers swallowing their own leaves. The 'Augen', which link the doll and the ice patterns, are a regular description of soups as well as a frequent symbol of the ever-watchful and oppressive norms of the village community.[67] These connections link individual, contiguous images rather than structuring the whole, a technique reminiscent of the dreams which are frequent motifs in Müller's texts and which are a cipher for literature.

In addition to the paratactic structures evident in the grammatical and narrative syntax of Müller's work, there are also deliberate and visible gaps in the texts. The most obvious and most basic of omissions in Müller's texts are syntactic. The opening pages of 'Niederungen' are densely packed with sentences which have no conjugated verb, creating impoverished linguistic structures which are to be found throughout Müller's work:

> Die lila Blüten neben den Zäunen, das Ringelgras mit seiner grünen Frucht zwischen den Milchzähnen der Kinder.
> Der Großvater, der sagte, vom Ringelgras wird man dumm, das darf man nicht essen. [...]

---

[67] See *FJ* 153, 260; *BF* 7; *MFW* 69. I presume the 'eyes' are globules of fat or bubbles.

Der Käfer, der mir ins Ohr kroch. [...]
Die Akazienblüten in den Dorfstraßen. Das eingeschneite Dorf mit den Bienenvölkern im Tal. Ich aß Akazienblüten. (*Nd* 17)

The lack of verbs points both to timelessness and a lack of movement; the repetition of the definite article furthermore suggests the images have intrinsic significance. These are the overwhelming images of trauma, which do not coalesce into a whole picture (blossom, snow, and bees are surely incongruous together) and which are not situated in time. In this passage, as Michael Günther notes, the significance lies in 'Er-innerung', in the dissolution of the boundaries between the child narrator and nature (the children eat grass, the beetle enters her ear).[68] The images also point to the refusal of 'Erinnerung', memory, which results from this traumatic merging of self and world. Here this collapse of boundaries is not only thematized, but enacted by the narrative: the descriptions displace the narrator from the central position within the text. The interpenetration of inner and outer worlds is, however, not reflected in undifferentiated language, but in staged disjunction.

Specific events—particularly acts of violence—are also left out of the text, and left to the reader to reconstruct. These semantic gaps have a paradoxical effect in the text, signalling, according to Claudia Becker, both 'Betroffenheit *und* (ästhetische) Distanz'.[69] The apparent lack of emotion in the language (also evident in Kerstin Hensel's later texts) is precisely an effect of trauma, a form of numbness which is as much a sign of affect as it is of distance. This becomes evident in the description of the slaughter of the calf in 'Niederungen':

Als der Onkel den dicken Hammer hochhob, lief ich in den Hof und stellte mich unter den Pflaumenbaum und hielt mir mit beiden Händen die Ohren zu. Die Luft war heiß und leer. Die Schwalbe war nicht mitgekommen, sie mußte brüten über einer Hinrichtung.
    Ein Dorf voll fremder Hunde war da im Hof. Sie leckten das Blut aus dem Stroh des Misthaufens [...]. (*Nd* 58)

Although the child narrator does not refer to her emotional state directly, it is clearly portrayed in her actions (covering her ears)

---

[68] Michael Günther, 'Froschperspektiven. Über Eigenart und Wirkung erzählter Erinnerung in Herta Müllers *Niederungen*', in Eke (ed.), *Die erfundene Wahrnehmung*, 42–59, here 43–4.
[69] Becker, '"Serapiontisches Prinzip"', 35.

as well as in the human connotations of the term 'Hinrichtung'. The layout of the narrative, and the self-conscious reference to the empty air emphasize the absence of the traumatic event, which is nonetheless evoked by the explicit reference to blood. The gap in the text is repeated on the following page, in a parallel act of violence:

> Mutter brachte jeden Mittag warme, kuhwarme Milch in die Küche. Ich fragte sie, ob auch sie traurig wäre, wenn man mich ihr wegnehmen, mich schlachten würde. Ich fiel an die Kastentür, ich hatte eine blaue Beule auf der Stirn, ich hatte eine geschwollene Oberlippe und einen violetten Fleck auf dem Arm. All das von der Ohrfeige. (*Nd* 59)

Here, the child confuses human and animal once more, using the term 'schlachten' which refers to the killing of animals. The clip round the ear remains unrepresentable; it is shown not through the mother's actions, but through the child's reaction and injuries. The child's apparent incomprehension is reflected in the narrative—the semantic explanation is given belatedly, and only after a description of the physical effects—and is implicitly critical of this unexpected, undeserved maternal violence. The external perspective—how could the child see she has a 'blaue Beule auf der Stirn'?—is a further indication of trauma, where the self is projected outside the body in extreme situations. This effect also signals a split within the 'ich', between the child and her older self who narrates this tale; the narrative 'ich' moves between these two perspectives. Additionally, the gap engages the readers, whose involvement in the narrative impels them to judge and to criticize this violence.

Other, more poetic structures which permeate Müller's writing draw attention to the surface of the text, and, further, to the page itself. Texts play with symmetrical sentence structures closer to poetry than narrative: the repeated phrase 'was glänzt, das sieht' (*FJ* 27 and *passim*) describes the omnipresence of the dictator ('Die Stirnlocke glänzt. Sie sieht jeden Tag ins Land', ibid.) and, by implication, the secret police. Repetition makes the narrative appear stylized, rather than realistic, and there is often tension between the significance implied by repetition and the insignificance of those elements repeated. In 'Das Schwäbische Bad' and 'Die Meinung', this is used for satirical purposes. Simple repetition of terms ('Die Mühle ist stumm.

Stumm sind die Wände, und stumm ist das Dach. Und die Räder sind stumm': *MFW* 6) contributes to the density of the text; the reordering of elements within passages highlights the issue of articulation; frequent anaphora disrupts narrative chronology by suggesting simultaneity. Conjunctions are occasionally repeated, producing a set of dependent clauses which similarly highlight simultaneity (the repetition of 'während', *Hz* 39) and the complex, unexpected interrelations which underlie apparently unrelated facts (the repetition of 'daß', *Hz* 57–8). These techniques rely on the visual impact of repetition to point to similarity and difference.[70] Certain narrative techniques employed by Müller further draw attention to the 'palpability' of the text, that is, its status as an artefact, echoing the move from referential to poetic function.[71] Physical textuality is evident in chapter titles which form a meta-commentary to the action of the text: Müller's are evocative and often epigrammatic (as in *Der Fuchs war damals schon der Jäger*), repeated as motifs throughout the text (an authorial wink to the reader, as in *Der Mensch ist ein großer Fasan auf der Welt*), or form a slogan whose startling punchline is supplied at the end of the text itself (see 'Überall, wo man den Tod gesehen hat' and 'Damit du nie ins Herz der Welt gerissen wirst' in *Barfüßiger Februar*).

The most significant form of narrative interference involves the use of the page layout and typography to engage with the physical text as it stands on the page of the book. Müller uses the spaces in page layout to emphasize the paratactic structures of her texts and to highlight the concrete, physical state of the text. Individual sentences are set apart from the narrative, forming paragraphs of their own. In some, the visual effect emphasizes the content of the phrase: the separation of the list 'Die Küche, die Äpfel, das Brot' (*FJ* 199) from the rest of the paragraph reflects Adina's slow realization as she looks round her flat that the *Securitate* could have poisoned her food. Others make more oblique sense, such as 'Auf der Stirn des Diktators sitzt eine Blattlaus und stellt sich tot' (46), a phrase which stands alone

---

[70] See Thomas Roberg, 'Bildlichkeit und verschwiegener Sinn in Herta Müllers Erzählung *Der Mensch ist ein großer Fasan auf der Welt*', in Köhnen (ed.), *Der Druck der Erfahrung*, 27–42, esp. 32–3.
[71] The term 'palpability' is taken from Roger Fowler, *Linguistics and the Novel* (London: Methuen, 1977), 67.

(with blank space before and after), emphasizing its surreal imagery. The significance of the 'Blattlaus' is elaborated on the following page, as a symbol of fear (see above). However, what is the reader to make of the final sentence of one chapter: 'Sein Kamm hat blaue Zähne' (85)? It has no obvious meaning or symbolism. The injunction 'Leben wir im Detail' (*HuS* 61) is here taken to absurd extremes, as the narrative enacts the 'Fremde[r] Blick'. In such instances, there is a tension between the structures of the text which suggest meaning and significance and the intrinsic meaninglessness of the phrase itself. While it may alienate the reader, it also reflects the uncertain significance and the intrinsic absurdity of life in the totalitarian state, where the common interpretative framework which enables language to function as communication has collapsed.[72]

Der Fuchs war damals schon der Jäger makes particular use of typographical changes and the manipulation of space on the page, especially to point to other forms of writing within the narrative. Official forms and the state bureaucracy are frequently signalled in capital letters:

Ich habe den Kugelschreiber angefaßt, und er hat durchs Fenster in den Fabrikhof geschaut und diktiert, ICH [...]. Er hat geschrien, schreib, was ich dir sag [...] schreibe ICH und deinen Namen. Ich hab es geschrieben, WERDE KEINER PERSON, UNABHÄNGIG VON DER NÄHE ZU IHR, SAGEN, DASS ICH ZUSAMMENARBEITE. (*FJ* 214)

This act of writing, renarrated and staged within the narrative, is highlighted by the capital letters, which also suggest the coercion and threat which accompanies dealings with bureaucracy (cf. *FJ* 241–2). The capital letters also subvert the dictation: in the text cooperation with the secret police is not only revealed against their orders, it is shouted about, made visible. Song lyrics, rebellious poetry, and old sayings suppressed by the regime are also visually distinct from the narrative (*FJ* 107, 126, 268), emphasizing the text as a montage of other poetic texts.

Narrative structures such as parataxis and poetic forms disrupt the transparency of the narrative, representing within the 'discours' the effects of repression thematized within Müller's texts. Hers is an implicitly political understanding of literary texts,

---

[72] Cf. the dreams in *Herztier* where days of the week are meaningless, or a crossword puzzle is insoluble.

which is bound up with the concerns of narrative itself and the possibilities of expression within a language already complicit in power structures. Müller uses forms which emphasize the visual poetic function of the text over the referential; this poeticization does not counteract the text's political engagement, but reinforces it. Müller's narratives challenge textual conventions, collapsing the distinction between the real and unreal, 'discours' and 'histoire', and presenting the text as a physical artefact.

Collage

The culmination of narrative fragmentation and the emphasis on the visual, physical elements of a text is collage. In *Reisende auf einem Bein* Irene produces collages of pictures cut from newspapers, which function as an expression of her own fragmentary psyche, and as a metaphorical representation of the contingent nature of her immigrant life. The description of Irene's collage picture emphasizes contiguity and parataxis, highlighting the relation between aesthetic and linguistic syntax:

Ein großer Daumennagel neben einem fahrenden Bus. [...] Ein Gesicht, das flog von der Geschwindigkeit neben einem Mädchen im Schaukelstuhl. Eine Hand, die auf den Revolver drückte neben einem Mann, der auf dem Fahrrad durch das Spiegelbild der Bäume fuhr. Ein schreiender Mund, der bis zu den Augen reichte. [...] Eine Frau mit schwarzer Sonnenbrille. Ein Toter im Anzug. Eine Wassermühle. Ein durchwühltes Zimmer. (*R* 46–7)

The description recalls the impoverished syntax typical of Müller's impressionistic passages: verbs are absent, the sentences are not linked (just as nothing links the pictures), and the description is reduced to a list of nouns. Furthermore, individual, independent body parts are foregrounded. What does link these pictures, however, is their dissociation: 'So fremd war das Gebilde, daß es den Punkt traf, an dem das Lachen des Mädchens im Schaukelstuhl denselben Abgrund auftat wie der Tote im Anzug' (*R* 47). The 'Abgrund' which opens up in the collage is clearly a cipher for trauma—Eleanor Kaufman refers to its 'abysslike structure'.[73]

---

[73] Eleanor Kaufman, 'Falling from the Sky: Trauma in Perec's *W* and Caruth's *Unclaimed Experience*', *Diacritics*, 28/4 (1998), 44–53, here 49.

Müller herself produces collages, which are of increasing importance in her oeuvre. Her first collages were primarily picture based, and introduced the essays in *Der Teufel sitzt im Spiegel*; two independent collections of primarily text-based collages have followed, *Der Wächter nimmt seinen Kamm: Vom Weggehen und Ausscheren* (1993), a boxed set of postcards, and more recently *Im Haarknoten wohnt eine Dame* (2000), a book. This move from intra-textual metaphor to aesthetic structure—from thematized collages within the texts, to the production of texts as collage—echoes the movement between 'histoire' and 'discours'; the connection suggests, moreover, that collages have a similar symbolic and therapeutic function for Müller to that which they perform for Irene.

André Breton, in his account of Surrealist collage, emphasizes its capacity to 'nous dépayser en notre propre souvenir'.[74] Significantly, the disorientation Breton invokes here encompasses both a form of exile—being displaced from one's 'pays'—and a disruption of memory, clearly analogous to the effects of trauma. Collages are associated with exile and distance in Müller's work through the figure of Irene and in the use of postcards as a ground for the collages.[75] Müller's collage technique also draws on methods which displace the self as source of writing, as selection replaces composing: 'Die Worte der Collagen müssen einem nicht einfallen, sie liegen alle gleichzeitig auf dem Tisch. Es ist eine andere Entscheidung, aus dem Vorhandenen zu nehmen, als wenn man Wörter aus dem Kopf schreibt.'[76] Expression is reduced to a chance encounter: 'es gibt Wörter, die mich fangen, die ich ausschneide', Müller notes, and she likens the cut-out words to objects, occupying a similarly uncanny position between belonging to the self or body and existing independently.[77] In this way, the words do not come from inside, from the individual, but rather from outside, the external world; the process of creating a text entails a further reversal of inner and outer: Müller remarks, '[diese gedruckten

---

[74] André Breton, quoted in Elza Adamowicz, *Surrealist Collage in Text and Image: Dissecting the Exquisite Corpse* (Cambridge: Cambridge University Press, 1998), 4.
[75] Stephan Düppe ('Geschicke der Schrift') sees postcards—Irene's preferred medium of communication—as a motif symbolizing *différance* and a form of deterritorialization.
[76] Müller, in interview with Driver Eddy, "Die Schule der Angst", 336.
[77] Ibid. 337.

Wörter] lassen mich draußen und ich bin *doch* drin', positing the process as a form of interior experience of language.[78] Müller's emphasis on language reflects what she sees as the collage's function as preparatory work for writing, a form of 'literarische[s] Handwerk'.[79] The collages must be considered as artefacts, however, not merely individual texts and images but the sum of the relations between the verbal and the visual.

Der Wächter nimmt seinen Kamm consists of ninety-six postcards, each comprising a collage of text, with individual words cut out from newspapers, and images ranging from photographs to crude silhouette forms. The assembled text stages visibly the contiguity and juxtaposition of parataxis, while the whole emphasizes the work's status as artefact. Just as the typographical changes in *Der Fuchs war damals schon der Jäger* draw attention to the physical text precisely at politically significant moments, however, so too does *Der Wächter nimmt seinen Kamm*. Formal experimentation is combined with a highly politicized text, containing many direct references to political repression and violence in Romania. Texts on the postcards take up themes familiar from the literary texts: 'die Freundin war längst vom Geheimdienst gekauft das Gehirn nie mehr Eigentum' (*WK* 2); 'daß Freunde keine Selbstmörder sind sondern Dahinter ein Holzmann stand' (*WK* 40).[80] The visual format is reminiscent of ransom letters, adding a slightly sinister, detached air to Müller's already disconcertingly bald wording.

Text passages from *Im Haarknoten* likewise touch on emigration, war, suicide, and death and contain allusions to the secret police, but they also mark a significant shift towards poetic form as well as playfulness. Although the texts adhere nominally to rules of syntax, this is subverted by the production of phrases which are semantically incoherent, as, for instance, 'im schwarzen Hemd die Pappel beim Spazieren | dazwischen muß der Mond in seinen Fahrstuhl steigen | und seine Höfe schneiden im Erfrieren | und von der Milch die weiße Seite stricken'.[81] Many of the texts in *Im Haarknoten* use poetic metre

---

[78] Ibid. 338.   [79] Ibid.
[80] All capitals and lack of punctuation reproduced as in the original.
[81] As the pages in *Im Haarknoten* are not numbered, references to individual collages are by the first words; no further reference will be given if the lines quoted are the first of the text.

and both end and internal rhymes; the surreal imagery of the texts often gives the impression of having been chosen simply because of the rhyming potential: 'Laien Trottel Schurken | alle zahlen mit Metall | einer hat nur Gurken' (*HD* 'einer verlangt Krähe'); or 'Hitze gelb wie die Zitrone | wo der Wind die Esche schüttelt | heißt sie Krone'. Texts apparently written in the form of prose also contain frequent rhymes, creating tension between the two formal structures, between the linear narrative and the repetitions of rhyme. Taking linguistic games even further, one text uses only the vowel 'a' (*HD* 'Anna war kalt'). These rules, along with syntax, provide constraints which facilitate, rather than hinder, poetic associations. Choosing to submit to formal rules of poetic composition is, for Müller, both a liberating step and a sign of liberation:

> In der Prosa bin ich noch nie so weit weggekommen, es lähmen mich die Beschädigung und der Schrecken. Aber hier kann ich raus davon. Es ist ein ganz anderes Feld, da kann ich außerhalb davon, ja fast außerhalb meiner Beschädigungen, meiner ganzen mitgebrachten Person, in diesen Collagen turnen.[82]

The texts embody the notion of fragmentation in their physical state, as words cut out and pasted onto the page, visibly staging the 'Riß' in language; variation of typeface, size, and colour provides a further level of disruption and subversion within the text. Müller's comment makes it clear, however, that the poetic strategies are her real interest here, as a means of overcoming the trauma which induces fragmentation.

Nonetheless, the images which feature on the collages in both collections are striking in their focus on the human form and, particularly, on the body in fragments. *Der Wächter* contains a large number of postcards which feature a crude, stylized human figure cut from plain black paper; the figures are frequently distorted, with missing limbs (arms especially) and disproportionate or uneven legs in impossible positions. Images of the body are also cut in two: a head and neck are separated from the shirt collar (*WK* 65), and a woman's body is separated from a (different) head (*WK* 81), or the middle section of a body is removed (*HD* 'der Tag zieht Aprikosenbacken'), giving the impression that the figure is swimming through

---

[82] Müller, in interview with Driver Eddy, "Die Schule der Angst", 338.

carpet. Collages in both collections focus on individual body parts—eyes, mouth, and especially legs—in cropped images or as incongruously isolated objects, such as the two sets of toes which are superimposed on an image of table legs (*HD* 'als die Gabel'). These images recall the radical metonymy of Müller's literary texts and her focus on detail, an appropriate term which, as Eliane DalMolin reminds us, 'names the actual gesture of cutting, not just fragmenting or separating but cutting the body into minute pieces with a sharp object, as the verb *détailler* signifies in French: to cut into pieces'.[83] Some of the images resemble the 'cadavre exquis' of Surrealist collage, where a body is suggested through substitute images: a kneeling headless figure on postcard 11 is superimposed on a picture of a jacket, so that the jacket's button replaces the head; a reclining torso has a toothbrush (brush, i.e. head, end) attached where a head would be (*HD* 'verrückte Blaumeise im Staub').[84] Elza Adamowicz sees such substitutions as a form of metaphor and explains that

> The *cadavre exquis* is structured as both a rule and a transgression [...]: the basic rules governing the articulation of the body are followed (head + shoulders + arms...), while the standard lexicon of the body is partly replaced by random elements which flout the rules of anatomical coherence.[85]

Müller's 'cadavres exquis' function in the same way as the texts on her collages, attending to self-imposed linguistic rules, whilst undermining the meaning of the ensemble. The metaphorical images she chooses also hark back to concerns of her literary texts—toothbrushes are a motif in *Herztier*, as a sign of always being prepared to be arrested by the *Securitate* or to flee them. However, while these particular images do uphold the human form, they are interspersed with images which fundamentally challenge the articulation of the human body as a discrete, integral entity. Whereas the Surrealists sought to subvert prevailing orthodoxies, Müller's work reflects a reality which already

---

[83] Eliane DalMolin, *Cutting the Body: Representing Woman in Baudelaire's Poetry, Truffaut's Cinema, and Freud's Psychoanalysis* (Ann Arbor: University of Michigan Press, 2000), 19.
[84] See Adamowicz, *Surrealist Collage*, 78 f. for a full analysis of the 'cadavre exquis'.
[85] Ibid. 80.

distorts and damages the individual, and it does so by inflicting violence on the human form.

The basic signifiers of the human form are reduced to a head and a pair of legs and feet, from which peculiar hybrid, grotesque objects emerge: card 57 appears to feature a cross between a table and a person, an image repeated in the collage 'was weiß ich'; the collage 'gezeugt hat mich doch einer' in *Im Haarknoten* similarly shows a table-like composition with a tree in the middle and a pair of feet in each corner; and two images suggest crosses between a human and a trumpet, and a human and a lamp, respectively (*HD* 'der Mann vom Tiefbauamt' and the following collage, 'außerdem haben zwei Quitten'). In this latter image, it is the outline of the shape which suggests the human body, while the picture from which the shape is cut features a lamp, signalling another form of visual interference, that between the original image and its transformed shape in Müller's collage. These different representational levels are frequently incongruous: human figures are cut from images of woodwork, fields (notably with a rabbit sitting in what would be the brain, *HD* 'kurz darauf sagt Barbara'), and a paper aeroplane (which resembles a cloak in the new image, *HD* 'wenn alle gegangen sind'). Images of people are also transformed into new objects: a sleeping (dead?) man is cut into the shape of a dog (the 'Heimwehhund' referred to in the text, *HD* 'und der nicht mehr zu Hause war'), a close-up of a nose becomes a pear, an ear is the shell of a snail. In one disconcerting composition, three figures are cut from images of people, but with the cut head shape slightly off centre, so that the heads are blank, although the rest of the bodies coincide with the original image (*HD* 'Vater kommt vom Dienst'), a striking image of dissociation. Müller plays with the two levels of image, recalling the role of mirrors and reflective surfaces in her texts as both surface image and representational depth. One collage has a photo of a landscape placed 'inside' one of a cup, acting as the mirror image reflected on the surface of the drink; reflections are referred to in the text: 'die Pferde trinken am Fluß | weil sie im Wasser den Himmel sehen'. The double vision which the collages demand is further disrupted by the rough edges and obvious scissor cuts which foreground the visible signs of production.

The interaction of text and image in the collages varies, and the relationship between the visual and the verbal is more often one of incongruous juxtaposition rather than a productive dialectic. In *Der Wächter*, where the text layout is less conventional and departs from literary lines, text and image interact spatially. Postcard 59 shows two small male figures from the hips up, one placed upside down directly underneath the other; the figures are separated by text, which reads 'Noch einmal, weil's so schön war' and underneath the second figure, text reads 'nach unten'. Here the text refers to the images as they stand on the card, self-consciously pointing to the whole as visual artefact. More frequently, images either clearly relate to the words of the accompanying text, such as the montage of clock and twiglike slug creature in the text 'immer gehen wir zu Tisch', which illustrates the line 'kriecht der Drehwurm durch die Uhr'. Or, the images have no obvious connection to the text, as, for instance, the watermelon accompanying the text beginning 'und in der einen Hand' or the many stylized human figures in both collections. Both the subordination of image to text (as mere illustration) and the absence of a link between the two, however, reinforce the distinction between the verbal and the visual, characterizing their relation too as one of incongruity and interference.

Although the intrinsic artistic or poetic merit of Müller's simple collages is unclear, they are interesting because they share themes and structures with her literary work, extending these into more literal forms. The collages develop the notion of fragmentation as an aesthetic strategy and point to the kind of interaction between levels of the work (text or artefact) which derives from the dissolution of boundaries. Whereas this latter is characterized in the literary work by the commingling of the levels of the text—'histoire' and 'discours'—and by movement between the two, in the visual work, this interaction is disruptive and characterized by difference. The different levels of the artefact—text and image, surface outline and representational space, syntax and semantics, perception of the physicality of the production and engagement with the meaning of the elements—constantly resist resolution into a single interpretation or viewpoint.

'LITERATUR IST DOCH IMMER VON DORT AUSGEGANGEN, WO BEIM AUTOR DIE BESCHÄDIGUNG AM TIEFSTEN WAR':[86] CONCLUSION

Structures of trauma pervade Müller's work, and are testimony to the lasting damage inflicted by the repressive Banat community and the Ceauşescu regime. In her work, the effects of trauma are reproduced in imagery and literary form; these disrupt, but do not preclude, the increasingly direct articulation of the horrors of the Ceauşescu regime. That the narrative strategies deriving from trauma have achieved recognition, and indeed acclaim, as literary effects strikes a blow against the state which would determine all signification. However, it also demonstrates the extent to which this trauma can be overcome—that is to say, it cannot be escaped, only resignified.

Trauma is represented by the dissolution of boundaries and fragmentation, figures which find expression both in representations of the body and in narrative structures. They are also repeated on a structural level in Müller's oeuvre. Müller's collages are emblematic of the way in which boundaries between levels of text and between different forms of writing become fluid: significantly, her first collages appeared interpolated within the poetological essays in *Der Teufel sitzt im Spiegel*, in a type of productive interference; moreover, Eke also notes a further commingling of discourses in *Teufel*, where '[p]oetischer und theoretischer Diskurs durchdringen sich'.[87] Müller's artistic output has split into two parallel developments, literary prose and collage work, evident in her two most recent publications, *Heute wär ich mir lieber nicht begegnet*, the most straightforward of her prose works to date, and *Im Haarknoten wohnt eine Dame*, composed entirely of Müller's text and picture collages. The publication of *Im Haarknoten* as a book—more accessible and mainstream than the box of postcards, *Der Wächter nimmt seinen Kamm*—indicates that the visual is to be given equal weight in Müller's oeuvre. I suggest that this split can be traced back to

---

[86] Müller, in interview with Haines and Littler, 'Gespräch mit Herta Müller', 23–4.

[87] Eke, 'Augen/Blicke oder: Die Wahrnehmung der Welt in den Bildern. Annäherung an Herta Müller', in Eke (ed.), *Die erfundene Wahrnehmung*, 7–21, here 18.

Reisende auf einem Bein, the one text exceptionally set outside Romania and one which, as Brigid Haines has recently argued, prefigures the trauma narratives and testimony of the later novels.[88] Irene's collages in *Reisende* also provide the transition into Müller's own. Separating these two strands allows Müller to testify increasingly directly to the horrors of Ceauşescu's Romania in prose, whilst retaining and further codifying the aesthetic of fragmentation in her collages, which have taken on a playful aspect as a result. Müller's most recent prose work, *Heute wär ich mir lieber nicht begegnet*, moreover also evinces a new development in narrative form: it rejects the paratactic, episodic structure of the earlier texts in favour of 'dramatic structure, with its strong forward momentum and final undermining twist'—in other words, a plot.[89] Finally, Müller's journalistic work constitutes a third distinct strand of writing. Her essays focus on repressive regimes and their victims, and can be seen as preserving traumatization in outrage: as Henry Krystal observes, 'moral and ethical judgement is often substituted for self-healing'.[90] This aspect of her work has attracted criticism for conflating different regimes—another totalizing gesture like the coercive metaphors identified by Schmidt.[91] Such splitting is, of course, itself one effect of the dissociation produced by trauma; the trajectory of Müller's oeuvre reflects the structures underlying the imagery and textual strategies in individual works.

Müller's work is not simply about the transcription of trauma, however. For all that her texts reflect its very real effects, and draw on autobiographical information, they are fiction, aware of their status as literary texts, within literary traditions. Müller's texts consciously invoke pre-existing literary forms such as fairy tales.[92] In *Herztier*, the reader cannot fail to be struck by the

---

[88] Haines, 'The Alien Gaze'.
[89] Haines, "Leben wir im Detail", 118. Predoiu suggests that Müller's later works show a similar development on a linguistic level, increasingly moving away 'von parataktischen Sätzen zu kompliziert gebauten Satzgefügen', *Faszination*, 186.
[90] Krystal, in Caruth (ed.), *Trauma: Explorations in Memory*, 85.
[91] See for example Haines, "Leben wir im Detail", 111.
[92] Cf. references to Snow White in 'Niederungen' (*Nd* 32) and, in *Fasan*, 'das Märchenmotiv der Rosen- und Dornenhecke', Norbert Otto Eke, ' "Überall, wo man den Tod gesehen hat". Zeitlichkeit und Tod in der Prosa Herta Müllers. Anmerkungen zu einem Motivzusammenhang', in Eke (ed.), *Die erfundene Wahrnehmung*, 74–94, here 85–6.

parallels with the tale of Snow White in the death of the 'singende Großmutter':

> Als die Mutter aus der Stadt kam, lag sie mit einem Stück Apfel im Mund tot auf dem Boden. Sie war aus der Aussteuer wie für eine Braut herausgestorben. Der Bissen steckte zwischen den Lippen. Sie war nicht daran erstickt. Der Bissen hatte eine rote Schale.
> Am nächsten Tag fand der Polizist im ganzen Haus keinen Apfel, von dem der Bissen fehlte. (*Hz* 242)

Müller also situates her texts in relation to other writers, in her critical essays, such as her speech for the Kleist prize in *Hunger und Seide*, or *In der Falle*, where she writes about 'Autoren [...], die an Diktaturen zerbrochen sind: Theodor Kramer, Ruth Klüger und Inge Müller', as well as within her literary texts.[93] 'Überall, wo man den Tod gesehen hat. Eine Sommerreise in die Maramuresch' (*Barfüßiger Februar*), as Antje Janssen-Zimmermann demonstrates, takes up themes and motifs from Paul Celan's 'Todesfuge', which evokes the trauma of the Holocaust.[94] Italo Calvino's *Le città invisibili* offers a parallel to Müller's own city tale, *Reisende auf einem Bein*, when Irene is identified with one of Calvino's cities. Ingeborg Bachmann provides the motto for *Fasan*, Gellu Naum the poem on the frontispiece to *Herztier*, which the friends cite within the text. Kafka's writing is invoked by an official in *Herztier*: 'Sie fühlen sich unschuldig. Ohne Grund wird doch niemand verprügelt' (*Hz* 216).[95]

The later texts are more self-conscious: words and literature have concrete functions within the dictatorship, and are given the potential to affect reality. *Fuchs* includes folk songs and a poem is credited with predicting the downfall of Ceauşescu. The narrator of *Herztier* is a translator and collects words to send to her friends, dissidents who read banned German literature; and the existence of 'Lolas Heft' is a parallel with the text of *Herztier* itself. Müller's work is thus consciously literary and intertextual, opening out onto a network of references to other authors

---

[93] Müller, in interview with Haines and Littler, 'Gespräch mit Herta Müller', 23.

[94] See Antje Janssen-Zimmermann, '"Überall, wo man den Tod gesehen hat, ist man ein bißchen wie zuhaus." Schreiben nach Auschwitz—Zu einer Erzählung Herta Müllers', *Literatur für Leser*, 4 (1991), 237–49.

[95] Cf. interpretations of Kafka's *Schloß* peculiar to Eastern Bloc countries (*HuS* 57).

and texts. Müller's carefully circumscribed use of literary allusion differs substantially from Libuše Moníková's and Kerstin Hensel's transgressive and transformational parodies. Although these references introduce extra-textual discourses into both levels of Müller's texts, in the same way that elements of the 'discours' and 'histoire' intrude into each other, they remain distinct, alien elements; only in *Reisende*, where sentences from unnamed books frequently occur to Irene (*R* 24, for example), do they begin to resemble the kind of postmodern consciousness evident in Moníková's *Pavane für eine verstorbene Infantin*. Even Irene's literary memory may ultimately be a product of repression: as Müller explains in *In der Falle*, memorizing literature was a way, 'eine Weile nur für sich zu sein'; poems were 'ein tragbares Stück Halt im Kopf' (*IF* 18).

Müller's work as a whole raises the question of to what extent it is possible to challenge and subvert the structures of trauma or, on a wider level, of language itself, which are always already imposed on the subject from outside. Does Müller merely reproduce these structures, or does her work manage to bring them into question? Müller is aware of the subject's implication in discourse: 'Auch, wenn wir uns aufs Innere beziehn, begreifen wir die Ränder nur, weil wir sie mit Äußerem verbinden. Auch, wenn wir über uns selber nachdenken, denken wir über uns im äußeren Zusammenhang nach' (*TS* 40). Her formulation points to a necessary, unconscious collusion and complicity in external structures. It recalls feminist theory, such as that of Luce Irigaray, who argues that it is impossible to think outside of patriarchal discourse, or Sigrid Weigel's notion of the 'schielende[r] Blick', the double vision which women must employ in order to be aware of, and counteract, their image under patriarchy.[96] The result, for Irigaray, is that a woman's voice is to be heard in the gaps of a text—which recalls Müller's 'Riß'. Irigaray also advocates mimicry as a form of subversion. In Müller's work, the structures of trauma are in turn revealed in the repressive tactics of the state, which induce trauma through, in Scarry's terms, a 'mime of uncreating'. By making these connections visible,

---

[96] Sigrid Weigel, 'Der schielende Blick: Thesen zur Geschichte weiblicher Schreibpraxis', in Sigrid Weigel (ed.), *Die verborgene Frau* (Berlin: Argument Verlag, 1983), 83–137.

Müller's texts mime this mimicry, in a move which opens up a space for the individual voice.

Literature cannot overcome the effects of trauma, but it can make them legible. By recreating and enacting them as fiction, it can reinscribe a tentative and contingent sense of subjectivity, which underlies Müller's political resistance.[97]

Vielleicht war in den Jahren des Frosches die Erfindung der Wahrnehmung die einzige Möglichkeit, die Umgebung zu verändern. Sie wurde nicht erträglicher. Sie wurde bedrohlicher. Doch hatte mindestens dieser Zusatz mit mir selber etwas zu tun. (*TS* 29)

While this small but significant shift allows Müller to salvage a minimal notion of selfhood, it also accounts for her texts' occasional compulsion of the reader. The reader is forced to approach her texts from within, by entering into Müller's 'erfundene Wahrnehmung', and experiencing the literary effects, that is, the effect of trauma.

[97] In Haines (ed.), *Herta Müller*, the following all take up aspects of the concern with integrity, subjectivity, and political agency: Littler, 'Beyond Alienation'; Haines, "Leben wir im Detail"; and John J. White, ' "Die Einzelheiten und das Ganze": Herta Müller and Totalitarianism', 75–95.

3
LIBUŠE MONÍKOVÁ:
'ICH BIN AM ORT MEINES URSPRUNGS', 'INNEN BIN ICH HOHL'

The body, and particularly the female body, is at the heart of Libuše Moníková's texts. Her first two texts centre on damaged bodies: *Eine Schädigung* (1981) begins with the rape of a female student by a policeman; *Pavane für eine verstorbene Infantin* (1983) focuses on the narrator's psychosomatic limp and her subsequent decision to take to a wheelchair. In a more positive light, the protagonists of her last two completed texts, *Treibeis* (1992) and *Verklärte Nacht* (1996), exercise their bodies in their respective professions as stuntwoman and choreographer-dancer. This physicality does not imply an entirely unmediated experience of the body, however; each of these manifestations is overlaid with, and constructed within, many forms of discourse. The bodies signify in different ways, and on different levels: Jana's rape functions at least in part as allegory; Karla's stunts and Leonora's dance routines are part of narratives within the 'histoire'. By far the most complex representation of the body, however, is in *Pavane*, where narrator Francine's hysterical mimicry (her limp) and performance (the use of the wheelchair) are a form of 'Körper-Sprache'.

Hysteria does not only manifest itself through the figure of Francine Pallas. It underlies representations of the body in Moníková's work and, further, it informs the narrative strategies she employs. The text of *Pavane* brings together these concerns with body-language and textual strategies of imitation. The two sections of this chapter deal with these two aspects, looking first at images of the body, focusing on the performance of identity, and specifically gender identity; and then at the mimicry of other texts and languages which are textual forms of hysteria. I begin by elaborating the aspects of hysteria which are relevant to Moníková's texts; in particular, I relate hysteria to the notion of exile which is a recurrent theme in her texts.

Hysteria and exile

Hysteria famously eludes definition: a psychosomatic disorder, with no organic lesions, its symptoms differ down the ages, from one individual case to another, and within each case. It is a catch-all term, covering what cannot be defined by medical discourse, and through history has incorporated anything, or anyone, designated as 'other'. Located in the intersection of medical discourse, the supernatural, and religious mysticism, as Cristina Mazzoni argues, 'The very story of hysteria is a series of displacements of its dominant hermeneutic metaphor—organic or functional, corporeal or spiritual, natural or supernatural'.[1] Mazzoni's statement suggests that the interpretation of the illness is as mutable as its symptoms; she also reminds us that hysteria is linked to stories of the body. The illness was originally considered to be caused by the womb wandering around the body—hence the term 'hysteria', from the Greek for the uterus; both Plato and Hippocrates saw the womb as like an errant little animal. These peregrinations are echoed in Moníková's texts, in her characters' travels and continual displacements.[2] The notion of 'wombsickness' marked the illness out as a female malady, and linked it to female sexuality and sexual desire, an association which has continued through the ages. In her recent study, Elisabeth Bronfen moves away from conventional gendered discourse predicated on female sexual dissatisfaction, however, and returns to Freud's initial studies of the disorder in order to trace a traumatic aetiology of hysteria.

According to Bronfen, whom I follow here, hysteria arises in the face of an unrepresentable and inaccessible 'Urtrauma', which remains as a gap in the psyche.[3] Hysteric symptoms are memory traces, façades which both encode and bar memories of that traumatic impact.[4] Hysteria is a form of bodily expression, a psychosomatic response to trauma played out on the body itself; it is both physical and symbolic. Typical physical

---

[1] Cristina Mazzoni, *Saint Hysteria: Neurosis, Mysticism and Gender in European Culture* (Ithaca, NY: Cornell University Press, 1996), 3.
[2] See Marven, 'Women in Wheelchairs', 515–16.
[3] Bronfen, *The Knotted Subject*, 34–42.
[4] Vedder, "Ist es überhaupt noch mein Prag?", identifies memory as a key theme in Moníková's work; the association with hysteria points to memory as a narrative after the fact, rather than the guarantor of discernible, historical truth.

symptoms include feelings of numbness or paralysis, suffocation, and, in the hysterical fit, loss of consciousness. Hysteria signals the vulnerability of the body, displaying its mutability and mortality, and revealing the unstable nature of identity. It can also express social discontent: Francine's limp in *Pavane* symbolizes her marginalization within society. Hysteria is a series of inconsistent, ever-changing self-representations, which stage their own fictionality; it is a fragmentary and discontinuous narrative. Like trauma, it is structured around a gap: Bronfen, who looks at specific narrative and visual representations of hysteria, characterizes it as 'much ado about nothing'. The hysteric's performance is one of imitation and simulation, which convey the self even whilst acknowledging that it remains a set of roles. In this, it recalls Judith Butler's idea that subjectivity is only a performance, an imitation without an origin.

Hysteria offers an image of the body participating in discourse, as its symptoms represent a form of non-verbal language, and emphasize the body's constructedness. Bronfen furthermore describes it in literary terms:

Freud emphasized that hysteria should be seen as the psychosomatic language a subject uses to articulate how she is haunted by the memories and stories she has incorporated and cannot shed—texts occupying her body as though it were their host, using the body to speak their alterity, regardless whether these nonabreactable psychic traces are inherited phantasies or conversions of actually inherited events.[5]

Francine is the only protagonist whose body 'speaks' in this way. The memories and stories which interrupt her narrative intertwine the personal and the national, like those of other protagonists who 'inherit' memories.[6] Francine's narrative is also occupied by other, literary texts, the traces of literary forebears. Hysteria is thus linked to intertextuality, particularly as Moníková's texts allude to other famous hysterics: *Pavane* contains oblique references to Ophelia,[7] and Ingeborg Bachmann's

[5] Bronfen, *The Knotted Subject*, 386.
[6] Karla in *Treibeis* describes events happening while she was still in her mother's womb, saying she was 'gewissermaßen auch dabei' (*T* 222).
[7] See Marven, 'Women in Wheelchairs', 527; also Katherine Roberts, 'The Wandering Womb: Classical Medical Theory and the Formation of Female Characters in *Hamlet*', *Classical and Modern Literature: A Quarterly*, 15/3 (1995), 223–32.

Franza Ranner in *Der Fall Franza* is invoked in both *Pavane* and *Verklärte Nacht*.[8]

The hysteric's symptoms stage the vulnerability of identity: as Bronfen suggests, she broadcasts a message of 'the insecurity of gender, ethnic and class designations'.[9] In Moníková's work, both gender and national identity are at stake. While the two concepts cannot be entirely separated, I concentrate in this chapter on the former because it is played out on the body.[10] But precisely because the two aspects are intertwined, I conclude these introductory remarks by considering the hysterical origin of Czech national identity in Moníková's texts.

Moníková's exploration of Czech history and national identity is one of her most frequent, and widely commented, themes; I believe that this very prominence already suggests it is a hysterical performance. Czech identity is linked with trauma, the source of hysteria, in two ways in Moníková's work. The first is through events in national history, notably the 'nationales Trauma' (*PF* 81) of the Munich Agreement in 1938, which saw Czechoslovakia handed over to the Nazis by the Western powers, and what Moníková calls 'die Quelle, das Urtrauma, aus dem ich schreibe', the invasion of Warsaw Pact troops in 1968.[11] Secondly, the Czech identity of Moníková's female protagonists (Francine, Karla, Leonora) is defined by their being in exile, which also shares with hysteria an origin in trauma. That her protagonists' Czech/exile identity is the most insistent and dominant of self-representations does not guarantee its authenticity, it merely suggests that it offers the best chance of reunifying their fragmented identity. The restatement and intensification of attachment to the country of origin, Czechoslovakia, is an attempt to overcome the specific 'Trauma der Entortung'; in this sense, it is a hysterical self-representation which both stages

---

[8] Ingeborg Bachmann, *Der Fall Franza* [with *Requiem für Fanny Goldmann*] (Munich: dtv, 1981).

[9] Bronfen, *The Knotted Subject*, p. xiii.

[10] In Moníková's texts national identity (Czech) is superimposed with an ethnic (Slav) identity, which *is* written on the body: the female protagonists have Slav dark colouring, but this is of less importance than their identification with the history, politics, and culture of the state of Czechoslovakia.

[11] Moníková in interview with Frank Dietschreit, 'Sehnsuchtsort: Libuše Moníková über tschechische Alpträume, Heimatliebe, Leben und Schreiben im Exil', *Wochenpost*, 26 Sept. 1996, 36–7, here 37.

and screens the vulnerability of national identity. To interpret Moníková's texts solely in relation to exile as a structure and metaphor would therefore be to take as authentic fact what is a hysterical performance.

Moníková's decision to write in German further demonstrates the overlap between the two figures of exile and hysteria. For her, the representation of trauma—the rape in *Eine Schädigung*, which can be seen as an allegorical representation of the Warsaw Pact troops' invasion—was a way into writing. The text forced her to find a language in which to write. She states:

> Das Deutsche ist für mich ein Filter. Ich habe nämlich angefangen, habe die *Schädigung*, die von einer Vergewaltigung handelt, tschechisch angefangen, aber das erste Kapitel war mir wortwörtlich peinlich. Und nur durch das Deutsche, weil ich mehr Abstand hatte und genauer sein konnte, merkte ich, das ist die Sprache, in der ich schreiben kann. Nicht enthemmter, das Deutsche ist für mich die Sprache, in der ich mehr Distanz habe und genauer sein kann. Das Tschechische ist mir zu ... ich habe auch keine Erfahrung.[12]

Moníková's adoption of German is a linguistic enactment of exile, and echoes Caruth's claim that 'trauma is a repeated suffering of the event, but it is also a continual leaving of its site'.[13] It also signals the hysteric's mimicry of language, a fact highlighted by the many other languages used in Moníková's texts.

Treibeis, set outside Czechoslovakia, is the novel which most explicitly thematizes Czech history; national identity comes undone as a result. Whereas in *Pavane* national concerns are subordinate to the narrative of Francine's hysteria, in *Treibeis*, historical discourse takes centre stage—and the exaggerated national identity reveals itself to be a form of hysteria. Historical facts emerge through dialogue between the two protagonists, Prantl and Karla, in the form of their own memories (a performance of the self) or, significantly, read out from other sources, as scripts which allow them to act out their differences. The penultimate chapter consists almost entirely of dialogue between Prantl and Karla, much of it quoted from second-hand, patriotic books on Czechoslovakia, with the narratorial comment that, 'Sie

---

[12] Moníková, in interview with Sibylle Cramer, Jürg Laederach, and Hajo Steinert, 'Libuše Moníková im Gespräch', *Sprache im technischen Zeitalter*, 119 (1991), 184–206, here 203.

[13] Caruth, in Caruth (ed.), *Trauma: Explorations in Memory*, 10.

gelangen an den Punkt, wo jeder ein anderes Land vor sich hat, das sie Tschechoslowakei nennen, mit schiefem Mund auch "Heimat"' (*T* 215). This oft-quoted line is generally taken by critics to indicate the incompatibility of the two lovers, the fact that they have no common history. Brigid Haines sees it as highlighting the opposition between language and experience, and the power of words to determine consciousness.[14] Ulrike Vedder, in a similar vein, touches on what I see as the crux of the matter: she suggests that, 'angesichts eines leeren, wenn auch nicht namenlosen Zentrums', the statement undermines the possibility of positing a notion of 'Heimat' against which exile can be constructed.[15] The construction of an identity around a gap is, I suggest, the notion of hysteria. National identity is here revealed to be a performance: each character constructs it according to, and as part of, their own self-representations.

The vast historical tracts which bolster Prantl and Karla's national identity, and which form part of the self-consciously pedagogical side of Moníková's texts (especially in *Treibeis* and *Verklärte Nacht*), are never fully assimilated into the narrative; indeed, the wealth of facts often hinders the progress of the narrative, pointing to the overwhelming, traumatic nature of this information. This is something that is justifiably criticized as an artistic failure by Sibylle Cramer, amongst others, in her review of *Treibeis*:

> Die Integration des Geschichtsverlaufs durch die Liebenden und die Verklammerung von nationaler und personaler Identifizierung macht die Figuren zu nationalen Bauchrednern und Ideologen einer durchgestrichenen Heilsgeschichte. Die Autorin gerät in einen Spagat zwischen historischer und poetischer Geschichtsschreibung, zwischen Volkshochschulekurs und Romanze.
>
> Als Gespräch hat die Geschichtserzählung die formalen Voraussetzungen für eine Konflikthandlung. [...] Die beiden Figuren wechseln sich in der Rolle von Referent und Lehrgangsteilnehmer ab.[16]

Cramer's criticism of what she sees as 'eine nostalgische Inszenierung von Diskursen' evokes aspects of hysteria: in references

---

[14] See Haines, 'New Places from Which to Write Histories of Peoples', 509–11.
[15] Vedder, "Mit schiefem Mund auch Heimat", 479.
[16] Sibylle Cramer, 'Triumphbogen für ein Opfer der europäischen Geschichte: Libuše Moníkovás Versuch, ein tschechisches Nationalepos zu formen: *Treibeis*', *Süddeutsche Zeitung*, 30 Sept. 1992, p. 8.

to roles and theatricality, to ventriloquism, and to the enactment of a gap, the unbridgeable divide between poetic and historical narrative. These excessive historical accounts point up their own nature as props and scripts to a performance within a hysterical narrative.

Although the trauma of exile may be the underlying source of the hysteria in Moníková's texts, there are other possible causes—trauma is defined precisely by being inaccessible and unrepresentable—and I examine other configurations of exile and hysteria in relation to Francine in *Pavane*.[17] I concentrate in this chapter on another construct, that of gender, which hysteria also reveals to be unstable. While several critics—most notably, Vedder, Braunbeck, and Jankowsky—have approached the question of gender in Moníková's texts, they have presented it primarily as an inflection of nationality, considering it only insofar as it modifies national identity. I concur that the two cannot be considered entirely independently of each other, but as my interest is in images of the body, I focus here first and foremost on gender.

The first section of this chapter deals with the representation of the body. I begin by looking at Francine Pallas in *Pavane*, before turning to the self-representations where Francine, Karla, and Leonora identify with mythical figures. Finally, I examine what I term the 'gender expatriation' of Moníková's female protagonists, and consider how the performance of gender is refracted through other peripheral characters in Moníková's texts. The representation of gender demonstrates key aspects of hysteria, namely mimicry and performance, and the lack of authenticity or 'Ursprünglichkeit', in both senses: a lack of origin as well as a refusal of naturalness. These aspects are also to be seen in the textual strategies which I examine in the second section: Moníková's use of quotation and intertextual allusion, and foreign languages. These strategies entail the adoption of another, or, more precisely, another's discourse, precisely the

---

[17] One possible interpretation which I can only raise here is the loss of the mother, which Bronfen suggests is the psychoanalytic analogue to exile; Bronfen, 'Exil in der Literatur', 174. This is a recurrent, albeit minor, motif in the texts; in Karla's case, her mother died just before she left the country, further linking these traumatic events. Moníková's own mother died suddenly just before she left Czechoslovakia.

mimicry which Irigaray posits as the strategy of woman and the hysteric under patriarchal discourse.

BODY

Moníková's work emphasizes the irreducible physicality of the body, through episodes and motifs, common to all her texts, of physical movement (running, dancing, and swimming), intoxication and delirium, or menstruation. This insistence on the body as an 'organ of experience' and on the embodiedness of her protagonists is at its most extreme in *Eine Schädigung*.[18] Jana's gradual reassessment of her identity after being raped, her transformation into a vulnerable, but embodied subject, is based on the notion of an 'eigentliche[-] Schädigung' (*S* 101), a version of original sin and the price of knowledge. It is a form of authenticity, of subjecthood and language gained through suffering—not a new theme in women's writing, as Weigel demonstrates in *Die Stimme der Medusa*. In Moníková's work, the physicality of the body is also linked to the structures of the text: bodies provide the impetus to the narrative action, in the form of Jana's rape, or Leonora's dip in the Vltava, which ultimately sparks her relationship with Thomas. In a wider sense, the physical and topographical displacements of the protagonists also structure the texts, most notably the artists' travels across the USSR in *Die Fassade*. More than this, the bodies in the texts participate in discourses about gender and the naturalness of the human form, which are my interest here.

I begin this section by looking at the figure of Francine, the most visible of Moníková's hysterics, and whose narrative reveals the hysterical textual strategies. I then analyse Francine's, Karla's, and Leonora's imaginary scenes of identification with mythical figures. These scenes represent symptoms of hysteria, and stage the instability of gender and of identity. The figures mark a shift in emphasis away from the authenticity of the body as source and site of identity, a shift expressed in the translation of Francine's declaration as Libuše, 'Ich bin am Ort meines Ursprungs' (*P* 79), into Leonora's realization as Hatshepsut,

[18] Adelson, *Making Bodies*, 23.

'Innen bin ich hohl' (*VN* 119). The function of these figures as a multiplicity of performed identities and alternative subject positions for the three protagonists is reflected by a range of other characters who challenge the nature of gender and show it to be a performance. Finally, I look at the ways in which Moníková's protagonists move from mimicry to a thematization of performance within the 'histoire' in the way that Irigaray proposes. Considering these last two aspects also enables me to demonstrate that elements of hysteria are already present in *Eine Schädigung*.

'*Geringe Anpassung? Ich hinke ja': Francine Pallas*

The figure of Francine represents the transition from Jana's investment in the authenticity of her body, to the more playful and performative identities evident in the later texts.[19] This transition is enacted within the text, in the progress from her 'Hinken' in the first part of the text to her use of the wheelchair in the second section. Both are manifestations of hysteria and mark her out most clearly of all Moníková's characters as a hysteric. The pain in Francine's hip is psychosomatic, a hysterical symptom produced by the body acting as a metaphor; her use of the wheelchair is a performance of her damage and marginalization. The idea of hysteria is explicitly raised in *Pavane*, where Francine's sister not only gives her the nickname Franza, thus linking her with Bachmann's Franza Ranner, but also, in her capacity as a psychiatric doctor, diagnoses her as hysterical:

> du bist völlig unbeherrscht, unberechenbar, etwas paßt dir nicht, und du schmeißt alles hin, guckst weder links noch rechts, nimmst keine Rücksicht—immer das gleiche: geringe Frustrationstoleranz, bis zur hysterischen Steigerung der Nichtidentifikation mit der Rolle. (*P* 37)

Francine demonstrates the shift from mere imitation (the position of the hysteric, or of woman within patriarchal discourse) to a deliberate mimicry, which constitutes the subversive strategy posited by Irigaray. As Toril Moi puts it, this is 'a theatrical staging of the mime: miming the miming imposed on woman,

---

[19] For a more detailed reading of *Pavane*, see Marven, 'Women in Wheelchairs'.

Irigaray's subtle specular move (her mimicry *mirrors* that of all women), intends to *undo* the effects of phallocentric discourse simply by *overdoing* them.'[20] Francine's limp is a symbol of her outsider status, her inability to conform to social norms, and an example of 'Körper-Sprache'; it cedes to a fake, fictional, and performed disability in her use of the wheelchair.

Francine is a figure on the margins of society, as a Czech immigrant in West Germany, a woman in a patriarchal society, and an academic within a male-dominated environment. The pain in her hip is a physical emblem of her marginality and difference; it is a response to the exclusion she herself experiences and which she notes around her—she feels 'wie sich [...] jeder einzelne Konflikt in diesem Punkt sammelt' (*P* 12). Francine relates the episodes which preceded her developing a limp, where she is met with unfounded distrust and discrimination because of her accent and appearance: her dark colouring points to her Czech nationality, which Francine refers to as the fact 'daß ich aus dem Sozialismus komme' (*P* 128), an odd displacement; and she is not feminine in appearance, therefore falls outside cultural norms.[21] Her limp also represents a resistance to conforming: responding to her friend Geneviève's question, 'there are so many *crippens* in Germany! How is it possible?', Francine asserts, 'Ich weiß es jetzt, ich gehöre auch schon dazu. | Ich habe mich angepaßt, ich kann manchmal vor Schmerzen kaum gehen' (*P* 12). This curious notion is not the pain of conforming to social norms, but rather of conforming to the image of the outsider, who is excluded in order to define the norm. Francine adopts an overt disability as a sign and displacement of psychological damage, making visible—as hysteria does—the way in which society deforms the individual who does not fit in. Her 'wilfully asymmetrical gait' is both a sign of resistance to society, a refusal to fit into predetermined forms and rhythms, and a sign that she has fitted in, and been damaged as a result.[22]

The pain Francine feels in her hip is a form of physical metaphor. It could also be seen as a textual metaphor for

[20] Moi, *Sexual Textual Politics*, 140.
[21] In both cases, Francine compares herself implicitly with her sister, who is blond and plays on her femininity and attractiveness.
[22] Littler, 'Beyond Alienation', 44.

the trauma of the invasion of Czechoslovakia in 1968 (represented allegorically in *Eine Schädigung*), where Francine's body takes on the paralysis of the Czech nation. Her disability is a visible enactment of the manifold 'Verstümmelung' (cf. *P* 7) of Czechoslovakia; the violence done to the language and culture of the Czechs; and a displaced representation of the Nazis' amputation of the country's name to 'Tschechei', a term which Germans persist in using to Francine. Such allegorical interpretations are given less weight within the text than the psychosomatic causes, which may still be bound up with national identity. Francine is an exile from her native Czechoslovakia, having left after the 1968 invasion, and her hysteria arises in response to that trauma: she declares that the pain has endured precisely 'seit einem nicht mehr feststellbaren Tag, seit meiner Ankunft hier' (*P* 12), a formulation which acknowledges that the trauma is inaccessible. The gap in the text which renders invisible (and therefore also visible) the purchase of the wheelchair is a retrospective representation of this unrepresentable, untouchable trauma. Her hysteria might also develop out of mourning for Czechoslovakia: Bronfen explains that melancholic forms of mourning lead to hysteria, as it is

> eine psychosomatische Sprache, die den Prozeß der Trauerarbeit—Rückzug aus der Außenwelt, übersteigertes Interesse an der Auseinandersetzung mit den Verstorbenen oder mit den Ereignissen der Vergangenheit—zum *modus vivendi* erhebt, der nicht nur nicht abgeschlossen werden kann, sondern sogar in seiner endlos fortdauernden Schmerzenslust zelebriert wird.[23]

Azade Seyhan refers to Francine's 'crippling exilic melancholy', although she suggests that this is something Francine overcomes in the course of the text.[24] Francine herself remarks, 'ich bin aus der Trauer einer ganzen Nation weggegangen, und das war zwingender. | Sie war damals auch nicht mehr in Trauer, nur lethargisch, aus der Trauer wäre ich nie weggegangen' (*P* 134).

The form of Francine's hysterical symptom is significant. As a disability, 'Hinken' signals the fact 'daß es den ungebrechlichen Körper nicht gibt', according to Elisabeth Strowick's

---

[23] Bronfen, 'Mourning becomes Hysteria', 33.
[24] Azade Seyhan, *Writing outside the Nation* (Princeton: Princeton University Press, 2001), 83.

etymological analysis.[25] It broadcasts the hysteric's knowledge of vulnerability and mortality which society wishes to repress: Francine complains that disabled people are falsely portrayed as 'Lebenskämpfer, als Zukunftsmodell' (*P* 119). In the essay 'Portrait aus mythischen Konnexionen', in *Schloß, Aleph, Wunschtorte*, Moníková discusses Jorge Luis Borges's tale 'Funes el Memorioso' ('Funes the Memorious'), where the protagonist, Ireneo Funes, has a perfect memory as the result of an accident (a head trauma) which crippled him:

Die Lähmung als Verminderung einer bis dahin indifferenten Gesundheit, eines Zustandes, der Funes rückblickend als ereignis- und bedeutungslos erscheint, ist der mythologischen Variante der *produktiven Reduktion* vergleichbar, von der Lévi-Strauss schreibt:
'Blinde oder Lahme, Einäugige oder Einarmige sind auf der ganzen Welt häufig vorkommende mythologische Gestalten, die uns deshalb verwirren, weil ihr Zustand als ein Mangel erscheint. Aber so, wie ein mittels Subtraktion von Elementen diskret gemachtes System logisch reicher wird, obwohl es numerisch ärmer ist, so verleihen die Mythen den Krüppeln und Kranken oftmals eine positive Bedeutung: sie verkörpern Modi der Vermittlung'. (*SAW* 109)

In this sense, Francine's limp—and also her acted disability in the wheelchair—make visible the system of marginalization and exclusion by which society operates. Margaret Littler sees Francine's disability in the light of Lévi-Strauss's argument as 'a self-imposed limitation which facilitates Francine's establishment of an identity in the city', in other words, 'a positive attempt to fix meaning'.[26] I would suggest that this interpretation applies to her use of the wheelchair, the later, self-conscious enactment of disability; however, I see the limp, her initial psychosomatic symptom, as a conduit, not only for her marginalization but for that of others. Francine draws attention to the damaging and deforming structures of society, evident in the academics with their medical complaints, war veterans, even the statues around the town: she diagnoses one with 'Hüftengelenkluxation' (*P* 143). The marginalization experienced by other outsiders and foreigners similarly manifests itself in physical symptoms: Francine observes 'eine türkische

---

[25] Elisabeth Strowick, 'Hinken, zur Atopie der Metapher', *Frauen in der Literaturwissenschaft Rundbrief*, 45 (1995), 33–8, here 33.
[26] Littler, 'Beyond Alienation', 44 and 55 n. 31.

Albino-Familie. Die Kinder haben rötlich helles Haar, unterscheiden sich deutlich von den einheimischen. [...] Die einzige Anpassung an die Umgebung sind die Brillen, die drei von ihnen tragen' (P 13). Francine, like Franza Ranner in Ingeborg Bachmann's *Der Fall Franza*, is the outsider per se, the embodiment of all victims of oppression.[27] Such self-mythologization is consistent with Francine's self-conscious interest in literary disabilities, of which her own is one.

Whereas Francine's 'Hinken' functions on one level as a kind of 'Körper-Sprache', manifesting damage inflicted by society and the fragmented nature of her psyche, her decision to take to the wheelchair represents a move towards notions of performance and theatricality. Moments of exaggeration and performance precede her retreat into the wheelchair, such as her greetings to '[d]ie Irren': 'ich grüßte laut zurück, mit überdeutlicher Mimik, damit sie meiner Antwort sicher sein konnten [...] nur eine übertriebene Form konnte genügen' (P 15–16); or her reply to an old Turk, who asks her 'Du Kaffee trinken mit mir', in similarly ungrammatical style, 'ich nicht allein' (P 55–6); and finally in her drunken protest 'ich kann nicht gehen' (P 88) which prefigures her decision to abandon walking. In one scene, she washes her curtains, and responds to the feeling of vulnerability by acting: 'ich habe jetzt keinen Schutz und fühle mich gesehen, auch aus den anderen Fenstern. Nach einer Weile merke ich, daß ich ein freundlich konzentriertes Gesicht habe und das Vergnügen, das mir die Arbeit nicht mehr macht, mime' (P 63). This mimicry, the doubling of her own actions, is significant. It is precisely this which Irigaray sees as the female strategy in the face of the male (phallic) gaze, the tendency of men to see women as their mirror, and to deny their difference. Francine's impulse to mimic her own actions in the face of the (patriarchal, outside) gaze culminates in her taking to the wheelchair. The wheelchair is mimicry of her exclusion from society writ large, and all the more powerful because it is entirely staged.

[27] Cf. the references to Bachmann in *Verklärte Nacht* (see below), where Leonora, remembering a trip to the Dead Sea, also momentarily takes on exemplary victim status: 'Daß ich keine Jüdin bin, ist nur ein Mißverständnis' (*VN* 80). Francine and Leonora may well be one and the same person: they share memories and Leonora was an academic before taking up dance.

Francine's move into the wheelchair immediately problematizes 'Körper-Sprache' by challenging the notion of the authentic body. Hers is a faked disability—she can walk without the wheelchair, but references to 'uns Krüppel' and 'normale Behinderte [...] wie ich' (*P* 133) undermine the idea of a 'genuine' physicality. Francine thrives on the dualities of her position in the wheelchair, and plays on the theatricality of her performance by equipping herself with the necessary props for the wheelchair, debating the worth of 'Anti-Decubitus-Gel-Auflagen gegen Wundsitzen' and 'Sonderrichtungen fürs Duschen' (*P* 109). She develops a kind of fetishism towards these accoutrements, buying some prismatic glasses, and perusing a catalogue of prosthetics and medical equipment, which are reminiscent of the artificial trappings of femininity worn by the legendary queen Libuše, with whose image she identifies.[28] Fetishism, as a psychological displacement, focuses on peripheral objects; it is an extreme example of the emphasis on fakery.

Francine's hysterical symptoms are a self-representation and a fiction which are further linked to textuality through the literary manifestations of disability which are thematized within the text. Francine, an academic specializing in Kafka and Arno Schmidt, has an avowed interest in 'Behinderungen als literarisches Thema' (*P* 22). This is evident in her psychological approach to Kafka, particularly to 'Ein Landarzt', which depicts a young boy with a symbolic 'Wunde in der Hüftegegend' and 'Der Bau', in which she sees 'nicht weniger Zwang als in einer Körperlähmung oder Beinlosigkeit' (*P* 59).[29] These intertextual references point self-consciously to Francine's own status as an invalid within a literary text. The conjunction of literature and illness is further emphasized in references to Virginia Woolf and Susan Sontag; to the schizophrenic Vera, who copies texts into her diary; and in Francine's expectation that writers must be ill, or at least psychologically unsound. 'Ich stelle mir Schriftsteller immer nur im Gespräch über Literatur vor, und dabei sind das Hypochonder, oder Vegetarier, chronisch Entlobte, Söhne

---

[28] Interestingly, when she shows this catalogue to her lover Jakob, it is the 'perfekter Robotarm' (*P* 116) which captures his attention, a motif taken up in the fight scene in *Treibeis*, where Karla uses a prosthetic hand.

[29] Franz Kafka, 'Ein Landarzt' and 'Der Bau', in *Sämtliche Erzählungen* (Frankfurt am Main: Fischer, 1970), 124–8, here 127, and 359–88 respectively.

ihrer Väter—oder Mütter; mit Trinkern ginge es noch' (*P* 93), she muses, when she sees visions of Kafka in her room as a result of a stinking hangover. Her 'Hinken' is an allusion to her own literary aspirations, as narrator of *Pavane* and rewriter of Kafka.[30]

In choosing to use the wheelchair, Francine transforms her own life into literature, deliberately and consciously enacting her earlier recognition that her life is merely a copy of literature:

> Mein Leben ist eine Abfolge von Literatur- und Filmszenen, willkürliche Zitate, die ich nicht immer gleich einordnen kann. Manchmal denke ich, daß ich die unerkannten, mit Literatur nicht resonierenden Stellen aufschreiben müßte,—auf die Gefahr hin, daß es dann eine bestimmte Art Langeweile oder Verzweiflung doppelt gibt, wenn sich das fiktive Pendant dazu nachträglich findet. (*P* 19)

Francine's life—precisely like her use of the wheelchair—is a series of roles for which literature provides the template. This statement of a postmodern consciousness is reflected in the text of *Pavane* itself—which Francine produces and performs—which is littered with intertextual references and (often unacknowledged) citations, not least the title itself, a reference to the piece by Ravel which is mentioned within the text. But the Kafka versions Francine produces take this imitation to a second degree. Her wheelchair doubles as a writing desk, and is the impetus for her to begin her task of the 'rectification of literary fates' (*P* 10). Francine produces a set of versions of Kafka's *Das Schloß*; she mimics Kafka—and in doing so, manages to shake off his influence. The end of the text shows her destroying the wheelchair, in a ritual enactment of the banishment of death, and, at the same time, casting off her literary 'Stützen' (*P* 147). I return to intertextuality in the second section of this chapter; I turn now to one particular manifestation of hysteria which Francine shares with the other female protagonists: her identification with a mythical figure.

Self-representations

Although Francine is the only character whom one might call a hysteric, hysteria is also represented in the texts through

---

[30] Mansbrügge analyses Francine as the author of the text of *Pavane* in her section on the text, *Autorkategorie*, 26–47.

the thematization of mimicry and performance, and images of artificiality and a lack of authenticity. The series of identifications with mythical figures which link Francine with Karla and Leonora draw on physical symptoms of hysteria as well as its symbolic manifestations. Francine identifies with Libuše, legendary founder of Prague; Karla with the bearded female Christ figure Kümmernus, a seventh-generation android, and Cleopatra; and Leonora with Elina Makropulos, Hatshepsut, and Leni Riefenstahl. These scenes are textual performances, which continually stage and refract an inaccessible, unrepresentable trauma into a series of hysterical self-representations. Specific features of the imaginary scenes suggest that they represent hysterical episodes: they occur during moments of semi- or unconsciousness (dreams, fevers), like the hysteric's fainting fit which stages the loss of self; and they represent the self, feelings, and characteristics as (partly) other. Francine's first scene of identification with Libuše is a response to feelings of sexual convulsion (aroused by a piece of music by Janáček), and stages her being buried alive, 'den Leib nach dem Brauch zur Atemlosigkeit verschnürt' (*P* 41). This is echoed in Leonora's experience as the mummified Hatshepsut: paralysis, lack of breath, and suffocation all signal typical hysterical symptoms. Finally, these scenes also emphasize the mortality of the physical body.

These identification scenes undermine the authenticity and naturalness of gender and the female body. The hysteric's body is a mode of expression, a performance, a set of mutating symptoms, and not an authentic, organic entity. Francine, Karla, and Leonora explore aspects of their identity—national and gender—through projecting themselves into these figures, fundamentally challenging the perceived essential nature of such identities. Francine as Libuše stages her attachment to Prague, her desire and inability to influence its future; Karla is an android, afraid that her feelings and body have become separated, or Cleopatra, bereft of her lover; Leonora's peripheral position with regard to Prague is represented through the nomadic Makropulos, her power in Hatshepsut, a female Pharaoh. Like the self-representation of the hysteric, these scenes mask and reveal identity at the same time. As a series, they demonstrate the mutation and modification of certain thematic concerns—with the naturalness or artificiality of the body, for example—through the texts, while also highlighting narrative strategies such as intertextual references which are also a form of hysteria.

Francine imagines herself as Libuše, legendary founder of Prague, on several occasions. On the first, she is listening to Janáček, and then Ravel's *Pavane pour une infante défunte* (source of the title of the text). Francine imagines a sacrificial funeral ceremony for herself, as the queen. The queen embodies her people and country; her death gives them life, and assures her of a place in history: 'ich [höre] die Stimme aus der Chronik: Da stirbt die große Königin von Böhmen' (*P* 41). Francine focuses on the body of the monarch, whose regal paralysis is in contrast to the physical emotions aroused by the two pieces of music: Janáček's 'Listy důvěrné' evokes intense, sexual convulsions which end 'in Erschöpfung, nicht Erleichterung'; Ravel's piece evokes mourning and 'das Suchen nach einem authentischen Schmerz in den Rippelungen und Windungen des eigenen Körpers als Antwort auf das Sterbegerümpel' (*P* 40). Here Francine still upholds the possibility of an authentic pain which would subsume the psychosomatic one. A second scene finds Francine tracing the history of Prague through its catacombs and underground network; a metaphor for an exploration of her own psyche, this journey transforms her once more into 'die Fürstin', 'am Ort meines Ursprungs' (*P* 79). Again, the identification with Libuše is linked with the question of origins, something which breaks down in the final scene.

Finally, chapter 14 is given over to the image of the queen 'in all her state and magnificence' (*P* 139).[31] Here she embodies the national aspirations of Bohemia, naming as her intention, among others, to arrange for the return of Kafka's manuscripts from the Bodleian Library (something Francine has already

[31] Helga G. Braunbeck, 'The Body of the Nation: The Texts of Libuše Moníková', *Monatshefte*, 89/4 (1997), 489–506, identifies this first image of the queen in ch. 14 as Elizabeth, 'the winter queen', not Libuše (she is the only critic to do so). Elizabeth was the daughter of James I of England (James VI of Scotland), which explains the use of English to describe her; as a non-Bohemian figure of identification, she would represent a loosening of the bonds of nationality. While Braunbeck's suggestion is persuasive, my focus here is on body and gender, and the actual identity of the queen is of less consequence. The final apparition of the queen is in any case a fictional construct of Francine's—see the references to Graf West-West, from Kafka's *Das Schloß*—and in this respect, resembles the mythical Libuše more than the historical Elizabeth.

called for). In this scene, Moníková has transposed the mythical figure into a modern setting; her version is 'a consciously (indeed corporeally) artificial construct', as John Pizer suggests in his essay on the figure of Libuše in German literature.[32] In the second half of the chapter, the queen disrobes, and the mental affinities between her and Francine, evident in the political polemic, cannot be fully reflected in physical similarity. The queen is dying, and her body is neither whole, nor natural:

Die Königin entkleidete sich.

Zuerst kamen die schweren Ringe und Gehänge, die steife Halskrause, der seidenschwarze Überhang, das schwere perlenbordierte Kleid aus Seidenbrokat.

Die Gestalt löste sich aus den Stützen von Fischgrat, aus den Schuhen, stand nun abgesunken vor dem dunklen Quecksilber-Spiegel, in weißen Strümpfen, in denen sie die Zehen frei bewegte, ohne sie zu spüren.

Als ihr die Perücke abgesetzt wurde, war die Kopfhaut gerötet, gereizt, verschwitzt, das wenige rötliche Haupthaar am Schädel angeklebt. Die Haut um die Augen war aufgerauht, echsenhaft facettiert, ein leichtes Tremolo auf den vorgewölbten Lidern. Von den schadhaften Zähnen war eine Reihe unten mit einem verdrillten Draht im Kiefer befestigt.

Die rechte Brust war Attrappe, sie nahm sie vor dem Schlafengehen selbst ab. An ihr versagte der Graf West-West; auch andere Höflinge hatten sich nicht bewährt, so sehr sie auch vom Glanz der verlotterten Majestät geblendet waren, von den Platin-Nieten in ihrer Schulter, von dem Gerücht des goldenen Nagels in ihrer Hüfte, von dem Karfunkel in ihrem Nabel [...]. (*P* 140–1)

The queen's body is created artificially; it is damaged and incomplete. Her magnificence is the effect of jewels and clothes as well as a wig, false teeth, and a prosthetic breast; her body contains metals and precious stones inside its ageing flesh. Significantly, this artificiality is also the signification of gender: the clothing and prostheses which the queen removes are the symbols of her femininity which is constrained by her position. The 'natural' femininity of the queen is suppressed (she is not allowed to get pregnant); but on assuming power, she must also assume the trappings of conventional femininity (beauty; two

---

[32] John Pizer, 'The Disintegration of Libussa', *Germanic Review*, 73/2 (1998), 145–60, here 157.

breasts), and is thus again denied her own identity. Even in a conventionally male position of power, she cannot forsake her gender, but must embody it.

However, the depiction of the queen whose 'rechte Brust war Attrappe' also evokes the Amazon, the self-mutilated female warrior, and hence a sign of power and the rejection of ideals of femininity (both physical and behavioural).[33] Neither her decrepit body nor her artificial public image offers an image of original, essential femininity; the emphasis on costume and artificiality points rather to Butler's notion of performative gender. Butler contends that gender is an effect of repeated gestures and acts, which produces the identity it purports to express. She continues:

> That the gendered body is performative suggests that it has no ontological status apart from the various acts which constitute its reality. This also suggests that if that reality is fabricated as an interior essence, that very interiority is an effect and function of a decidedly public and social discourse, the public regulation of fantasy through the surface politics of the body, the gender border control that differentiates inner from outer, and so institutes the 'integrity' of the subject.[34]

The queen's body participates in the very public, social discourse of nationhood, which also regulates her body's interiors. According to Butler's understanding of performativity, it would seem that by acting out her gender, by taking on the exaggerated and artificial signs of femininity, the queen is also enabled to transcend them.[35] The disjunction between her real body and the public one signals the non-authenticity of gender, and further highlights the mortality of the body underneath the signs of the immortal monarch.

The accoutrements of majesty and nationhood resemble nothing so much as the prosthetics and metal supports Francine

---

[33] Maria Kublitz-Kramer gives the Amazon as one of many female images alluded to in the text, here through the association of Francine Pallas and Pallas Athene: 'Athena verbindet mit Libussa, deren Name "Jungfrau" bedeutet, die Doppelgestalt von Kriegerin (Amazone) und Jungfrau', Kublitz-Kramer, *Frauen auf Straßen*, 188.

[34] Butler, *Gender Trouble*, 173.

[35] This particular passage reminds me of the final scene in Shekhar Kapur's 1998 film *Elizabeth*, where the young Elizabeth dons artificial and exaggerated signs of femininity—make-up, wig, dress—in order to transcend her womanhood (but also as a sign of her maturing into a woman) and become The Virgin Queen, a paradoxically gender-neutral monarch.

begins to fetishize. Francine's wheelchair is a display of imperfection; the artificial limbs of the Queen of Bohemia hide hers. Both are damaged mentally and physically by the constrictions of society, but they have inverse reactions. Accordingly, it is in looking in the mirror that Francine distinguishes herself from the body image of the queen, and where the attempt at identification—Francine's use of 'ich' to refer to herself *as* the queen—breaks down. The vulnerability of the naked body, which creates the semantic transition from 'sie' (the queen) to 'ich' (Francine/the queen, and then Francine alone), prevents the allegorical identification with the nation: it is the artificial majesty which constitutes the head of the nation.

Ich trete vor den Spiegel, zähle meine Öffnungen, es sind zehn, durch jede bin ich sterblich.

Ich taste nach Verhärtungen, fremden Körpern unter meiner Haut—ich suche den metallenen Mantel, der mir die devoten Ansprüche des Hofs und der Außenwelt abspiegelt, mich zwingend umschließt und zur Perfektion nötigt. Aber ich bin kein gepanzerter Skorpion, ich habe gebrechliche Rippen. [...]

Ich wippe vor dem Spiegel, hüpfe auf dem inkriminierten Bein, vollführe einen 'dupák'—einen Trampeltanz, dann die slovakische Variante 'odzemok'—zu Ehren von Jánošík und Matica Slovenská.

Ich blecke die langen Zähne, Zeichen der Klugheit bei den Römern, grimassiere, habe Ringe unter den Augen, bin gesund. (P 141–2)

Interestingly, Francine begins by referring to the borders of the body, the 'Öffnungen' between inner and outer which are implicated in the regulation of the body and gender, according to Butler. The imperfections of Francine's body reassert her bodily existence, as does her dance. Unlike the slow and stately pavane of the title, these are lively steps, reminiscent of her irregular 'Hinken'. Significantly, Francine embraces mortality: to be 'sterblich' is to be human—she recalls the Sibyl at Cumae, who, immortal, wishes only to die (P 142). The living death in the images of the queen is rejected: neither the legendary immortality of the queen who sacrifices herself for her people, nor the artificial extension of life through the gradual replacement of the body, is a productive stance for the would-be writer. Francine's destruction of the wheelchair, staged as a ritual driving out of death, marks the end of her tendency towards this kind of symbolism; it enables her to get on with writing, specifically rewriting Kafka's *Das Schloß* in a similarly liberating vein.

Treibeis follows the travels of two expatriate Czechs, Jan Prantl, who teaches in Greenland, and the young stuntwoman Karla, who meet in one of the random encounters typical of Moníková's texts. The final chapter is narrated by Karla, who has previously appeared only in the third person; the sudden switch in narrative puts the rest of the text into new light (the narrator of the main body of the text shares Karla's sensitivity towards misogyny).[36] Her narrative draws on two earlier scenes, a visit to a museum in Graz, where Karla admires the armour, weapons, and masks on display, and the moment when Prantl calls Karla a robot, as she plays the memory game perfectly (*T* 207). In Karla's imaginary, stream-of-consciousness monologue which forms the final chapter, these elements coalesce in the image of a seventh-generation android, whose death is both simulated and real. Central to the imagery is deconstruction: of the body, language, and the notion of a natural, original identity, precisely those constructs which underlie the 'ich'.

Haken, die mich weitergeben. Mich? [...] [D]ie Berührung und der sterile Ölgeruch machen mich schaudern. Mich?
Womit schaudern? Womit roch ich sie, womit spürte ich das Kitzeln der Stahlfedern, die sich blitzschnell spannen konnten und wieder lockern, bei der Anspannung drangen sie unter die Haut, ohne sie zu ritzen, zu verletzen, das Schaudern war natürlich wonnig. Natürlich?
In welcher Sprache erinnere ich mich? War ich vor der Sprache da, meine Empfindungen, die Stahlhaare, die Fließbänder, oder war zuerst die Sprache da, durch welche auch diese metallene Welt erschaffen wurde, das geräuschlose Gleiten der Haken, Räder, Glieder, die sich so fließend bewegen, als wären sie durch Blutkreislauf, Muskeln, Sehnen und Knochenskelett gesichert und gehalten, ohne Mechanik, noch die Erstbeweger, die sie in der siebten Generation von Androiden nicht mehr sein können, dazu lag ich als Beweis da.
Ich? (*T* 229)

Karla is a paranoid android, constructed with metal to resemble the human form, but with no essential humanity, in the form of emotion or memory; she experiences sensations at one remove (a form of dissociation), questioning them even as she records

---

[36] See also Mansbrügge's section on 'Die Figur Karla als fiktive Autorperspektive', *Autorkategorie*, 182–5.

them. Her imaginings are in reaction to the gradual realization, prompted by her discussions with Prantl, that their pictures and memories of Prague are unassimilable: no 'real' Prague exists outside them. The absence of this central image—central to both their lives and the text—and its essential unknowableness is reflected in the image of the android, which embodies the lack of essence and memory. The scene also highlights the fact that language determines consciousness, and does not correlate to experience, in Karla's questions, 'In welcher Sprache erinnere ich mich? War ich vor der Sprache da [...] oder war zuerst die Sprache da.'[37] Karla's questions signal two key concerns in Moníková's work, namely the construction of identity—and memory, which is the narrative of identity—within and through discourse; and the relativity and contingency of all individual languages, none of which approaches 'reality'. This latter is apparent in Moníková's use of other languages, which I examine below.

The cold, distant, metal image of the android is contrasted with Karla as she lies thinking: 'Ich bin wie zerschlagen, alle Gliedmaßen angespannt, in meiner Hüfte knackt es, wenn ich über P. steige, mit nackten Beinen, noch weich, verschwitzt von seiner Wärme und Last' (*T* 229). Karla's humanity is indicated physically as warmth and softness, and also through eroticism. Interestingly, the reference to Karla's hip cracking recalls Francine: the pain in Francine's hip—the result of 'falsche Anspannung' (*P* 12), the doctor tells her—also surfaces during love-making. Moreover, the post-coital air, the android imagery, and the duel which ends the chapter come together in a citation from Borges, '[d]as ineinandergreifende Triebwerk der Liebe' (*T* 230), which is also used in *Pavane*, where Francine's wonky hip acts as a spanner in the works, as it were, of sex: 'Das sporadisch *ineinandergreifende Triebwerk der Liebe* rastet manchmal aus; das ist meine Hüfte' (*P* 12). Both Karla and Francine refer to their lovers and partners in this mechanism as 'mein Gegner' (*P* 12 and *T* 232).

Karla's reverie continues with religious images of women: St Kümmernus (Uncumber), and mythically innocent Madonnas,

---

[37] See also Haines, 'New Places from Which to Write Histories of Peoples', 509–11.

both imperfect models of femininity which foreground psychosomatic disorders.[38] Uncumber is the bearded, female Christ-like figure who fascinates Karla in the museum in Graz:

Die Heilige Kümmernus im Museum, ein Christus in Frauenkleidern, mit goldbesticktem Mieder und Brüsten, die Unterarme, am Kreuz gebunden, muskulös und sehnig, weiche Hände, große Füße in goldenen Pantoletten, langes blondes Haar, Bart. [...]
Eine rätselhafte Gestalt, in den kanonischen Schriften nicht verzeichnet; der Legende nach eine christliche Prinzessin, die sich der Heirat mit einem Heiden entzogen hatte, indem sie sich von Gott einen Bart erbat. Daraufhin ließ der entsetzte Vater sie kreuzigen. (*T* 230)

Kümmernus escapes an unwanted marriage by growing a beard, a sign of male potency and a challenge to paternal (patriarchal) authority; she is crucified for her refutation of her femininity, which is still visible in her clothes, breasts, and long hair. Uncumber is more of a legend than a historical figure, but her condition of hirsutism is recognized medically as a psychosomatic symptom of stress.[39] The figure could be the patron saint of Moníková's female protagonists, an archetype of their rejection by society. In the following duel, Karla's already uncertain gender identity disintegrates along with her body as she identifies increasingly with male figures.

The mechanics of love are translated into a duel between the lovers in a scene combining Karla's memories with invented details. Choosing her armour for the fight, Karla takes the model of Götz von Berlichingen's iron hand, which had fascinated her in the museum, and attaches it to her own. Thus she recreates the image of the android or cyborg using centuries-old prosthetics, and crosses genders to identify with a masculine figure. Prantl also has a deformed hand, the result of an injury incurred on a parachute jump during the Second World War; when Karla puts on the immobile prosthetic hand, she both mimics Prantl and takes him on as an equal, reconciling herself to his different experiences of Czech history. During the duel, Karla takes a direct hit and her armour disintegrates:

---

[38] According to Mary Jacobus, the figure of the hysteric is sublimated in the Madonna, which is an image of the phantom (hysterical) pregnancy, Mary Jacobus, 'Madonna: Like a Virgin; or, Freud, Kristeva and the Case of the Missing Mother', *Oxford Literary Review*, 8/1-2 (1986), 35-50, here 41.
[39] Harry S. Lipscomb and Hebbel E. Hoff, 'Saint Uncumber or La Vierge Barbue', *Bulletin of the History of Medicine*, 37 (1963), 523-7.

Auch die linke Brusthälfte klappt ab; unter dem zerrissenen Kettenhemd kommt eine zweite Schicht von Drähten zum Vorschein und ein metallener Kern, glatt, ohne getriebene Ornamente—ein Herzschrittmacher, entblößt unter einer Schicht Silikongewebe. Ich reiße den verzierten Plunder ab, meine Eingeweide haben den schimmernden Glanz des Funktionalen, Feinmechanik, die pulst, dagegen ist die eiserne Hand einfach.

Von dem rosa Gewebe tropft eine Art roter Sirup, es ist mir zu viel der Simulation [...]. (*T* 232)

Underneath her armour Karla is not human, but robot; her heart and her insides are made of metal—the recurring image of the android. But Karla, the stuntwoman, recognizes the image as a simulation and rejects it. Like Francine, she pictures her own death using imagery with regal associations: 'zwischen den Zähnen kommt mir die Flüssigkeit heraus, rot, rot, konnten sie nicht blau nehmen? Oder flüssiges Gold. Blattgold. Ich wäre lieber in meinem goldenen Mantel gestorben. Is this well done? It is well done, and fitting for a princess...' (*T* 233). The citation in English is from Shakespeare's *Antony and Cleopatra*: the servant Charmian refers to Cleopatra's suicide as 'fitting for a princess | descended of so many royal kings' (v. ii). Karla, like Francine before her and Leonora afterwards, assumes the identity of the queen who occupies a male position.[40] Cleopatra was renowned for her beauty and sexuality, although this belongs as much to myth as to historical fact; Cleopatra remade herself in the image of the people she addressed, exactly as the self-performance of the hysteric mutates along with her interpellator's expectations.[41] This staged, cinematic death distances the mythical from the physical, as Karla asserts her own mortality: 'ich bin doch nicht so unverwundbar [...] wo ist mein schwacher Punkt? Überall. Ich bin also sterblich' (*T* 232–3). Again this recalls Francine's 'durch jede [Öffnung] bin ich sterblich' (*P* 141); Karla's reference to her 'abgerissenen aufgeklafften Panzer' (*T* 233) similarly echoes Francine,

---

[40] The reference also provides fuel for the debate as to whether Karla and Prantl's relationship is dying, or continues: Antony and Cleopatra are one of the greatest pairs of lovers in history, reunited in death.

[41] A 2001 British Museum exhibition, 'Cleopatra of Egypt: From History to Myth', showed how statues of her took on different features in different countries; see the catalogue, Susan Walker and Peter Higgs (eds.), *Cleopatra of Egypt: From History to Myth* (London: British Museum Press, 2001).

who declares 'ich bin kein gepanzerter Skorpion' (*P* 142). Having passed through symbolic death, Karla too turns to writing: 'Noch lebe ich. Es heißt, sich zurückzuziehen, sich die Wunden zu lecken, die Geschichte unserer Liebe aufzuschreiben' (ibid.). Vulnerability—the hysteric's message—is the source of both love and writing.

Whereas both Francine and Karla explore these mythical images respectively at the end of *Pavane* and *Treibeis*, the equivalent sequence in *Verklärte Nacht* is in the middle of the text, suggesting that the images conjured up by Leonora are more easily, or more completely, assimilated into her narrative. Leonora's visions are not the waking reveries of Francine, nor the dream pictures of Karla—Leonora is delirious, having fallen into the Vltava; the images are more rooted in her own body as a result. Three figures loom large in her delirium, Elina Makropulos from Janáček's opera *The Makropulos Case*, the Pharaoh Hatshepsut, and photographer Leni Riefenstahl; I focus here primarily on Hatshepsut.[42] These three are less loaded as national figures than Libuše and, not being products of Leonora's imagination, are also less personal than the metaphor of the robot, which inspires Karla to see herself as an android. The sequence of imagery in Leonora's delirium moves back in time, and away from Prague: the journey is by the number 22 tram (trams are an enthusiasm shared by Moníková's protagonists). One of the first stops on the imaginary journey is the 'Tal der Wilden Šarka', site of the mythical 'Mädchenkrieg', a battle between a band of women led by Vlasta and Libuše's widower Přemysl. The mythical figure who was so significant for Francine is now absent. The women are overpowered and defeated, their castle razed to the ground, 'auf daß kein Beleg existiere von der einstigen Macht und Wehrhaftigkeit der Frauen. Der Widerstand wurde ins Mythische abgeschoben' (*VN* 117). The mythologization of women diffuses their real, historical power into imagery; Leonora's personal re-creation, renarration, and, most importantly, re-embodiment of the various mythical female figures is an attempt to counteract this disempowerment.

---

[42] Helga G. Braunbeck, ' "Der Roman muß sich die Bilder holen"': Film Discourse in the Texts of Libuše Moníková', in Haines and Marven (eds.), *Libuše Moníková*, looks at the significance of Leni Riefenstahl, emphasizing the text's distance from her as a figure.

The 22 tram travels further in time and space to the Egyptian kingdoms ruled by the queen Hatshepsut, a figure who combines myth and history. Historical ruler of Egypt (*c.*1473–1458 BC), Hatshepsut was considered to be descended from the gods. 'Ich bin Hatschepsut, Maatkarê Hatschepsut, von dem widderköpfigen Gott Chnum auf seiner Töpferscheibe modelliert, während der Gott Thot meine Entstehung schriftlich fixiert. Hatschepsut, zu Füßen von Amun-Re, dem König der Götter [...]. Ich trinke aus dem Euter der Muttergottheit Hathor' (*VN* 118–19), declares Leonora as Hatshepsut. Hatshepsut has mythical aspects; her form and existence are fictional, artificial, created in language and image. She is also a woman in a male position of power, reflected in the confusion of signs of gender: Hatshepsut wore the false beard of the pharaohs. After her death, Hatshepsut's nephew destroyed all traces of her, her pictures, statues, and inscriptions. In Ingeborg Bachmann's unfinished novel *Der Fall Franza* the hysteric Franza Ranner undertakes a journey to Egypt in the hope of being healed, and identifies with the figure of Hatshepsut.[43] Both Franza and Leonora experience being buried alive, a fact which further links them with the dead queen; for the former, buried in Dead Sea mud which hardens, the traumatic experience triggers another breakdown; the latter projects herself self-consciously into the mummified body. For Franza, Hatshepsut is symbolic of the annihilated woman, whose voice is suppressed but cannot be totally erased: 'Siehst du, sagte sie, aber er hat vergessen, daß an der Stelle, wo er sie getilgt hat, doch sie stehengeblieben ist. Sie ist abzulesen, weil nichts da ist, wo sie sein soll.'[44] Hatshepsut, whose absence signifies her presence, is revived in Moníková's text, her deeds recorded. She is no longer an abstract, mythologized symbol, but is re-embodied:

Der Deckel des dritten Sarges schlägt über mir zu. [...] Die salbengetränkten Binden und Tücher pressen mich fest. Ich kann mich

---

[43] As Vedder points out, Bachmann's fragmentary sketches 'Berlin und die Wüste' (a preliminary version of *Berlin: Ein Ort für Zufälle*) depict an imaginary tram journey into the desert, Vedder, 'Mit schiefem Mund auch Heimat', 485. The fragments are also closely related to *Der Fall Franza*, even citing it: Ingeborg Bachmann, 'Berlin und die Wüste', in Ingeborg Bachmann, '*Todesarten'-Projekt*, ed. Monika Albrecht and Dirk Göttsche (Munich: Piper, 1995), i. 179–83.
[44] Bachmann, *Der Fall Franza*, 104.

nicht bewegen. Innen bin ich hohl, die Eingeweide wurden durch die Öffnungen, durch den Mund und die Nase herausgezogen. Ich gebe keinen Laut von mir. Die Augen, ob ich sie schließe oder öffne—die gleiche Dunkelheit. Geräusche? Das Blut in den Ohren? Das Herz? Mein Herz liegt gebettet in einer Alabasterschale hinter einer vergoldeten Mauer neben dem Sarg, mit Lapislazuli, Obsidian, Saphiren, Perlen und Smaragden ausgelegt. Auf meinem Sarg liegen Blumengirlanden.

Meine Zunge? Ich taste im leeren Mund. Womit taste ich? Die Zähne sind da. Meine Augen habe ich. Es ist mühsam sie zu öffnen, die Tücher liegen fest an, die Nasenlöcher sind bedeckt wie der Mund. Es ist stickig. Womit atme ich? Habe ich eine Lunge? Sie ist herausgerissen, wie der Magen, die Leber, die Galle, die Nieren. Das Hirn? Entfernt. Durch die Nase. Ich habe keine Schmerzen. Ich bin leicht.

Schwer ist nur die goldene Maske auf meinem Gesicht, mit der königlichen Kobra und dem Geier auf der Stirn. (*VN* 119–20)

The staged burial in state echoes Francine as Libuše, bound and motionless; and the questioning, the itemization of an alien body, harks back to Karla as the android. The decorations, the jewels and garlands and the golden mask, are the symbolic props of royalty, like those worn by Libuše in the final scene in *Pavane*; they are no less artificial or necessary. Where Karla-the-android had a metal heart and innards, Leonora's have been removed as part of the process of mummification; Leonora-Hatshepsut is literally hollow, though human, whereas Karla-the-android is inhuman and unemotional. As with both Karla and Francine, the two bodies of Leonora and Hatshepsut do not fully coincide: the sensations of the 'ich' do not correspond to her body, in an image of dissociation ('Womit taste ich? Womit atme ich?'). Unlike Francine-Libuše, who hears the voice of history calling, Leonora-Hatshepsut hears the sound of the destruction of history (her story) from her tomb.

Leonora wakes up from her delirium to find she is menstruating. Hatshepsut's hollow body is superseded by Leonora's period pains, pointing to a functioning womb, historical cause of hysteria, as the point of difference, and indeed identity, between the two. The scene reconfigures elements of a scene in *Eine Schädigung*, where Jana experiences excruciating period pains: she experiences an 'aushöhlende[r] Schmerz', 'als sollten die vom Schmerz durchgebrannten Organe ausgespien werden' (*S* 53), recalling the process of mummification. When her friend Peter finds Jana writhing and vomiting in pain, the text presents us with their two respective views of her suffering: for Peter, confronted with her irrefutable femininity, Jana seems to be 'ins Mythische gerückt' (*S* 56); Jana herself feels 'zum Ursprünglichen zurückgeworfen' by the pain (*S* 55). Their two irreconcilable perspectives demonstrate how 'Ursprünglichkeit', the idea of origin and naturalness, is overlaid with, and inseparable from, images of femininity—and vice versa. The conjunction of the mythical and the bodily recurs in subsequent novels, in these sequences where the protagonists identify with, and assume the identity of, mythical or historical figures. Only Jana, for whom these two aspects are split into her own view and Peter's external perspective, does not do so. Instead, she idealizes and mimics Mara, whose function and appearance within the text resemble a mythical figure: that of Jana's guardian angel.[45]

Even though none of these figures is taken up and worked into the narrative—they mark the end of the novels, in *Pavane* and *Treibeis*, and do not surface again in *Verklärte Nacht*—they do nonetheless represent possibilities of literature. It is only once Karla becomes the narrator that we see her reverie, and her narrative incorporates references to *Pavane* as well as Borges and Shakespeare. Leonora's scene as Hatshepsut alludes to previous scenes within Moníková's oeuvre, as well as to Bachmann and the history and mythology of ancient Egypt. The passages point to the text as the performance of all these references, and suggest that intertextuality is a significant element of the hysterical narrative.

[45] Mara resembles an angel in her features, with 'honigfarbenem Haar' and 'ein massives Gesicht, mit aufgewälzten Wangen über breiten Backenknochen, es wirkt auf den ersten Blick hart und gleichzeitig verschlafen. Ein befremdendes Gesicht, daneben sind die anderen wie zerkocht oder winzig, man vergißt sie' (both *S* 19). Mansbrügge notes that Jana senses Mara's presence before she sees her (*S* 38), 167 n. 57. Mara appears to Jana suddenly, seems to know everything that has happened, asks no questions, and cleans Jana's wounds. Mara offers to take Jana to their 'Kolonie' on the border, an offer which Jana does not take up, but whose utopian potential comforts her. Wise woman and artist, Mara facilitates Jana's return to her self, body, and the city; while Jana sleeps, with the radio on, 'kann sie aus dem Sender Maras Stimme hören, in unzähligen Sprachen wiederholt sie, daß ihr nichts mehr passieren wird' (*S* 102).

The scenes of identification by Francine, Karla, and Leonora demonstrate a move away from national identity, as the imaginary figures embodied by the three protagonists grow ever more contingent throughout Moníková's work: Francine's investment in the mythical Libuše is far stronger than the detached fascination with which Leonora views Leni Riefenstahl, whose history is given in the third person, indicating distance. In addition, the scenes subvert the equation woman–body, bringing into question both gender and the body as a source of identity. The significance of these sequences as images of the body is twofold: first, the figures undermine the notion of an authentic and essential physicality, deconstructing the body from the outside in (Libuše's prosthetics) or the inside out (Hatshepsut's mummified form), or staging the disjunction of the human and the corporeal (the android). Secondly, in the rulers Libuše, Cleopatra, and Hatshepsut, they represent gendered bodies within history, and the strategies of women in conventionally male positions of power: Libuše exaggerates and constructs conventional femininity, Cleopatra exploits her 'natural' beauty, Hatshepsut adopts traditionally male accoutrements of power. In the following, I analyse the representation of gender in more detail, looking first at how Moníková's female protagonists are already alienated from conventional gender roles and images—something which underlies their identification with these figures—and then examining the other gender images in the texts.

Gender/expatriation

The images of Libuše, Cleopatra, and Hatshepsut demonstrate how gender is implicated in narratives of nation. National identity interacts with gender identity as only two of the many discourses within and against which subjectivity is constructed. In Moníková's texts, these constructs are problematized and implicated in the hysterical performance; both are structured around a gap. Jana, Francine, Karla, and Leonora—all, notably, characters who display physical and biographical similarities with Moníková herself—are radically alienated from conventional images of femininity, in both their appearance and their behaviour. All of the women are described as looking like, or are mistaken for, boys. Tellingly, their names are also feminized versions of male names: Jan (as in Palach), Franz (as in Kafka), Karl (as in Karl IV); Leonora is the exception here, although there are hints within *Verklärte Nacht* that this is not her real name, but an assumed stage one. (Her initials, LM, are of course those of Moníková herself.) The protagonists' experience of gender is one of alienation from their 'natural' gender: one could say it is a form of expatriation, a topographical metaphor already suggested in the conventional image of woman as a 'dark continent'. Whereas the exiled protagonists shrilly reassert their national identity in exile, however, they are less concerned to recoup their gender. I would suggest that, on the one hand, national identity thus (over-)compensates for gender identity, which is the more fundamental construct, being inscribed on the body. On the other hand, representations of gendered bodies in Moníková's texts express loss (and therefore also the loss of the nation) far more directly.

In *Eine Schädigung*, Jana is initially mistaken for a boy by the policeman who rapes her. He addresses her twice as 'Junge' (*S* 12), before recognizing her gender by her voice, when Jana protests at his attempt to search her; and when she fights back against his advances, he again categorizes her with the masculine term '[d]er Täter' (*S* 14). Jana's body and face clearly do not signal her gender: what follows—the rape—can be seen on one level as the policeman's attempt to impose conventional images of gender onto Jana's body. As he realizes she is female, the policeman 'leuchtet [...] ihr ins Gesicht, fährt mit dem Lichtkegel an ihrem Körper entlang, langsam, kehrt mehrmals zurück, mit Wohlgefallen richtet er das Licht auf ihre Hose und zeichnet in der Luft einen riesigen imaginären Hintern nach' (*S* 12–13). The policeman gives Jana an exaggerated feminine form which she does not possess, his torch symbolizing the male gaze and its power to enact its own vision. Just before he rapes her, the policeman tells Jana, 'Jetzt werden wir sehen, was für ein Weib du bist' (*S* 15); afterwards he addresses her as 'du Hure' (*S* 17). These exaggerated stereotypes of femininity are invoked precisely because Jana does not conform to a conventional female body image; they are enforced by the non-consensual act of (heterosexual) sex. Later in the text, when Jana encounters a student who is her mirror image, a 'Doppelgängerin' with similar build, haircut, and clothes, she reflects on the collusion of society in gender images:

das Mädchen war sonst allzu ernst und schlank, mit schmalen Hüften und ohne Riesenbusen, es kannte die Verwechslungen, die den anderen Jux bereiten: 'Ist das ein Kerl oder ein Weib?' Dann fressen sich die Blicke an der Brust und am Hintern fest, durch empört zur Schau getragene Verwirrung gesichert. Diejenigen, die mit ihr gehen, fühlen Unbehagen, schämen sich für sie und verübeln nicht den anderen ihre Frechheit, sondern dem Mädchen das Aussehen. (S 78)

The shift from the imperfect to the present tense highlights the traumatic immediacy of the scenario for Jana, as well as its universal validity. The aggressive, bestial gaze ('fressen') echoes the policeman's torch, behaviour which is tacitly sanctioned by the embarrassment of the bystanders.

Moníková's other protagonists are equally unfeminine. Francine describes herself as 'zu groß, zu mager, zu dunkel, nicht attraktiv' (P 56), a litany of excess; she is 'düster, aus schwarzen Eiern gekrochen, aus schwarzem Mehl gemacht' (P 145). Her lack of femininity is only implied; she is not mistaken for a boy (although, answering the door to a salesman, she is once asked 'Ist die Mutter zu Hause?' (P 55), which suggests that neither does she look like a mature woman). It is Francine's job as an academic which makes her into a 'male' figure: for her pseudo-feminist students, Francine is a figure of privilege and authority, perceived as a masculine role which perforce excludes her from being a woman. Karla, in *Treibeis*, is a tomboy by nature; her appearance—she too is thin, dark, short-haired—is similarly unwomanly: 'Karla sieht in kurzer Hose wie ein Junge aus' (T 82). Even Prantl, her lover-to-be, on first meeting her, admits that she is 'häßlich' (T 75), and he is later disconcerted by her unwomanly fascination with weapons and instruments of torture in a Vienna museum (T 204). Karla gives her occupation as 'Stuntmännin' (T 216), an awkward formulation, highlighting the essentially male nature of the job. Despite her androgynous appearance, however, Karla is still excluded from male circles as a woman, particularly in Japan. Finally, Leonora is also thin and 'düster'. *Verklärte Nacht* opens with her description of the state Spartakiada, in which she took part twice as a child, a time when gender roles are more fluid and the body's form is less clearly marked: 'da in der Klasse die Schülerzahl nicht aufging, turnte ich als Junge, mit gelbem Würfel in roter Turnhose und weißem Träger' (*VN* 8). Leonora's early interest in reading was not welcomed by her parents, who saw it as adding to her already unfeminine aspect: 'Sieh dich an, wie du aussiehst. So düster. So unmädchenhaft. Andere Mädchen sind wie Funken' (*VN* 109). While her failure to signify femininity has violent consequences for Jana, for the other protagonists it underlies a general sense of non-belonging. Francine's lack of 'Anpassung', symbolized by her limp, is echoed in Karla's critical, outsider's perspective, and particularly her unwillingness to accept misogynist traditions: 'Prantl stellt fest, daß sie es überall schafft, nicht hinzugehören' (*T* 199). Leonora remarks of herself, 'Ich versäume jede Zugehörigkeit, jede Gemeinschaft' (*VN* 136): her inability to belong is reflected in her continuing awkwardness in her native city, and is particularly obvious in her encounter with other women in a municipal sauna.

Moníková explores and subverts conventional narratives of gender in her texts, and the dislocation between gender and the body, or gender and identity, can be seen in other figures in the texts, who at once reflect and modify the expatriation of gender experienced by the female protagonists. In *Die Fassade*, which has no central female protagonist whose embodiment as a gendered subject is in doubt, gender images are at their most playful, seen in the humour with which André Nordanc's homosexuality, or Podol's playing a female part in a play, are treated. Even in the other texts, these peripheral reflections, as in the hall of mirrors which Leonora and Thomas visit (*VN* 146), offer new perspectives. Not all of the performances of gender in the texts are viewed positively, however. In *Eine Schädigung*, Jana's ordeal means she is all the more concerned to avoid displays of femininity. When she watches a crowd of girls, dressed in fashionable flares and platforms, she is shocked that they choose to wear clothes which explicitly emphasize their femininity and vulnerability. For Jana, still suffering after her physical ordeal, the girls seem to be 'asking for it': 'Wollten sie vergewaltigt werden, auf der Straße umgestoßen und benützt werden, da sie sich schon im voraus jeder Widerstandsmöglichkeit entledigt hatten? Niemand müßte sie fesseln' (*S* 33). As Margaret Littler rightly argues, Jana sees fashion here 'unequivocally as a means of oppression, not an opportunity for playful feminine masquerade'.⁴⁶ Perhaps Jana is right to be concerned at the grotesque display of the female body, the contortions the girls are forced into by their clothing—but the charge of provocative clothes has long been levelled at women as a way of shifting the blame for male aggression onto the victim. In any case, as I have argued, Jana's assailant initially mistook her for a boy: she was 'punished' for her lack of femininity, rather than an excess emphasized by clothing.⁴⁷ Jana projects her guilt and shame at her own complicity onto the other girls. The reported speech, and the use of the question form, make it quite clear that this is Jana's traumatized viewpoint, not the narrator's.

The same thinking colours Jana's view of her 'Doppelgängerin' whom she watches in the mirror as she applies make-up, in an altogether more ambiguous later scene. The girl—like Jana, skinny, with dark short hair—draws onto her features an exaggerated image of femininity: long black eyelashes, a fuller, redder mouth, and a beauty spot; she is 'süßlich starr' (*S* 78), and almost unrecognizable. This is a physical example of the mimicry Irigaray espouses. Jana sees the girl immediately afterwards hiding her height, and laughing at the conversation of two unattractive, shorter boys: adopting the female role, but self-consciously—Jana hears 'ein lautes hohes Lachen, das Mädchen von unten machte Jana auf sich aufmerksam' (ibid.). Jana interprets this scene, like the earlier one, as analogous to rape: she remarks that 'das Mädchen schien gefesselt' (*S* 79). The fact that Jana watches this girl, her own double, in a mirror, as she applies an 'ablehnendes Gesicht' or 'Maske' (*S* 78) suggests, however, that this could be a useful strategy for Jana: to hide behind conventions of femininity, to imitate them without necessarily embracing them, as a means to social interaction. As I explain below, Jana does turn to a kind of mimicry in order to communicate with the outside world.

A second encounter, with Jana's schoolfriend Irene, further emphasizes the theatricality of gender identity. Irene, attractive

---

⁴⁶ Littler, 'Beyond Alienation', 42.
⁴⁷ Jana's clothes could hardly have been the constrictive shoes and trousers of these girls, either—she had been running.

and self-confident, grew up surrounded by the theatre; grown-up, she acts her gender for effect:

> Sie konnte Mannequin oder Schauspielerin sein, aber derzeit fuhr sie mit einer Straßenwalze am Stadtrand, wo sie sich in einer Baracke gemeinsam mit den Bauarbeitern umzog und wusch, getrennt durch ein paar Latten, denn es gab dort keine extra Einrichtung für Frauen. [...]
> Sie trug den Monteuranzug mit Stil, und die großen Handschuhe verstärkten die Wirkung. Niemand von ihren Bekannten nahm das ernst, und sie spielte auch damit [...]. (*S* 83)

Irene plays with the juxtaposition of her attractive and feminine features with masculine work (and work-clothes). In private, Irene performs an 'Ausziehszene', a choreographed, theatrical striptease, intended to arouse the misogynist lecturer Svidor, although he may only look, not touch; in return, she gets the keys to his flat. Irene appears to be in control of the situation. Her displays are merely performances: she calls it 'ein Spiel', stresses her 'Professionalität' and her balletic training, and is 'unpersönlich, sie bezog es nicht auf sich' (all *S* 89). Irene represents another possibility of non-authentic, theatrical identity: she manipulates inequality and sexism for her own benefit, although this is not without its pitfalls and cannot effect change. However, Irene can play her gender as an exaggerated role precisely because her gender identity is not in question. Jana is unable to adopt these masks and performance, traumatized as she is after the rape, but the theme recurs increasingly within Moníková's texts.

While the four female protagonists' uncertain signification of gender is portrayed as alienating, male characters who experience the same show a more positive, and more light-hearted perspective. Gender can become a performance, however, only when the identity of the character is not in doubt. *Die Fassade* demonstrates this, presenting gender-bending on several levels as a matter of theatricality. Uncertainty and ambiguity of gender are introduced by the motif of André Nordanc's cat: christened Max, it turns out that the cat is in fact female (but she refuses to answer to her full name Maxine). Grammatical genders as well as biological ones are mixed in Nordanc's reference to Max as 'eine Katze', which is a generic, rather than gendered term—the pedantic biologist Qvietone corrects it to 'eine Kätzin' (*F* 180). This confusion follows a comment from a worker, about Nordanc himself, 'Er kann aber dafür sehr gut tschechisch, auch wenn er die Geschlechter manchmal durcheinanderbringt' (*F* 176), a remark which refers to Nordanc's Luxembourg nationality and his homosexuality. As an openly gay Luxembourger, who chose to stay in Prague even after his Czech lover deserted him, Nordanc embodies the successful adaptation to both national and gender exile. Strictly speaking, it is Nordanc's sexual orientation, rather than his gender, which is at issue, but as Judith Butler argues, gender is produced and regulated precisely within and through a 'heterosexual matrix'.[48] Homosexuality is perceived as a threat to, because a corruption of, masculinity. It potentially short-circuits the signification of gender, taking up a position 'outside' conventional gender norms, although in Butler's analysis, this is a purely hypothetical possibility. Nordanc's status as national outsider diffuses the threat of his 'other' sexuality, and he provides a foil for the artists working on the façade, who wear their Czech nationality (and nationalism), heterosexuality, and masculinity very much on their sleeves.

The specific interaction of gender constructs in the narrative of national identity is exposed and undermined in a satirical playlet put on by the artists during a lull in their restoration work. Podol, one of the four, dresses as Magdalena Dobromila Rettigová, an author of patriotic cookbooks; the play lays bare the historical constraints on Rettigová as a woman and patriot.[49] Podol clearly relishes the contradictions of his role, as do the others, using their characters' voices and opinions for thinly veiled attacks on each other, but his is a special case. Cross-dressing allows Podol to take liberties with the women who are playing minor roles: 'Hier gibt es nur vertrauliche Gespräche von Frau zu Frau (er drückt Hanna an seinen Busen), kurz, von Patriotin zu Patriotin' (*F* 128). The dramatic irony serves to emphasize Podol's underlying identity as a heterosexual

---

[48] Butler, *Gender Trouble*, 9. See her ch. 2 for a fuller explanation.
[49] See Karen Jankowsky for a more detailed analysis of Rettigová and her representation in this scene, in 'Between "Inner Bohemia" and "Outer Siberia": Libuše Moníková Destabilizes Notions of Nation and Gender', in Jankowsky and Love (eds.), *Other Germanies*, 119–46, esp. 135–7.

male, rather than confuse it: the sudden shift in register in an exchange with Maltzahn (playing historian Alois Jirásek) shows where Podol draws the line.

> Jirásek schaut behaglich der Gastgeberin nach, die mit einem Tablett herumgeht und Kaffee kredenzt: 'Korpulent seid ihr, Frau Rätin, eine hübsche Person noch.'
> 'Aber Herr Alois', droht ihm Rettigová mit dem Finger, 'vergessen Sie nicht, ich könnte Ihre Mutter sein.'
> 'O ja, Mami', er schmiegt seinen Kopf an ihre Brust.
> Podol: 'Verpiß dich, Mensch, nein wirklich, Olbram, du bist noch schlimmer als Jan! [...] Du weißt, wie gern ich dich an der Brust habe, wie eine Natter!' [...]. (*F* 128)

Podol presents Rettigová as a mother figure, but construes his role as limited to a speaking part: actions are his own. Podol/Rettigová plays with the apparent disjunction between the body (and his actions) and discourse (in terms of his performed female gender, and his role as Rettigová). Podol's transvestism undermines the absolute nature of gender roles, collapsing the opposition of male and female and exposing gender per se as a performance.

Moníková plays with Podol's appearance—some kind of pantomime dame—in her use of the conventions of dramatic script writing, emphasizing the theatricality. Podol is referred to variously as 'Podol', 'Podol/Rettigová', 'Rettigová', which generally correspond to the tenor of his speech. Almost all of the stage directions use the masculine pronoun, however, as in the scene with Hanna above, which creates comic distance. Podol also uses as a prop—by definition an unreal object—'die original Haube der M. D. Rettigová' (*F* 121), highlighting the confusion between fake and authentic. When the artists revert to their own voices, Moníková continues to use the script convention for their conversation, which reminds us that their usual banter is also a form of role-playing. The Gogol version the 'Czech delegation' put on in Akademgorodok later in the text is similarly deconstructed and alienated: the Czech artists play it in Russian, a foreign language for them, they read straight from the text, improvise with Russian popular songs, and allow the audience to participate. In this play, Podol plays husband and wife, 'Ein Ehepaar in einer Person, wie Schistosoma, der Pärchenegel' (*F* 303), Qvietone comments on this unexpected human hermaphroditism. Qvietone's biological interjections make it clear that binary genders are a human, cultural construct; in nature there are many, more varied roles for the sexes.

The doubling effect of the Gogol, where both actors and characters are visible, and the meaning of the text refers both to the action of the play and to the situation of the actors/artists, makes transparent the nature of role-playing itself. Role-playing is not limited to a theatrical context, but underlies social interaction and the construction of identity. As Karen Jankowsky shows, in their relationship, Qvietone and Marie attempt to follow 'gendered scripts' drawn from popular wisdom—Qvietone 'hat gelesen, daß ein Mann sehr viel wissen sollte, damit die Frau sich mit ihm nicht langweilt' (*F* 66) —or Hollywood romance.[50] Marie in particular feels that, in her professional life as a doctor, she is genderless. However, role-playing cannot impose the authentic essence they both seek; neither Qvietone, detached scientific observer of his own mating habits, nor Marie can embrace the theatricality required for a successful performance. Alienated from her gender, Marie resembles in some ways the female protagonists in the other texts (although she is peripheral to the narrative of *Die Fassade*), but she looks for an identity in the chimera of socially determined notions of femininity.

In the later novels, the question of gender is less fraught, and the issue seems to reach a form of resolution in *Verklärte Nacht*, Moníková's last completed publication. Moníková's oeuvre contains only two substantial descriptions of sex: the first is the rape with which *Eine Schädigung* opens, the other is the love-making in the final scene of *Verklärte Nacht*, which rewrites many of the gender issues of the first. Towards the end of the text, both Leonora and Thomas become aware of their having swapped conventional gender roles. Thomas has cared for Leonora during her illness, doing the cooking, cleaning, and shopping; when she turns down a carefully prepared meal, he responds with camp irony: ' "Da steht man den ganzen Tag am Herd...", er geht in die Küche' (*VN* 145). Dr Thomas Asperger of the 'Europäische Musiktheater Akademie' (*VN* 140) describes his

[50] Jankowsky, 'Between "Inner Bohemia" and "Outer Siberia" ', in Jankowsky and Love (eds.), *Other Germanies*, 132. Braunbeck, "Der Roman muß sich die Bilder holen", deals further with the significance of film for Marie and Orten's romance.

job as '[e]ine Art Faktotum, Mädchen für alles' (*VN* 141), which in this light points more to his feminized view of himself than to the association of women with menial jobs. Thomas's feminine characteristics are translated into physical ones in the final scene; his body carries both masculine and feminine markers:

> Er hat breite Schultern und einen schweren Brustkorb, hält mich fest und vorsichtig umklammert, lange, schlanke Beine. Ich lege den Kopf auf seinen Bauch [...]. Sein Busen ist fast größer als meiner, mit feinem gekräuseltem Haar, ich sauge mich an einer Brustwarze fest, schließe die Augen. Er ist mütterlich. (*VN* 147–8)

Instead of the violent enforcement of conventional gender roles and images, as in *Eine Schädigung*, the combination of Leonora's masculine, and Thomas's feminine, physical and psychological features evokes harmony and euphoria. Thomas's transformation into a mother-figure harks back to Leonora's admission that for her, the purpose of a boyfriend was to provide a mother: 'Ich war der Schwarm der Mütter unverheirateter Söhne. Ich konnte sie betören. Die Söhne, die waren unwichtig, aber eine Mutter—meine war zu früh gestorben. Ich wollte an eine Mutter heran, nicht an den Sohn' (*VN* 23). Thomas is both in one. The patriarchal power structures reinforced by the rape are subverted by the ambiguous genders of Leonora and Thomas. The final dissolution of boundaries, instigated by the slippage of gender attributes, takes place during sex: 'Wir wissen nicht, wem welcher Körperteil gehört, es gibt keine Teile' (*VN* 148). In stark contrast to *Eine Schädigung*, where Jana experiences her body as fragmented and alien as a result of the trauma of the rape, Leonora and Thomas merge into one undifferentiated whole.

Moníková's representation of gender undermines assumptions of 'essential' gender attributes; her characters experience conventional gender roles and appearances variously from positions of expatriation or alienation. Gender is seen to be performed, as a theatrical role or script adopted by a character which cannot be translated entirely onto the body. The characters' attitudes, and the aspects of their identity which they act out in the scenes of identification, undergo a shift. In Moníková's early texts, the protagonists reject the performance of gender as a response to the gender expatriation they have experienced: they cannot act or overact what they have never fully possessed. Jana rejects the images of femininity which surround her; Francine, as Libuše, exaggerates feminine corporeal signifiers. In the later texts, the protagonists move towards an acceptance of their lack of femininity, signalled in the figure of Hatshepsut, while at the same time evincing a more sophisticated conception of performativity. It is this aspect of performance, which differs from, but develops out of, mimicry, to which I turn now as the final aspect of the hysterical body in Moníková's work.

Performance

Jana represents an extreme of investment in the body as the unitary, authentic site of subjectivity; her sense of identity is shattered by the rape, and is only partially renegotiated within the text. Moníková's other female characters, not subject to such a crisis, are able to explore, and increasingly embrace, the possibilities of performance and theatricality. The texts follow a trajectory away from the mimicry of the early work towards a notion of performance which is linked with an authentic bodily experience. In their choice of careers, Karla (a stuntwoman) and Leonora (choreographer-dancer) develop a relation to their body through performance and theatricality. At the same time, the notion of the text as performance—which first arises in *Pavane*—becomes increasingly important.

Even in her first text Moníková raises the possibility of performed identity, in images which surround and reflect Jana. What is more, Jana herself, at the beginning of her rehabilitation, mimics Mara, the woman who takes her in and helps her after the rape. Having borrowed Mara's jumper, in exchange for her own blood-stained one (which Mara washes), Jana also borrows Mara's life and her friends. When Mara arranges for her to meet Palzer, a sculptor, she (Mara) is the only connection they have, and this has an odd effect on Jana:

Sie gab ihm ein Buch von Mara zurück und wiederholte noch, weshalb sie nicht kommen konnte, obwohl er es schon wußte. Er nahm es an und fragte belebt, wie es ihr gefallen hatte. Jana hatte das Buch erst am letzten Abend bekommen und nur hineingesehen, aber sie wollte nicht, daß das Gespräch wieder stockte und äußerte deshalb Maras

Meinung; Palzer war damit nicht einverstanden, und sie diskutierten eine Weile darüber. Jana war in Maras Ton gefallen, sie verwandte ihre Ausdrücke und ihre Mimik, ohne daran zu denken, und Palzer antwortete mit Sätzen, die auf Maras Argumente zu passen schienen. (*S* 67–8)

Jana uses Mara's opinions and voice as a way of distancing herself from the world, but also as a means of facilitating interaction. When Jana tries to speak to Palzer directly, as herself, the conversation falters. Jana's mimicry is short-lived; she similarly grows out of the mask which Mara has given her, a portrait that she draws soon after the rape. The non-coincidence of image and identity highlights the body's mutability; it is a dichotomy which both Karla and Leonora attempt to overcome.

Although Karla only really comes into focus in the final chapter of *Treibeis*, which she narrates, her initial appearance already marks a shift in Moníková's representation of the body. Karla is a professional 'Stuntmännin', a film double: she is the literal embodiment of the disjunction between the real and the inauthentic, between her body and the image she represents and projects. Karla's body is made up (in all senses) in order to stand in for the actress: when Prantl first sees her, during his comic rescue attempt, every aspect of her body is dissimulated. As they roll away from the film set, her make-up begins to disintegrate:

> Er starrt in ein braunes und ein blaues Auge. Auch das andere blaue Auge geht verloren, die Kontaktlinse gleitet unter dem Lid hervor und ragt heraus, unter Lachtränen. Sie fährt sich ins Gesicht, ihr angemalter Mund ist schief, unter der Farbe blaß, nach unten gezogen.
>
> Sie wird immer nackter: unter dem langfasrigen blonden Filz kommt kurzes dunkles Haar zum Vorschein, jetzt merkt er erst, daß sie eher mager ist, ihre Brust, die unter den Stricken so aufreizend wirkte, ist ziemlich klein. [...]
>
> Sie wird immer brauner, die weiße Paste, mit der sie beschmiert war, bleibt auf der Plane und an Prantl haften. (*T* 74–5)

Karla's eye, hair, and skin colour is faked, her face made up, she has a wig and a pair of wings (she is a harpy); the blonde, blue-eyed, busty maiden collapses into Karla's small, dark figure. Karla emphasizes that she would prefer to do her stunt work than play the actress's role: 'ich weiß, daß sie nie so springen würde. Ich möchte das, was sie in dem Film tun muß, nicht spielen. [...]

Wir machen reale Arbeit und sind nicht so abhängig' (*T* 77). Her work is not real, in that she is standing in for another actor, being the double of a person already playing a role. And yet it is also real, as it puts her in real physical danger. In a profession based on doubling and disguise, Karla has a relation with her own body based on actions, not appearance, and which combines physicality and performance.

Leonora Marty in *Verklärte Nacht* similarly combines body and performance in art. She is a choreographer and dancer, who has brought her peripatetic ballet troupe to Prague to perform her adaptations of literary or musical works, specifically, *The Makropulos Case* by Janáček, adapted from the drama by Čapek. In choreography the real, physical act of dancing is overlaid with the acting out of a story; body and narrative are united in performance. In the figure of Leonora, portrayed in the title role of Elina Makropulos on a poster for the show, these aspects are fused: she is, as Helga Braunbeck states, 'body and image in one'.[51] This fusion is reflected later in the text, when Leonora imagines herself as Makropulos (also called Emilia Marty) during her delirium. Leonora's art—her choreography and her dancing—is contrasted in the text with the spectacle of the Spartakiada, which she took part in twice as a young girl and where the individual body was subsumed within the bigger picture and the narrative of the nation. Even in her day-to-day activities, the split between body and image is evident:

Meine Aktivitäten, wenn ich die Pflanze gieße oder mit dem kaputten Staubsauger versuche die Wohnung wohnlicher zu machen, ähneln einer Inszenierung. Ich setze eine Pflanze unter Wasser und komme mir nützlich vor, während die anderen im Haus Kinder vom Kindergarten und vor der Schule abholen, Einkäufe in Netzen herbeischleppen [...].

Sie leben unmittelbar ins Reine, ohne zu probieren, während ich immer noch auf dem Schmierpapier das Konzept durchstreiche. (*VN* 72)

Leonora's doubled vision is symptomatic of her experience of Prague: she is neither visitor (as she was born there) nor inhabitant (she has been away too long, and is only renting a flat). The city is both familiar and different—'Ist es überhaupt

---

[51] Braunbeck, 'The Body of the Nation', 502.

noch mein Prag?' (*VN* 125), she asks—and her perspective on the city, like her deconstructive view of the Spartakiada, takes in both detail and the panorama. Leonora's view of the city, as both panorama (the narrative of the cityscape) and immediate surroundings, and overlaid with histories and imaginary tales, which she accesses by walking around the city, points to choreography as her mode of experience. Vedder suggests that the visions of Leonora's delirium—literally, her mind wanders—similarly constitute a form of choreography.[52]

Braunbeck sees dance, the product of choreography, but not identical to it, as central to the text: she describes Leonora and Thomas's relationship as a pas de deux, and the breaking up of Czechoslovakia as a 'necrology, dance of death'.[53] Dance is a momentary, transcendent fusion of narrative and movement, dancer and character, body and image. Leonora does not dance in the text but the text is a performance of her time in Prague. In the following section, I take up the idea of the text as performance, and examine textual strategies which reflect hysteria, focusing in particular on the distinction between mimicry and performance.

NARRATIVE

Textual strategies employed by Moníková manifest the structures of hysteria in different forms: gaps in the text (such as Francine's purchase of the wheelchair) represent the trauma which engenders hysteria, and the paratactic, episodic structure of Moníková's texts points to the ever-changing performance of the hysteric. The first-person present tense narrative used for Francine, Karla, and Leonora's stories is furthermore a performative tense, creating the narrative at the same time as relating it, and allowing their mimicry to be projected onto the text. One might expect that *Die Fassade*, as a third-person narrative, would correspondingly show less concern with hysteria, but the novel is in fact the most successful transformation of hysterical concerns onto a textual level. *Die Fassade* is written under the sign of the hysteric: it is divided into three sections, whose titles evoke

---

[52] Vedder, "Mit schiefem Mund auch Heimat", 484–5.
[53] Braunbeck, 'The Body of the Nation', 502.

hysteria. 'Böhmische Dörfer' is the German term for something unknown, unidentifiable, or incomprehensible, a gap in one's knowledge; the 'Potemkinsche Dörfer' were façades erected by Potemkin to simulate settlements for Catherine the Great's journey through the wilderness; 'ohn' Unterlaß' is a quotation from the Internationale. Together the three clearly signal hysteria: something inaccessible, unknown, and other, an incessant progression of inauthentic images and quotations.

The titles also refer to the work on the façade of the text's title. The façade is a postmodern palimpsest, continually reworked, its original features long since effaced. It is not a monolithic, authentic artefact, but a constantly changing work of art (as soon as the artists have finished it will be time to start again at the beginning), whose original identity is lost under layers of representation. Whereas Graf von Thurn und Taxis's restoration attempt aims at historical accuracy, which tries to collapse the modern copy into an original which no longer exists, the artists accept the transitoriness of their work. They playfully refabricate, alter, and add images, using references from modern sources (Kafka, Moby Dick), personal meanings (Maltzahn, as a motorcyclist, uses traffic signs), and incidental images like the ham that Podol draws because he is hungry. The 'Geheime Geschichte der Mongolen', rewritten by Liu Chu ts'sai, an old Chinese man that the artists meet in Irkutsk, is similarly inauthentic: the Chinese destroyed Mongol culture, so only fragmentary traces of this history exist, which Liu Chu ts'sai reconstructs from 'chinesische Abschriften' (*F* 402). Even this recreated narrative is incorporated into the façade: 'Podol schreibt die Geheime Geschichte der Mongolen an der Fassade von Friedland weiter' (*F* 440). The façade symbolizes the text of *Die Fassade*, as well as representing the experiences of the artists on their travels: like Moníková's work as a whole, it is full of quotations, parodies, and the relativization of cultures.

In this section, I focus on intertextuality and the use of other languages, which manifest the concern with mimicry and performance. These two strategies represent literally, and literarily, the hysteric's relation to patriarchal discourse, where she imitates another's words, or speaks in a language which is not her own. Carolyn Burke states, 'when a woman writes or speaks herself into existence, she is forced to speak in something like a foreign tongue, a language with which she may be personally uncomfortable'.[54] In a similar vein, Moníková refers to German as 'eine[-] Sprache, die nicht die meine war, in der ich nie sicher bin' (*SAW* 142). In the previous section I suggested that, in *Pavane*, intertextual references and parodies arise from a narrative of hysteria; in this section I examine those references, and ones from subsequent texts, in more detail. Intertextuality, which in Moníková's texts takes the form of direct quotation and parody, represents the mimicry of the hysteric and her double-edged relationship to patriarchal discourse. The text becomes polyphonic—Bakhtin's term for the mode of the novel with its multiple discourses—in a very literal fashion in Moníková's work: non-literary discourses and foreign languages are deliberately and self-consciously employed.[55] Moníková often quotes from other literary sources in the original language (unsurprising given her academic background and her wide range of references). Her use of foreign languages (Czech, although her own mother tongue, must also be considered as foreign to the German text) goes well beyond that usage, however, to include free composition. Although these two aspects cannot be kept entirely separate, I start by considering those references which invoke a specific work of art before looking at Moníková's use of other languages.

Intertextuality

Intertextual references in Moníková's work take several forms: they can be located within the 'histoire', as references made by characters in dialogue, or as descriptions of other pieces of art (other literary texts, film, music), within the 'discours', as allusions made by the narrator, and even in characters' names, titles of the texts, and the frontispieces to the books. References can be descriptive, parodic, explicit, or implicit, quotations are both signalled and attributed or neither. Their function is both to refer to specific source texts, setting up implicit comparisons, and more generally, to open the text out onto a web of

[54] Carolyn Burke, quoted by Showalter, in Showalter, *The New Feminist Criticism*, 253.
[55] Mikhail Bakhtin, *The Dialogic Imagination*, trans. Caryl Emerson and Michael Holquist (Austin: University of Texas Press, 1981).

intertextual allusions. Intertextual references, particularly quotations, disrupt the singular, hierarchically ordered narrative, as Heinrich Plett explains: 'The seams between the quotation and its context do not only endanger the homogeneity of the literary structure, but also the unity of perception. The perception is diverted by something alien and unexpected which requires integration.'[56] Quotations also draw attention to the literariness of the text, for, as Sigrid Weigel contends,

Das Zitat verkörpert gleichsam die Sprache *als* Literatur, ein Stück Text, herausgebrochen aus einem Diskurs, um als Bruchstück Teil einer anderen Schrift zu werden, ohne doch in dies integrierbar zu sein. Dabei ist die doppelte Attribuierung des Zitats bedeutsam, durch die es zu einer Figur des Widerstreits wird, genauer zu einer sprachlichen Figur, die den Widerstreit von Ursprung und Zerstörung in sich aufgenommen hat [...]. Indem das Zitat den Bruch erinnert, dem es seine Existenz als Zitat verdankt, sperrt es sich auch, an der Konstruktion eines neuen Ganzen teilzuhaben.[57]

The terms Weigel uses to signal the disruptiveness of the quotation recall hysteria—in particular, the 'Widerstreit von Ursprung und Zerstörung', and the refusal to construct a whole.

The most obvious and visible type of intertextual reference are the citations found on many levels and in many forms in Moníková's work. The titles of two of her novels are quotations: *Pavane pour une infante défunte* is the title of a work by Ravel; *Verklärte Nacht* is the title of an 1899 symphonic poem by Schoenberg. Characters' names could also be seen as quotations: in the context of the opera references in *Verklärte Nacht*, 'Leonora' could refer to Beethoven's cross-dressing heroine Leonore in *Fidelio*.[58] Within the texts themselves, citations are given on the level of the 'discours', or by characters in dialogue, generally in first- and third-person narratives respectively. The self-consciousness of the latter is a step towards parody, and it occurs for the most part in *Die Fassade*; the

[56] Heinrich F. Plett, 'Intertextualities', in Heinrich F. Plett (ed.), *Intertextuality, Research in Text Theory/Untersuchungen zur Texttheorie*, 15 (Berlin: de Gruyter, 1991), 3–29, here 16.
[57] Sigrid Weigel, *Entstellte Ähnlichkeit: Walter Benjamins theoretische Schreibweise* (Frankfurt am Main: Fischer Taschenbuch, 1997), 199.
[58] Ludwig van Beethoven, *Fidelio* (1805). Leonore dresses as a man in order to rescue her husband from prison. Moníková's musical references, which I cannot deal with here, deserve more attention.

former is a more literary usage, a distinction made by Udo J. Hebel:

> The analysis of allusions presented as part of the fictional world emphasizes the meta-textual dimension of the text because these allusions are narrated, and thus commented upon, just as the events and characters of the fictional world are narrated and commented upon.[59]

In addition, individual citations function differently, depending on whether or not they are attributed (their author named) and marked (signalling their status as quotes within the narrative). Unmarked quotations within the narrative enact Barthes's view of intertextuality as described by Moníková: 'nicht die Menschen, die Autoren, sondern Texte kennen sich. Was geschreiben ist, das ist in der Luft und das trifft sich.'[60]

In *Pavane*, Francine's narrative is littered with quotations in varying degrees of visibility. She quotes Kafka (whom she teaches at university) frequently: '"... oder Beweis dessen, daß es unmöglich ist zu leben"—Kafkas "Belustigungen". Ich bereite mich für das Seminar am nächsten Tag vor' (*P* 9), she remarks, and, '"Die Logik ist zwar unerschütterlich, aber einem Menschen, der leben will, widersteht sie nicht." Welcher Lebenswille? Der Satz ist schön, aber in diesem verlassenen Steinbruch, wo K. stirbt—*wie ein Hund*, ist er unwahr' (*P* 10).[61] In this second quotation, Kafka is quoted directly but not named, although the appended description of (Josef) K.'s death make it clear that *Der Proceß* is the source text. Two typographical markers signal the citations, quotation marks and italics, the latter disrupting the narrative visually as well as signalling a semantic disruption. Several lines later, another phrase is italicized, '*Ja, sie hetzen mich*', the italics being the only indication that it, too, is a quotation—and, indeed, from the same source: both Francine and K. are disturbed by a telephone call, and respond with the same phrase.[62] These citations develop from a self-conscious, framed reference (motivated by the 'histoire')

---

[59] Udo J. Hebel, 'Towards a Descriptive Poetics of *Allusion*', in Plett (ed.), *Intertextuality*, 135–64, here 147.
[60] Moníková, in interview with Cramer et al., 'Libuše Moníková in Gespräch', 198.
[61] Cf. Franz Kafka, *Der Proceß*, ed. Malcolm Pasley (Frankfurt am Main: Fischer, 1993), 244, 245.
[62] Cf. ibid. 218.

indicating Francine's academic interest in Kafka, to a partially concealed citation within the 'discours' demonstrating that Francine identifies with Josef K. This last quotation sets up a second level of engagement with Kafka's writing, complementing Francine's more explicit concern with rewriting *Das Schloß*.

The same graphemic marker, italics, is used to signal a citation from Borges, *The Aleph*: 'Das sporadisch *ineinandergreifende Triebwerk der Liebe* rastet manchmal aus' (*P* 12). Here the italics signal that this is a quotation, but there is no indication of the author or the source text. The quotation as used in *Pavane* has been modified slightly in two ways: it is itself in translation (from Spanish into German) and the second half of the phrase is missing. The whole phrase is given in a longer citation in 'Portrait aus mythischen Konnexionen', and reads 'das ineinandergreifende Triebwerk der Liebe und die langsame Entstellung des Todes' (*SAW* 116).[63] In *Treibeis* the same citation appears in Karla's narrative, where it is the image of the 'Triebwerk', rather than its origin in the text by Borges, which is most important: 'Das ineinandergreifende Triebwerk der Liebe. | Kolben, Transmissionsriemen, Räder' (*T* 230). The suppressed reference to death also fits the tone of the passage.[64] Here the citation is without italics, and it functions as a reference to both the Borges source text and the earlier Moníková text. Manfred Pfister, concerned with specifically postmodern intertextuality, notes, 'Quoting a quote [...] is a device that in itself foregrounds intertextuality and substantiates the poststructuralist view, according to which each text refers to pretexts and those in turn refer to others and so on *ad infinitum.*'[65] This postmodern notion of a chain of signification underlies the multiple adaptations which feature in the texts: in *Die Fassade*, Orten and Marie listen to Janáček's String Quartet No. 1, composed after Tolstoy's novella, in turn written after Beethoven's 'Kreutzer Sonate'; and in *Verklärte Nacht*, Leonora has adapted for her dance troupe Janáček's version

---

[63] Cf. the Spanish original, 'el engranaje del amor y la modificación de la muerte', Jorge Luis Borges, *El Aleph* (Madrid: Alianze/Emecé, 1971), 171.
[64] See also the allusion to death in Shakespeare's *Antony and Cleopatra*, discussed below.
[65] Manfred Pfister, 'How Postmodern is Intertextuality?', in Plett (ed.), *Intertextuality*, 207–24, here 217.

of *Makropulos*, which was composed after Čapek's play. The lack of an original reality, the postmodern condition, and the breaking down of the distinction between literature and reality is also self-consciously foregrounded within the narrative. Not only does Francine declare that her life is 'ein Abfolge von Literatur- und Filmszenen, willkürliche Zitate'; Podol, referring to the artists' attempts to speak Russian, explains 'Alles, was man sagt, sind Zitate. Ich bringe keinen eigenen Satz zuwege' (*F* 282), touching on Bakhtin's notion that every word has already been spoken and bears the traces of its previous use.[66] In *Der Taumel*, the idea surfaces once more: Jakub Brandl recalls, 'Assoziationen aus unzähligen Büchern. Seine Lektüre platzte wie ein Sandkasten in seinem Kopf auf. Namen zerstreuten sich, Zitate, die Grenze zwischen dem Gelebten und dem Gelesenen verlief unmerklich' (*Tm* 6). Brandl's confusion, this uncontrollably proliferating dialogue of texts, is the consequence of the violent 'Gespräch' he has just attended.

In both *Pavane* and *Treibeis*, quotations from English sources are given in the original language. Francine refers twice to the Beatles, once proposing to play Kafka (who appears as a vision in her room) '*for the benefit of Mr. K.*' (*P* 93) — a play on 'For the benefit of Mr Kite' and (Josef) K.—and the final line of the text, 'she's leaving home, bye bye', is from the song of the same title, also from *Sergeant Pepper's Lonely Hearts Club Band*. Although the first instance is clearly signalled, both framed and in italics, the second is only apparent in the use of English. Similarly in *Treibeis*, linguistic interference indicates the quotation from Shakespeare's *Antony and Cleopatra*, 'It is well done and fitting for a princess...' (*T* 233). Whereas the Beatles references are light-hearted, significant primarily for the change in register and discourse, the reference to *Antony and Cleopatra* invokes the context of the original. The line is spoken by Charmian, the servant of the dying Cleopatra; the intimation of death, clear only from the context and not from the content of the quotation, fits the scene in *Treibeis*, where Karla is imagining her own death.

Intertextual references are closely linked to the narrative of hysteria in Moníková's work: while *Eine Schädigung* does not

---

[66] Bakhtin, *The Dialogic Imagination*, 293.

feature quotations, *Pavane* and the final chapter of *Treibeis* demonstrate the use of quotations within the 'discours', where they are a form of mimicry. By way of contrast, *Verklärte Nacht* is notably lacking in direct quotation. This change is inherent in the shift from a notion of mimicry to performance: Leonora performs her intertextual references literally and physically, in her own choreographed adaptations. *Die Fassade* contains the most intertextual references, largely on the level of the 'histoire'. The line from Arno Schmidt, 'Wer nicht liest, kennt die Welt nicht' (*F* 230), stands as a motto for both text and characters. As in the other texts, citations are given within the narrative—such as the unattributed Camus quote, 'Wir müssen annehmen, daß Sisyphos glücklich ist' (*F* 25) or the reference to *Candide*, 'Wir müssen unseren Garten bestellen' (*F* 440).[67] Quotations are to be found most frequently in the dialogue between the characters, lending an air of self-consciousness which is appropriate for this more postmodern text. Quotations are often used for comic effect—like the exchange between Nordanc and Podol:

'Herr Podolský, nehme ich an.'
　'Haben Sie Livingstone erwartet? Was gibt's?'
　'Ich habe Ihnen Material gebracht.'
　'Also doch Stanley.' (*F* 143)

Here familiarity with Stanley's line, 'Dr Livingstone I presume', is attributed to the two characters, and it is the characters' (often improbable) knowledge and discussions of other texts which frequently frame quotations. Thus intertextual references are motivated by the 'histoire', with the effect ranging from realism to self-conscious meta-textual reference, depending on the context. Qvietone's reference to Freud's 'Was will das Weib' (*F* 190), for example, is merely a literary equivalent of the scientific data littering his speech; the Mayakovsky poem (*F* 283) is cited in an exhibition in Akademgorodok; and Maltzahn's quoting of a Red Army Choir song and the lyrics from *Parsival* is practically involuntary—the filling in his tooth acts as a radio receiver—and reinforces the comedy of his situation by enacting this unwanted intrusion within the narrative. Maltzahn's

---

[67] The quotation from Camus's *Le Mythe de Sisyphe* also appears in 'Die Wunschtorte: Über literarische Wunscherfüllung', this time attributed (*SAW* 138).

predicament, picking up radio stations right across the USSR, from Riga to Kamchatka, is termed an 'akustischen Aleph' (*F* 351), another allusion to Borges.

Other citations work on a meta-textual level: citations from Gogol are part of the performance given by the artists, although the Russian which they read out is translated into German within the narrative. At the end of the chapter where the characters dress up as figures from Czech history, and which Moníková gives in the form of a dramatic script, Podol self-consciously quotes a fragment of Puck's speech from the end of *A Midsummer Night's Dream*, 'Wenn wir Schatten Euch beleidigt' (*F* 142).[68] Their 'script' also encompasses a poem by Czech Romantic poet Karel Hynek Mácha amongst a roll-call of Czech figures and their artistic and scientific achievements. Orten cites Mácha's poem at length, amid protests from the other characters, complaining that the poet is undeservedly ignored outside Czechoslovakia; it is clear that intertextual references form a significant part of Moníková's pedagogical address to her German audience. The text acts as a form of collective remembering: like the historical details which pervade the texts, literary quotations introduce Czech political and cultural history, and often feel as forced. However, quotations are also drawn from many other languages and literatures, and the concern to preserve within the text aspects of cultural heritage is extended to the inclusion of Inuit songs in *Treibeis*, to Nordanc's French nursery rhymes, and to folk songs, legends, and fairy tales across the Soviet Union in *Die Fassade*. 'Wer nicht liest, kennt die Welt nicht' becomes Moníková's attempt to represent the (nations of the) world through literature. 'Ich habe überhaupt kein Vertrauen in die Welt, ich habe Vertrauen in die Literatur, nach wie vor', she states: for her, literature *is* the world.[69]

Moníková employs a range of intertextual devices, from paraphrase and description to allusion and parody, on all levels of the text. Even the frontispiece of *Pavane* is a copy of Velázquez's *Las meninas*, a self-referential work (the artist himself is in

---

[68] Also quoted in English in *Treibeis*, 'If we shadows...' (*T* 209), where the content rather than the context is relevant—Prantl watches shadows lengthening at sunset.

[69] Moníková, in interview with Cramer et al., 'Libuše Moníková im Gespräch', 200.

the picture).⁷⁰ Films, music, and operas, other art forms translated into language, are brought into the narrative, along with newspaper articles (*Verklärte Nacht*) and history books (*Treibeis*). Intertextual references which form part of the 'histoire'—as characters view or listen to works—are mirrored in the dialogue of the characters, in frequent discussions of film or literature. Francine's discussions of Kafka, for example, are academic criticism written into the text; her psychoanalytic approach to *Die Verwandlung* and *Der Bau* prefigures a similar interpretation of *Pavane*. Such explicit references are absorbed into the narrative; they necessarily demand no prior knowledge of the source work, instead the narrative stages the process of intertextuality through the characters' discussions. Allusions and parodies on the level of the 'discours', however, point beyond the narrative, implying a relationship with another parallel text which the reader must construct, and preventing the foreclosure of the text.

Kafka is the main source of allusion and parody in Moníková's work. In her 1989 'Rede zur Verleihung des Kafka-Preises', Moníková cites Kafka as her inspiration to write, and write in German: 'mein Schreiben verdanke ich ihm. | Er hat mich ermutigt zu schreiben, in einer Sprache, die nicht die meine war' (*SAW* 142). The episodic structure of *Eine Schädigung* which formed a template for her later texts was drawn, she claims, from *Der Proceß*; and talking about *Treibeis*, she remarks,

ich weiß, wo man [Kafka] finden kann. Ich höre ihn, ich höre den Duktus, den Ton, das sind die Bierpfützen im Schloß, wo K. mit Frieda liegt und das ist dieses Abrollen den Berg hinab, wenn man will. [...] Kafka ist sowieso überall. Bei mir ohnehin. [...] Ich meine jetzt vom Rhythmus her, von der Stimmung.⁷¹

Prantl and Karla's tumbling embrace is but one example. The schoolgirls who pursue Prantl are reminiscent of the girls who throng round Titorelli in *Der Proceß*: like Titorelli's girls, they are a combination of giggly playfulness and corrupt sexuality: 'Jung, zerzaust' (*T* 40), 'eine Mischung von Kindlichkeit und Verworfenheit'.⁷² They reek of violet scent where Titorelli's girls painted their mouths, and sneak into Prantl's bedroom while

---

⁷⁰ Mansbrügge analyses *Las meninas* in her introduction, *Autorkategorie*, 17–25.
⁷¹ Moníková, in interview with Cramer et al., 197–8.
⁷² Kafka, *Der Proceß*, 149–50.

he is out, just as the girls clamour to be let into Titorelli's studio and have secretly got hold of a copy of his key; the leader of Titorelli's band is a hunchback, the leader of the Greenland girls is bandy-legged.

Der Proceß is invoked several times in *Pavane*. When Francine imagines exploring the catacombs under Prague, it is Josef K. who points the way:

> Auf der Südseite des Berges Petřín sehe ich in einem verlassenen Steinbruch einen Mensch liegen, über einen Stein rückwärts gelehnt, mit einem Messer in der Brust, spitze Knie unter dem festlichen Anzug, erstarrt in der Erfrierung die gebrochenen Augen von undefinierbarer Bleichheit, im Frost nicht ganz augelöscht, sie starren zum Himmel, zeigen aber in der Rückbiegung des Kopfes in den Spalt, der in der abgesprengten Wand geöffnet ist; ich gehe in der Richtung dieses ehemaligen Blickes [...]. (*P* 76)

The details here follow Kafka's text exactly—the location, K.'s black suit, his position 'nahe der Bruchwand', and the method of execution—even using phrases which refer to the original text: the 'kleiner Steinbruch, verlassen und öde' or K.'s 'brechende[-] Augen'.[73] Francine's subsequent ritual destruction of the wheelchair takes place in a quarry on the other side of the river, in a further reference to the Kafka text (K. and his executioners also cross a bridge); she watches from above as the effigy in the wheelchair burns at the bottom of the quarry, just as an unidentified figure watches from above as K. dies. If previously Francine had identified with K., evident from the direct quotation, then the allusion indicates that this is no longer the case. Immediately following on from this scene is Francine's version of *Das Schloß* which allows Olga too to escape the fate Kafka had planned.

When Francine takes to the wheelchair, her hysterical performance, she also begins to write—turning her involuntary mimicry (quotation) into a voluntary imitation; in this way she hopes to cast off her literary 'Stütze', Kafka. Her revisions of *Das Schloß* both confirm and undermine Kafka's authority. Linda Hutcheon describes 'a central paradox of parody', the fact that 'its transgressions are always authorized. In imitating, even with

---

[73] Kafka, *Der Proceß*, 243, 244.

critical difference, parody reinforces.'[74] In this respect, then, parody resembles hysteria and its relation to authority:

> The hysteric sustains the system of knowledge proclaimed by the figure representing paternity. Furthermore, it is a mode of communication that both sustains and calls into question the symbolic, specifically paternal authority. Supporting the father's desire, at the same time, the hysteric also calls into question the consistency of his law, endlessly demanding that he prove the authority of his power.[75]

Parody points to a specifically literary strategy, one which is directed at other literary texts and authors; it reproduces the structures of hysteria on a purely textual level.[76] The Kafka versions produced by Francine in *Pavane* are reprinted in *Schloß, Aleph, Wunschtorte*, with commentary by Moníková herself, and an additional, comic version which reveals her parodic, irreverent, and notably physical focus—entitled 'Anpassung', it reads simply 'Gräfliche Landpost | Amalia B. schwanger!' (*SAW* 92).

Babel

Not only are Moníková's texts full of quotations—which signal language as literature, according to Benjamin—and references to other texts, they are also full of other languages. There is some area of overlap between these categories, as foreign languages often mark direct quotations, but Moníková's use of other languages goes far beyond this limited use: she composes freely in other languages. Characters often speak in other languages, something which may be reproduced in the 'discours' or 'récit', or may be implied within the 'histoire'. Multilingualism in the texts is furthermore accompanied by images of Babel. Moníková's use of German is implicitly invoked in such passages, which represent difference within the text and form part of Moníková's pedagogical agenda, as many phrases (notably Czech words) are followed by a translation. It can be

---

[74] Linda Hutcheon, *A Theory of Parody: The Teachings of Twentieth-Century Art Forms* (London: Methuen, 1985), 26.
[75] Bronfen, *The Knotted Subject*, 39.
[76] Moníková's collection of plays *Unter Menschenfressern. Ein dramatisches Menu in vier Gängen* (Frankfurt am Main: Verlag der Autoren, 1990) parodies Nestroy, Shakespeare, and Arno Schmidt, as well as citing Freud, Lacan, and Lévi-Strauss, and merits further study with regard to Moníková's use of parody.

said of Moníková, as of Qvietone, in his element in Russian in Akademgorodok, 'es macht ihm [ihr] einfach Spaß, polyglott zu sein' (*F* 253).

The incorporation of foreign languages into the text begins, appropriately, with Francine in *Pavane*: Francine speaks a mixture of English and French with her friend Geneviève in Paris, although some of their conversations are reported in German. The first exchange between the two sets the tone: ' "Elle est gâtée", sage ich, "spoiled, verwöhnt." | "Tu exagères", antwortet Geneviève' (*P* 66). The use of English leaks into the narrative from the dialogue: '[ich] sage zu Geneviève in unserem basic idiom: "You can say to your ... *zigzag* ... good bye" ' (*P* 69). Other conversations are given in the appropriate language as a matter of realism—an exchange with an Englishman in English, and Francine imagines talking to Kafka in Czech as well as German—where the content is of less importance than the fact of it being in another language. Most striking in *Pavane* is the description of the Queen of Bohemia (*P* 139), which is written in not quite perfect English. Part of Francine's imaginary identification sequence, the passage sits uneasily with the Czech nationalism of the scene, highlighting the incongruity of the German narrative as well.[77] It is clear from the italicized English that this is not just an imaginary scene: the passage is also a composition by Francine.[78] The English enacts a degree of distance, evident in the whole scene, where the queen is referred to as 'sie': the use of the foreign language stages the perception of the self as other, showing Francine taking on a role. In this, her use of English mirrors Moníková's use of German, 'dieser Filter, das Deutsche, das ich kaum beherrschte'.[79] The foreign language enables representation at the same time as denying immediate access to the experience, the function of hysterical representations.

Die Fassade, which is set partly in the USSR, contains the most sustained and complex use of other languages: the artists' stay

---

[77] The use of English backs up Braunbeck's claim that this figure is the 'winter queen', Elizabeth, rather than the mythical Libuše.

[78] A passage written by Jan is also in italics (*P* 137).

[79] Moníková in interview with Sibylle Cramer, 'Die Dauer der Welt beruht auf dem Fleiße des Schriftstellers: Ein Gespräch mit der deutsch schreibenden tschechischen Autorin Libuše Moníková', *Süddeutsche Zeitung*, 19/20 Sept. 1987, p. 164.

in Akademgorodok in particular is reported in German, Russian (Cyrillic and transliterated), and English. Russian is used primarily for cultural references — to songs, plays, and music — but also has a realist function when used as dialogue, to enact within the text the difficulties the artists have in understanding. The exchanges with the lorry driver who mistakenly takes them to Akademgorodok are a case in point. Qvietone's determination to speak Russian under the influence of hallucinogenic mushrooms leads to confusion: 'Seit einiger Zeit spricht Qvietone ungehemmt und ziemlich perfekt russisch, er erklärt, daß er Biologe, Wissenschaftler sei. "Forscher", fällt ihm noch ein. "Akademija Nauk". "Ja ponimaju", der Fahrer gibt Gas' (*F* 248). And so the driver takes them to the research enclave Akademgorodok, rather than back to Novosibirsk, as they had wanted. The German-speaking reader is left in the dark as to what is happening and why, just like the artists (whose Russian is much weaker than Qvietone's). Particular features of Russian are preserved, such as occasional interjections, phatic elements which need no translation: 'Fühlen Sie sich nicht wohl, *golubtschik?*' (*F* 275) Dobrodin asks Maltzahn. In places, this realism segues into a more technical interest, a combination which leads to incongruity and humour in Podol's altercation with Russian bureaucracy:

> Podol schreibt tschechisch und soll einen neuen Bogen in Druckbuchstaben ausfüllen, er knallt seinen Paß, auf den er jetzt geradezu stolz ist, hin, faßt sich dann aber und sagt mit Lächeln: 'Du Kuh blöde, füll es selber aus.' Die Attributiv-Umstellung ist ein Zugeständnis an den Ton russischer Märchen, die er einmal illustrieren sollte, spontan aktualisierte Satzgliederung im Dienst der poetischen Funktion der Sprache, während ihr appellativer und konnotativer Charakter hier verloren sind. Die Komsomolzin wird unsicher: Einerseits sind das Wort kráva und das russische korova zu nahe aneinander, um mißverständlich zu sein, andererseits ist Podols Lächeln zu gewinnend, sie hat sich wahrscheinlich verhört, oder es heißt noch etwas anderes. (*F* 241–2)

Specialist knowledge is part of the joke here, although the humour arises more from the juxtaposition of Podol's crude insult with the academic discourse than from the specific reference to the poetic syntax of Russian fairy tales. In the following exchange between the artists and the researcher Roger Snafu, the humour presupposes a knowledge of English:

Snafu lehnt an seinem Tisch und kaut Kashew-Kerne. Er zwinkert Qvietone zu und hält ihm die Tüte entgegen. 'What's your fuckin' business here?'
'I ... I am an entomologist', stottert Qvietone überrascht, sein Englisch ist wesentlich schwächer als sein Französisch oder zur Zeit Russisch.
'A what—?'
'He is interested in ... devoted to ... bugs', Nordanc meint, einspringen zu müssen.
'So am I. Doin' a lot of debugging here. Them Russian [sic] need it badly', Snafu grinst seinen russischen Kollegen an und beide lachen.
'Was hat er gesagt?', fragt Qvietone.
'Er entfernt hier irgendwelche Käfer', übersetzt Nordanc verwirrt.
'Du meinst, er entlaust es hier?', grinst Podol.
'Nein, er entfernt Wanzen', Maltzahn zieht sich um.
'Er bringt sie eher an', sagt Orten. (*F* 272)

The bilingual, punning translation also highlights, as do many of the exchanges in 'Russian', the missing Czech language— although textual reality and narrative coincide in the use of English, Nordanc's translation is into Czech in the 'histoire', but German in the 'récit'. The absence of the Czech language is alluded to self-consciously when Podol remarks, 'Merkst du übrigens, wie verlogen alles klingt in einer Fremdsprache? Sogar "Wie spät ist es?" oder "Guten Tag". Ich komme mir wie ein Heuchler vor' (*F* 281). Podol's term 'verlogen' recalls Irigaray's contention that the hysteric lies, further suggesting that Moníková's use of German is a hysterical performance.

As is clear from Moníková's frequently repeated diatribes against tourists who do not learn Czech when visiting the country, language use is implicated in power structures and national identity. Moníková claims 'Bei mir schreiben die Verlierer die Geschichte': she gives a voice to minorities, literally, in using or alluding to their languages; in this sense, the foreign languages, like intertextual references (and here the two are almost inseparable), are also cultural artefacts to be preserved in the name of diversity.[80] In *Die Fassade*, the Ewenks and the 'Geheime Geschichte der Mongolen' both evoke a language which is, in Bachmann's Franza Ranner's words about

---

[80] Moníková, in interview with Cramer, 'Die Dauer der Welt', 164.

Hatshepsut, 'abzulesen, weil nichts da ist, wo sie sein soll'.⁸¹ The Ewenks are a nomadic native Eskimo people of Siberia, whose customs and language are slowly being superseded by modern Soviet practices. Although Moníková's narrative contains no examples of what is presumably an oral language, its existence is alluded to, in an old woman's speech, 'Ihre Sprache klingt wie gedämpftes Kichern, der Junge, der es übersetzt, bleibt aber ernst' (*F* 358), and the shaman's incantation, 'Oronka Tagir [...] ruft in einer vergessenen Sprache die Große Bärin an' (*F* 365).⁸² However, no claims are made for the absolute authenticity of the people, their language, or customs; their culture is giving way to relativization and parody. 'Häuptling Suruj, bei Verhandlungen in Tura auch Genosse Vorsitzender genannt' (*F* 358) is in reality head of '[e]ine staatliche Rentierzuchtgenossenschaft' (*F* 363), complete with quotas and scientific data, not just a tribe of nomads; he performs the traditional ceremonies but does not believe in them.

In contrast, Moníková's treatment of the Inuit on Greenland does include instances of their language and history, by way of Prantl's explanations to Karla. The text includes Inuit songs, 'taqigdlune name atúngiveqaoq...' or 'Unmöglich noch weiter in Ruhe zu verweilen...' (*T* 35) and 'ilippuaalaa qiliniarsinngaalaa...' or 'Hilf mir ich falle' (*T* 38), a refrain repeated in the narrative later in the text (cf. *T* 209). Prantl, true to his self-designation as 'ein mährischer Inuk' (*T* 186), is knowledgeable about the vocabulary and grammar of their language, its regional variations, paralinguistic gestures, customs, and legends. What emerges is again a lack of authenticity or 'Ursprünglichkeit': 'Du stellst dir die Grönländer als ein reines Naturvolk vor, aber das sind sie nie gewesen' (*T* 95), he tells Karla. The Greenlanders are descended from several different races; their language is a mixture of Inuit and Danish, whose spelling is not fixed and varies from coast to coast, its written form having only been introduced in 1851 by a German dictionary compiler; and their beliefs are an incongruous combination of ancient and modern, pagan and Christian: 'Früher glaubten sie an den Mond und an die Sonne und daran, daß

---

⁸¹ Bachmann, *Der Fall Franza*, 104.
⁸² A reference also to Ingeborg Bachmann's *Anrufung des Großen Bären* (1956).

sie im Himmel mit Seehundschädeln Fußball spielen werden' (*T* 192). The situation of the Inuits reflects the wider postmodern trends evident in the novel, according to Brigid Haines, where 'master discourses are discredited and weakened; modern life is shown to be dominated by inauthenticity, the superficial and the watering down of distinct cultures'.[83] Indeed, it seems that the Inuks never had a distinct culture.

At the heart of this concern with the weakening of cultural boundaries is Prague, continually overlaid with new names, politics, and even language: Prantl and Karla 'gelangen an den Punkt, wo jeder ein anderes Land vor sich hat, das sie Tschechoslovakei nennen, mit schiefem Mund auch "Heimat"' (*T* 215). The parallels between Czechoslovakia and Greenland make it clear that the validity of the former is also at stake: a state invented in 1918, which has been part of several political landscapes (*Treibeis* was written after the Velvet Revolution of 1989), whose boundaries and street names have changed, and whose history is revealed in a foreign language (German, language of one of the aggressors towards the state). Czech is the unspoken language underlying Moníková's texts—as elusive as Prague itself for Karla and Prantl—a fact alluded to in self-conscious references. Czech, like the other foreign languages, is used as an 'effet de réel': titles of songs and films are often given in Czech, followed immediately by a translation within the narrative.[84] In *Verklärte Nacht*, the act of translating between the two languages becomes part of the narrative itself. Leonora and Thomas initially speak Czech, which she remarks upon; the conversation is narrated in German. After their unplanned dip in the Vltava, Leonora speaks German: 'Wir reden durcheinander, wechseln die Sprachen, eine Mischung aus Deutsch und Tschechisch, er will bei Tschechisch bleiben, aber ich werde ungeduldig und schreie deutsch, es geht schneller' (*VN* 101); no further reference is made to the language in which they converse.[85] The weakening of cultural boundaries which Brigid Haines identified in *Treibeis* is here enacted by the relationship

---

[83] Haines, 'New Places from Which to Write Histories of Peoples', 510.
[84] Roland Barthes, 'L'Effet du réel', *Communications*, 11 (1968), 84–9.
[85] Cf. also Karla and Prantl's first meeting, 'Sie reden schnell, lassen das Englische, in dem sie beide mit Akzent sprechen, überspringen das Deutsche, da ist sie besonders stur, es bleibt das Tschechische' (*T* 75).

between the expatriate Czech who lives in Germany and speaks German (Leonora), and the German of Sudeten parentage, who lives in Prague and speaks Czech (Thomas), and embodied in the language they use to speak to one another: either Czech, German, or a mixture of both, represented in the text by German which functions as a translation of this linguistic utopia.

There are also frequent references to multiple languages, not least, in *Pavane*, in a discussion of Kafka's 'Das Stadtwappen', a short text about the building of the Tower of Babel.[86] Francine identifies a logical inconsistency in the text, the fact that the need for 'Dolmetscher' was foreseen even though building work on the Tower never began—according to the biblical version, the confusion of languages was a punishment for man's attempt to realize his ambition. She comments,

> Der Vorgriff kann mehreres bedeuten: Entweder war die Sprachverwirrung, die Differenzierung der Rede voraussehbar oder sie war als Ziel des Unternehmens eingeplant; oder Kafka reflektiert seine örtliche Situation, das Gemisch von Tschechen, Juden und Deutschen—Prag hat eine Faust im Wappen. (*P* 58)

Images of Babel are found throughout Moníková's texts, in Francine and Geneviève's conversations, in the international linguistics conference in *Treibeis*, and Karla's meeting with an old Samurai in Hiroshima, 'wir schwelgten in Dostoevskij, in basic english, gebrochenem Deutsch, mit Russisch-Brocken, manchmal fiel er ins Französische' (*T* 150–1). There is a difference, though: in these instances the multiple languages facilitate communication, rather than hinder it, as in the biblical Tower of Babel.

The story of the Tower of Babel is also a fantasy of origins: in attempting to explain the existence of different languages, it posits an original, originary language which the Tower's builders must have spoken. Moníková's multiple languages highlight the opposite—Karla and the Samurai illustrate this particularly well—namely that all languages are relative, contingent, and artificial. Moníková's texts suggest that all language is foreign, to the subject as well as to others. Moníková writes in German, not her mother tongue, yet her mother tongue is a foreign language to her text. But one must speak, even though this

[86] Kafka, *Sämtliche Erzählungen*, 306–7.

means speaking in a language which always already determines the speaking subject. This is the paradox at the heart of the hysteric's performance: that there is only performance and inauthentic forms of expression.

'DIE LITERATUR IST SELBST DER ORT, AN DEM ICH MICH ALS SCHRIFTSTELLERIN BEFINDE':[87] CONCLUSION

Hysteria is foregrounded in Moníková's texts through the figure of Francine Pallas, whose decision to overact her hysterical symptom (the limp) by taking to a wheelchair evinces the shift from mimicry to performance evident on a wider level in Moníková's work. This shift is precisely the strategy advocated by Irigaray: the hysteric represents the position of women in patriarchal discourse, forced into mimicry; deliberately staging this mimicry allows women to undo it, by overdoing it. This process is mirrored in Moníková's oeuvre, which follows a trajectory from Jana's mimicry of Mara in *Eine Schädigung* to the images of performance offered by Karla and Leonora. In their respective professions as stuntwoman and choreographer-dancer these latter two combine a form of genuine physicality with an awareness of the non-essential nature of identity. The movement from mimicry to performance is also evident in Moníková's use of intertextual references and other languages, strategies which represent woman-as-hysteric's imitation of patriarchal discourse. Parodies and allusions, as well as free composition in other languages, constitute a textual performance; their self-consciousness draws attention to the literary nature of the text itself and, further, to Moníková's use of German.

The hysteric's succession of self-representations underlies the scenes of identification with mythical figures (Francine with Libuše, Karla with an android and Cleopatra, Leonora with Hatshepsut), which problematize the notion of gender. On a textual level, too, figures representing alternative subject positions with regard to gender (Uncumber, Nordanc, Podol, and Thomas) both present different roles and display their nature *as* roles. One could similarly analyse a set of figures

---

[87] Moníková in interview with Helga G. Braunbeck, 'Gespräche mit Libuše Moníková 1992–1997', *Monatshefte*, 89/4 (1997), 452–67, here 452.

who problematize national identity and offer other ways of constituting identity (Nordanc again, the nomadic Elueneh in *Die Fassade*; Elina Makropulos and Thomas in *Verklärte Nacht*; Tereza, Halina, and the elusive 'Hüterinnen des Feuers' in *Der Taumel*). Moreover, Francine, Karla, and Leonora act as Moníková's self-representations within literature: all act out her identity or alternative versions of it. Not for nothing does Sibylle Cramer, in her laudatio for Moníková as recipient of the 'Chamissopreis' in 1991, refer to the 'Schauspiel [des kollektiven Ich] Moníková'.[88] Leonora in particular, as an academic-turned-dancer, is a form of wish-fulfilment for Moníková, who maintains that had she stayed in Prague, she would have been a dancer not an academic.[89]

The repetition of the imaginary identification scenes not only allows the notion of hysteria to resurface in later texts, having been raised in *Pavane*, but also points to the fact that the later texts, particularly *Verklärte Nacht*, themselves perform a version of the earlier ones, taking up and reworking scenes, shared memories, and motifs. Moníková's texts share certain overarching concerns, such as the structures of hysteria and exile; her main female protagonists are strikingly similar in their physical features and characteristics—such as the love of trams and cinema, also attributed to the most sympathetic male protagonists (Orten and Prantl). Even seemingly insignificant scenes, events, and details appear identically in several texts. In *Die Fassade*, Orten's reluctance to give a speech mirrors the sculptor Palzer's page-dropping performance at a similar event in *Eine Schädigung*; ex-Nazi Jirse's wooden leg is a comic reprisal of Francine's limp.[90] In *Die Fassade*, the 'kommunistische Halbblut' (F 269) Roger Snafu travelled from America to Siberia in order to trace the migration of tribes back to its origins, and in *Treibeis*, a half-blood Eskimo makes the original journey to America. *Treibeis* also sees a translation of the Ewenks' ritual of the bear (in *Die Fassade*) into an Inuit ceremony celebrating 'Bruder Seehund'.

[88] Sibylle Cramer, 'Lobrede auf Libuše Moníková' (Laudatio zur Verleihung des Adalbert-von-Chamisso-Preises), *Akzente*, 38/3 (1991), 229–35, here 229.
[89] See Moníková, in interview with Frank Dietschreit, 'Sehnsuchtsort', 37.
[90] Moníková's humour, which is often overlooked, is something she has in common with Hensel. Beth Linklater analyses Moníková's humour in ' "Könnten so nicht politisch Träume in den Himmel wachsen?" Women's Writing and Humour in *Die Fassade*', in Haines and Marven (eds.), *Libuše Moníková*.

Verklärte Nacht is the culmination of this type of reference through repetition. There are several references drawn from *Die Fassade*, such as Leonora's adaptation of the 'Geheime Geschichte der Mongolen', and the tale of Makropulos which Marie mentions. More frequent are the repetitions from *Pavane*, however—further suggesting that Leonora may in fact be an older Francine. Both talk about the Spartakiada; both identify with, or refer to, the Sibyl of Cumae; both relate a dream where a butterfly (*Pavane*) or moth (*Verklärte Nacht*) represents physical vulnerability; the drowning of Virginia Woolf, alluded to by Francine, is evoked in Leonora's visit to the swimming pool, and accidental dip in the Vltava; and both recall a disabled childhood friend who wished they were in a wheelchair—what is a passing reference in *Pavane* becomes a whole scene in *Verklärte Nacht*, as Leonora pays a surprise visit to the same friend.

The effect of this repetition is to turn what are apparently 'effets de réel' into a form of self-quotation. It may be tempting to conclude that these anecdotal details point to Moníková's own experience, an impression strengthened by the fact that so many of the thematic concerns, as well as the attributes of the female protagonists, appear to have their origins in her autobiography. To do so would be to ignore the process of fictionalization and the imitative structures of Moníková's texts. Biddy Martin's analysis of the autobiographical elements in Lou Andreas-Salomé's work can usefully be applied to Moníková's too:

> As in much of her fiction, she integrates anecdotes from her more explicitly autobiographical writings as well as her essays. These characteristic intertextual references challenge interpretative claims to biographical referentiality by virtue of their appearance in so many different forms and genres.
>
> Particular anecdotes do seem to take on a certain centrality for her conception of self and for others' perceptions of her. [...] It is simply not clear where the original version is, which version is a copy, and even less clear whether the story in the memoirs comments on an actual incident. What matters is Salomé's proliferation of such stories and her particular reflections on them.[91]

Repetition thus becomes intertextuality. Moníková treats her own texts, whether fictional or non-fictional, as intertexts; the

---

[91] Biddy Martin, *Woman and Modernity: The (Life)Styles of Lou Andreas-Salomé* (Ithaca, NY: Cornell University Press, 1991), 178.

repetition of content is not meant to refer outside the text to autobiographical detail, but is rather intended to signal the fictionality and self-referentiality of the texts. This is a reversal of Francine's declaration that her life is a copy of literature. Indeed, many of the repeated elements are already intertextual references—most obviously the startling tale of 'Urdunkel', given in full in *Pavane, Die Fassade*, and the essay 'Das totalitäre Glück' in *Schloß, Aleph, Wunschtorte*, which is in turn a citation from the Tao Te Ching. Martin's analysis suggests that this kind of self-reference becomes a copy without an original—'an imitation without an origin', as Butler describes the performance of gender—and thus another manifestation of hysteria's problematizing of origins.

The trajectory of Moníková's texts evinces both mutation and repetition. Sibylle Cramer, writing in 1991, describes Moníková's oeuvre in a way which recalls the structures of hysteria:

Das Schreibkollektiv Moníková [...] ist eine unzeitgemäße Spezies der Literatur, nämlich von Buch zu Buch sich wandelnd, eine alles andere als unverkennbare Autorin. [...] Ich spreche über die Mehrheit namens Libuše Moníková in den Kategorien eines sc.: [*sic*] monographischen Entwicklungsromans. Allerdings ist er verwildert, ein episodenhaftes Gebilde, sein Material in totalen Bruchstücken zeigend, additiv, akkumulativ, parataktisch.[92]

Cramer cites the variety of publications at that date: *Eine Schädigung, Pavane*, and *Die Fassade*, the collection of dramas *Unter Menschenfressern*, and the volume of essays *Schloß, Aleph, Wunschtorte*. The three novels are distinct and dissimilar, *Eine Schädigung* the most straightforward, with allegorical overtones and *film noir* atmosphere; *Pavane* a dense, psychoanalytically aware first-person narrative set in Germany; and *Die Fassade*, the picaresque tale of a group of male artists in Czechoslovakia and the USSR. The dramas in *Unter Menschenfressern* are similarly dissimilar, each parodying a different author. Moníková's subsequent publications are, however, much less varied: *Treibeis* and *Verklärte Nacht* take up many elements of narrative from the earlier work; *Prager Fenster*, a collection of journalistic essays, revisits in different form—often as personal memories—events and issues raised in the literary texts. The overall structure of

---

[92] Cramer, 'Lobrede auf Libuše Moníková', 230.

Moníková's work shifts from parataxis and mutation to reprisal and reconfiguration—a performance which highlights in retrospect elements of similarity within the early works.

Brigid Haines suggests that the Velvet Revolution marks a turning point in the treatment of power and personal agency in Moníková's work, and the historical moment also seems to signal, and possibly even trigger, the shifts from mimicry to performance on all levels of her oeuvre.[93] The trajectory of Moníková's work appears to reach a form of resolution, though, and a real paradigm shift occurs between *Verklärte Nacht* and the fragments which constitute *Der Taumel*. The five completed novels mirror each other, with both first and last set in Prague, second and fourth revolving around the absence of the city; the middle text, *Die Fassade*, is relatively unconcerned with the city—there is no central female character, therefore Prague has no role as a place of identification. Furthermore, there is a notable symmetry in the scenes at the beginning and end of Moníková's published work, between the rape which opens *Eine Schädigung* and Leonora and Thomas's lovemaking which ends *Verklärte Nacht*.[94] This final scene stages the coupling of the masculine Leonora, an expatriate from Prague who lives in Germany, with the feminine Thomas, a Sudeten German who is living in Prague; it brings together and neutralizes the two most insistent elements of the performance of identity in Moníková's texts, gender and national identity. After this apparent resolution of hysteria, *Der Taumel* moves to a more direct representation of trauma, both in the historical setting—Prague during the repressive period of 'normalization' after the violent suppression of the Prague Spring—and in the image of the protagonist's epilepsy. A physiological condition, where hysteria is psychosomatic, it nonetheless recalls hysteria in the epileptic fit, the blackout which is a physical enactment of the traumatic gap in the psyche. It is also notable that the text deals with internal affairs of the state, as opposed to

---

[93] Haines, 'New Places from Which to Write Histories of Peoples', 511.

[94] Graham Jackman, ' "Kde Domov Můj?" Nation, Exile and Return in *Eine Schädigung* and *Verklärte Nacht*', in Haines and Marven (eds.), *Libuše Moníková*, also notes the symmetry between these two works, and sees the union between Leonora and Thomas on one level as an allegory of national reconciliation, but also as a triumph of warmth and togetherness over Leonora's 'icy solitariness'—which would further suggest a resolution of some of the concerns in *Treibeis*.

Eine Schädigung's allegorical representation of the invasion of Czechoslovakia by Warsaw Pact troops. Brandl's epilepsy is an internalization of trauma, in contrast to the external trauma of the rape in the earlier text. Although *Der Taumel* does take up many motifs and themes from Moníková's previous texts, it places them in a different context, that of trauma. It would have been interesting to see where she went from here.

4
KERSTIN HENSEL:
'WER "DRAUSSEN" STEHT, KANN DEUTLICHER SEHEN'

In her review of *Hallimasch*, Kerstin Hensel's first prose publication, Eva Kaufmann describes the characters as 'unheimliche Sonderlinge'.[1] She points to the obese 'Nilpferdpaar', identical twins Liese and Lotte Möbius (in 'Hallimasch'), with their incestuous relationship, and the abused Jutta Gallwitz (in 'Katzenbericht'), who mistakes her cats for her children. The eccentricity of Hensel's protagonists, Kaufmann suggests, consists in physical oddity as well as emotional deformity, barely suppressed sexuality, and violent tendencies. Eccentricity—etymologically, 'out of the centre'—is a particularly apt term for these characters on the margins of society. Their difference, as well as the reaction they evoke—they are 'unheimlich'—marks these characters as grotesque: the grotesque deals with the excluded other, who transgresses both physical form and social norms. Furthermore, these characters are at the centre of grotesque texts, which play with the reader's expectations of narrative and plot.

In this chapter, I look first at grotesque representations of the body, which encompass images of the body as well as bodily functions and acts. These aspects of the bodily grotesque are reflected in disrupted language, in exaggerated descriptions and monologues where the communicative function of language is problematized. This linguistic disruption is furthermore mirrored in the disruption of narrative discourse which I examine in the second half of the chapter. Hensel plays with conventions of narrative both in grotesque—exaggerated, unpredictable—plots and in literary parodies. I begin by looking at the mode of the grotesque in more detail and delineating its relation to irony, which has

---

[1] Eva Kaufmann, 'Kerstin Hensel, *Hallimasch: Erzählungen*', in Siegfried Rönisch (ed.), *DDR-Literatur '89 im Gespräch* (Berlin: Aufbau, 1990), 230–40, here 234.

become a more significant aspect of Hensel's narrative voice in her work since 1989.

The grotesque and irony

The grotesque is a product of its historical context: it draws on the cultural and social values of a particular time and place, and often precedes or signals imminent change. Alexander von Bormann, writing in 1988, notes a resurgence of the grotesque in contemporary poetry in the GDR. He explains:

> Das Groteske bringt einen Widerstand gegen einen zu eng gezogenen Vernunftbegriff zum Ausdruck und wird sozusagen erst 'böse', wenn es (das, wofür es steht) abgedrängt werden soll, wenn die symbolische Ordnung sich exklusiv versteht. Das ist recht ausdrücklich die Situation der DDR-Kultur, die kaum bereit ist, sich den aufklärerisch-sozialistisch-humanistischen Vernunftbegriff pluralisieren zu lassen.[2]

Hensel's narrative perspective is a response to the experience of a grotesque political reality, to '[d]ie Staatssicherheit in ihrer Absurdität, Simplizität, in ihrer Kleinheit und komischen Monströsität',[3] and 'die Absurditäten des DDR-Alltags'.[4] As she says: 'Der Irrsinn unseres Alltags, die wahnwitzigen Abläufe einer jeden auf dieser Welt herrschenden Gesellschaft sind durch Literatur nur faßbar, wenn sie groß und übertrieben dargestellt werden (und des öfteren zeigen sich die realen Geschehnisse selbst so)'.[5] Hensel's texts continually invoke their context, directly and through allegory, and the grotesque vision which pervades her work, from images of the body to her depiction of the state's exploitation and physical abuse of individuals, is rooted in the reality of life in the GDR. Her intention is not to portray the effects of this reality on the individual's psyche, as Herta Müller does with her narratives of trauma, but rather to show how the individual is determined

---

[2] Alexander von Bormann, 'Das Groteske in der deutschen Gegenwartslyrik', *Études germaniques*, 43 (1988), 142–57, here 151.
[3] Kerstin Hensel, 'IM Positiv', *Freitag*, 23 Apr. 1993, p. 12.
[4] Kerstin Hensel, 'Weiß der Teufel, was Glück ist: Über den Briefwechsel von Brigitte Reimann und Christa Wolf', *Freitag*, 9 Apr. 1993, p. 18.
[5] Kerstin Hensel, in interview with Karin Néy, '"Letzlich will ich nichts, als Aufklärer sein": Gespräch mit Kerstin Hensel', *Temperamente*, 3 (1989), 3–7, here 5.

by its structures and values. In order to do so, she employs an external perspective, as opposed to trauma's necessarily internal one.

The grotesque is characterized by its dual structure and its ambivalence. As the psychoanalytic critic Carl Pietzcker explains, it is the result of the continual creation and disruption of expectations, maintaining 'Zerstörung und Erhaltung des Erwartungshorizontes in gespanntem Gleichgewicht'; and it provokes a reaction between laughter and horror.[6] Although persons or objects are labelled grotesque, this characterizes the effect they have on others: it is the structure of the experience of an observer, rather than the object observed, which is grotesque. Recurring images relate to fundamental notions of what it means to be human, and of how we make sense of the world. These pertain to the human form and the human mind, on the one hand, and to language and narrative (in the sense of storytelling) on the other. Applied to literature, the text mediates and determines the experience of the grotesque in the former case; in the latter, the strategies of the text itself are grotesque.

The grotesque derives its force from representations of the human body, challenging its form and signification. Frequently these images of the body recall the effects of trauma, but in the grotesque they are represented from outside. In his work on Rabelais, Mikhail Bakhtin analyses images of the bodily grotesque; he links the grotesque with carnival, suggesting that it is both positive and subversive. Bakhtin describes as grotesque 'that which protrudes, bulges, sprouts or branches off (when a body transgresses its limits and a new one begins)', or which 'ignores the impenetrable surface that closes and limits the body as a separate and completed phenomenon'.[7] The grotesque body cannot be contained; its transgressions take the form of extra limbs or growths on the body, or bodily fluids which blur the boundaries of the body—this is not as extreme as trauma's dissolution of boundaries, and in the grotesque it is observed from the outside. As the boundaries of the body ultimately represent—and can therefore guarantee or

[6] Pietzcker, 'Das Groteske', 200.
[7] Bakhtin, *Rabelais and his World*, 320 and 318 respectively.

unsettle—the limits of intelligibility of language, the grotesque also effects linguistic disruption.

Other manifestations of the grotesque threaten the delineation of what is considered human. In his influential early study of the grotesque, Wolfgang Kayser identifies combinations of the human and animal, human and the organic world, or human and machine, which call into question the definition of the human.[8] The grotesque demonstrates that definitions of the human are discursive constructs which are constantly renegotiated and redefined against what is 'other', and that these constructs uphold, and are upheld by, society. Still other forms of the grotesque challenge conventional signification of the body, problematizing gendered physical attributes such as beauty or strength; according to Pietzcker, 'das "Häßliche", "Abstoßende" gehört in einer Kultur, die das "Schöne" zum Wert setzt, zu den Ingredienzien des Grotesken'.[9]

The grotesque is also concerned with human psychology. Kayser identifies madness as a fundamental experience of the grotesque, because it implies a lack of physical control, and the loss of the self. Madness enacts physically the separation of body and mind as the alienation of the self from the physical body: 'Ins Unheimliche verwandelt erscheint das Menschliche im Wahnsinnigen; wieder ist es, als ob ein "Es", ein fremder, unmenschlicher Geist in die Seele gefahren sei.'[10] Here 'es' implies the id, as well as an impersonal, other 'it'. Conversely, the attribution of a mind to an inanimate object is also grotesque, 'alles, was als Gerät ein eigenes, gefährliches Leben entfaltet', such as the lift in 'Grus', in *Hallimasch*, which appears to have a mind of its own.[11] Similarly, depictions of 'Triebe' which take over the body and overrule the rational mind are grotesque, as they manifest 'die Verfremdung in der Gespaltenheit des Ich und in seinem Beherrschtwerden von namenlosen Kräften'.[12] This 'Gespaltenheit' recalls the splitting characteristic of trauma; there it is experienced by the individual, rather than observed. Hensel's characters are often subject to uncontrollable urges or drives, which take the form of insatiable appetites (for both food and sex) and, not infrequently,

---

[8] Kayser, *Das Groteske*, 22. [9] Pietzcker, 'Das Groteske', 208.
[10] Kayser, *Das Groteske*, 198. [11] Ibid. 197. [12] Ibid. 157.

lead to violence, murder, and suicide.[13] These acts of excess also form part of the narrative grotesque, as they generate grotesque plots.

The grotesque possesses the potential for social criticism. It enables us to examine social structures by representing their margins and outcasts, 'denn das in einer Gesellschaft Verdrängte ist, wenn es ins Bewußtsein tritt, am besten geeignet, den von der Autorität getragenen Entwurf in Frage zu stellen'.[14] The grotesque represents repressed elements within society; it reveals social values to be contingent, whilst also confirming their existence. Like the hysteric's ambivalent relation to authority, it can therefore be interpreted as either reactionary or subversive: Kayser suggests that it is 'der Versuch, das Dämonische in der Welt zu bannen und verschwören'.[15] Pietzcker suggests the opposite, that it rather undoes repression, allowing that which has already been banished by society to return.

Unlike trauma and hysteria, the grotesque is an aesthetic mode. However, some recent critics have extrapolated it into a phenomenon of reality. Arnold Heidsieck suggests that its source is the contemporary world: 'Das groteske Bild der Welt, wie es vor allem in der zeitgenössischen Dramatik heraustritt, stellt sich als das Bild einer grotesken Welt dar.'[16] Heidsieck's ethical grotesque centres on 'die produzierte Entstellung des Menschen, die von Menschen verübte Unmenschlichkeit', particularly the image of the human (body) as an object.[17] Pietzcker takes issue with Heidsieck's definition, emphasizing the importance of the encounter: 'Der entstellte Mensch ist nicht grotesk, er kann lediglich so wirken, falls ihm ein Bewußtsein begegnet, das seine Verfassung als Entstellung wahrnimmt und nicht bewältigen kann, weil sie mit seinem Bild des Menschen nicht übereinstimmt.'[18] The aspect of 'nicht bewältigen', the possibility that this image cannot be overcome, shows where the grotesque may tip into trauma—precisely at the point where the focus shifts from the object (or the content of the text)

---

[13] See also Pietzcker, 'Das Groteske', 208, 'Die anarchische Komponente des Grotesken bringt es mit sich, daß die grotesken Werke in unserer patriarchalisch strukturierten Gesellschaft häufig von Sexualität und Verbrechen bestimmt sind'.
[14] Ibid. 208.   [15] Kayser, *Das Groteske*, 202.
[16] Heidsieck, *Das Groteske*, 15.   [17] Ibid. 17.
[18] Pietzcker, 'Das Groteske', 201.

onto the effect on the reader. Pietzcker's distinction between 'sein' and 'wirken' highlights the role of the 'discours': narrative strategies such as humour or irony counteract the effects of images which, unmediated, would be horrific. In this sense, the grotesque is a function of the interaction, or, frequently, the disjunction, of 'discours' and 'histoire'.

Grotesque images must belong to, and distort, a recognizable reality in order to have an impact—'Deshalb gehört das Normale, Gewohnte, notwendig zum Grotesken', Pietzcker declares.[19] This also characterizes it as a literary mode: the grotesque distorts the mode of realism. Hensel's work does so by emphasizing the fictionality of the text, either through implausibility or self-referentiality, or by focusing attention on the 'discours' and thus undermining the transparency of the narrative. The degree of humour or horror which greets the grotesque varies in relation to the significance of the ideas which are threatened; a threat to notions of what it is to be human, to have an autonomous identity and recognizable human form (thematic concerns), will necessarily induce more horror in the reader than a threat to literary form—unless, of course, this literary form is as highly politicized as was the case in the GDR. Reactions to Hensel's early tale 'Katzenbericht' (later published in *Hallimasch*) focused on the purportedly decadent form as much as the grotesque content. The tale was labelled 'entartet', a politically loaded term which signals recognition of grotesque distortion and deformation.[20] Hensel's narrative grotesque takes the form of disproportionate plots and parody: her plots are unpredictable, revolving around surprising events (often of a grotesque nature), and play with the reader's expectations of logic and coherence. The grotesque work is unstable, it is a 'Form im geformten Zustand ihrer Auflösung'.[21] Hensel's plots and parodies continually threaten to, and occasionally do, collapse into unreadable forms.

The grotesque plot also has wider implications. In his survey of postmodern theories of narrative, Mark Currie declares that 'the enquiry into plot is an enquiry into a collective psyche, a social

---

[19] Ibid. 205.
[20] See Hensel, in interview with Hammer, 'Gespräch mit Kerstin Hensel', 93.
[21] Pietzcker, 'Das Groteske', 200.

desire for plotting and telling'.[22] If Hensel's individual plots offer a perspective on the society they depict—from the early years of the century through fascism, the Second World War, the GDR, to post-unification Germany—the tendency of her plots in general can be read against the 'desire for plotting and telling' in the GDR, specifically against the socialist teleology and its manifestation in literature as the 'Perspektive' of Socialist Realism. There is a certain sense of glee about the inexorable but still unforeseen progress towards complete destruction in the pre-1989 texts 'Herr Johannes' and 'Stinopel', for example, which becomes more apparent when read against these GDR forms. The 'social desire for plotting and telling' is also ours as readers: narrative is, on a more general level, the way in which we approach the world and make sense of it. The disruption of narrative in Hensel's prose texts disconcerts and alienates the reader.

Language is implicated in the grotesque in several ways. As a system which determines our world-view, it can be subjected to the same distortion and disruption as other cultural forms. Techniques such as the literalization of metaphors can be considered grotesque, as Kayser explains: '[die Sprache], das uns vertraute und für unser In-der-Welt-Sein unentbehrliche Mittel, erweist sich plötzlich als eigenmächtig, fremdartig, dämonisch-belebt und reißt den Menschen ins Nächtliche und Unmenschliche'.[23] In Hensel's work, hybrid combinations of human and other are usually suggested through metaphor and simile, implicating language in the creation of the grotesque. Metaphor and simile rely on the stability of the two distinct terms of the linguistic device, but this breaks down in Hensel's descriptions when the two cannot be reconciled. In more extreme cases, the communicative function of language is disturbed, in particular through the disruption of syntax by, in Weigel's words, 'ein Einbruch der Triebe in die Sprache'.[24] The bodily grotesque returns to disrupt language, a connection made evident in several passages of Hensel's work where thematic and linguistic grotesque coincide.

The most significant aspect of linguistic grotesque in Hensel's work is irony. Irony and the grotesque have structural similarities: the most basic definition of the grotesque as irreconcilable

---

[22] Mark Currie, *Postmodern Narrative Theory* (Basingstoke: Macmillan, 1998), 143.
[23] Kayser, *Das Groteske*, 168. [24] Weigel, *Die Stimme der Medusa*, 117.

opposition is echoed in D. C. Muecke's definition of irony as 'an opposition that may take the form of contradiction, incongruity, or incompatibility'.[25] The rhetorical techniques and markers which signal irony can be considered grotesque in their own right. Pietzcker characterizes as grotesque a 'Gegensatz von Aussageweise und Aussageinhalt': verbal irony. Irony, like the grotesque, relies on expectations based on previous experience in order to recognize oppositions and incongruities; this is the 'competence' referred to by Linda Hutcheon:

> irony requires of its reader a triple competence: linguistic, rhetorical or generic, and ideological [...] the reader has to comprehend what is *implied*, as well as what is actually stated. Such linguistic sophistication would be assumed as a given by a genre like parody that employed irony as a rhetorical mechanism. The generic or rhetorical competence of the reader presupposes a knowledge of rhetorical and literary norms in order to permit the recognition of deviation from those norms that constitute the canon, the institutionalised heritage of language and literature.[26]

Ideological competence furthermore implies a set of extraliterary values which are shared by both writer and reader. The function of irony thus corresponds closely to the way in which the grotesque facilitates social criticism. Much of Hensel's oeuvre can be categorized as ironic in a wider sense, as it deals with discrepancies between stated values and implied ones. Irony lends itself to representing the GDR, where official declarations were at odds with everyday experience; indeed, Hensel attributes her desire to write to 'der früh wahrgenommene Widerspruch zwischen den offiziellen Berichten über den Zustand unserer Gesellschaft, beziehungsweise über den "neuen Menschen" und dessen Wirklichkeit'.[27] Because of their structural similarities, verbal irony is a form which is particularly suited to manifesting the grotesque, and in Hensel's texts there is considerable overlap between the two. Irony can be used to establish the grotesque, as it creates the necessary distance. Unlike the grotesque, though, irony intends to invoke judgement and implies more distance from the values at stake; it is a linguistic technique, which has an intellectual effect, rather than

---

[25] D. C. Muecke, *The Compass of Irony* (London: Methuen, 1969), 19–20.
[26] Linda Hutcheon, *A Theory of Parody*, 94.
[27] Hensel, in interview with Hammer, 'Gespräch mit Kerstin Hensel', 94.

provoking physical or emotional affect. Significantly, Hensel's oeuvre displays a shift over time away from the physicality of the grotesque towards linguistic and literary irony.

In this chapter, I explore some of the interlinked manifestations of the grotesque in Hensel's prose. In the first section, I analyse images of the bodily grotesque, which encompasses both representations of the body and the depiction of uncontrollable urges. The representation of the body in Hensel's work draws on four key aspects of the grotesque: the transgression of the body's boundaries; the distorted body; attributes such as ugliness and strength, which are grotesque when they contradict conventional social signification of the body; and finally hybrid combinations of the human and other. Both descriptions of the body and representations of drives result in linguistic grotesque, where language and, ultimately, the text are rendered unstable. In the second section, I look at instances of narrative grotesque: Hensel's unpredictable plots, her parodies of 'Märchen', and the parody of the montage novel in *Auditorium panopticum*.

BODY

Hensel's texts emphasize physicality in many ways. Her third-person narratives focus not primarily on the psychology of her characters, but rather on their corporeal existence—they are characterized by their appearance, their bodily functions and acts. Frauke Meyer-Gosau notes that Hensel's work contains 'Lust, Sinnlichkeit, Genuß—es wird gefressen, gesoffen, gevögelt, daß es eine Art hat'.[28] These resemble the activities performed by the grotesque body, according to Bakhtin:

Eating, drinking, defecation and other elimination (sweating, blowing of the nose, sneezing), as well as copulation, pregnancy, dismemberment, swallowing up by another body—all these acts are performed on the confines of the body and the outer world, or on the confines of the old and new body.[29]

---

[28] Frauke Meyer-Gosau, 'Aus den Wahnwelten der Normalität: Über Brigitte Kronauer, Elfriede Jelinek und Kerstin Hensel', in Heinz Ludwig Arnold (ed.), *Vom gegenwärtigen Zustand der deutschen Literatur* (Munich: text + kritik, 1992), 26–37, here 35.

[29] Bakhtin, *Rabelais and his World*, 317.

In this section, I focus on grotesque images of the body and grotesque acts. These two aspects are concerned with the physical form and the boundaries of the body, as well as its social signification. I look first at laughter, then bodily fluids and childbirth, before turning to the gendered attributes of strength and beauty. As Butler and Kristeva suggest, an unstable body also threatens the stability of society. Hensel's texts demonstrate that the transgression of norms of the body calls into question the social system and the definition of the human; ultimately, both grotesque representations of the body and its acts unsettle language.

Images of the body

One of the key forms of physical expression in Hensel's texts is laughter. Laughter is grotesque as it enacts a lack of control over one's own body, and, in extreme forms, distorts the faces of those who laugh; it is a motif within the 'histoire' which mirrors the humour of the narrative 'discours'. By its very corporeal nature, the physical aspect of laughter is opposed to the logocentric reason which constitutes society. Just as the grotesque has the potential to subvert social norms but not replace them, laughter cannot formulate an alternative to these norms—this is, however, precisely its power. Marianne Schuller explains:

Das Lachen läßt sich nicht formulieren zu einer kritischen Gegenstimme der Opposition, die einen ausmachbaren Platz und eine kalkulierbare Funktion im Machtspiel zugewiesen bekommen könnte. Vielmehr setzt das Lachen auch noch diese machtfunktionale Regel der Bipolarität außer Kraft. Sie fällt gewissermaßen ins Leere. Denn das Lachen ist nur die andere Wahrheit als 'Wahrheit des Anderen'.[30]

In 'Ritter Rosel oder Das nullte Gefecht', in the GDR edition of *Hallimasch,* Diether the blacksmith finds strength in laughter to resist the taunts of 'Weibs-Mann' which his weakness provokes in the village, and to reject the social norms which exclude him. His laughter is uninhibited and uncontrollable:

Da war es auch schon wieder, jenes Lachen, das durch die Schmiede lief. Von innen kam es, aus der Feuerglut hervor, aus dem Werkzeug,

[30] Schuller, in Stephan, Weigel, and Wilhelms (eds.), '*Wen kümmert's, wer spricht*', 68.

aus den Armen den Beinen dem Kopf und dem Mund des Schmiedes. Hahahahaha! Es dröhnte wie Donner, es lachte der Schmied, und das war seine einzige wirkliche Kraft. (*H* 212–13)

The impersonal formulation 'es lachte der Schmied' is the sole reference to Diether, in contrast with the active associations of the disembodied laughter which invades him: 'lief', 'dröhnte wie Donner', and the force suggested by the omission of commas (a device Hensel uses frequently) in 'aus den Armen den Beinen dem Kopf'.

In Hensel's texts, laughter is more frequently associated with female figures who attempt to reject their culturally prescribed role, such as Ritter Rosel and Mechthild, in 'Kotterba'. The physicality of laughter is closely linked to sexuality, as well as to the expression of subjectivity. Mechthild's laughter is a denial of male authority, and specifically a response to her husband's attempts to subjugate her sexually. After she discovers he has raped her while she was asleep, she 'begann zu lachen und lachte, sie lachte eine Koloratur' (*H* 118). In laughing, Mechthild rejects her husband's sexual advances and undermines his power over her. Hers is an extreme laughter, a form of 'Lachkrampf' which contorts her features: 'sie sieht dabei so häßlich aus, furchtbar rot und verzerrt' (*H* 112). Mechthild Labuhn's are reminiscent of the contorted features Bakhtin notes as being typical of the 'grotesque life of the body'.[31] She is not recognizably human and frightens her son Gösta. Such contortion is all the more horrifying in the case of Ritter Rosel, whose face is already scarred and deformed: 'Harald sah zwei Dinge, die ihn abermals lähmten: Rosel zitterte nicht, sie kicherte unablässig und hemmungslos. Und sie tat es mit einem furchtbaren Gesicht' (*H* 218). Her face is distorted into a threatening, bestial pose when she laughs: 'so tat sie, wenn sie lachte, entblößte Zahnfleisch und Zähne wie eine Stute' (*H* 223). Rosel's laughter is just as terrifying as her deformity; both signal a woman outside the bounds of social acceptability.

In Hensel's texts, the body is a mutable object, whose margins are unstable. Bodily fluids and excretions highlight the permeability of the body and its border with the outside world. The repulsion experienced on encountering these fluids has

---

[31] Bakhtin, *Rabelais and his World*, 308.

its origin in the threat of pollution; female bodily fluids are a particular source of threat, due to their association with sexuality. Childbirth also demonstrates that individual bodies are not discrete, separate objects. Bakhtin considers childbirth as a crucial image of the grotesque, as the body has to expel something which is alien to it, which begins as a kind of growth within the body, and which crosses the boundary of life and death.[32] Although these functions are natural, society suppresses displays of the body's physicality, with the result that they come to be considered grotesque. Hensel's texts do contain images of male bodies whose boundaries are transgressed—Gero Schloff (*Auditorium panopticum*) gives birth to Ingrid Tabea through his chest and Herr Botho in 'Ritter Rosel' walks around impaled by a lance—but more frequently, the grotesque images are of female bodies and bodily fluids, pointing to the particular suppression of women's bodies in society.

Grotesque depictions of bodily functions in Hensel's texts vary in the reaction they provoke, between humour and horror; the narrative perspective mediates the effect. Bodily fluids can be a sign of physical intimacy: comically, the twins in 'Hallimasch' urinate together to seal their inseparability: 'Das begießen wir' (*H* 84); and in *Tanz am Kanal*, Katka shows Gabriele her menstrual blood in the toilet as a sign of friendship. However, where intimacy with an other is undesirable or forbidden, bodily fluids are perceived as physically threatening and reactions tend towards horror rather than humour. They provoke disgust, a visceral, instinctive reaction, and one of the elements of the grotesque. Disgust is the flipside of desire: it is a response to uninvited, excessive intimacy and is linked to a fear of contagion.[33] Hensel parodies this fear in the speech of the Valkyrie Ingrid Tabea, where menstrual blood is portrayed as toxic and contaminating: 'Wenn das Weib den Samen, so geht ihr das Blut da herum, das heißet "Menstrualis". [...] Wo man es hingießt, dorret das Kraut davon, die Bäume welken davon, und welcher Hund das Blut frißt, der wird tobend' (*AP* 57). Such obvious

---

[32] Ibid. 320.
[33] See Konrad Paul Liessman, ' "Ekel! Ekel! Ekel!—Wehe mir!" Eine kleine Philosophie des Abscheus', *Kursbuch*, 129 (1997), 101–10. Marven, "Wie ein Festmahl nach langer Hungerszeit", deals with the links between disgust, eating, and sex.

exaggeration is humorous, rather than threatening, all the more so as these outdated beliefs are expounded in archaic language. In other contexts feminine excretions are still experienced as threatening. The lonely Frau Richter in 'Grus', for example, has one 'Hoffnung', for physical intimacy, and her desire is expressed physically:

> Sie harrt und an ihr läuft die Hoffnung zusammen. Aber die Hoffnung riecht. Sie riecht ein wenig, wie Frau Richter riecht. Etwas dunstig, ein bißchen nach Fisch und Schmalz [...] die Hoffnung läuft in Strömen [...] es riecht, riecht nach Fisch und Schmalz und Blüten vom Schellenbaum, die Hoffnung läuft die Beine herab auf den Flurboden. (*H* 41)

As an old woman and a single female, Frau Richter's desire is not sanctioned by society; this social transgression is mimicked physically by her body, whose boundaries are not stable and which therefore encroaches upon the outside world. The appeal to the reader's sense of smell is striking: the formulation 'riechen *nach*' is stronger than any metaphor or simile and the cumulative effect of the repetition recreates the horror felt at the bodily excretion.

The ambiguous reaction which characterizes the grotesque can be seen in two contrasting depictions of childbirth within *Hallimasch*, which veer from comic to horrific. The first is the birth of Uschka's child in 'Grus', a satirical 'DDR-Zeitgeschichte'.[34] Pregnancy and childbirth demonstrate a lack of control over one's own body; the growing child distorts the body and is an unknown entity: 'aus Uschka will etwas heraus' (*H* 50). In the description of the birth, humour is created by the reversal of priorities:

> [Uschka] öffnet sich ein wenig. Nach einem langgezogenen Uuuuh!, das sie ausstößt, ergießt sich ein Schwapp Fruchtwasser auf ein schon von vierundzwanzigtausend Schuhen zertretenes Löwenzahnbüschel am Wiesenrand Ecke Friedrich-Ludwig-Jahn-Allee. (*H* 50)

The physical involvement of the mother is an inarticulate, involuntary noise, signalling her reduction to a physical, rather than rational being. Her effort is dwarfed by the inordinate length of the participle construction and the street name, as well as the

---

[34] Hensel, in interview with Hammer, 'Gespräch mit Kerstin Hensel', 108.

enormous figure, which all detract from the immediate physicality of the birth, and make the disproportionate description comic. This depersonalized picture is mirrored in the following scene, when Uschka is hailed as the winner in the sporting contest as a result of her physical achievement. The commodification of motherhood is founded on the suppression of the bodily functions and pain involved in childbirth.

Whereas this passage is humorous, deliberately playing down physical suffering, the second allusion to birth is horrific. In 'Kotterba', a text which deals with the inhumanities of fascism, Mechthild Labuhn foretells the violent nature of her son in the unembellished description of his birth: 'Gott schickte Gösta, und Gösta zerriß ihr den Damm' (*H* 103). The simple paratactic structure emphasizes the violence of 'zerriß', and the unexpected connection of God and the perineum, the sacred and the intimate, further intensifies the scale of the damage. The matter-of-fact reportage makes this a repulsive, rather than humorous, image: without any distancing effect in the 'discours', the intimate physicality is immediate and unavoidable. *Gipshut* contains a third birth scene, which demonstrates the shift away from the physicality of the grotesque towards irony. As the dead-pan narrator of *Gipshut* reports Veronika Dankschön's weight gain and her inexplicable craving for fish, the reader cannot misinterpret what the backward Veronika obviously does: she is pregnant. The lack of control over one's body is, in Veronika's case, a lack of knowledge about her body. The drawn-out birth scene highlights not her physical ordeal, but the fact that Veronika got pregnant without knowing what was happening:

Dieser Krampf im Bauch! Veronika dachte, daß etwas in ihr vorgehe, was noch kein Mensch derart erfahren habe und was vielleicht, so dachte sie allen Ernstes, etwas mit dem zu tun habe, wovon jedermann im Dorf sprach, was sie nicht verstand, weil sie es nicht zu verstehen brauchte, um glücklich zu sein. (*G* 8)

Irony is signalled by the use of the subjunctive for Veronika's thoughts, and by the narratorial comment 'so dachte sie allen Ernstes'; the complex sentence structure is similarly evidence of the narrator's distance. However, this irony does not judge her ignorance, but those who have kept her ignorant, as the second half of the sentence makes clear. The real target here, as in much of Hensel's work, is the society which allows such discrepancies in power and knowledge to persist.

These images of bodies which overrun their boundaries touch upon concerns with female physicality. Hensel engages with expectations of femininity, as they relate to physical features as well as character traits and social roles. In her texts, the refusal to comply with social prescriptions of female beauty is coupled with resistance to the gender roles allocated by society. Almost all of her female protagonists are ugly (Lilit is the exception), and many possess the masculine attribute of strength; very few accept the restrictions placed on them as women. Hensel uses humour to defuse expectations of the feminine (rather than female) body, and to reveal the cultural standards which inform these expectations. The figure of Isolde in the short text 'Zurzach', in *Neunerlei*, exemplifies this approach: far from being the romantic beauty invoked by her name, she suffers from water retention and a skin complaint as a result of her job as a kitchen maid. Humour arises from the incongruity of her evocative name and her appearance, not least in descriptions of her obesity and 'die schwammigen Schenkel' which 'wie Pudding wabbeln' (*Nl* 119). Isolde's search for love is comic, rather than romantic, a fact which highlights the way in which love is implicitly associated with beauty. A similarly comic, pathetic hope for love is shown by Heike, in the landlord's tale in 'Lämmerdeern' (also in *Neunerlei*). Heike has a hook and pin for hands, after an accident: 'Sie war ein Wunder, obgleich ein Krüppel und auch im ganzen häßlich wie—' (*Nl* 110). By presenting that which is undesirable (ugliness, obesity) in an exaggerated form, the grotesque points to the socially prescriptive body images which exclude it, and challenges the authority of this exclusion.

In Hensel's prose texts the link between the visual expression of gender and conformity to socially determined gender roles is explored by means of grotesque connotations: aberrant female characters such as Rosel, Ulriche, and Ingrid Tabea are likened to animals or are associated with unruly nature. 'Ritter Rosel' illustrates that the transgression of norms of appearance and of behaviour is connected. The eponymous heroine is disfigured and by her status as an outcast is marked both by her appearance and by her rejection of conventional feminine attributes. Rosel has a 'furchtbar[es] Gesicht [...] gelb und fleckig [...] mit bräunlichen Narben überwachsen' (*H* 218), and is dubbed 'die Pferdegesichtige' (*H* 272): her lack of femininity is translated into a grotesque image of the non-human. Rosel seeks fulfilment in two non-sanctioned ways, through expressing her sexuality openly and by surreptitiously taking on the masculine role of 'Ritter', in which guise she saves her husband, the knight Harald. The fear provoked by Rosel's appearance and behaviour is the superstitious fear induced by the woman as outsider, uncontrollable and unpredictable. Her power to disrupt social order is symbolized by her tearing down a church with her bare hands. Rosel is compared to a witch and attributed with supernatural powers:

Wer es mit Rosel, der es mit einer Hexe. Kinder würde sie gebären mit Spiegelköpfen, kürbisgroß und Lügen zeigend. Wer diese Kinder anblickt, der würde sich selbst in ihnen sehen: verzerrt und verharnischt, seine wütendsten Träume könnten darin zu lesen sein, die verdrängten Wünsche: Verführer oder Mörder sein, Ritter oder in feinstem Adel. (*H* 222)

Several grotesque tropes are involved in these threats: the children's heads are not human; their mirror heads reveal distorted images; and they reflect repressed desires for sexual or violent excess. However, Rosel still arouses sexual reactions in the men who see her, despite, or more likely because of, her deformity and outsider status. Women also reject her: the beautiful Barbara believes Rosel's disfigurement is contagious; her face reveals the precariousness and superficiality of social acceptance. In a way, the disfigurement is catching: during the fight from which Rosel rescues him, Harald is badly scarred, but as a sign of his knightly prowess, this does not exclude him in the same way as she is excluded.

In *Ulriche und Kühleborn*, Ulriche also does not conform visually to the expected standard of beauty, just as she initially refuses to take on socially prescribed female characteristics. Ulriche is a grotesque image of Undine, the arch-feminine, mythical figure in Ingeborg Bachmann's 'Undine geht'; *Ulriche und Kühleborn* is a response to Bachmann's text.[35] Bachmann's is a short and sustained poetic monologue, portraying a state of being; Hensel's is a longer third-person narrative, which focuses on the physical processes of becoming and depicts the (incomplete) transformation of Ulriche into Undine. Her text starts from a point of difference: in opposition to Undine's traditional attributes, Ulriche is human, seems to possess a soul (she is 'Ulriche die Seelenreiche', *UuK* 5) and initially lives within society; it is only in being cast out and marginalized that she becomes 'fischig' (*UuK* 5) and takes to the water. 'Undine geht' is based on binary oppositions of earth/water, nature/culture, and art/society which, as Hélène Cixous argues, resolve into the fundamental binary pair of male/female.[36] While Undine represents one half of each set, Ulriche embodies both terms, undoing these oppositions. As her feminized male name (reminiscent of Moníková's protagonists) indicates, Ulriche is female but has male physical features: 'Nicht, daß ihr Leib reizend war: der Hintern flachplattig, die Brüste dünn, die Schultern breiter, als schön zu nennen wäre, die Beine mit starker Fessel' (*UuK* 15–16). Although her build and strength are ideal for her chosen trade, Ulriche is still judged against criteria of femininity—and found lacking. Moreover, Ulriche moves between land and water, belongs in society, and stands for both civilization and art in her work as stonemason. The difficulty she encounters is summed up in her self-definition as a 'Steinmetze' (one thinks here too of Moníková's Karla, the 'Stuntmännin'). The awkward feminized form points to the traditionally male nature of the stonemason's job and, in the pejorative 'Metze' (prostitute), to the fact that working women are still defined by sexuality.[37]

In the course of the text, Ulriche is forced by the community and Kühleborn into traditional spheres, but even when she becomes an undine, Ulriche resists mythicization by displaying an unsettling superimposition of the piscine on a human

---

[35] Ingeborg Bachmann, 'Undine geht', in *Das dreißigste Jahr* (Munich: dtv, 1966), 140–7. See also Mererid Puw Davies, 'Fishy Tales: Kerstin Hensel, *Ulriche und Kühleborn*', in Dahlke and Linklater (eds.), *Kerstin Hensel*, 51–66.

[36] Hélène Cixous and Catherine Clément, *La Jeune Née* (Paris: Union Générale des Éditions, 1975), see esp. 115–16.

[37] Dahlke, *Papierboot*, 165 n. 580.

body: 'Sie hat sich rücklings gedreht, paddelt leicht mit den Füßen und gleicht mit den zur Seite gehaltenen Armen ihre Lage aus' (*UuK* 13). Although her movement is that of a fish, Ulriche retains human arms and legs. Hybrid figures such as mermaids clearly have grotesque origins, in the combination of woman/fish, but in becoming a conventional literary image, they have lost the threatening aspect. Hensel's text restores the threat in the figure of Ulriche. Where Undine exists as the disembodied poetic voice of a familiar mythical figure, Ulriche, called 'Ungeheuer', in reference to Bachmann's text, is described as a 'Muräne' with 'Giftdrüsen an der Gaumenschleimhaut' (*UuK* 5), terms which point to an unpleasant physicality. Ulriche is a 'fischige[-] Abart' (*UuK* 29), a disturbingly literal translation of the half-woman, half-fish.

Like Ulriche, Regina in 'Ritter Rosel' and the Valkyrie Ingrid Tabea von Toracks, in *Auditorium panopticum*, challenge prescriptive notions of femininity by displaying the masculine attribute of strength. Regina 'war das Weib nicht' (*H* 229): she has 'baumstarke[-]' or 'schlächterstarke[-] Armen' (*H* 205 and 241) which are more suited to the work of a smith (her husband's job, although he is too weak to carry it out successfully), but she can only use this strength clandestinely. In *Auditorium panopticum*, Valkyrie Ingrid's dimensions and strength contradict expectations of a 'feminine' form. Just as Ulriche is a grotesque, because literal, version of Undine, the Valkyrie is reborn in a literal and very graphic enactment of the creation of Eve, emerging from between the fourth and fifth ribs of the unsuspecting Gero Schloff. Her physical appearance arouses fear in other characters—Gero is reduced to a gibbering wreck at the sight of her naked body—which is projected onto her body, in the similes used to describe her 'weißkohlgroße Brüste, die sie, wie Atlas die Weltkugel, von unten her anhob' and 'ihre Scham, aus welcher die inneren Lippen wie kleine rosa Elefantenohren heraushingen' (*AP* 38). The connotations of Atlas, the 'Weltkugel', and elephants all combine to create an image of gigantism. However, the over-exaggerated nature of the comparisons and the bathetic reference to the banal 'Weißkohl' deflate the threat posed by the grotesque associations, and distance is implied by the repeated 'wie', which focuses attention on the 'discours' rather than Ingrid in the 'histoire'. As a result, the effect is humorous not threatening (although not to Gero, who is hiding under the bedclothes). The Valkyrie leaves a physical token of her power over him:

> Er fand es in Form eines cirka fünfzig Zentimeter langen Haares, das, drahtig, an seinem Hosenbein haftete und das er sogleich als das Haar der Walküre identifizierte: allein die enorme Länge des Gewächses und dessen Durchmesser von einem Millimeter waren Beweis genug für die gesellschaftliche Untragbarkeit seines Ursprungswesens. (*AP* 86)

The hair, in a suggestive position, is unnatural, associated with danger and imprisonment ('drahtig', 'haftete') and of exaggerated dimensions. The Valkyrie, who embodies the danger of unbridled, predatory female desire, is 'gesellschaftlich untragbar': she must be excluded from society.

Hensel challenges the conventional association of woman and Nature in her descriptions of Ingrid the Valkyrie, undermining it by means of humour and exaggeration. Woman symbolizes nature in patriarchal discourse because of her marginal status as the Other; as such, she fluctuates between being part of human society, and merging with nature. Ingrid presents the grotesque implications of this trope. When she takes her apprehensive beloved, Gero, into the park to give him a lesson in human nature, she literally merges with nature in the shape of an elder bush:

> 'Guck mich an', befahl Ingrid Tabeas donnernder Baß. Gero senkte gehorsam den Kopf und sah mitten in den Hollerbusch hinein. Zwischen den Lenden der Walküre wuchs er, schwarz-fruchtig, zwei bis auf den Boden hängende Dolden, die Gero augenblicklich stark beeindruckten. [...]
> 'Ich vertrag's nicht, aber...' Gero sagte es zu den Dolden, die zu glänzen begannen, zart aromatische Blütenstände. Ingrid Tabea brachte ihren Leib noch einmal in die richtige Lage, drückte die Schenkel fester auf die Erde, daß Gero das Innere des Busches studieren konnte, wie ein Modell aus dem Biologischen Kabinett. (*AP* 56–7)

While the previous descriptions of Ingrid do not affect the reader, here both Gero and the reader are left unsure of the relationship between Ingrid and the elder; they cannot be disentangled. Significantly, this confusion arises in the face of women's sexual nature, reflected in the double entendre of the 'bush'. I return below to other, more exaggerated passages from *Auditorium panopticum* where grotesque images of the body entail a grotesque distortion and disorder in language.

'Das Licht von Zauche' draws on less extreme grotesque images of the distorted body in order to make visible social expectations of femininity. The short text, a satirical fairy tale about women who resort to magic in their pursuit of husbands, demonstrates the shift towards irony in Hensel's later work:

> Es ergab sich, daß die einsamen Frauen von Zauche eines Abends in der Nähe des Lustigberges auf einer Wiese zusammentrafen. Sie hatten ihre Tagesgeschäfte erledigt und waren alle gekommen: die Dünnhaarige, die Großköpfige, die Zweimeterfrau aus Oberjünne, die Rotäugige, die Schiefzahnige, die Grauhäutige, die dicke Margit, das Mädchen mit den Fadengliedern, die Mineralienforscherin, die Bücherleserin und natürlich die einbeinige Sylphe.[38]

The irony draws on expectations of genre, contrasting fairy-tale elements with comically banal, contemporary realist touches. The characterization of one character as 'die einbeinige Sylphe' (a phrase which got a huge laugh at a reading of the text by Hensel in Swansea) is ironic: the connotations of 'Sylphe'—a mythical, ethereal, graceful, beautiful creature—are entirely contradicted by the unattractive physicality of being one-legged. The other women have similarly grotesque features: they are excessively tall ('die Zweimeterfrau'), thin ('das Mädchen mit den Fadengliedern') or fat ('die dicke Margit'); they have odd proportions ('die Großköpfige') and possess demonic aspects ('die Rotäugige', 'die Schiefzahnige'). The list itself is ironic, initially defining the women by these abnormal physical characteristics, but suddenly changing topos with 'die Mineralienforscherin' and 'die Bücherleserin'. The comic shift suggests that scientific jobs and a predilection for reading are as abnormal as these physical aberrations, and therefore account for the women's unmarried status. Here Hensel plays on stereotypes of female scientists and bluestockings, whilst mocking such prejudice.

---

[38] Kerstin Hensel, 'Das Licht von Zauche', in Dahlke and Linklater (eds.), *Kerstin Hensel*, 1–4, here 1. The text was read by Hensel at 'Der Langsame Blick', conference at the University of Wales, Swansea, 30 Sept.–1 Oct. 2000.

The irony in 'Das Licht von Zauche' relies on linguistic markers such as register and lexical field in order to function. In other passages, descriptions of grotesque bodies enact other, more extreme forms of linguistic disruption. Kayser states that language becomes grotesque when it no longer represents the world, but misrepresents it or appears to act independently: 'Es ist die Sprache selber, die hier, genau verhört, die Welt verfremdet.'[39] Literalization of metaphors is one such technique, which presents the human as a mere element of speech and one wholly subsumed by the logic of language. In *Auditorium panopticum*, two staged descriptions of the naked male body bring into question both the human form and the use of metaphor to describe it. Self-styled poet Egmont eulogizes the vagabond Jonatan, and the anachronistic Friederike describes Egmont in passages which draw on typical manifestations of the grotesque to challenge conventional views of the sexual body and particularly the male genitals; the passages reverse gender conventions on several levels.[40] Hensel's work questions the ability of language to describe the human body, and here the grotesque is used to explore the erotic possibilities of language.[41] Carefully framed and written in character, the two descriptions emphasize the narrative voice and fictionality.

The erotic description of Jonatan by Egmont is a full three pages long, and is marked by a clear shift into a first-person narrative voice. Linklater calls the passage, which she refers to as a laudatio, 'an ironic comment on writing such as Verena Stefan's', where the attempt to create a new, positive form of language was rooted in the association of nature and woman.[42] Hensel's piece swaps the gender in question, and the exaggeration of Jonatan's features and the metaphors used to describe them further deconstructs this association. The reader's attention is focused on the 'discours', while the body itself is obscured.

---

[39] Kayser, *Das Groteske*, 177–8.
[40] The systematic reversal of gender in *Auditorium panopticum* is also apparent in a rape scene, where Egmont is gang-raped by a group of girls during the re-enactment of the battle of Waterloo (*AP* 169–70).
[41] See Linklater, '*Und immer zügelloser wird die Lust*'; and Dahlke, *Papierboot*, 216–18, and also Hensel, in interview with Dahlke in the same volume, 277.
[42] Linklater, '*Und immer zügelloser wird die Lust*', 197.

The main metaphor, to which Egmont returns throughout his panegyric, is the comparison of Jonatan's body to nature and to the landscape. This is Bakhtin's cosmic conception of the grotesque body, which is, and represents, the whole world: 'This body can merge with various natural phenomena, with mountains, rivers, seas, islands, and continents. It can fill the entire universe.'[43] Herta Müller's description of the child as a marsh in 'Niederungen' draws on this same topos, but is presented from within, in a first-person narrative. Here observer Egmont's eye travels 'den süßen Hügel hinauf, der sich, wo das Feld dichter zu werden beginnt, sanft aus der unteren Bauchseite erhebt' (*AP* 96) and he addresses 'mein Berg mit dem rötlich strahlenden Gipfel' (97). His gaze 'schwenkt [...] von des kühnen Astes Eichel in die Tiefe der Landschaft, wo sich das Feld in dichter Bepflanzung fortführt und an beiden birnengroßen Scrotii ihre Vollendung findet' (ibid.). The combination of man and nature is an archetypal motif in grotesque literature and sculpture, but here it is constructed solely through language. Jonatan's body becomes a whole landscape, external and internal, 'ein herrliches Plateau starker Muskulatur durchzieht wie eine Kastanie groß die Prostata' (98). The accumulation of words evoking large features suggests abnormal bodily proportions: the 'Krater' of his navel, 'Lichtungen' in his body hair, the 'Straße' of the urinary tract, and the 'Labyrinth' of his internal ducts and canals. Egmont's metaphors are grotesque in the discrepancy between the size of the object described and the enormity of the object to which it is compared, but the scale also keeps shifting, with the result that the relation between metaphor and subject becomes unstable.

Bakhtin's grotesque body experiences 'an interchange and an interorientation' with other bodies and the world.[44] Egmont experiences Jonatan as part of the surrounding landscape; 'Nicht genug kann ich von diesem Feld bekommen—will nicht innehalten—gehe ich weiter, so ist es ein Stück dem Ende entgegen. Die Stachelbeeren duften. Sehe ich den süßen Hügel hinauf [...]' (*AP* 96). Egmont's description jumps from metaphor (Jonatan's torso as a field or hill) to factual statement about the immediate surroundings, the gooseberries in

---

[43] Bakhtin, *Rabelais and his World*, 318.   [44] Ibid. 317.

the garden where Jonatan is standing. Jonatan appears as the backdrop against which Egmont sees the garden. More significant is the collapsing of the distance between the two men, something which is akin to intercourse: 'Doch nicht länger will ich verweilen am äußeren Anblick des vornehmenen Ortes—' exclaims Egmont, 'hindurch!' (97). Egmont's metaphorical penetration of Jonatan is the culmination of his eroticized, hyperbolic portrayal. His transgression of the boundaries of the body is mirrored in disruption of linguistic and syntactic order. The register shifts from formal references to the 'corpus penis' and 'ductus deferenz' to the scientific 'die hellsten Strahlen geradewegs—299 792,42 km/s hineinfallen' (ibid.) and technical, 'der Vorstehergang, dessen seltsamen amtlichen Namen ich lächelnd quittiere' (98). The hyperbolic invocation of 'die Römischen Götter' and the 'Urgrund der Zeugung, des Daseins Gänze und den Halt der Poesie bestimmt' (96 and 98) is deflated by the bathetic effect of Egmont's repeated use of diminutive forms: 'Löckchen', 'Säckchen', 'Löchlein'. In addition, the syntax of the passage is interrupted and incomplete, with frequent ellipsis. The continual shifting of register, focus (from Jonatan to Egmont), and plane (from the physical to the abstract philosophical), combined with the hyperbolic metaphors, prevents the reader from gaining a clear picture of Jonatan himself.

In a second scene, Egmont's disciple and secretary Friederike narrates her discovery of his naked form. Humour stems from Friederike's ignorance of the physical differences between the two sexes, and her inability to articulate these differences when she encounters them. Specifically, it arises from the gap between Friederike's perception of Egmont's body and what the reader knows to be the reality. The focus here is again diverted to language and the 'discours', the metaphors Friederike employs, rather than the ostensible subject of attention, Egmont's penis: Linklater aptly comments, '[a]s this scene progresses to orgasm the penis shrinks away to nothing'.[45] But this scene has an altogether more disturbing effect than the previous one. On first seeing Egmont naked, from behind, Friederike remarks: 'Es war mein erster Männerleib, und ich

---

[45] Linklater, '*Und immer zügelloser wird die Lust*', 199.

war nicht schlecht verwundert, daß er—von hinten—dem unsrigen, nur im geringem Maße anders gebildet, ähnelte' (*AP* 185). In accordance with Friederike's naive viewpoint, the male body is presented as deviating from the female model (and not vice versa), which leads to a comic reversal of Freud's view of the female genitals as a lack of the penis. Friederike's first impression of Egmont's manhood is of 'ein mir unbekannter, weicher, milchweißer Nabelfortsatz, den ich zwischen Egmonts Schenkeln entdeckte' (187). Here the penis is not only seen as an aberration from a female bodily norm, but also as a grotesque outgrowth from the body, an idea compounded when Friederike describes it as an independent entity, '[s]olch hilfloses Wesen' (187). To add insult to injury, this protrusion is given unmasculine connotations: it is vulnerable ('weich' and 'milchweiß') and arouses pity in Friederike, 'sogleich ob seiner lästigen Funktion, nutzlos zu sein' (187).

The imagery then shifts to another grotesque topos, that of the displaced member of the body, or the 'free play with the human body and its organs'.[46] Friederike discovers 'das Auge des Gebildes, das fast vollständig von einem faltigen Hautlid verdeckt war'; the metaphor of the penis as an eye is extended to comprise the 'zugegeben: unnatürliche[-] Pupille' and 'ein paar trübe Tränen' (187). Deciphering the image is part of the reader's enjoyment, and engagement; although it is an effective metaphor, there is no mistaking the penis for an eye. Even this metaphor is disrupted, however, as it cannot encompass the behaviour of Egmont's penis. A new one is needed: Friederike reports, 'da schoß ein Strahl warmer Tränen aus ihm heraus. Im nächsten Moment biß es mich in die gewölbte Handfläche' (188). An eye becomes a mouth, reflecting Friederike's confusion. The juxtaposition of the two separate images and their inadequacy as metaphors for the penis appears to reinforce the separation of the aesthetic from reality. However, the violence ('biß') is not figurative but literal: Friederike's hand 'blutete tüchtig' (188). The literalization of the metaphor disconcerts the reader, seeming, as it does, to collapse the distinction between the literary and the real. It is

---

[46] Bakhtin, *Rabelais and his World*, 345–6.

no longer clear what 'really' happens: the metaphor appears to create the action, rather than describe it (a device that Müller also uses). Friederike's description confronts the reader with two disconcerting possibilities, which are both funny and horrifying: that Egmont's body is abnormal, and Friederike's description is not metaphorical but literal; and that language does not reflect reality, but determines it.

Hensel's images of bodies emphasize that language is the medium through which the grotesque can be experienced, at the same time as problematizing its ability to describe. Bodily and linguistic manifestations of the grotesque are thus interlinked and their structures mirrored on different levels of the text. I now turn to the body's grotesque acts, the uncontrollable urges which are the dynamic counterpart to the static images of the body. These drives similarly entail a disruption in the movement and syntax of language and, ultimately, narrative discourse: they generate the grotesque plots I examine in the second section of this chapter.

Destructive desires: eating and sex

The acts of eating and having sex both have grotesque aspects, which are highlighted in Hensel's texts. Both take place on, and reconfigure, the boundaries of the body, through consuming food, or merging with another body in intercourse. These two processes become interchangeable in Hensel's texts: eating becomes a sexual act, and sex resembles the consumption of another body. The two acts are also connected in being generated by bodily drives and appetites, which, when taken to excess, can overrule the rational mind. In this way, they stage a loss of control and subjectivity in the individual, and in Hensel's texts both eating and sexual desire lead, in extreme cases, to violence and death. In this section, I examine grotesque depictions of eating and food; then the connections between eating and sex, appetites which culminate in violence; and finally, representations of sex and sexuality.

In Hensel's work, eating is a necessity which becomes a desire, one which takes over the individual. Hensel's reworked version of 'Hänsel und Gretel', 'Da ward gutes Essen aufgetragen' in *Hallimasch*, shows how the children collude in their imprisonment in order to get 'die berühmte Speise, die fett machen sollte' (*H* 147). They repress their knowledge of danger in order to satisfy their greed; it is only when the food gets worse and, finally, stops coming (because the old woman has died) that they formulate plans of escape. In the Rabelaisian orgy in 'Ritter Rosel', greed is a self-destructive impulse; the body's limits (its boundaries as well as its capacity) are ignored, transgressed, or overridden. When the poor villagers are invited to a feast by Herr Botho, they indulge themselves to excess. In one orgiastic scene, the villagers devour '[e]ine 80 Zoll lange und 5 Zoll dicke Blutwurst' (*H* 284), one after the other in a long line:

> Plötzlich fühlte der Bursche Druck auf seinem Darm. Und noch, bevor er den nächsten Bissen Wurst geschluckt hatte, öffnete sich sein Anus und entließ das eben Gegessene durch die Hose [...] dem Burschen kam die Blutwurst wieder—noch immer warm und duftend, vollkommen unversehrt und unverdaut. Das machte Appetit. Während der Bursche von der Wurst nach hinten weiter aß, biß ein nächster in die aus ihm wiedererscheinende Spitze. (*H* 285)

Needless to say, this is grotesque: the body's boundaries are transgressed in two ways simultaneously, as defecation and consumption merge. Harald watches the scene from the sidelines, while his mother gorges herself until she is literally fit to burst:

> Regina war die, die sich im Feste füllte bis an den äußersten Rand ihrer Haut. Und am Ende zog sie noch ihre Finger durch die Zähne, um das letzte mögliche zu erheischen. Es schmeckte ihr, geladen zu sein. Sie leckte kaute füllte sich auf. Sie rollte von der Bank, als ihre Haut nichts mehr einlassen wollte und riß. (*H* 286)

Regina '[hatte] sich totgefressen' (*H* 287), demonstrating how far this greed overrules the mind and ignores the body's limits. The 'Unmaß der Bauern [...]. Diese Sucht, zu fressen, zu naschen und alles nochmals und nochmals zu wiederholen' (*H* 285–6) is their own downfall. Like 'Da ward gutes Essen...' and 'Herr Johannes', 'Ritter Rosel' contains satirical allusions to the GDR, and these orgiastic scenes are an extraordinarily prescient depiction of the excesses of capitalism which engulfed the GDR after the fall of the Berlin Wall.

In texts with more modern settings, the focus is on what is eaten, rather than how it is eaten. During the Second World War, the normal order of things no longer holds and texts set during the war feature grotesque foodstuffs: a cat in 'Katzenbericht', and a pet tortoise in 'Vogelgreif', illustrating the desperation of the population. In 'Hallimasch', the poisonous Hallimasch mushroom is the last recourse of a starving folk. It becomes shorthand for deprivation: '1902 ist ein Pilzjahr' (*H* 90). In an interview, Hensel says the Hallimasch represents the 'Wucherung des Gewöhnlichen [...] des Eßbaren, aber doch latent Schädlichen, des Lebensnotwendigen, das keinen delikateren Kompromiß zuläßt'.[47] Hensel's description of the 'Wucherung des Gewöhnlichen' sums up the grotesque precisely. While these foodstuffs are grotesque because they are culturally unacceptable, other, more normal foodstuffs are made grotesque by anthropomorphization. Human characteristics possessed by animals, and their appeal to human sexuality, problematize their status as food. In the screenplay script 'Der Wasserwalzer', in the GDR edition of *Hallimasch*, the heroine Bettina is confronted by a lobster:

der Hummer muß der Hotelküche entlaufen sein, denn er ist rot und dampft und trägt eine Zitroneschale mit sich herum. Bettina ist erst erschrocken, dann belustigt, sie schluckt voller Appetit. Der Hummer klappt aufgeregt mit den Scheren. (*H* 28)

The colour and condition of the lobster (complete with lemon) are consistent with its being dead, and therefore edible, yet it is running around and even speaks. The anthropomorphization makes the act of eating the animal more akin to cannibalism, something that the lobster itself points out, saying its eyes are 'blind und schwarz' (i.e. not recognizably human) 'damit du mich besser fressen kannst' (*H* 28).[48] At this, Bettina kisses the lobster: her appetite is transformed into a desire for sexual consumption.[49] In an early prose text, 'Die Kette der Ricke', the hunted doe exists simultaneously as animal and food: 'Vierfüßiges Suppenfleisch ist die Bedingung für den

---

[47] Hensel, in interview with Hammer, 'Gespräch mit Kerstin Hensel', 107.
[48] The play on the wolf's words in 'Rotkäppchen' points to the grotesque motifs in fairy tales; see below for Hensel's versions of 'Märchen'.
[49] In Hensel's little-known play 'Thaiwans Leibchen: 12 Tee Aberstücke', the reverse happens: a talking cow is 'totgeküßt' and then 'am Spieß gebraten', Kerstin Hensel, 'Thaiwans Leibchen: 12 Tee Aberstücke', *INN Zeitschrift für Literatur*, 10/31 (1993), 67–9, here scenes 9 and 11.

mangelnden Geschmack meiner Gedanken.'[50] The projection of its fate as meat onto the animal is grotesque, as it makes its imminent demise visible: the animal is simultaneously dead and alive.

The converse image of the human as food presents the individual as mere object to be consumed. In 'Die Kette der Ricke', a revolution is described in terms of eating: 'Wir haben den Kaiser gegessen, Himmel! [...] O wir haben den Kaiser gegessen, die Kronen geraspelt. Die Paläste auf dem Landsitz der Mägen.'[51] The Kaiser is dehumanized by being compared to food, which is the necessary precondition for his demise and the consequent reversal of power. More frequently, the connotations are sexual. In 'Das Spiel der Billabohne', in *Neunerlei*, the naive Billabohne fails to register sexual desire, but instead wants to eat Anke. It is the visual similarities between the girl and food which attract him.

Er schaute Anke an. Die so spontan war und die wie ein Hühnchen aussah. Das fiel ihm plötzlich ein. Anke trug die Schultern entblößt.
Sie war so zart. Wie ein Hühnchen, das Billabohne jedes Wochenende im *Ranstädter Büfett* aß, ohne Appetit, hastig und genußlos. Nun sah er Anke. [...] Billabohne schmeckte Hühnchen nicht, das einzige, was er empfand beim Biß in das Fleisch: zart, glatt, weiß. Anke hatte nackte Schultern. In die wollte Billabohne hineinbeißen, irgendwie, wollte Geschmack empfinden, endlich einmal Geschmack! (*Nl* 53)

Billabohne's childlike behaviour is seen in his lack of appetite, and he fails to recognize his desire to eat Anke as sexual. Other male characters are not so reticent. In 'Lilit', Hensel's rewriting of the myth of Lilith in *Hallimasch*, the sexually voracious Adam sees Lilit as his possession and her 'Leib wie eine Frucht' (*H* 8) for his delectation. Ritter Rosel makes this point at her wedding banquet: as a knight's bride, she is a mere commodity, and she makes the connection explicit by proffering herself as part of the sumptuous feast. Jumping suddenly onto the table, Rosel 'raffte den Rockschoß und hockte sich schnittgerecht mit blankem Arsch gegen die Messer' (*H* 252). The illustration to this text shows Rosel next to a roast pig's head, giving the two visual equivalence.

[50] Kerstin Hensel, 'Die Kette der Ricke', *Sinn und Form*, 42/1 (1990), 528.
[51] Ibid.

In Hensel's most recent text, *Im Spinnhaus*, a similar occurrence draws its impact from its context during the Second World War: women forcibly prepare a shopkeeper as a joint of meat for roasting, covering him with salt, herbs, and bacon—'Die alte Uhligen stopfte in jede Wunde einen Speckstreifen. Schweigend, als ob sie nicht wußte, was sie tat.'[52] He is saved by the Russians: 'Die Russen sahen den gespickten Mann vor sich und stürzten sich auf ihn.'[53] Far from the bawdy comedy and vague historical setting of 'Ritter Rosel', this passage verges on horror, mitigated only by distancing effects in the 'discours', the echo of biblical language, 'she knew not what she did' in the first quotation here, and our realization that (as an earlier draft of the novel made clear) the Russians might not be rushing to free the man, but to eat the bacon.

The desire to consume the other metaphorically links eating and sex; in Hensel's texts, it becomes the attempt to devour and destroy the other. Critic Jean-Pierre Richard describes this relationship as:

> la voration: engloutissement primitif d'un être par un autre, puis sa digestion, son assimilation [...] l'interpénétration, prenant alors valeur cosmique, devient une des catégories de l'appétit: Toute la nature que nous avons sous les yeux est mangeante et mangée. Les proies s'entremordent.[54]

In the pursuit of the other, which cannot be fully assimilated (devoured) during sex, individuals are dehumanized by being reduced to the level of predator/prey. The combination of sex, consumption, and killing is at the heart of the tale 'Das Mittwochsmenü', in *Neunerlei*. Museum curator Endenthum's desire for the artist Katka Lorenz is unrequited and repressed. It resurfaces as murderous intent: he kills her with poisonous sugar, and by gorging himself on confectionery as she expires, he is able to join her in death. Endenthum's sudden inexplicable craving for confectionery is another expression of the 'Triebe' which led to his murder: 'Plötzlich verspürt Endenthum rasenden Appetit. Noch nie im Leben hatte er einen

---

[52] Kerstin Hensel, *Im Spinnhaus* (Munich: Luchterhand, 2003), 180.
[53] Ibid.
[54] Jean-Pierre Richard, *Essai sur le romantisme* (Paris: Seuil, 1970), 187, cited as a frontispiece in David Bevan (ed.), *Literary Gastronomy* (Amsterdam: Rodopi, 1988).

solchen Appetit' (*Nl* 102-3). The formulation 'verspürt' suggests Endenthum is possessed by this appetite, just as he was obsessed by his desire for Katka. The symbolism of the confectionery is clear: the food is a substitute for the female body. Endenthum's first dish is 'ein rosa umzuckertes Törtchen', decorated with a 'Zuckergußrosette' which Endenthum savours. The language of the passage reveals the sensual pleasure in his eating: 'Schiebt die Gabel flach darunter, hebt die Rosette ab. Steck sie in den Mund. Endenthums Zunge drückt die Rosette gegen den Gaumen. Sie löst sich auf, breitet ihre ganze Süße aus' (*Nl* 103). The careful prose and concentration of detail shows the sensuality of the experience, and the shape and colour of the rosette are an obvious reference to the female sex. The sexual connotations are made even more explicit with Endenthum's next dish, an éclair, '[a]uch Liebesknochen genannt' (*Nl* 103). Consumption is the consummation of Endenthum's desire, and its ultimate sating.

In 'Das Mittwochsmenü', eating is a substitute for sex, although both are subordinate to the death drive. The balance shifts in the case of Ingrid Tabea, whose uncontrollable and indiscriminate eating signals an equally voracious sexual appetite:

> Nackt wie sie war, [...] durchstöberte sie das enge Wohnzimmer und suchte nach Eßbarem. In einem Nachtisch fand sie eine angebrochene Packung Keks, auf dem Fensterbrett eine halbe, in fettiges Papier gewickelte Leberwurst, unter der Heizung schließlich zwei Stück Würfelzucker. Sie steckte alles in den Mund, kaute Keks, Leberwurst und Zucker. (*AP* 37)

Ingrid's desire is initially expressed through eating. Gero fears, 'augenblicklich von der Dame gefressen zu werden' (*AP* 39), and as Ingrid consumes seven sausages in a row, she exhorts Gero not to flee: '"Nix da, Liebster. Hier bleibste. Ich will mich nur schnell stärken, dann sollst du die Freuden des Lebens erfahren." Sprachs und biß in die Wurst, daß es spritzte' (*AP* 47). The phallic symbolism is obvious—Ingrid's ravenous appetite is to be matched by her sexual one—but its exaggeration is comic. When Gero and Ingrid eventually have sex, these associations are taken further:

> WEHR DICH! rief sie, wenn Gero Anstalten machte, in ihr zu versinken. Sein Leib wurde von Ingrids Ausmaßen geschluckt—ihre

Schamlippen schlossen die Hälfte seiner Hüftpartie ein, stülpten sich pulsierend um sommersprossige Haut. (*AP* 252)

The overt play on the function of the 'Scham*lippen*' suggests another connection between sex and eating, which is demonstrated in the sexual connotations of Ingrid's 'appetite'. Gero is 'geschluckt', and disappears physically into her body. Moreover, when he is made impotent by Ingrid's powers, this is translated into a loss of appetite: 'Seit Wochen keinen Bissen herunterbekommen. Auch keine Verdauung. Zwar Hunger, aber nie Appetit' (*AP* 147). Interestingly, Sigrid Lange sees this impotence as having other oral connotations: 'Impotenz als Oppositionsbegriff zu Lust metaphorisiert nichts weniger als "selbstverschuldete Unmündigkeit".'[55] The mouth is the locus of concerns with sexuality, eating, and expression; the ability to express sexual desire is a key aspect of subjectivity.[56]

In Hensel's work, however, sexuality is one of the 'Triebe' which Kayser saw as inherently grotesque because they take over the body and the individual. Hensel depicts sexuality not as the expression of identity, but as a force which takes over the individual and subsumes their identity. The figure of Don Juan, a recurrent motif in Hensel's work, illustrates the interrelation of sexuality and the grotesque.[57] Hensel deals with the mythical figure in the analytical essay 'Abschied von Don Juan', in *Angestaut: Aus meinem Sudelbuch*, and the character appears as 'Herr Johannes' in the eponymous tale, and in the poem 'Monolog des Herrn Johannes', also in *Angestaut*. Hensel's theoretical view of Don Juan, the fictional embodiment of destructive desire, recalls the phenomenon of the grotesque. Hensel sees Don Juan as the anomalous product of a system in collapse: he is both one of the nobility, whose values and existence are threatened, and also the exaggerated reflection of the 'Verkommenheit der Leute' (*An* 19). According to Bakhtin, the grotesque as a phenomenon appears when the values of a society are no longer seen as absolute, and this is precisely the

---

[55] Sigrid Lange, 'Topographische Irritationen: Frauenliteratur nach dem Ende der DDR', *Colloquia Germanica*, 27 (1994), 255–73, here 266.

[56] Towards the end of the novel, Ingrid goes on hunger strike in protest at the conditions in the briquette factory, breaking it only after having sex with Gero, illustrating the conjunction of eating, sex, and the expression of subjectivity.

[57] See also Marven, "Wie ein Festmahl nach langer Hungerszeit".

moment when Hensel's Don Juan emerges: 'Befindet sich das System in Auflösung, erlischt die Fiktion des Adels, wird Juan, beim ersten Anzeichen der *maroden* Macht, der er angehört, besinnungslos und startet sein Geschäft' (*An* 19). Juan both embodies and accelerates the collapse of the value-system which produced him: he is the expression of a greater power, the 'marode Macht' of sexuality itself. The overthrow of a familiar system provokes an ambivalent reaction and Juan, who undoes the cultural suppression of sexual desire, is no exception: he 'both fascinates and appals'.[58]

Hensel's grotesque representations of sex and sexuality show the latent tendencies of a society where the body is suppressed: the fear of sexuality (a fear of losing control) finds an outlet in the very excess which it seeks to contain. Don Juan is the grotesque product of society's values: he is 'nicht der Sieger über die Dumpfheit und Indolenz der Gesellschaft, sondern der andere, unerträgliche Pol derselben' (*An* 26). He is a symbol of extremity and 'Unmaß', a term which recurs in 'Herr Johannes' in relation to Johannes himself; the sexuality Johannes embodies and awakens in the women he encounters is forbidden by society, because its all-encompassing nature threatens the existence of society itself. It is impossible to incorporate 'das, was von der Gesellschaft als Sünde deklariert ist' (*An* 21) into the fabric of society, because it is precisely its sinfulness which makes it desirable. When the character of Herr Johannes is invited back into the city in Hensel's tale, in other words, he is made part of the ruling symbolic order, he dies and the city is destroyed.

The destruction of the city is the result of the sexual desire which Herr Johannes arouses in the women, who 'geraten außer Kontrolle' (*An* 26), and it is the destructive potential of unleashed female sexuality which is Hensel's real focus. In some texts, conventional gender roles are reversed, and women like Ingrid Tabea are perceived, and feared, as sexual predators; in other tales, like 'Herr Johannes' and 'Stinopel', grotesque imagery and exaggeration are used to stage the 'befürchtete[-] ordnungszerstörende[-] Lust' projected onto women by men.[59]

---

[58] J. W. Smeed, *Don Juan: Variations on a Theme* (London: Routledge, 1990), 4.
[59] Lange, 'Topographische Irritationen', 264.

The threat posed by female sexuality is sublimated into more tangible notions of physical danger and played out in mythical scenarios of destruction, in which desire is represented as cosmic force.

One way of signifying and thus controlling female sexuality is to portray it as illness or madness. When the women of Sankt Veit rediscover their carnality, each husband initially 'tat seine Pflicht, um sie nicht zu kränken' (*H* 151). Lange observes a connection between the sexual desire rediscovered by the women of Sankt Veit in 'Herr Johannes' and the medical phenomenon of 'Tanzwut' or 'Veitstanz':

> Benannt nach dem ursprünglich therapeutischen Heiligen, Sankt Veit und seines auch Johannistag genannten Feiertages [...] bezeichnet der Veitstanz eine vom 13. bis ins 17. Jahrhundert hinein nachgewiesene mittelalterliche Epidemie. Ihr medizinisches Krankheitsbild hat unverkennbar kulturelle Konturen: 'Müßiggängern' und 'abenteuerlichen Weibern' zugeschrieben, äußert sie sich in einem zwanghaften Trieb zu bacchantischen Tänzen mit ansteckender Wirkung—die Weltordnung geriet aus den Fugen.[60]

The condition reflected (the disruption of) social norms—in her essay, Hensel describes the women's despair and desire similarly as driving them to 'hexischen Grenzen' (*An* 26). Women's disorderly sexuality was reinscribed as a medical condition—here verging on hysteria—and pathologized as a lack of control over their own bodies, again denying them subjectivity.

In 'Stinopel', the pathologization of female sexuality is taken further, and it is linked to madness: the sexual desires of Gretel take the form of hallucinatory fantasies. Untouched by her husband Mäxi Mühe, she is visited nightly by his diabolical alter ego Henry, and conjures up exotic locations—Baghdad or the Nile—in her own bedroom. Gretel's imagination and her sexual desire are seen as insanity: 'Grausam war das Weib, verleiert, krachidiotisch' (*Nl* 160). Not only is 'Stinopel' interesting for this conflation of sexual fantasy and madness, but it also suggests a further connection between sexual liberation and the imagination. One of the key ideas expounded by Sandra Gilbert and Susan Gubar in *The Madwoman in the Attic* is that the figure of the madwoman is a cipher for female creativity, as

---

[60] Lange, 'Topographische Irritationen', 265.

well as sexuality.[61] Applying this to Hensel's text, one might say that Gretel is the author of her own desires, who gives herself another name (Else) and, for a short while at least, creates a fantastic world in which she can express her own sexuality. Refiguring female sexuality as Other (exotic, ill, mad) cannot however neutralize its power—far from it. The infernal power which allows Gretel to fulfil her dreams and desires ultimately destroys not only her, but the whole village of Stinopel. When she receives the 'Höllenjunge' Henry, she is taken to, and comes to be identified with, the gates of hell itself:

> Henry fing 's Gretel von nun an nächtlich ab. Er gab sich großmütig wie ein Prinz, hielt sich schwefelfrei und närrisch. Das liebte sie. Immer taten sie ihres gleich an der Pforte. Weiter hinten lärmte die Hölle ungewohnt, krachte und knackte und dehnte sich. Nächtlich holte sich 's Gretel das teuflische Vergnügen. (*Nl* 158)

Sexuality is seen as the expression of more potent powers: the individual is only a channel. Gretel drowns one night—Mäxi 'hatte den zärtlichen Nildamm gebrochen' (*Nl* 160). The ambiguous and suggestive term 'Nildamm' confuses fantasy and reality: the image functions simultaneously as Gretel's hallucination and as a euphemism for Mäxi attempting to penetrate his virginal bride, and manifests in Gretel's death. When Gretel drowns, hell itself opens up and engulfs the village in a cosmic revenge for her repression.

Female sexuality, synecdochically the female genitalia, is considered dangerous because it threatens to engulf the male and swallow everything up: the vagina becomes a grotesque image of the maw of hell. In her essay on Don Juan, Hensel makes clear the sexual connotations of his demise in an abyss: 'Mit *Blitz* und *Donner* geht er in die sich *spaltende* Erde, die Geovagina gibt Juans Abschiedsvorstellung und nimmt ihn auf ewig' (*An* 27, Hensel's italics). The topographical and the bodily converge, as the conventional conflation of woman and nature assumes grotesque dimensions. In Hensel's Don Juan version, 'Herr Johannes', the destruction of society by the uncontrollable female desire unleashed by Herr Johannes is superseded

---

[61] Sandra M. Gilbert and Susan Gubar, *The Madwoman in the Attic: The Woman Writer and the Nineteenth-Century Literary Imagination* (New Haven: Yale University Press, 1979).

by nature's devastation of the city. Gretel, whose pleasure is demonic, is—along with the insatiable 'Magd Konstanze', who sleeps with the entire village in the same tale—a female image of Don Juan's sexual excess. The petty, materialistic village of Stinopel forms a modern, capitalist counterpart to Sankt Veit, and, like Sankt Veit, Stinopel is destroyed when the gates of hell open. In Bakhtin's grotesque cosmic body, the gaping entrance to the underworld which swallows Juan is also an image of the mouth. Writing about the myth of Don Juan, Shoshana Felman suggests that it is 'le mythe de la bouche, en tant que la bouche est précisément le *lieu médiateur entre le langage et le corps*'.[62] And so we return to narrative: the repeated image is ultimately a symbol of the exaggeration of storytelling which both 'Herr Johannes' and 'Stinopel' display. Don Juan's legacy in Hensel's work is not only that of a concern with the 'lebensnotwendigen Exzeß' (*An* 23), the grotesque drive which all too frequently proves destructive. More significantly, it is also a legacy of narrative excess, the taking to extremes of characters, plot, and narrative structures, a tendency Herr Johannes himself, in the 'Monolog des Herrn Johannes', sums up: 'Die Dinge laufen ungeahnte Bahnen' (*An* 16).

Desire and language

I return to Hensel's narrative grotesque in the second half of this chapter, but first I wish to explore in more detail the links between sex and language in Hensel's texts, in particular, two different manifestations of desire in language. In 'Lilit', language manifests the uncontrollable drives to which the protagonists of Hensel's tales succumb. Drawing on Kristeva's theory of the 'sujet en procès', which expresses itself by incorporating 'Triebe' into language, Weigel describes a form of 'Körper-Sprache' which can clearly be linked to the grotesque:

Diese Momente, die [Kristeva] unter dem Begriff des 'Semiotischen' faßt, sind z.B. Gestik, Mimik, Rhythmus des Sprechens und der Atmung, Intonation, Melodie, Reim, Lautmalereien und Artikulationen, die wie die 'Glossolalie', das Zungenreden, der Wortgestaltung

---

[62] Shoshana Felman, *Le Scandale du corps parlant: Don Juan avec Austin ou la séduction en deux langues* (Paris: Seuil, 1980), 76.

vorausgehen. Impliziert das Sprechen, indem es das Dargestellte in Bildern, Worten bzw. eindeutigen Benennungen festhält, immer einen Schnitt gegenüber der pulsierenden Bewegung des Lebendigen, so vollzieht sich in den Äußerungen des 'Semiotischen' ein Einbruch der Triebe in die Sprache. Soweit die genannten Momente die Materie der Sprache bzw. den Sprach-Körper betreffen, läßt sich eine entsprechende poetische Praxis vor allem als sprechende, d.h. mündliche Sprache denken oder aber in Schriftformen, die dem Lyrischen verwandt sind. Für Prosa oder erzählende Genres wird damit der Bezug zur Materie und zum Körper um so bedeutsamer.[63]

The radically disrupted syntax and oral language which Weigel posits can be seen in 'Lilit'. Written entirely without punctuation, the short text is a breathless stream of consciousness narrated in the third person. The metaphor of a 'stream' of consciousness is reflected in the text, as the river in Eden functions as a symbol of Adam's unbounded sexual desire. The narrative further reflects this desire in its continual forward movement; in this, it manifests the process of continual deferral which underlies the Lacanian assertion that desire behaves like a language. In particular, the text blurs the lines between discrete syntactical units, as the opening few lines demonstrate: 'Sie sieht was ihr auserwählt wurde stumm und zweifelnd sieht sie unfähig zu empfinden was der Vater ihr zugedacht hat an Glück ja womöglich soll es Glück sein nach Erfüllung drängend in diesem Zeitalter der Schöpfung' (*H* 7). The text further displays the semiotic in the rhythm which underlies the words, in the repetition of phrases, and finally also in the use of capitals and italics as a form of hysterical, physical gesture within the written language.[64]

'Lilit' appears to equate body and language directly. However, this early piece is atypical of Hensel's work; her other texts resist and undermine the mythologizing at work here. I would argue that 'Lilit' may represent a citing, or even parodying, of such a radical style. In this, it resembles the other sustained instances of linguistic grotesque, Egmont's laudatio to Jonatan's body and Friederike's diary entry about Egmont's body in *Auditorium*

[63] Weigel, *Die Stimme der Medusa*, 117.
[64] Cf. also the emphasis on the physicality of the text of *Ulriche und Kühleborn*. As I have argued elsewhere, unconventional typography is one way of representing the hysteric's gestural language, Marven, 'Women in Wheelchairs', esp. 526–7.

panopticum, both of which are intended ironically. 'Lilit' displays a level of self-consciousness lacking in the other two passages: the phrase 'geht sie jetzt rastlos und immerfort ohne Ruhe ohne einen Punkt an dem sie haltmacht kein Zeichen gebietet ihr Rast' (*H* 9) self-referentially points to the lack of punctuation ('Punkt' or 'Zeichen'). Furthermore, Hensel's comments about the text also signal a form of ironic distance:

> Hier erzähle ich nicht. Es ist irgendwie ein Drive, dichterische Prosa in der Ich-Form. Ich erzähle nicht, beim Erzählen hat man doch eine bestimmte distanzierte Haltung, hier ist es etwas sehr Gedrängtes, das ist eine Art von Distanz. 'Lilit' muß ja nicht ich sein, es ist ein Rollenstück: 'Ich. Lilit' ist eine Rolle.[65]

That Hensel refers to the piece as being in the first person (although it is in fact a third-person narrative) is telling; it is a poetic voice which must be considered with the same ironic distance as Friederike and Egmont, or even the unreliable first-person narrator of *Tanz am Kanal*, Gabriele von Haßlau. The description of the text as a role-play suggests theatricality, a deliberate performance, which is evident in the style—it is not a spontaneous outpouring, but a literary monologue.

The second manifestation of desire in linguistic structures occurs, appropriately enough, in 'Herr Johannes'. The text consists of a framework third-person narrative, and, within this, a first-person account by Leo of Johannes's appearance in the city. Leo is an alter ego of Johannes, and his oral narrative is his means of seduction. Like Johannes's sexual activity, it is a result of forces beyond his control: Leo appears 'durch seinen inneren seltsamen aufstoßenden Drang, genötigt worden sein zu erzählen'.[66] The two impulses (sex and storytelling) are related: Leo notes that the people of the city stop telling and reading aloud stories at the same time as they stop having sex. His own storytelling is thus a declaration of intent. Desire manifests itself in the manipulation of tension through narrative structure. Leo breaks off at key moments, deliberately leaving cliff-hangers to keep his audience interested, such as, 'wie es kommen mußte, so kam es. Herr Johannes wurde gesehen'

---

[65] Hensel, in interview with Dahlke, *Papierboot*, 275.
[66] This telling phrase appears only in the early version of 'Herr Johannes' published in *Sinn und Form*, 39/2 (1987), 972–95, here 972 (cf. *H* 126).

(*H* 142). This fragmentary narrative also stages the process of continual deferral. There can be no ultimate satisfaction, no fulfilment of desire. The reader of Hensel's text is tantalized by the gradual seduction of the landlady by Leo, which is narrated in the intervals between Leo's episodes. This strand of narrative fails to reach a satisfactory conclusion, however:

> Die Hausherrin könnte ihm das alles geglaubt und ein wenig Sehnsucht empfunden haben. Und vielleicht hat sie die Mädchen einfach wieder hinausgeschickt und zu ihrem Gast gesagt: *Komm*. Und der Gast, der sich gestärkt hat, könnte zur Antwort gegeben haben: *Ja*. Oder, was wahrscheinlicher ist, der unmäßige Genuß an Wein hat ihn zu Boden getrieben, selig und beflügelt für den kommenden Tag. (*H* 163)

In this, the final passage of the text, the reader is denied the consummation of the narrative strand. The repetition builds up to a deliberately anticlimactic ending, the textual equivalent of the non-ending of Don Juan's repetitive actions.

However, the use of the conditional also draws attention to the fictionality of the tale. What remains constant throughout the text is a pleasure in storytelling, something which underlies Hensel's work as a whole; Hensel herself talks of '[e]in Drang eben zum Gestalten, zum Fabulieren'.[67] Through self-conscious references to the act of composing and narrating, the narrative stages the very process of invention. I turn now to the ways in which the grotesque is manifested in the very stuff of fiction: plot.

NARRATIVE

In Hensel's first-person narratives, the disjunction and discrepancy between the 'discours' and the 'histoire' focus attention on the characters' voices. Hensel's more frequent third-person narratives also highlight the narrative voice through irony; her tales are predominately in an oral mode of storytelling. Far more so than either Herta Müller or Libuše Moníková, Kerstin Hensel plays with the idea of a narrative, that is, a story told. For her, the acts of plotting and telling are fundamental to the text—quite unlike Müller's tales of Ceaușescu's Romania,

[67] Kerstin Hensel, *Diana! Zeichnungen von Karla Woisnitza mit einem Gespräch von Elke Erb und Kerstin Hensel* (Berlin: KONTEXT Verlag, 1993), 45.

where the unpredictable actions of the *Securitate* and the lack of personal freedom in the oppressive state determine the text as similarly unmotivated; and unlike Moníková, whose texts rely on random encounters to generate the action which allows her to display her real interests. Hensel's narratives manifest the structure of 'Zerstörung und Erhaltung des Erwartungshorizontes', in Pietzcker's terms, in two ways. First and foremost, the plots of her texts play with the expectations of the reader, with regard to plausibility as well as literary conventions. These plots are not only grotesque in the reaction their exaggeration and understatement arouse, but frequently the unexpected developments also centre on grotesque acts. Secondly, Hensel parodies myths, fairy tales, and specific texts, most notably Bachmann's 'Undine geht' and Irmtraud Morgner's *Leben und Abenteuer der Trobadora Beatriz*. These parodies represent a specific example of the setting up and disrupting of expectations, as Hensel's texts mimic, reverse, and exaggerate the plots, motifs, rhetoric, and, in the case of Morgner's montage novel, the form of the source texts.

Plot: tales of the unexpected

In her texts, Hensel challenges the notion of plot, playing with its conventions self-consciously and parodistically. This section considers how Pietzcker's definition of the grotesque can be applied to plot, and I draw here on Peter Brooks's influential *Reading for the Plot* for a definition of plot which can support the grotesque.[68] A plot is an interconnected sequence of events, a structure, or rather a structuring principle, which is open to exaggeration, distortion, and disruption. Plot implies intentionality and causality; it is 'goal-oriented and forward moving'.[69] A plot is therefore grotesque where it disrupts the reader's expectations of logical progression, presents effects which are out of proportion to their causes, or comes to a different climax from that which had been suggested by the text. Two further elements are also implicated here: the genre of the text necessarily creates expectations of a plot appropriate to that style; and the narrative voice holds the dialectic of expectation and disruption 'in

[68] Peter Brooks, *Reading for the Plot: Design and Intention in Narrative* (1984; Cambridge, Mass.: Harvard University Press, 1992).
[69] Ibid. 12.

gespanntem Gleichgewicht' (Pietzcker). Other connotations of the word 'plot' offer useful analogies with the bodily grotesque. In its spatial definitions—the plot of land, or the verb 'to plot' e.g. a graph—the term also denotes a demarcation of space, the drawing of boundaries and limits. The bodily grotesque is concerned with the transgression of limits, the overstepping of boundaries; narrative grotesque manifests this same tendency, continually exceeding itself with regard to the conventions of plot or in the relation of text and intertext, but always within the bounds of recognizability, that is, within the bounds of readability.

As Peter Brooks suggests, what unites the different levels of the text is desire. Focusing on 'the temporal dynamics that shape narratives in our reading of them, the play of desire in time that makes us turn pages and strive towards narrative ends', Brooks concludes that 'Desire as narrative thematic, desire as narrative motor, and desire as the very intention of narrative language and the act of telling all seem to stand in close interrelation'.[70] As Brooks demonstrates, desire is the basic dynamic structure, first, of life itself, which Freud conceived of as the interplay of the pleasure principle and the death instinct; this desire is manifested in literature in the content and the schematics of the plot. Secondly, desire is the underlying structure of language, according to Lacan: the structure of difference which creates this desire is also evident in the metonymic transformations of plot, and is, furthermore, the source of the narrative impulse itself. Plot is the attempt to balance the desire for an end, for satisfaction, with the desire for repetition and an avoidance of the 'short-circuit', which is untimely death or the too-short, too-direct narrative. 'The desire of the text (the desire of reading) is hence desire for the end, but desire for the end reached only through the at least minimally complicated detour, the intentional deviance, in tension, which is the plot of narrative'.[71] Deviation is implicitly linked with deviance: the narratable is frequently that which falls outside the norm; it is the criminal act, the story of the outsider. Proper to narrative is the need to 'bind' textual desire through repetition and the working through of the plot. The failure to bind energy released within the text—on the level of content

[70] Ibid., pp. xiii and 54.   [71] Ibid. 104.

or the 'discours'—is a key element of Hensel's grotesque plots, and contributes in part to their social critical function. Narrative desire is also, Brooks suggests, itself transferable and never fixed: 'the movement is one of "contamination": the passing-on of the virus of narrative, the creation of the fevered need to re-tell.'[72] This points to 'Herr Johannes', the grotesque plot par excellence in Hensel's work, dealing with the grotesque figure of Don Juan, where desire manifests itself both as (hysterical) illness and as narrative drive.[73]

Hensel's texts employ several different forms of plot which can be considered grotesque, based on structures of excess and lack, exaggeration and understatement. These grotesque plots follow developments *ad absurdum* ('Hallimasch', 'Das Mittwochsmenü'); contain surprising and unmotivated developments ('Vogelgreif'); or end in unexpected or overly dramatic climaxes (*Gipshut*, 'Das Spiel der Billabohne'). Alternatively, they deny the reader the consumption of a narrative strand (the framework narrative of 'Herr Johannes') or do not follow up suggestions given in the narrative ('Neunerlei', *Im Schlauch*), leaving the text open or ambiguous.

The first type of grotesque plot, the paradoxically 'unreal, weil folgerichtig' narrative, as Hensel describes 'Hallimasch', is the most clearly linked to a thematic grotesque and to out-of-control desire: the plot displays the same uncontrollable 'Triebe' which also prompt the characters to transgressive actions.[74] The two are inseparable: the grotesque acts are the impetus to, and constitute the action of, the exaggerated, grotesque plot. 'Hallimasch' presents the tale of Liese and Lotte Möbius, twins born into a poor family in the village Katzgrün in the Vogtland at the end of the nineteenth century; the ironic narrative of their isolated lives is brought to an abrupt end when Lotte murders Liese after the Führer comes between them. The twins' names already suggest they are neither individuals—'Lieselotte' is a single, contemporary name; the Möbius strip is a piece of paper with one continuous side, formed by twisting the paper through 180 degrees so that one side meets the other—nor,

---

[72] Brooks, *Reading for the Plot*, 221.
[73] See Marven, "Wie ein Festmahl nach langer Hungerszeit".
[74] Hensel, in interview with Hammer, 'Gespräch mit Kerstin Hensel', 107.

as a consequence of this overt symbolism, realist characters.⁷⁵ However, the rural setting of the text and its domestic, anecdotal focus seem to place it in a realist mode. For thirteen of the eighteen pages of the tale, the twins' life is narrated as if they were a single entity, through a distanced and ironic third-person (plural) narrative punctuated with occasional heavily accented direct speech, giving details of inconsequential events in their schooling, puberty, and the upkeep of the farm after the death of both parents. Only one short passage, the final one in this section, is out of the ordinary—an ambiguous scene of incest. Incest commonly features in narratives, Brooks suggests, as a symbol of the threat of narrative short-circuit, the collapse of the plot into an untimely end.⁷⁶ In 'Hallimasch', the ambiguous moment—introduced by 'vielleicht', a signal of the act of storytelling—presents the potential short-circuit of sameness, where the two become one. The release of textual desire in this scene is the (belated) impetus for plot.

Two and a half pages are then dedicated to the visit of the Führer to Katzgrün, where Liese comically falls for this man with a spot hiding in his facial hair. The final two and a half pages chart the twins' sudden falling out as a result of Liese's irrational infatuation, beginning with the observation:

Liese und Lotte Möbius gehen die Dorfstraße hinauf, wie immer schwerfällig, rrsch rrsch, Schritt für Schritt. Aber wenn Liese nach rechts wankt, fällt Lottes Körper nach links. Sie laufen einzeln, hintereinander, in einem halben Meter Entfernung. (*H* 99)

From the potential over-sameness of incest, the twins rebound into an over-exaggerated difference; they are no longer mirror images, but opposites. The rapid decline of their relationship follows: the next evening the twins have a violent fight, in a passage which sees the narrative focus shift dramatically from direct speech to historical distance: 'Wenn jetzt net gleich de Gusch halten tust... | Da hat Lotte schon eins auf der Gusch sitzen, daß ihr der Kopf dröhnt. Im Spätherbst vierundvierzig schlagen sich die Möbius-Zwillinge in der Küche die Augen blau' (*H* 100). The comic, incongruous mimicry of Liese's

---

⁷⁵ Hensel describes the twins as 'ein Gleichnis, da geht es um das Gleichsein bis ins Letzte, als gesellschaftliches Gleichnis', in interview with Dahlke, *Papierboot*, 277.
⁷⁶ Brooks, *Reading for the Plot*, 109.

dialect, and the sudden zooming out, ensure that the reader does not view this development seriously. The narrative then jumps to winter, where Liese is packing her bags ready to set off in search of the Führer and Lotte is mucking out in the stable. Now separation and difference determine the narrative. Lotte's attempt to do away with her twin is both a denial of this difference, as well as its ultimate enactment: the twins will become one, not through the forbidden incest, but through radical asymmetry, as only one will survive.

No prior indication is given in the narrative of Lotte's murderous intent, and indeed the murder is only suggested rather than depicted:

Von Katzgrün läuten die Glocken herauf. Das Vieh beginnt zu dösen. Feierlich ist es im Stall. Lotte nimmt die scharfgablige Harke auf. Es ist genug. Prüfend wiegt sie das Gerät in den Händen, hebt es hoch über den Kopf und hängt es an den krummen Nagel über der Tür. Still ist es. Die Harke hängt. Alle Arbeit ist getan. Stille, selbst die Glocken hört man nicht mehr. Und Liese Möbius öffnet von außen den Stall. (*H* 102)

In this, the final passage, the narrative becomes ever more elliptical, building up suspense with short, repetitive sentences. Only the phrase 'Es ist genug', Lotte's thoughts intruding into the narrative, suggest that anything untoward is afoot, and the remark 'Alle Arbeit ist getan', which may be another of Lotte's thoughts or simply a narrative statement, derives a sinister double meaning in retrospect. The reader has to interpret Lotte's actions and fill in the missing ending. Hensel herself acknowledges the reader's effort: 'Ich will die Anstrengung der genußvollen Dechiffrierung von Texten; kein Rätselraten, aber die Mühe, hinter Geheimnisse zu kommen.'[77] The reader is drawn into solving the mystery of the text—a pleasurable task, as Hensel suggests—but is repulsed by the solution itself, exactly like the process of apprehending the grotesque as Pietzcker describes it.

It is not only the ending, and the discrepancy between the content and narration, which characterizes 'Hallimasch' as grotesque: the plot displays other grotesque features. The

[77] Hensel, in interview with Hammer, 'Gespräch mit Kerstin Hensel', 107.

developments towards the end are not only comically improbable, but also entirely out of proportion to the rest of the tale. The detailed, anecdotal, but uneventful narrative of the first thirteen pages is followed by a sudden acceleration of events, and the complete breakdown in the twins' relationship is compressed into a mere two and a half pages; the apparent plotlessness of the first, longer section is succeeded by what is almost a parody of a plot. However, the non-events take up most of the narrative and, as a correlative of this reversal in significance, the relation of narrated time (the duration in the life of the twins) to narrative time (the time it takes the reader to read that section of text) also counters expectations: in descriptions of the foot massage the twins give farmer Kuczmat or their first Christmas dinner alone, the narrative time approaches narrated time, conventionally a signal of importance. In contrast, the odd deaths of their father and mother are passed over quickly: the humanly and emotionally significant is suppressed. After the blow-by-blow account of the twins' fight, the abrupt leap in the narrative from late autumn to winter implies (misleadingly) that there were no after-effects. The systematic reversal of significance forces the reader to focus on the things which remain unsaid: the motivation for the murder, but also the historical conditions which are represented in the text and which underlie the desperation—the poverty symbolized by the 'Hallimasch' mushroom, last-resort food for a starving population. As in other tales in *Hallimasch*, particularly 'Kotterba', the grotesque highlights the inhumanity of the seemingly harmless, albeit difficult, social conditions. Here, then, the grotesque narrative serves the purpose of social criticism by disrupting the normal order of the text in order to make the reader think.

'Das Mittwochsmenü', in *Neunerlei*, follows a similar structure to 'Hallimasch', taking twenty-six pages (out of thirty) to work up slowly to a murder committed for the simplest of motives, jealousy. Again, the narrative concentrates on detail—the ritual meeting of an unlikely group of friends over lunch, the ludicrous dishes served by the restaurant, Endenthum's obsession with the details of his own funeral and his scientific explanations which accompany the exhibits in his Sugar Museum, only one of which has any narrative significance: the deadly 'Melasseschlempe durch Pyrolyse zersetzt [...] trauriger Gipfel der

Zuckergeschichte' (*Nl* 94), which Endenthum uses to kill the artist Katka. As in 'Hallimasch', the murder is out of proportion to Endenthum's feelings as well as the narrative; both his plans and their execution are merely alluded to, leaving the reader in the dark. Additionally, potential elements of plot are inexplicably ignored by both characters and narrative alike. When Katka unexpectedly announces that she has got married, this news is not even discussed until the following week; when Barmer is apparently found dead and something unknown happens to Frl. Nawlonski, the characters and the narrative carry on as if nothing had happened and there were no mystery. What by conventional standards would seem to be events with a story behind them, potential subplots representing the need for deviation, are rejected by the narrative. Only the waiter comments: 'Es passieren ja schreckliche Dinge in der Stadt' (*Nl* 102), validating the reader's recognition that the plot has gone awry. The text of 'Das Mittwochsmenü' undermines our expectations of narrative coherence and logic—not just in the literary text, but in real life. It frustrates our need to solve, explain, and to some extent control grotesque aberrations in human behaviour, such as murders, through turning them into a narrative.

In addition to these tales which transgress the limits of storytelling by exaggeration, so that things happen which were not anticipated, there are others which function in the opposite way: nothing happens, precisely where the narrative leads you to expect something. This can take the form of explicit suggestion, as in 'Neunerlei', or implicit, signalled primarily by the convergence of narrated time and narrative time, or by the excess of detail which implies significance. In 'Neunerlei', a simple narrative of a male teacher's generosity towards his young pupils is introduced from a perspective beyond the projected end of the tale: 'Wo das Pöhlwasser durchs Erzgebirge fließt [...] lebte bis zum Jahre 1994 der Lehrer Dörfler' (*Nl* 32). From this initial distance and the suggestion of a change in circumstance, the narrative proceeds to be infected by the suspicion of the teacher's neighbours, aroused in part by his good nature: 'Sein freundliches aufgeschlossenes Wesen war für die Gegend untypisch und weckte Mißtrauen' (*Nl* 32). When Dörfler invites four schoolchildren round for an old-fashioned Christmas Eve supper, references to his feeling faint and forgetting why he was doing this combine with the repeated suspicion—'Es war dieser haderlumpengraue Gegend. Er war heiterer, als es sich hier gehörte' (*Nl* 37)—to produce unease in the reader. The more detailed the narrative becomes, the more the reader searches for the catch, until it seems that those suspicions will be confirmed: 'Er platzte förmlich vor Heiterkeit, obwohl seine Gedanken seltsame Signale ausschickten, solche, als dürfe er die Kinder nie wieder aus dieser Stube herauslassen, als könne ihnen auf dem Heimweg etwas zustoßen, oder ihm' (*Nl* 38). But instead Dörfler sends the children off home with a present of 'Schwarzbeerkompott': 'Die Kinder hatten rote Wangen und blaue Zähne, als sie Abschied nahmen' (*Nl* 39). Which would appear perfectly harmless, were it not for the postscript to the tale—that the police picked the teacher up on his way to school some days later.

The ambiguous ending neither fully confirms the suspicions which the narrative has fostered, nor does it deny them; it does not explain why the teacher only lived in the village until 1994. Is it just that the villagers cannot accept someone who is different, or is there really something sinister in the teacher's actions? Are we, the readers, simply too quick to suspect people and to jump to conclusions? The narrative is intentionally incomplete and ambiguous, deliberately comparing the reader's reactions to those of the distrustful neighbours and raising questions about the state of a society—both the intra-textual and extra-textual one—where such apparently innocent qualities foster suspicion. 'Neunerlei' also raises questions about our expectations of such anecdotal narratives. Many of Hensel's texts do indeed come to a dramatic, sinister, or gruesome end, often with much less textual motivation than in 'Neunerlei': her tales condition the reader to expect the unexpected, as it were. The absence of a twist here, or rather, the suppression of the nature of that elided development, is just as grotesque.

The refusal to resolve all the aspects of the plot is a common, though frustrating, feature in Hensel's writing. This leads to conspicuous loose ends such as the existence of the child in 'Herr Johannes' or of Herr Fischer in *Im Schlauch*.[78] It also leads

---

[78] The small child Leo finds among the ruins of Sankt Veit could be the offspring of Lucie and any of the three men—himself, Herr Johannes, or King

to the apparently random sequence of events in 'Vogelgreif' and the unexpectedly unrealistic ending, when Katinka is carried off by an owl. Gaps, leaps, uncertainties, and unexpected developments all turn attention back onto the narrative voice. The more the plot of a text becomes unpredictable, the more the narrative voice holds—has to hold—the interest of the reader. These three texts display a more intrusive and clearly oral narrative voice than 'Hallimasch' and 'Das Mittwochsmenü'—none more so than 'Herr Johannes', where the majority of the tale is narrated by the character Leo.

Im Schlauch is a short narrative about the 16-year-old daughter of a party official, who runs away from home and squats in a condemned house. Interspersed in the tale of her banal adventures are scenes from the typical GDR life of her parents, both of whom commit adultery. Among the few vestiges of a plot that remain in this text with its stylized 'discours' is the figure of Herr Fischer, whom Natalie hears coughing in the condemned house which will be her home for the two days she is away. 'Nebenan hustete der Tote' (*ImS* 11), we are informed, an oxymoron indicating a grotesque merging of life and death. She hears him for a second time shortly afterwards, and then no further mention is made of the man until Natalie returns to the house at the end of the text, to find it has been boarded up:

Sie legte ein Ohr ans Brett, sie konnte es im Hause husten hören. Fäustetrommeln. Sie warf sich noch einmal gegen die Barrikade.

Ein Polizeibeamter fing Natalie Kulisch auf. Sie biß ihm in den Handrücken, dann antwortete sie: 'Hier wohne ich!' Der Polizist lachte, gutmütig: 'Wegen Einsturzgefahr baupolizeilich verschlossen.'

'Aber hier wohnt auch Herr Fischer!' rief Natalie unter des Polizisten festem Griff.

'Hier wohnt seit Jahren kein Mensch.' Der Genosse wußte, was er sagte. (*ImS* 66)

The authority of the older male figure is invoked to cast doubt on her story, but the narrative appears to support Natalie's view, as the text concludes 'nur am Abend, ganz im Inneren der Stadt, schlug leise bellend ein Greis an' (*ImS* 67). This sinister throwaway line uses a familiar technique from horror tales, the

Otmar; the child's parentage is one of many aspects of the text which remain tantalizingly unresolved.

twist in the last words, as well as the common motif of being walled up or buried alive. By leaving the tale hanging on this incongruous note of horror, the narrative also fails, in Brooks's terms, to bind and thus discharge the intensive textual energy released by the plot. Moreover, the ending gives disproportionate significance to a seemingly unimportant strand of plot: the narrative discourse mirrors Natalie's teenage melodrama, as the insignificant is overdramatized and effects are intentionally excessive in relation to their causes.

Im Schlauch deflates Natalie's dreams of adventure by showing the mundane and inconsequent reality of her running away. Herr Fischer aside, there is no plot to speak of, and what actions there are have little effect—even her parents' past adultery, interspersed in the narrative, has little bearing on the present. But again, that is the whole point: her running away does not make a difference, her desire for plot, for adventure, is frustrated and life carries on as 'stinknormal' (Stinopel). As the family is reunited in the Stinopel festival, where the whole town comes together as one ('Stinopel hielt den Atem an [...] atmete aus', *ImS* 67), the parody of the GDR solidarity is undermined by the lack of progress within the text. In 'Grus', which Hensel describes as 'eine DDR-Zeitgeschichte, über die man in ein paar Jahren vielleicht lacht—oder nicht', the apparent change at the end of the text, also accompanied by a town festival, is undermined by the repetition, rather than linear progress, which structures the rest of the text: nothing has changed at all.[79] That we should extrapolate from the text to its context is clear: the GDR has lost the/its plot.

At times these exaggerated structures tip the balance of expectation and disruption too far. Ambiguous and obscure endings, such as those in 'Hallimasch' and 'Das Mittwochsmenü', are occasionally unconvincing when taken further: the ending of *Gipshut*, for example—Hans blows up the Berlin Stadtschloß where he works—is simply too surprising to be effective. Other texts exaggerate plotlessness and slip into mere character sketch, simple anecdote, or pure atmosphere—'Das Rathaus' and 'Der Graf am Tisch' in *Neunerlei* in particular illustrate the unsatisfying result of taking this tendency to extremes.

---

[79] Hensel, in interview with Hammer, 'Gespräch mit Kerstin Hensel', 108.

As the plot-centred grotesque disturbs conventional forms, it falls to the act of storytelling to sustain interest and belief. The potential pitfalls of the reliance on narrative voice can be seen in *Gipshut*, where the distanced, ironic narrative, typical of the grotesque and of Hensel's texts, undermines the interest in the characters and their fates which is necessary in a longer novel. At the other extreme, *Auditorium panopticum* presents the proliferation of plot: the multiple strands of narrative in this highly self-conscious montage novel represent the excess of deviation, the total devolution of narrative movement into subplot upon subplot and ever-diverging strands of narrative. It even fails to end definitively, incorporating into the narrative responses to the fictionalized book written by Egmont Köhler (which of course resembles the actual text by Hensel). I look at the form of *Auditorium panopticum* in more detail in the following section, where I examine parody, which is concerned with the specific characteristics of individual texts, rather than textual conventions in general.

Parody

Hensel's plots are grotesque where they disappoint the reader's expectations of narrative, but yet some energy in the text, to use Brooks's terms, keeps the reader reading. This results from the attempt to read the text against pre-existing conventions of narrative. It may also take the form of interest in the narrative voice, or the act of narration. Finally, textual energy may be derived from the recognition that this frustration can be located within the text's content and context (here in particular the implicit comment on GDR society). This applies in general to Hensel's texts, which play with patterns of plot, but specifically and particularly to her revisions of other texts: fairy tales; the legend of Lilith, and the myth of Don Juan; her response to Ingeborg Bachmann's 'Undine geht', *Ulriche und Kühleborn*; and finally the problematic *Auditorium panopticum*, which contains multiple individual parodies and pastiches as well as setting itself explicitly against Irmtraud Morgner's celebrated montage novel, *Leben und Abenteuer der Trobadora Beatriz*.

In the chapter on Moníková, I explained how parody can be interpreted as reflecting hysteria. The structures of parody also resemble those of the grotesque. Parody has a dual nature: it is both transgressive and reverent, its imitation contains critical distance but is authorized by the very text it parodies—this is the tendency which can also be interpreted as a hysterical strategy. It is, as Linda Hutcheon suggests in *A Theory of Parody*, 'a boundary work', 'overtly hybrid and double-voiced', terms which recall Bakhtin's bodily grotesque.[80] Like the grotesque plot, the parody continually exceeds its limits (the source text), but never goes so far as to render the references unrecognizable or redundant; it transgresses, but still remains within certain boundaries. Necessarily, the parody oscillates between confirming and denying the reader's expectations which derive from knowledge of the intertext. The reader's work, which Hensel acknowledges and which underpins the grotesque, is necessary for a parody to function: it relies on being given enough clues about the intertext—not too many, nor too explicit. Parody is furthermore linked to irony and satire: its imitation is 'characterized by ironic inversion', and it can be used 'to satirize the reception or even the creation of certain kinds of art'.[81] Hensel's parodies are both ironic and satirical, and are particularly directed at the conditions of cultural production and the understanding of art represented by the source texts. In *Ulriche und Kühleborn* and *Auditorium panopticum*, the two texts which exemplify this satirical bent, parody's role as a way of 'com[ing] to terms with the weight of the past' is not only reflected in the concern with literary influences and forebears.[82] Parodies set their own historical and political context against that of the source texts, and the reader must decode the context of Hensel's tales as well as their literary references.

One of the most frequent sources of intertextual references in Hensel's work is fairy tales, particularly those collected by the Brothers Grimm. 'Vogelgreif', in *Neunerlei*, refers to an otherwise unrelated Grimm tale, 'Der Vogel Greif', with a literalization of the title supplying its ending; 'Das Licht von Zauche' alludes to the dancing princesses of 'Die zertanzten Schuhe'.[83] In addition to these passing references, Hensel writes parodies of 'Märchen',

---

[80] Hutcheon, *A Theory of Parody*, 13, 28.   [81] Ibid. 6, 16.   [82] Ibid. 29.
[83] Brüder Grimm, 'Die zertanzten Schuhe' and 'Der Vogel Greif', in *Kinder- und Hausmärchen, Jubiläumsausgabe*, 2 vols. (Stuttgart: Philipp Reclam, 1980, 1984), ii. 217–21 and 296–303 respectively.

both as specific tales and as a genre, this latter serving to highlight the satirical aspect. Individual tales she tackles, and which I analyse below, are 'Hänsel und Gretel', in 'Da ward gutes Essen aufgetragen' in *Hallimasch*, and 'The Emperor's New Clothes' (a Hans Christian Andersen tale), in 'Des Kaisers Rad' in *Neunerlei*; and she parodies the Grimm's tales generally in 'Ein Hausmärchen', a short piece published in 1990.[84]

The parodic rewriting of 'Hänsel und Gretel' in 'Da ward gutes Essen aufgetragen' begins with a quotation from the Grimms' version. Hensel's narrative, consisting of a single breathless sentence, is an alternative ending to the tale. Several elements of the original are altered: both of the children are imprisoned, whereas in the original it was only Hänsel. The children make no attempt to trick the old woman: in the original, the witch feels Hänsel's fingers to see if he needs more fattening, so Hänsel offers her bones to feel; Hensel's children scold the old woman for her bad food, and even when she dies of old age, they do not immediately try to free themselves. When they do, it transpires that the door had been open all along. It is greed which motivates the children: instead of using their cunning to escape, they are complicit in their imprisonment. Hensel's tale is a self-conscious parody, which quotes its source text directly and refers to 'die berühmte Speise, die fett machen sollte' (*H* 147), relying on and acknowledging the reader's prior knowledge.

Like 'Da ward gutes Essen', 'Des Kaisers Rad' also provides an alternative ending for a familiar tale ('Des Kaisers neue Kleider' in German). Beginning with the cry 'Aber der Kaiser ist ja nackt', by a 6-year-old child, Hensel's version is less concerned with the trickster tailors (who supply the invisible 'cloth' in the original) and the individual's desire not to look stupid, than with the collusion of the crowd in the Emperor's delusion. As the child insists on the truth of what it is saying, his father reprimands the mother, 'Daß du so viel Aufhebens um unser dummes Kind machen mußt! [...] Wir sind unser Leben lang nicht aufgefallen' (*Nl* 130). Instead of the child's revelation allowing the crowd to admit what they are all too aware of, the Emperor has the child killed on the wheel. Jubilant, the

---

[84] Kerstin Hensel, 'Hausmärchen', *Deutsche Volkszeitung*, 29 June 1990, p. 13; Brüder Grimm, 'Hänsel und Gretel', in *Kinder- und Hausmärchen*, i. 100–8.

'Oberzeremonienmeister' exclaims, 'keiner wird jemals wieder sagen, der Kaiser sei nackt' (*Nl* 132); even the possibility of his being naked is dangerous for the Emperor, and he orders the 'Oberzeremonienmeister', too, to be put to death. Someone else repeats the assertion, only to meet the same fate: the crowd act like automatons, a grotesque tendency. The cycle continues until only the Emperor himself is left and 'der letzte Mensch, den er noch lebend sehen konnte, ein sechsjähriger Knabe, folgte ihm und trug die Schleppe' (*Nl* 133). Now a child confirms the Emperor in his delusion, rather than shattering it.

'Ein Hausmärchen', as its title indicates, refers to the 'Kinder- und Hausmärchen' collected by the Brothers Grimm, and it draws on elements and motifs from several tales. The parody uses exaggeration, foreshortening (techniques used in the grotesque plot), and incongruity. The short narrative (although, given the lack of coherence and logical progression, narrative is perhaps a misnomer) starts *in medias res*, with a magical transformation typical of fairy tales: a 'Mädchen' is literally showered with gold. However, this is not entirely in keeping with convention: the gold comes from out of the blue, rather than as a result of a wish, a reward, or an adventure; and the 'Mädchen' has worked for 'sechs mal sieben Jahre', making her substantially older than the conventional young girl protagonist. The gold sets hard, eventually killing the woman, something described in grotesque physical detail: 'Drei Tage lang hatte sie nichts gegessen und getrunken, ihre Haut war vom Gold verstopft und fiel zusammen.' The narrative then piles on motif after motif, drawn from two Grimm tales, 'Tischchendeckdich, Zauberesel und Knüppel aus dem Sack' and 'Rumpelstilzchen'.[85] A 'Rumpelmüller' turns up, with a 'Zauberesel' who produces gold coins and a magic stick which moves on its own (here only two elements of the original tale). Taking the golden woman to his mill, he deposits her in the same room as the queen who has to spin the gold into straw; in the Grimm tale, the miller's daughter must spin straw into gold, and when she does this, with the help of Rumpelstilzchen, the king marries her, making her queen.

[85] Brüder Grimm, 'Tischchendeckdich, Zauberesel und Knüppel aus dem Sack', and 'Rumpelstilzchen', in *Kinder- und Hausmärchen*, i. 195–205 and 285–8 respectively.

Aside from exaggeration and comic reversal (spinning gold into straw is surely pointless), the parody also draws on grotesque bodily images. Hensel replaces the Grimms' coy formulation that the donkey 'speit Gold [...] hinten und vorn' with unconventionally literal, corporeal content.[86] Hensel's donkey produces coins by regurgitation—'es würgte ihm erbärmlich. Meistens verklemmte sich die Münze auch noch zwischen Gaumen und Oberkiefer'—or defecation: 'so kam die Münze aus dem Loch im Hintern, das aber, durch das scharfe Metall von vielerlei schmerzhaften Ragaden und Hämorrhoiden befallen war.' This graphic and grotesque transgression of the body's boundaries explains the magic words, 'Goldesel, reck dich!' and 'Goldesel, streck dich!', which parody and rhyme with the instruction 'Tischchen, deck dich' in the Grimms' tale. The ending also travesties fairy-tale narrative: when all the gold is spun into straw (by a 'Männlein' borne by the queen, collapsing two aspects of the Rumpelstilzchen tale), all at once, the donkey dies, the stick refuses to work any more, and 'Die Königin riß sich vor Freude mehrmals mitten durch'. They do not exactly live happily ever after: the traditional fairy-tale phrasing, 'und wenn sie nicht gestorben sind, dann leben sie noch heute', is invoked and reversed in the final sentence: 'Das Land aber versank bis zur Hälfte in der Erde, und wenn es gestorben ist, stinkt es zum Himmel'. Like Hensel's other tales, the hybrid 'Ein Hausmärchen' does not function as a 'compensatory image of reconciliation', as Jack Zipes characterizes the Grimms' tales; there is no protagonist who is integrated into society through their innate virtues and wits.[87] Instead, greed, meaninglessness, death, and stagnation proliferate. As an explanation of the world, it presents a particularly negative view.

It is in the interpretation of the tales that the complexity of the relation between the texts emerges, for Hensel's versions offer no simple moral. As a psychological template, 'Da ward gutes Essen' does not symbolize resolution and socialization, but rather repression: the children sleep 'hinter kunterbunten Stäben, von denen sie bald wußten, wozu sie gut waren und die

---

[86] Brüder Grimm, 'Tischchendeckdich, Zauberesel und Knüppel aus dem Sack', and 'Rumpelstilzchen', in *Kinder- und Hausmärchen*, i. 200.

[87] Jack Zipes, *The Brothers Grimm: From Enchanted Forests to the Modern World* (London: Routledge, 1988), 84.

sie hernach vergaßen' (*H* 147). 'Des Kaisers Rad' also focuses on the violent repression of knowledge—that the Emperor has no clothes on; ultimately death is necessary to uphold the delusion. Zipes reads the Grimms' tales as a critique of social and political conditions, but whereas their tales provide a realm where transformations can be realized, Hensel's are dystopian: all transformations are negative and brought about by the stupidity of the protagonists. Above all, what the changed elements in a parody highlight is its own contemporary context, hence its suitability for allegory, and the ending of 'Da ward gutes Essen' in particular suggests such an allegorical reading:

da standen sie auf ihrer Straße, von der sie gekommen waren, irgendwann vor Jahren, und sie erkannten die Straße auch wieder, und da fragten sie sich, wohin sie jetzt gehen sollen, NACH HAUS, sprach der Junge, und da sah ihn das Mädchen zum erstenmal an, zum erstenmal nach den Jahren, und sagte, WIE FETT DU GEWORDEN BIST, HANS, und da sah es auch Hans und sprach, WIE DUMM DU GEWORDEN BIST, MARGARETE, und da gingen sie und wußten nicht, wohin. (*H* 148)

Hensel parodies the rhetoric of fairy tales, and her tale ends not with arrival, but with a loss of direction. In the context of the publication of *Hallimasch* in 1989, it is tempting to interpret this old road as socialism, which has lost its way; the children display the complicity and greed which propped up the corrupt state of the GDR (the old witch?). The collusion of the crowd in 'Des Kaisers Rad' and the violent suppression of potential dissidence could also be read as an exaggerated depiction of the socialist state. Even more directly, the final lines of 'Ein Hausmärchen', from 1990—'das Land aber versank bis zur Hälfte in der Erde'—suggest the collapse of the rotten half of Germany ('und wenn es gestorben ist, stinkt es zum Himmel').

There are problems with these political readings, however, particularly in the weight of detail which cannot be assimilated into the allegory: the threat of being eaten in 'Da ward gutes Essen', for example, or the orgy of violence in 'Des Kaisers Rad'. But this, I think, is precisely the point. Hensel deliberately disrupts the symbolic reading, even while seeming to invite it. In the introduction to the 1996 edition of his *Kleine Literaturgeschichte der DDR*, Wolfgang Emmerich makes a telling comment which might shed some light on Hensel's parodies: he suggests that 'die sogenannten kritischen DDR-Autoren, die man veröffentlichen ließ, hätten vielleicht an einer "Verbesserung der Haftbedingungen" mitgewirkt, nicht aber die Haft selbst in Frage gestellt', exactly what the children do in Hensel's narrative.[88] The similarity between the names Hänsel and Hensel, which is surely intentional, seems to point to a concern with the role of literature within society. Hensel would appear to be criticizing the collaboration of 'Geist und Macht'. She is also criticizing the use of literature as substitute social dialogue—both the conventional utopian function of fairy tales, and the function of 'Ersatzöffentlichkeit' which literature in general fulfilled in the GDR—and she does this not through allegory, but by using grotesque structures to disrupt the text's ability to function as allegory.

In short texts such as these, it suffices to invoke the source text once; the rest of the text can then depart quite radically from its predecessor. In longer texts, the need to sustain the process of creating and destroying expectations necessarily leads to more complex interrelations between the texts. *Ulriche und Kühleborn*, the parodic text par excellence in Hensel's oeuvre, sustains multiple intertextual references. *Auditorium panopticum*, on the other hand, is substantially longer and the dynamic of parody alone is not enough to maintain interest. As Hensel's reworking of fairy tales shows, however, this may well be an intentional effect. I turn now to these two texts, looking first at *Ulriche und Kühleborn* in order to find a way of approaching the less discussed *Auditorium panopticum*.

Ulriche und Kühleborn was written as a response to Ingeborg Bachmann's 'Undine geht', in an explicit attempt to counteract what Hensel saw as the 'weinerliche Haltung' of the earlier text.[89] As Mererid Puw Davies demonstrates, the text alludes to two further intertexts, namely Friedrich de la Motte Fouqué's novella *Undine* (1811), the source of Bachmann's piece, and *Undine* by Albert Lortzing (1845), an obscure 'Romantische Zauberoper' also based on Fouqué's novella. The combination of these multiple intertexts is a key element of the grotesque nature of Hensel's text. *Ulriche und Kühleborn* is a protean text

---

[88] Emmerich, *Kleine Literaturgeschichte der DDR*, 14.
[89] Hensel, in interview with Dahlke, *Papierboot*, 270.

which contains citations from 'Undine geht', as well as borrowing characters' traits and names from both this text and Lortzing's opera (and therefore indirectly also from Fouqué's novella). These references do not constitute simple correspondences or straightforward reversals, however; as Puw Davies says, in terms which recall Bakhtin's bodily grotesque, 'Hensel's work shifts, magnifies, distorts and alters material from its intertextual antecedents.'[90] Expectations set up by the references to each of the intertexts are not only continually frustrated by the inconsistent, asymmetrical nature of these references and the fact that they are not sustained, but also by the incongruities arising from the combination of the multiple intertexts.

Hensel's text also displays hybridity in its form: in the variation of mode and register, from the ironic to the elegiac; in its vocabulary, which focuses on the material, scientific (the zoological terminology used to describe Ulriche as eel, or the geological terms applied to Metz Albert), and the physical; and in the range of references beyond the Undine myth (particularly in the odd Christ figure who appears in the workshop). These shifts are not seamless; as Puw Davies writes, Hensel's text 'emphasizes the process of textual construction by not masking the traces and joins', something which could also be said of Herta Müller's collages, which foreground visually the montage process.[91] *Ulriche und Kühleborn* further evinces a concern with aesthetic form in its intrusive typography, which foregrounds the text as physical artefact, in the use of capitals (often signalling a quotation, or pun, such as 'MĀNNSCHLICH', *UuK* 5), and in its unconventional font. The font, called 'Royal-Grotesk', is an oddly proportioned sans serif; the editor comments, 'Trotz dieser grafischen Mangel besitzt die Royal-Grotesk einen eigenartigen Reiz, den Reiz des Noch-nicht-Perfekten oder Noch-nicht-ganz-Ausgereiften, des Archaischen' (*UuK* 54). Both the text of *Ulriche und Kühleborn* and the figure of Ulriche exist in a state of physical flux and contradiction, of change and incompleteness. Ulriche's body and the body of the text thus both recall Bakhtin's description of the grotesque as 'reflect[ing] a phenomenon in transformation, an as yet unfinished metamorphosis'.[92]

---

[90] Puw Davies, 'Fishy Tales', 57.   [91] Ibid. 58.
[92] Bakhtin, *Rabelais and his World*, 24.

According to Bakhtin, the grotesque represents the crisis which precedes renewal, a notion echoed in the Russian formalists' understanding of parody as a signal that a particular form has degenerated into convention. Parodies 'hurry up what is a natural procedure: the changing of aesthetic forms through time'.[93] Hensel's text challenges Bachmann's, not simply through reversing her perceived 'weinerliche Haltung', but in the conception of art it presents. As Puw Davies suggests, art for Hensel is not timeless and monolithic, abstract and 'auratic', but rather a form of production, a process, which is manifested in the form of the text itself, as well as symbolized in Ulriche's work as stonemason, where her physical work is highlighted over the finished artefact.[94] Linda Hutcheon suggests that 'Parody can, of course, be used to satirize the reception or even the creation of certain kinds of art', and while I am not sure that Hensel goes so far as to satirize it, she certainly problematizes the creation of works of literature such as 'Undine geht'.[95] Her parody signals that it is no longer possible, nor, perhaps, even desirable, to produce such work. Hensel's text, written some thirty years after Bachmann's, bears the traces of its own contemporary context: an awareness of the ideological manipulation of narrative and the ways in which literature has been harnessed for non-literary purposes, and an increased self-consciousness and self-reflexivity. Myth has been demystified and mythologizing is no longer appropriate.

It is in this light that *Auditorium panopticum* needs to be (re)considered. Although initially well received by critics, the text has since largely been ignored and tends to be perceived as an imitation of Irmtraud Morgner's *Leben und Abenteuer der Trobadora Beatriz*. In her review of the novel, Ursula Vogel obliquely signals some of the problems inherent in the comparison:

Der Autorin Irmtraud Morgner, die, klug und gekonnt wie niemand anders, Bachtins Theorie vom polyphonen Roman nutzbar gemacht hat für moderne (nicht nur) DDR-Literatur, wird bewundernde

[93] Hutcheon, *A Theory of Parody*, 35.
[94] As Puw Davies points out, this is also reflected in the opera Ulriche conjures up, where material production is foregrounded, recalling the etymological origin of 'opera' as 'work', 'Fishy Tales', 58.
[95] Hutcheon, *A Theory of Parody*, 16.

Zustimmung entgegengebracht, indem Hensel nun ihrerseits einen polyphonen Roman schreibt, dessen eine Stimme die Thematisierung der Polyphonie selber ist.[96]

The apparent contradiction and self-consciousness of what Vogel calls a polyphonous novel whose single voice is the thematization of polyphony already hints at the problems of Hensel's novel. That *Auditorium panopticum* is self-consciously written against Morgner's monumental montage novel is not in doubt. Morgner herself appears in the text, attending the '1. Müggelseekonferenz' on 'Montage, Polyphonie, Maschentrennung und Musterdichtung' where Hensel is to give a paper entitled 'Der Frust der Epigonen' (*AP* 107). And Hensel has acknowledged Morgner's wider influence on her work in two essays, 'Trobadora passé' and 'Tanz in gefährdeter Welt', in *Angestaut*. Rather than being dismissed simply as an imitation or pastiche, Hensel's text needs to be explored as a grotesque parody which uses Morgner's original as a standard against which to measure, and satirize, contemporary reality. Analogous to the relationship of *Ulriche und Kühleborn* to 'Undine geht', the parody points ultimately to the impossibility of writing like Morgner in post-*Wende* Germany.[97] This intention underlies the parodic elements of style and structure, as well as informing the motifs and themes of the text: Hensel parodies and satirizes the montage form used by Morgner. Much remains to be said about this provocative text regarding Hensel's parodies of the character of Beatriz, in the figure of Ingrid Tabea, and major thematic issues from Morgner's novel, particularly her concern with history and the relation of fictional literature to political reality. In the following, I offer some suggestions for a rereading of the text, concentrating on the formal aspects of Hensel's parody which are pertinent to my concern with narrative grotesque.

In Morgner's novel, Laura Salman famously offers Aufbau-Verlag a montage novel on Beatriz's behalf, declaring: 'Was ich anbiete, ist die Romanform der Zukunft. Die zum operativen

---

[96] Ursula Vogel, 'Polyphoner Sirenengesang', *Neue deutsche Literatur*, 6 (1992), 130–2, here 132.

[97] It would be instructive in this respect to compare *Auditorium panopticum* with Kathrin Schmidt's *Die Gunnar-Lennefsen-Expedition* (Cologne: Kiepenheuer & Witsch, 1998). Schmidt's novel is also clearly influenced by *Beatriz* but does not invoke the critical distance which informs parody.

Genre gehört.'[98] The self-referential pronouncement, both tongue-in-cheek and serious, is echoed by Egmont Köhler in Hensel's text, who calls the 'polyphoner Roman' he is writing 'die Literatur der Zukunft' (*AP* 137).[99] But of course time has not stood still and the conditions which underlie Laura's and Morgner's use of the montage novel have changed. Half-jokingly suggested to be suitable for women writers because it fits the stop-start rhythm of their lives, the montage form was to represent an understanding of identity as continually developing (a 'sujet en procès', in Kristeva's terms) and to involve the reader in the book. Laura explains, 'Ein Mosaik ist mehr als die Summe der Steine. In der Komposition arbeiten sie seltsam zu- und gegeneinander unter den Augen des Betrachters. Lesen soll schöpferische Arbeit sein: Vergnügen.'[100] It was the reader's job to recognize and assimilate the symmetries, incongruities, and contradictions presented by the material within the text; this act of assimilation—like the involvement of the reader in the grotesque—underpins the novel's progressive aims. By the time of Hensel's text (1991), however, not only is the form itself outmoded, but these political implications and uses are also outdated. Even as early as 1984, in a study of the montage form in GDR literature, Ute Brandes signalled that the 'myth of the closed form' was coming to an end.[101] In the same way that certain grotesque hybrid figures like the mermaid have become literary tropes, what was once an anti-form, a reaction against linear narrative, is now a form in its own right.

Hensel's novel seeks to restore the original disruptive, grotesque intent of the montage novel. It attacks two main precepts of the form, namely that it draws on material from foreign sources, and that this material does not constitute a linear narrative but nonetheless contributes to a coherent meta-narrative or thematic whole. Where Morgner quoted from a range of documentary, non-literary, real sources, Hensel's text is composed

---

[98] Irmtraud Morgner, *Leben und Abenteuer der Trobadora Beatriz nach Zeugnissen ihrer Spielfrau Laura: Roman in dreizehn Büchern und sieben Intermezzos* (1974; Munich: dtv, 1994), 247.

[99] 'E. Köhler' is the authority Laura draws on in book 1, ch. 15, in order to prove Beatriz's existence.

[100] Ibid. 248.

[101] Ute Brandes, *Zitat und Montage in der neueren DDR-Prosa* (Frankfurt am Main: Peter Lang, 1984), 9 n. 22.

purely of fiction. Supposedly quoted texts—Gero's Protokolle, Friederike's diary, Egmont's rejection letters—are all invented, bringing into question the novel's basis in, and ability to refer to, reality. Furthermore, the parodies and allusions in *Beatriz* are more or less hidden; the quotations at the beginning of chapters in *Auditorium panopticum*, however, are attributed, and the parodies, pastiches, and allusions—to Remedios the Beauty, in Gabriel García Márquez's *Cien años de soledad* in Friederike's ascension, for example—are deflated by being revealed at the end of the text. In a letter to Egmont, one publisher lists the influences on his novel (which, even allowing for the exaggeration of the list, clearly resembles Hensel's); the parodic list includes Hensel, Morgner, and Simplicius simplicissimus, as well as other, real authors, García Márquez among them. Unusually for Hensel's work, this revelation denies the reader's involvement and also the reader's pleasure in interpreting and completing the work. Most importantly, these multiple parodies and allusions do not have the same function as those in Morgner's novel: instead of offering 'heterogene Blickpunkte zu einem übergreifenden Thema', they exist purely for their own sake and are not even thematically linked.[102] Hensel's parodies actually do what Morgner's parodies and conventional montage novels only appear to do: that is, they disrupt the narrative absolutely and cannot be assimilated into any thematic meta-narrative.

Auditorium panopticum overturns many of the precepts of the montage novel, as employed by Morgner. Where the parody of Bachmann's 'Undine geht' points to the problematic elements of that text and the literature it represents, however, I would suggest that the critical distance inherent in the parody of Morgner's *Leben und Abenteuer der Trobadora Beatriz* points rather to the problems of contemporary literature. The differences between the two are summed up in the way each author refers to her own work. Morgner uses the device of the found document to smuggle into her novel two previously censored works: *Rumba auf einen Herbst*, which was confiscated by the authorities in 1964, reappears as the intermezzos as 'copied' by die Schöne Melusine; and the 'Gute Botschaft der Valeska', rejected from the

---

[102] Ibid. 15.

anthology of sex-change stories for which it was commissioned, is introduced in the form of a manuscript given to Beatriz. These carefully framed excerpts represent subversive strategies which Morgner employs to confuse the politically sensitive issue of authorship. By way of contrast, in *Auditorium panopticum*, Ingrid finds a copy of Hensel's well-received prose debut, *Hallimasch*. Ingrid takes the work to be a history of Katzgrün, her putative ancestral home; and indeed, she finds nameplates by the houses of Katzgrün which feature the characters mentioned in Hensel's text. The fictional intermezzos in *Beatriz* offer a perspective on the history of the GDR—both international concerns, in the Cuban missile crisis, and domestic ones, in the changing views of the state. Hensel's self-reference, on the other hand, incorporates fiction as fictional history, short-circuiting the interaction of the real, historical, and political with literature. Moreover, her text foregrounds impotence, physical as well as political: both Gero and would-be writer Egmont are impotent; Ingrid's hunger strike is ineffectual; and even the protest march by the workers of the briquette factory, an image of those in 1989, is characterized by ignorance rather than activism: 'Mit uns zieht die neue Zeit HIER SINN MIR! WO SEID IHR! Keiner wußte, wer gemeint war' (*AP* 253). The utopian impulse of Morgner's *Beatriz* is no longer evident; Hensel is not measuring society against 'das Mögliche von übermorgen', but rather against what seemed possible in the past.[103] An often irritating, unsatisfying read, *Auditorium panopticum* forces us to consider why Morgner's approach is no longer possible, nor appropriate in post-*Wende* Germany. If nothing else, though, we can still see in this a vestige of Morgner's political concerns.

'ALLES, WAS ICH ERZÄHLE, IST ERFUNDEN':[104]
CONCLUSION

Hensel's prose texts are grotesque in both content and form. They evince the grotesque structure of 'Zerstörung und Erhaltung des Erwartungshorizontes' (Pietzcker) in representations

---

[103] This is a slogan from the sequal, Irmtraud Morgner, *Amanda: Ein Hexenroman* (1983; Hamburg: Luchterhand, 1992), 93.
[104] Hensel, in interview with Hammer, 'Gespräch mit Kerstin Hensel', 100.

of the body as well as in narrative strategies. Her texts portray distorted, unstable, or hybrid human forms; bodies which challenge conventional gender signification and perceptions of the human; and her characters perform grotesque bodily acts or are subject to urges which take over the body. Moreover, the representation of these grotesque images entails a disruption in language. Grotesque manifestations in language such as the breaking down of metaphors and syntax undermine its ability to refer to reality and its function as a medium of communication. On a narrative level, Hensel's plots and her literary parodies play with the expectations of the reader with regard to conventions of literature or knowledge of specific texts. The two are connected—her grotesque plots are, one could say, parodies of real plots. One might also suggest that her oeuvre demonstrates a grotesque trajectory, in that no two texts are the same: *Gipshut*, an ironic novel in the third person, is different from *Tanz am Kanal*, a first-person novella, is different from *Ulriche und Kühleborn*, the most poetic of Hensel's texts. The continual changing of narrative form, as well as Hensel's writing in a whole range of genres, mirrors on a large scale the jumps in register and vocabulary in texts such as *Ulriche und Kühleborn*; it disrupts her reader's expectations.

Hensel's texts also display a shift in mode, away from corporeal forms of the grotesque towards literary and linguistic forms and, ultimately, irony. This is in part a result of the change in the historical and political context of her work. Hensel's use of the mode of the grotesque was a reflection of the crisis in the state of the GDR. Her work written in the years preceding the collapse of the GDR—*Hallimasch* and the early texts included in *Neunerlei*, most notably 'Stinopel'—is the most clearly grotesque, something consistent with Bakhtin's view of the historical phenomenon of the grotesque. More recent work still deals with the now defunct state, but looks at it from an ironic perspective: distanced, judgemental, and without affect. Hensel's writing is a historical product of the GDR and, since its demise, the GDR can no longer sustain the grotesque. With increasing historical distance, representations of the GDR no longer present the threat which is intrinsic to the grotesque and therefore the texts lose some of their impact; the society portrayed in *Gipshut* is no longer the reader's society. *Gipshut* seems to lack the vitality of her earlier texts, which are more oriented towards a physical grotesque, a fact which may be related to the interpretation of Bakhtin's bodily grotesque as a kind of 'jouissance'.

The grotesque is an ambivalent mode, which both disrupts and confirms the potency of social norms and cultural signification. It may be seen as subversive or reactionary—a mere 'Ventil'—depending in part on its context and reception. It is true that Hensel's grotesque texts depended on the existence of the GDR, but this is not to say that they upheld it. I believe that Hensel's work demonstrates the subversive potential of the grotesque, in its representation of bodies, in its plots, and also in its structures. It is an attempt to challenge the absolute values of the GDR; she sees literature and art (as Alexander von Bormann suggests) as a form of 'Widerstand'.[105] Where images of the body are concerned, what the grotesque presents is not that which is outside humanity, but that which is without humanity, a telling semantic difference. Hensel's work shows how easily those who are considered different or outside society come to be dehumanized and treated violently, and in *Im Spinnhaus* in particular, she sets this within a specific historical context. According to Judith Butler, unthinkable human forms represent 'the persistent possibility of [the] disruption and rearticulation' of the human: in this view, the grotesque cannot help but be subversive.[106] The very existence and, more importantly, the visibility of grotesque, abjected beings—like Ritter Rosel—calls into question the validity of social norms which exclude them. Hensel's grotesque plots are likewise intended to provoke the reader:

Ich finde, man sollte im Wunsch nach Anderssein nicht immer den totalen Umsturz des Bestehenden sehen. Ich meine das nicht nur auf den einzelnen bezogen, sondern will in meinen Texten auch eine vorsichtigere, weil realisierbare Variante anbieten, die punktuelle Veränderung heißt. Mehr kann ein Text, Kunst, glaube ich, überhaupt nicht schaffen. Stockt einem Menschen beim Lesen eines Textes der Atem oder beschleunigt sich für Sekunden der Herzschlag, so ist eine

---

[105] See Kerstin Hensel, 'Das Eine und nicht das Andere: Zum Thema Schreiben in der DDR', *Neue deutsche Literatur*, 4 (1995), 19–23, here 20.
[106] Butler, *Bodies that Matter*, 8.

Veränderung in diesem vorgegangen, etwas Außergewöhnliches. Er ist anders geworden!¹⁰⁷

Surprise events and developments left hanging have precisely this momentary, but lasting effect on the reader. Here the ambivalence of the grotesque, the fact that it does not enact the 'totalen Umsturz des Bestehenden', is precisely its strength.

That Hensel should take this less radical approach also reflects on the political context of her work. In an article on the mode of the fantastic in GDR literature, Rainer Nägele considers the use of the metaphor of 'Boden' in the political rhetoric of the state: 'Wo immer er evoziert wird, geht es um Ausschließung, die als solche gleichzeitig verdeckt werden soll: innerhalb der Grenzen des jeweils abgesteckten Bodens ist alles erlaubt: Grenzenlosigkeit in Grenzen, ordentliche Freiheit.'¹⁰⁸ The metaphor expresses the political conditions of the GDR in terms which recall the conceptualization of the grotesque plot in spatial terms, as bordering on the limits of the readable. The metaphor underlies the literary debate about realism, according to Nägele. Freedom within bounds, transgression within limits, characterizes the position of the writer negotiating the state's literary policies, as well as the critic of the GDR's ideology. It is also the structure of the grotesque. Hensel follows this structure with regard to politics as well as literary mode. Writing in critical engagement with socialism, Hensel's texts draw on the grotesque, the fantastic and unconventional, anti-realist linguistic techniques, but they never wholeheartedly reject realism; these strategies of excess are ultimately incorporated into storytelling. Hensel's texts revel in exaggeration and foreground fictionality. But these are not purely literary strategies: Hensel's work demonstrates that telling stories is a political act.

[107] Hensel, in interview with Hammer, 'Gespräch mit Kerstin Hensel', 102.
[108] Rainer Nägele, 'Trauer, Tropen und Phantasmen: Ver-rückte Geschichten aus der DDR', in P. V. Hohendahl and P. Herminghouse (eds.), *Literatur der DDR in den siebziger Jahren* (Frankfurt am Main: Suhrkamp, 1983), 193–223, here 197.

5
INTERCHANGING INTERPRETATIONS:
CONCLUSION

My examination of the works of Herta Müller, Libuše Moníková, and Kerstin Hensel has pursued three main concerns: I considered ways of approaching the texts which recognize their social and political context as well as their aesthetic qualities, and the places where these coincide. I analysed images of the body, looking at how it can be represented in language and how these images participate in wider political discourses about the body within the Eastern Bloc countries of Romania, Czechoslovakia, and the GDR. Finally, I examined the narrative strategies employed by the three authors, which derive from their representations of the body and attempt to portray alternative views of reality. My focus has been the figures of trauma, hysteria, and the grotesque: in the works of Müller, Moníková, and Hensel, they are direct or indirect responses to the experience of the Eastern Bloc countries, and confirm 'Daß dies der Osten ist Was im Kopf nicht aufhört'.

The figure of trauma is central to Müller's work. Müller's distinctive poetic vision and narrative voice—'der Fremde Blick'—are in part the product of the repressive conditions in Romania; furthermore, for Müller, the body is the impetus to writing. The effects of trauma are represented through the dissolution of boundaries, and fragmentation, which manifest in representations of the body and narrative structures. Disembodiment, and ultimately displacement, of the self is portrayed as the body merging with the world, nature, or surrounding objects; at its most extreme, this leads to the splitting of the self and the reduction of the body to individual, autonomous parts. The dissolution of textual boundaries is seen in the interaction and mutual interference of the 'discours' and 'histoire'; impoverished syntax and gaps in the text are a form of fragmentation. These literary strategies are not abstracted from their context: alienation of the body and fragmentation are explicitly linked to physical threat, and effects such as parataxis or capitalization draw attention to the text at moments of traumatic impact or of political significance. Narrative fragmentation and emphasis on the text as a visual artefact culminate in Müller's collages, which were introduced as a motif in the 1989 text *Reisende auf einem Bein*, and have taken on greater importance in her recent work. *Reisende* is a pivotal text in Müller's narrative of trauma: through moving away from Romania in its setting, it prefigures and enables the representation of the Ceauşescu regime in subsequent texts. In Müller's work, unreal images of the body and textual disruptions reflect the reality of Romania under the Ceauşescu regime, which damaged the individual's psyche. The effects of trauma are refigured as literary and aesthetic strategies; they cannot be overcome, but they can be made legible. By splitting her artistic oeuvre into prose and collage Müller is able to testify increasingly directly to the horrors of the regime in narrative, while preserving the fragmenting, dissociating effects of trauma in literal and visual forms in collage.

Moníková's work draws on the figure of hysteria. Hysteria is a response to trauma and is linked to Czech identity in Moníková's work through the traumas of national history and the personal trauma of exile; it takes the form of mimicry and performance on both bodily and textual levels. The figure of Francine Pallas, narrator of Moníková's second text, *Pavane für eine verstorbene Infantin*, embodies both forms of hysteria: she moves from psychosomatic limp to performed disability in her use of the wheelchair, and, at the same time, her writing develops from involuntary citation of texts to parodic, irreverent revisions of Kafka. Francine displays the shift from imitation to intentional mimicry which Luce Irigaray posits as the subversive strategy of the hysteric, and which is repeated on a wider level in the development from mimicry to a thematization of performance in Moníková's later texts. Hysteria displays the vulnerability of identity and its nature as a role. The instability of identity, particularly gender identity, is highlighted by the protagonists' identification with mythical figures, in imagined scenes which draw on physical symptoms of hysteria. Additionally, Moníková's texts perform a multiplicity of gender positions through peripheral characters who reflect and modify the gender expatriation of the female protagonists. On the level of narrative, the hysteric's imitation of patriarchal discourse, the language which is not her own, is demonstrated in the use of intertextual references—from quotation to allusion and parody—and other languages. Many details of Moníková's work are drawn from autobiography; her female protagonists are her self-representation in literature and display her own concern with Czech (exile) identity. But these quotations from her own life do not bespeak authenticity: hysteria demonstrates that there is only the performance of identity and inauthentic forms of expression. Only the fragments of *Der Taumel*, Moníková's posthumously published novel, point towards a more direct representation of the trauma which is the source of hysteria.

The mode of the grotesque is evident in both the content and form of Hensel's prose texts. The grotesque challenges the form and signification of the body as well as language and narrative structures. Body, language, and narrative are subject to exaggeration and distortion; all three transgress their boundaries. Representations of the distorted or hybrid human form in Hensel's texts are strikingly physical. They focus on the body's unstable, permeable margins; portray literal combinations of the human and other; and problematize gendered attributes such as beauty and strength. The body is also grotesque in the acts which reconfigure its boundaries, in childbirth and particularly in eating and copulating, which frequently prove destructive. Physically and socially transgressive bodies in Hensel's texts also enact linguistic disruption: metaphors are literalized and syntax breaks down, undermining language's ability to refer to reality. These bodies are further implicated in narrative excess, the taking to extremes of character, plot, and narrative structures. The plots of Hensel's texts are based on structures of exaggeration and understatement. They play with the reader's expectations, refusing logic and coherence as well as literary convention. Parody might be considered a special case of narrative grotesque, which operates by simultaneously confirming and denying the reader's knowledge of the source text. Hensel's parodies highlight hybridity and physicality in both 'histoire' and 'discours', and restore the disruptive potential of forms which have become common literary tropes. Her work since the end of the GDR has moved towards irony, taking a more distanced and more judgemental perspective, which nonetheless still demonstrates an often grotesque disjunction between what is portrayed and how it is narrated. Structures in the authors' texts such as the fragmentation which is fundamental to trauma, the performance which underlies hysteria, and parody are often considered to be features of postmodern literature. This conjunction is not coincidental: both trauma and postmodernism characterize a historical moment, as Rosi Braidotti suggests, the post-war, post-Cold War time of displacement which is the background to the texts I examine.[1] In *Trauma: Zwischen Psychoanalyse und kulturellem Deutungsmuster*, Bronfen, Erdle, and Weigel contend further that trauma offers 'ein neues Deutungsmuster für Moderne und Modernität allgemein, oder wenigstens für das ausgehende 20. Jahrhundert'.[2] This is not to say that the two—trauma and postmodernism—are entirely congruent, nor that the one can simply be resolved into the other. Writing on contemporary transnational literature, although not specifically on trauma, Azade Seyhan cautions,

Although the contemporary tales of migration, exile and displacement are often seen as mirroring the fragmented consciousness of postmodern culture itself and certainly participate in many of the aesthetic and literary legacies of the latter, they part company with it in terms of certain historical and geographical boundaries. For if the postmodern is to be defined either as a sociohistorical epoch or a philosophical or aesthetic school of the late-twentieth century Western world, then it would be impossible to contain the culturally and temporally diverse articulations of diasporic experience in the postmodern syntax.[3]

As the interpretations of *Reisende auf einem Bein* demonstrate, the context in which the text is written, and which it also in turn generates, determines how we read it.[4] In the works of Müller, Moníková, and Hensel, literary devices associated with

[1] Braidotti, *Nomadic Subjects*, 2.
[2] Elisabeth Bronfen, Birgit R. Erdle, and Sigrid Weigel (eds.), *Trauma: Zwischen Psychoanalyse und kulturellem Deutungsmuster* (Cologne: Böhlau, 1999), p. vii.
[3] Seyhan, *Writing outside the Nation*, 4.
[4] See also the chapter on *Reisende* in Brigid Haines and Margaret Littler, *Contemporary German Women's Writing: Changing the Subject* (Oxford: Oxford University Press, 2004), where the two different readings—of the traces of trauma, and Irene as a postmodern city nomad—are held in balance and demonstrate that in this text, alone in Müller's work so far, it is possible and indeed necessary to read it in both ways.

postmodernism are rooted in a political and historical context, but are not limited to this context. Their works negotiate the boundary between trauma and the postmodern, demonstrating their productive interference and also the limits of that overlap.

Bringing together these three authors highlights their common ground in trauma. The three chapters of this study form a narrative, showing different responses to, and representations of, trauma. Trauma, hysteria, and the grotesque are related: hysteria is a reaction to trauma which both screens and stages traumatic impact; the grotesque, an ambivalent mode, is both a refusal of trauma and a first step towards admitting it. Their interrelation means that, although trauma, hysteria, and the grotesque are the dominant modes to date in the works of Müller, Moníková, and Hensel respectively, these interpretations are not fixed absolutely. Both Moníková and Hensel use parody, and it can be construed as either hysterical or grotesque. Certain images also cross over: the image of Karla as a woman-machine in *Treibeis* uses a common trope of the grotesque, for example, and the reaction of both the women and men of Sankt Veit, in 'Herr Johannes', resembles mass hysteria. More significantly, the authors' respective oeuvres show signs of developing away from, or towards, different modes. Müller's earliest and her most recent texts tend towards the grotesque; Moníková's later work comes increasingly close to trauma; and Hensel's texts also exhibit a growing concern with trauma, although this remains problematic.

Müller's earliest works verge in places on the grotesque, whose ambivalent nature indicates a more distanced perspective than the narratives of affect which otherwise characterize her texts. In 'Niederungen', old age is described as a gradual, uncontrollable metamorphosis of the body, the transformation of old women into old men:

Die alten Frauen schlürfen beim Frühstuck die dicke Haut von der Milch und kauen nasses Zuckerbrot und haben in den Augenwinkeln noch den Schleim der Nacht. [...]

An den Winternachmittagen sitzen sie am Fenster und stricken sich selber mit hinein in ihre Strümpfe aus kratziger Wolle, die immer länger werden und so lang sind wie der Winter selbst, die Fersen haben und Zehen und behaart sind, als könnten sie von alleine gehen.

CONCLUSION   249

Und die Nasen über den Stricknadeln werden immer länger und glänzen fettig wie gekochtes Fleisch. [...]
Während des Strickens wachsen schmächtige Barthaare aus ihrem Kinn, die immer blasser werden und grauer, und manchmal verirrt sich ein Faden davon in den Strumpf.
Ihre Schnurrbärte wachsen mit dem Alter, aus den Nasenlöchern und Warzen stehen Haare hervor. Sie sind behaart und haben keine Brüste mehr. Und wenn sie mit dem Altern fertig sind, dann gleichen sie den Männern und entschließen sich zu sterben. (*N* 33-4)

There are several grotesque images within this passage, whose basic, grotesque premiss is the mutation of the body with old age, and the instability of gender. Exaggerated or growing features (here, the nose), liminal fluids (the 'Schleim der Nacht'), the intertwining of the human and the inanimate (the beard hairs and the stockings), the description of human flesh as meat (noses are 'fettig'), and the animation of the inanimate (the stockings which could almost walk by themselves, an image which recurs as traumatic in later texts) are all grotesque. The 'dicke Haut von der Milch' also recalls Julia Kristeva's notion of the abject, closely linked to the grotesque: in *Pouvoirs de l'horreur*, she invokes precisely this image.

Müller's most recent work also seems to return to the grotesque, a sign that the damage which is constitutive of her work is no longer overwhelming. The figures in the collages can be considered grotesque: they are distorted or hybrid forms, and the 'cadavres exquis' follow a pattern of transgressing, but not breaking, rules about human bodies. Moreover, in a recent interview with Müller, Beverley Driver Eddy suggests that *Heute wär ich mir lieber nicht begegnet* displays a 'neue Leichtigkeit'.[5] Müller's reply is instructive:

Es vergeht Zeit, ich habe mich wahrscheinlich von vielem frei machen können. Und ich kann mich jetzt drauf stellen, es stellt sich nicht mehr auf mich drauf. Und das freut mich auch. Da wo sich Witz einschleicht, Sarkasmus, habe ich gesiegt.[6]

Humour is a key element of the grotesque, which is both a prelude to dealing with trauma and a measure of having overcome it. Laughter can signal denial (distance as defence mechanism)

---

[5] Müller in interview with Driver Eddy, "Die Schule der Angst", 333.
[6] Ibid.

or sovereignty. *Heute* ends with the narrator resigned, but still determined and defiant: 'Ha, ha, nicht irr werden' (*Ht* 240) are her last words.

The trauma of rape in *Eine Schädigung* was Moníková's way into writing, and her work appears to have been returning to the idea of trauma in the posthumously published *Der Taumel*.[7] *Der Taumel* is the first of her texts to depict directly the repressive regime in Czechoslovakia in the 1970s and opens with the protagonist having attended a violent interrogation. Trauma is symbolized by Jakub Brandl's epilepsy, which appears to be traumatic (or perhaps psychosomatic) in origin, as well as form. Brandl has his first fit when he catches sight of his uncle, who has returned from the Second World War: 'Als er nach zwei Monaten starb, behielt Brandl die fallende Krankheit als Erinnerung' (*Tm* 15). The description of the uncle's trauma clearly resembles an epileptic fit: 'Zum Trauern war die Leere und die Schwärze zu groß' (*Tm* 13). Significantly, Brandl inherits the trauma of his uncle's experience—perhaps, like Jan Prantl in *Treibeis*, the uncle had also been part of the Czech parachute troop—in the form of the illness known as 'falling sickness'. Cathy Caruth sees the device of falling in Paul de Man's work as a specifically modern emblem of trauma, representing spatial and temporal suspension.[8] Taking up Caruth's analysis of falling as a 'marker of the abysslike structure of trauma', Eleanor Kaufman sees its significance in linking both thought and the body; she thus characterizes the trauma itself as 'inner falling'.[9] This image also links *Der Taumel* with earlier texts: Ulrike Vedder identifies the image of falling as a key one in *Treibeis* in particular, and thus it may be a key to tracing earlier representations of trauma in Moníková's work.[10]

Given the trajectory of Müller's work, one might expect Hensel's oeuvre to display a similar progression from the grotesque to trauma. Certainly her most recent texts do contain images of trauma: the rape in *Tanz am Kanal* is one such

---

[7] See also Lyn Marven, 'Falling Down: Images of Trauma in Moníková's Fragmentary novel, *Der Taumel*', in Haines and Marven (eds.), *Libuše Moníková*.

[8] Caruth, *Unclaimed Experience*.

[9] Kaufman, 'Falling from the Sky', 49 and 52 respectively.

[10] Vedder, '"Mit schiefem Mund auch 'Heimat'"', 477–88; 'Die Intensität des Polarsommers', 16.

image, but it is problematic; Gabriele's unreliable account is as much about her writing as about trauma. *Gipshut* is more clear, with trauma represented by Veronika's unexpected, shocking suicide and Hans's destructive impulse which ends the text. On annual leave in the summer before the fall of the Wall, Veronika swims in the lake where she gave birth to Hans: 'Sie wartete auf den Schmerz. [...] Der Schmerz blieb aus' (*G* 178). Returning to her flat, she is visited by the mythical Pscheschpoldnitza, who demands that she tell a story—her story. Instead, Veronika drives her away by laughing. Typically for one of Hensel's characters, laughter is a form of release—'Es war, als platze etwas in ihr und ließe einen Schwall Heiterkeit sich ihr in den Leib ergießen' (*G* 179)—but this is not liberating, instead, it is the severing of ties. 'Nichts hielt Veronika am Leben' (ibid.), so she hangs herself. Veronika's suicide is disturbing because it reveals a capacity for despair which had up until this point been concealed, or denied, by the ironic narrative perspective.

Similarly, in post-*Wende* Berlin, Hans too seeks a form of verifiable pain: 'Der Wunsch nach einem Schmerz macht sich breit in Hans Kielkropf' (*G* 225). Hans's name illustrates the difficulty with Hensel's text: comic and exaggeratedly symbolic (of the misconceived GDR, the German changeling), it distances the reader; the continual repetition of Hans's full name refuses familiarity. Hans's and Veronika's search recalls Francine Pallas's 'Suchen nach einem authentischem Schmerz' (*P* 40), and when Hans spots the gas-leak which will blow up the Stadtschloß, 'wo einst der Bau seiner, Hansens, Zeit stand' (*G* 225), he has found what he was looking for: 'Mit freudigem Erschrecken merkt Hans, wie ein Schmerz vom Nacken über die Schläfen zur Stirn den Kopf einnimmt. Da sieht er den haarfeinen Riß im Betonfundament. [...] Die Gefahrenquelle ist entdeckt' (*G* 225–6). The pain, as well as the symbolic 'Riß' and 'Gefahrenquelle', point to trauma—explicitly linked with the GDR—which Hans can only articulate through an act of destruction. Neither is it articulated through the text: Hensel's narrative strategies do not reflect her protagonists' psyches, and the desperate measures of Veronika and her son sit uneasily in her customary ironic, distanced third-person narrative. *Im Spinnhaus*, which I have not been able to analyse in detail in this study, suggests that Hensel has a growing interest in the traumas of German history: this anecdotal, episodic narrative of rural Saxony combines the fantastic with the violence of history. In these later texts the disjunction between 'histoire' and 'discours' approaches the dissociation of trauma: in places, the laconic, distanced narrative becomes simply a literal, frank description, and the lack of emotion a form of numbness.

This examination of the relationship between representations of the body and narrative strategies in the works of Herta Müller, Libuše Moníková, and Kerstin Hensel demonstrates that these aspects are bound up with much larger concerns. The variety of their work demonstrates that 'Körper-Sprache' can take many forms, and that there is no single way of linking body and narrative. Their texts look at gender, identity, and the body, and the way these are realized in language; they are concerned with the representation of reality and the imbrication of political and narrative strategies. Bringing the three authors together, adding Hensel to the 'Kombination Müller-Moníková', as Sabine Gross phrases it, highlights both the similarity of their reactions to the common experience of the Eastern Bloc, and the differences in their representations of that experience.[11] The combination of the three different perspectives from the individual authors, far from relegating each to the specificity of their own context, rather opens out new perspectives for studying contemporary literatures in German.

[11] Gross, 'Einleitung', 441.

BIBLIOGRAPHY

This bibliography is organized as follows: primary literature by each of the three authors, subdivided into books, individual publications, and interviews; secondary literature on each of the three authors; and other sources.

Extensive bibliographies of primary and secondary literature by and about Herta Müller can be found in Norbert Otto Eke (ed.), *Die erfundene Wahrnehmung: Annäherung an Herta Müller* (Paderborn: Igel, 1991) (covering 1972–90) and in Brigid Haines (ed.), *Herta Müller* (Cardiff: University of Wales Press, 1998) (covering 1990–8). An extensive bibliography of work on or by Moníková will be published in Brigid Haines and Lyn Marven (ed.), *Libuše Moníková: In memoriam* (Amsterdam: Rodopi, forthcoming 2005). A bibliography of primary and secondary literature by and about Hensel can be found in Birgit Dahlke and Beth Linklater (eds.), *Kerstin Hensel* (Cardiff: University of Wales Press, 2002).

PRIMARY TEXTS

Herta Müller

Books

Niederungen. Prosa (Bucharest: Kriterion, 1982).

Niederungen (Berlin: Rotbuch, 1984; Reinbek bei Hamburg: Rowohlt Taschenbuch [rororo], 1993).

Drückender Tango (Bucharest: Kriterion, 1984).

Der Mensch ist ein großer Fasan auf der Welt (Berlin: Rotbuch, 1986; Reinbek bei Hamburg: Rowohlt Taschenbuch [rororo], 1995).

Barfüßiger Februar (Berlin: Rotbuch, 1987; Berlin: Rotbuch Taschenbuch, 1990).

Reisende auf einem Bein (Berlin: Rotbuch, 1989; Berlin: Rotbuch Taschenbuch, 1992).

Der Teufel sitzt im Spiegel: Wie Wahrnehmung sich erfindet (Berlin: Rotbuch, 1991).

Der Fuchs war damals schon der Jäger (Reinbek bei Hamburg: Rowohlt, 1992).

Eine warme Kartoffel ist ein warmes Bett (Hamburg: Europäische Verlagsanstalt, 1992).

Der Wächter nimmt seinen Kamm: Vom Weggehen und Ausscheren (Reinbek bei Hamburg: Rowohlt, 1993).
Herztier (Reinbek bei Hamburg: Rowohlt, 1994; Reinbek bei Hamburg: Rowohlt Taschenbuch [rororo], 1996).
Hunger und Seide (Reinbek bei Hamburg: Rowohlt, 1995; Reinbek bei Hamburg: Rowohlt Taschenbuch [rororo], 1997).
In der Falle (Göttingen: Wallstein, 1996).
Heute wär ich mir lieber nicht begegnet (Reinbek bei Hamburg: Rowohlt, 1997; Reinbek bei Hamburg: Rowohlt Taschenbuch [rororo], 1999).
Der Fremde Blick oder Das Leben ist ein Furz in der Laterne (Göttingen: Wallstein, 1999).
Im Haarknoten wohnt eine Dame (Reinbek bei Hamburg: Rowohlt, 2000).
Heimat ist das, was gesprochen wird (Blieskastel: Gollenstein, 2001).
Der König verneigt sich und tötet (Munich: Hanser, 2003).

Individual publications

'Auch das ist Schuld: das Hoffen ohne Grund' [Ricarda-Huch-Preis Rede], *Die Zeit*, 26 June 1987, p. 51.
'Rausschmisse und Entlassungen. Der rumänische Boß mehrt sein rechtmäßig erworbenes Eigentum', *die tageszeitung*, 8 Oct. 1987, p. 8.
'Wenn nur Luft berührt...', in Günter Kunert (ed.), *Aus fremder Heimat. Zur Exil-Situation heutiger Literatur* (Munich: Hanser, 1988), 78–82.
'Ich muß mir manchmal in den Finger beißen', *Die Zeit*, 11 Aug. 1989, Feuilleton p. 39.
'Der Preis des Tötens. Rumänien—Massaker und Tribunale', *Frankfurter Allgemeine Zeitung*, 29 Dec. 1989, p. 23.
'Geschichten einer nicht Erwünschten', *Neues Deutschland*, 15/16 Dec. 1990, p. 14.
'Wie Wahrnehmung sich erfindet. Poetische Überlegungen zum Prozeß des Schreibens', *Frankfurter Rundschau*, 11 May 1991, Feuilleton p. ZB2.
'Der Staub ist blind—die Sonne ein Krüppel. Beleidigt, verfolgt und in Elend gestoßen: Zur Lage der Zigeuner in Rumänien', *Frankfurter Allgemeine Zeitung*, 4 May 1991, Bilder und Zeiten.
'Das Land am Nebentisch', *Neue Zürcher Zeitung*, 6 Dec. 1991, pp. 41–2.
'Sie zittern vor Kälte und beten nicht. Zwei Jahre danach: Am Grabe Ceaucescus', *Frankfurter Allgemeine Zeitung*, 28 Dec. 1991, p. 25.
'Ahnungen sehen Tatsachen blind', *Karpaten Rundschau*, 23 Jan. 1992, pp. 4–5.
'Die Tage werden weitergehen. Nur eine militärische Intervention könnte jetzt die serbische Aggression stoppen', *die tageszeitung*, 8 Sept. 1992, p. 14.

'Staatskinder und Landeskinder. Der innere und äußere Schatten (I)', *Frankfurter Rundschau*, 15 May 1993, p. 2.
'Staatskinder und Landeskinder. Das Muster der deutschen Eigenschaften (II)', *Frankfurter Rundschau*, 22 May 1993, p. 2.
'Die Nacht sie hat Pantoffeln an: Über Inge Müllers Gedichte', *Literaturmagazin*, 34 (1994), 14–18.
'Das Ticken der Norm', *Die Zeit*, 14 Jan. 1994, pp. 49–50.
'Am Ende war es keiner gewesen. Vor zwanzig Jahren starb die Schriftstellerin Marieluise Fleißer', *die tageszeitung*, 2 Feb. 1994, p. 14.
'Von Menschen nicht mehr zu bewegen. Die serbische Landkarte ersetzt das Gewissen: Über die Wurzeln nationaler Propaganda', *Frankfurter Allgemeine Zeitung*, 27 Apr. 1994, Feuilleton p. 37.
'Meine Jahre mit Helmut Kohl', *Die Zeit*, 2 Sept. 1994, p. 56.
'Wachheit danach. Warum wir aus Diktaturen nichts lernen', *Frankfurter Allgemeine Zeitung*, 4 May 1995, p. 35.
'Wenn mein Körper mich im Stich läßt', *die tageszeitung*, 23 June 1995, Ausgabe Welt p. 17.
'Der Himmelschlüssel. Herta Müllers Rede bei der Übergabe des Stadtschreiberpreises von Bergen-Enkheim und des dazugehörigen Schlüssels am Vorabend des Berger Marktes', *Frankfurter Rundschau*, 4 Sept. 1995, p. 17.
'Es möge deine letzte Trauer sein. Notizen und Gedanken des iranischen Exilautors Said', *Die Zeit*, 11 Aug. 1995, p. 40.
'Das kleingewürfelte Gluck. Erinnerung an den Dichter Rolf Bossert', *Frankfurter Allgemeine Zeitung*, 17 Feb. 1996, p. 27.
'Das Haar auf der Schulter: Fünf Texte zur Messe in C-Dur von Franz Schubert', *Frankfurter Rundschau*, 25 May 1996, p. ZB3.
'Zungenspäße und Büßerschnee. Wie Helmut Böttiger mich durch "Orte Paul Celans" führte', *Die Zeit*, 6 Dec. 1996, Literatur p. 3.
'Heimat oder der Betrug der Dinge', in Gisela Ecker (ed.), *Kein Land in Sicht: Heimat — weiblich* (Munich: Fink, 1997), 213–19.
'Die rote Blume und der Stock', in Günther Rüther (ed.), *Literatur in der Diktatur: Schreiben im Nationalsozialismus und DDR-Sozialismus* (Paderborn: Schöningh, 1997), 53–7.
'Die Klette am Knie' (Gedichte), *Akzente*, 44/2 (1997), 104–12.
'Sarkuhi ist unschuldig. Wie halten wir es mit der Freiheit des Geistes? Ein Appell', *Die Zeit*, 1 Aug. 1997, Feuilleton, pp. 37–8.
'Minze Minze. Zum siebzigsten Geburtstag von Oskar Pastior', *Die Zeit*, 17 Oct. 1997, p. 58.
'Die Geschichte vom Huhn' (Rede zur Verleihung des Grazer Franz-Nabl-Literaturpreises), *Neue Zürcher Zeitung*, 21/2 Mar. 1997, p. 52.

'5 Collagen' and 'Einmal anfassen—zweimal loslassen', in Jürgen Wertheimer (ed.), *Zukunft! Zukunft?* (Tübingen: Konkursbuchverlag, 2000).

Interviews

AUFFERMANN, VERENA, 'Gerechtigkeit ist ein Unwort. Ein Gespräch mit der Schriftstellerin Herta Müller über die Staatssicherheit, die Sprache und die Macht', *Süddeutsche Zeitung*, 14/15/16 Aug. 1992, Feuilleton p. 15.

BEDNARZ, KLAUS, and MARX, GISELA, 'Der Fuchs war damals schon der Jäger', in *Von Autoren und Büchern: Gespräche mit Schriftstellern* (Hamburg: Hoffmann und Campe, 1997), 232–7.

DOBLER, ALEXANDER, 'Der Wind spricht nicht, sondern die Menschen sprechen. Die Erzählerin Herta Müller über menschliches Verhalten, die Macht und die Sprache', *Frankfurter Rundschau*, 12 July 1995, Feuilleton p. 7.

DRIVER EDDY, BEVERLEY, ' "Die Schule der Angst"—Gespräch mit Herta Müller, den 14. April 1998', *German Quarterly*, 72/4 (1999), 329–39.

ETZERSDORFER, IRENE, ' "Warum sind Sie enttäuscht, Herta Müller?" Ein Gespräch mit der rumäniendeutschen Autorin über ihr Land nach dem Umsturz', *Die Presse*, 24 Oct. 1992, p. vii.

FELDKAMP, HEINER, ' "Ich glaube, alle Diktaturen ähneln sich". Ein Gespräch mit der Schriftstellerin Herta Müller über Literatur, Politik und Sprache', *Strombinger Tagblatt*, 22 Jan. 1993.

HAINES, BRIGID, and LITTLER, MARGARET, 'Gespräch mit Herta Müller', in Brigid Haines (ed.), *Herta Müller* (Cardiff: University of Wales Press, 1998), 14–24.

HENKE, GEBHARD, 'Mir erscheint jede Umgebung lebensfeindlich: Ein Gespräch mit der rumäniendeutschen Schriftstellerin Herta Müller', *Süddeutsche Zeitung*, 16 Nov. 1984, p. 13.

HENSEL, KLAUS, ' "Alles, was ich tat, das hieß jetzt: warten." Die ausgewanderte rumäniendeutsche Schriftstellerin Herta Müller im Gespräch', *Frankfurter Rundschau*, 8 Aug. 1987, p. ZB2.

JAKOBS, KARL-HEINZ, ' "Das Wort 'Heimat' beanspruche ich nicht für mich." Im Gespräch mit Herta Müller', *Neues Deutschland*, 15/16 Dec. 1990, p. 14.

KROEGER-ROTH, ELISABETH, ' "Der Brunnen ist kein Fenster und kein Spiegel" oder: Wie Wahrnehmung sich erfindet. Ein Gespräch mit Herta Müller', *Diskussion Deutsch*, 26 (1995), 223–30.

MÜLLER, WOLFGANG, ' "Poesie ist ja nichts Angenehmes": Gespräch mit Herta Müller', *Monatshefte*, 89/4 (1997), 468–76.

MÜLLER-WIEFERIG, MATTHIAS, 'Kultur auf gepacktem Koffer', *die tageszeitung*, 24 Mar. 1987, pp. 11–12.
SCHOELLER, WILFRID, 'Es wird alles erstickt. Ein Gespräch mit der rumäniendeutschen Autorin Herta Müller', *Süddeutsche Zeitung*, 9/10 May 1987, SZ am Wochenende p. 1.
SCHULLER, ANNEMARIE, '"Und ist der Ort wo wir leben". Interview mit Herta Müller', in Emmerich Reichrath (ed.), *Reflexe II. Aufsätze, Rezensionen und Interviews zur deutschen Literatur in Rumänien* (Cluj-Napoca: Dacia Verlag, 1984), 121–5.
SOLDT, RÜDIGER, 'Fremder als eine Deutsche in Rumänien', *Badische Zeitung*, 20/1 Apr. 1991, BZ-Magazin p. 5.

Libuše Moníková

Books
Eine Schädigung (Berlin: Rotbuch, 1981; Munich: dtv, 1990).
Pavane für eine verstorbene Infantin (Berlin: Rotbuch, 1983; Munich: dtv, 1988).
Die Fassade. M.N.O.P.Q. (Munich: Hanser, 1987; Munich: dtv, 1990).
Schloß, Aleph, Wunschtorte. Essays (Munich: Hanser [Edition Akzente], 1990).
Unter Menschenfressern. Ein dramatisches Menu in vier Gängen (Frankfurt am Main: Verlag der Autoren, 1990).
Treibeis (Munich: Hanser, 1992; Munich: dtv, 1997).
Prager Fenster. Essays (Munich: Hanser [Edition Akzente], 1994).
Verklärte Nacht (Munich: Hanser, 1996).
Der Taumel (Munich: Hanser, 2000).

Individual publications
'Das totalitäre Glück. Franz Wedekind', *Neue Rundschau*, 96/1 (1985), 118–25.
'Und die Kirschfeste feiern, wie sie fallen. Über die Annexion Europas an Böhmen anläßlich des 50. Jahrestages des Münchener Abkommens', *Literaturmagazin*, 22 (1988), 56–62.
'Dies habe ich in den Felsen geritzt und jenes in die Mauer', *Der Literatur-Bote*, 6/23 (1991), 10–14.
'Feindbilder—Einige Überlegungen', *Jahrbuch Deutsche Akademie für Sprache und Dichtung Darmstadt*, (1993), 109–10, 179–82.
'Lebende Bilder', *Neue deutsche Literatur*, 44/3 (1996), 82–7.
'Über eine schwierige Nachbarschaft', *Die Zeit*, 7 Mar. 1997, pp. 49–50.
'Jakub Brandl', *Akzente*, 44/6 (1997), 512–36.

'Über die Kunst, greifbar zu verdächtigen', *Literaturmagazin*, 39 (1997), 22-30.
'Einige Thesen zu women's writing', *Frauen in der Literaturwissenschaft Rundbrief*, 50 (1997), 30-1.
'Der Leguan', *Literaturmagazin*, 44 (1999), 157-65.

Interviews

BRAUNBECK, HELGA G., 'Gespräche mit Libuše Moníková 1992-1997', *Monatshefte*, 89/4 (1997), 452-67.
CRAMER, SIBYLLE, 'Die Dauer der Welt beruht auf dem Fleiße des Schriftstellers: Ein Gespräch mit der deutsch schreibenden tschechischen Autorin Libuše Moníková', *Süddeutsche Zeitung*, 19/20 Sept. 1987, p. 164.
—— LAEDERACH, JÜRG, and STEINERT, HAJO, 'Libuše Moníková im Gespräch', *Sprache im technischen Zeitalter*, 119 (1991), 184-206.
DIETSCHREIT, FRANK, 'Sehnsuchtsort: Libuše Moníková über tschechische Alpträume, Heimatliebe, Leben und Schreiben im Exil', *Wochenpost*, 26 Sept. 1996, pp. 36-7.
ENGLER, JÜRGEN, 'Wer nicht liest, kennt die Welt nicht', *Neue deutsche Literatur*, 45/5 (1997), 9-23.

Kerstin Hensel

Books

Hallimasch (Halle: Mitteldeutscher Verlag, 1989; Frankfurt am Main: Luchterhand, 1989).
Auditorium panopticum (Halle: Mitteldeutscher Verlag, 1991).
Ulriche und Kühleborn (Stuttgart: Reclam Gutenberg Presse, 1991).
Im Schlauch (Frankfurt am Main: Suhrkamp, 1993).
Angestaut: Aus meinem Sudelbuch (Halle: Mitteldeutscher Verlag, 1993).
Diana! Zeichnungen von Karla Woisnitza mit einem Gespräch von Elke Erb und Kerstin Hensel (Berlin: KONTEXT Verlag, 1993).
Tanz am Kanal (Frankfurt am Main: Suhrkamp, 1994; Suhrkamp Taschenbuch, 1997).
Neunerlei (Leipzig: Kiepenheuer, 1997).
Gipshut (Leipzig: Gustav Kiepenheuer, 1999).
Der Tappeinerweg (Dresden: Die Scheune, 1999).
Im Spinnhaus (Munich: Luchterhand, 2003).

Individual publications

'Herr Johannes', *Sinn und Form*, 39/2 (1987), 972-95.
'Linie 1', *Neue deutsche Literatur*, 4 (1988), 78-9.

'Ein Maler will Hensel malen', *Deutsche Volkszeitung*, 8 Apr. 1988, p. 11.
'Wende', *Temperamente*, 1 (1990), 138.
'Ein Hausmärchen', *Deutsche Volkszeitung*, 29 June 1990, p. 13.
'Die Kette der Ricke', *Sinn und Form*, 42/1 (1990), 528.
'Das Kind. Funkmonolog', in Wilhelm Solms (ed.), *Begrenzt glücklich: Kindheit in der DDR* (Marburg: Hitzeroth, 1992), 19–26.
'Altmodisch, daß es zum Himmel schrie', *Deutsches Allgemeines Sonntagsblatt*, 8 May 1992, p. 27.
'Weiß der Teufel, was Glück ist: Über den Briefwechsel von Brigitte Reimann und Christa Wolf', *Freitag*, 9 Apr. 1993, p. 18.
'IM Positiv', *Freitag*, 23 Apr. 1993, p. 12.
'Thaiwans Leibchen: 12 Tee Aberstücke', *INN Zeitschrift für Literatur*, 10/31 (1993), 67–9.
'Über dem Jammertal', *Neue deutsche Literatur*, 1 (1993), 77–83.
'Meine Jahre mit Helmut Kohl', *Die Zeit*, 19 Aug. 1994, p. 46.
'Das Eine und nicht das Andere: Zum Thema Schreiben in der DDR', *Neue deutsche Literatur*, 4 (1995), 19–23.
'Kopfball und Verlängerung: Ein Meister aus Deutschland', *Freitag*, 5 July 1996, p. 2.
'Die Universale Hexe', *Freitag*, 2 Oct. 1998, p. v.
'Im Stoff der Parzen: Kunstdeutsch aus Zorn und Angst. Zum Roman-Fragment "Der Taumel" von Libuše Moníková', *Freitag*, 24 Mar. 2000 (source: *Freitag* web archive, **www.freitag.de/2000/13l/ 00132502.htm**).
'Das Licht von Zauche', in Birgit Dahlke and Beth Linklater (eds.), *Kerstin Hensel* (Cardiff: University of Wales Press, 2002), 1–4.

Interviews

DAHLKE, BIRGIT, 'Der Langsame Blick, der gute Text: Gespräch mit Kerstin Hensel', *Neue deutsche Literatur*, 48/4 (2000), 41–53.
DEIRITZ, KARL, and STEFANIAK, ROLF, ' "Ich teste meine Grenzen aus": Gespräch mit Kerstin Hensel', *Deutsche Volkszeitung*, 3 Nov. 1989, p. 11.
EBEL, SABINE, 'Die Schriftstellerin Kerstin Hensel: Für die Lyrik den Musenkuß, für die Prosa das Sitzfleisch', *Berliner Zeitung*, 13 Apr. 1993, p. 29.
HAMMER, KLAUS, 'Gespräch mit Kerstin Hensel', *Weimarer Beiträge*, 37/1 (1991), 93–110.
HARTINGER, WALFRIED, HARTINGER, CHRISTEL, and GEIST, PETER, 'Eine eigene Sprache finden', *Weimarer Beiträge*, 36/4 (1990), 580–616.
JAKOBS, KARL HEINZ, ' "Mein Thema ist die Dummheit": Gespräch mit Kerstin Hensel', *Neues Deutschland*, 22 Jan. 1993, p. 12.

NÉY, KARIN, ' "Letzlich will ich nichts als Aufklärer sein" ': Ein Gespräch mit Kerstin Hensel', *Temperamente*, 3 (1989), 3–7.
PASSOW, ANNE, 'Schreiben als Antwort', in Frank Hörnigk (ed.), *Stückwerk: Deutschsprachige Dramatik der 90er Jahre* (Berlin: Theater der Zeit, 1997), 51–4.
RICHTER, RONALD, 'Überall ist Grimma: Gespräch mit Kerstin Hensel', *Theater der Zeit*, 51/4 (1996), 86–7.
TRAUTH, VOLKER, ' "Indem ich schreibe, suche ich eine Antwort": Gespräch mit Kerstin Hensel', *Theater der Zeit*, 9 (1988), 59–60.
VON HALLBERG, ROBERT, interview in Robert von Hallberg (ed.), *Literary Intellectuals and the Dissolution of the State: Professionalism and Conformity in the GDR*, trans. Kenneth J. Northcott (Chicago: University of Chicago Press, 1996), 208–12.

SECONDARY LITERATURE

Secondary literature on Herta Müller

APEL, FRIEDMAR, 'Kirschkern Wahrheit. Inmitten beschädigter Paradiese: Herta Müllers *Herztier*', *Frankfurter Allgemeine Zeitung*, 4 Oct. 1994, p. L16.
—— 'Turbatverse: Ästhetik, Mystik und Politik bei Herta Müller', *Akzente*, 44/2 (1997), 113–25.
AUFFERMANN, VERENA, 'Gefahr, ins Leere zu stürzen. Westdeutschland, gesehen mit den Umsiedleraugen Herta Müllers', *Süddeutsche Zeitung*, 10 Oct. 1989, Literatur p. v.
AYREN, ARMIN, 'Lakonischer Satz, komplexe Welt: Eine Erzählung von Herta Müller', *Stuttgarter Zeitung*, 19 July 1986, p. 50.
BAUER, KARIN, 'Zur Objektwerdung der Frau in Herta Müllers *Der Mensch ist ein großer Fasan auf der Welt*', *seminar*, 32/2 (1996), 143–54.
—— 'Patterns of Consciousness and Cycles of Self-Destruction: Nation, Ethnicity, and Gender in Herta Müller's Prose', in Patricia Herminghouse and Magda Mueller (eds.), *Gender and Germanness: Cultural Productions of Nation* (Providence, RI: Berghahn, 1997), 263–75.
CRAMER, SIBYLLE, 'Provinz als mentaler Zustand: Herta Müllers neue Prosa *Barfüßiger Februar*', *Frankfurter Rundschau*, 7 Oct. 1987, p. 10.
CREUTZIGER, WERNER, 'Leidendes Land und politischer Weltschmerz', *Neue deutsche Literatur*, 41/4 (1993), 139–42.
DRIVER EDDY, BEVERLEY, 'Testimony and Trauma in Herta Müller's *Herztier*', *German Life and Letters*, 53/1 (2000), 56–72.
EKE, NORBERT OTTO, ' "Sein Leben machen | ist nicht, | sein Glück machen | mein Herr": Zum Verhältnis von Ästhetik und Politik in

Herta Müllers Nachrichten aus Rumänien', *Jahrbuch der deutschen Schillergesellschaft*, 41 (1997), 481-509.
—— (ed.), *Die erfundene Wahrnehmung: Annäherung an Herta Müller* (Paderborn: Igel, 1991).
ENGLER, JUERGEN, 'Erfahrung, leibhaft', *Neue deutsche Literatur*, 43/1 (1995), 174-6.
GLAJAR, VALENTINA, 'Banat-Swabian, Romanian and German: Conflicting Identities in Herta Müller's *Herztier*', *Monatshefte*, 89/4 (1997), 521-40.
GÖTZ, DOROTHEA, '"Vom Ende einer heilen Welt": Herta Müllers *Niederungen*', in Anton Schwob (ed.), *Beiträge zur deutschen Literatur in Rumänien seit 1918* (Munich: Verlag des Südostdeutschen Kulturwerks, 1985), 97-102.
GROSS, SABINE, 'Einleitung: Sprache, Ort, Heimat', *Monatshefte*, 89/4 (1997), 441-51.
GÜNTHER, PETRA, 'Kein Trost, nirgends: Zum Werk Herta Müllers', in Andreas Erb (ed.), *Baustelle Gegenwartsliteratur: Die neunziger Jahre* (Opladen: Westdeutscher Verlag, 1998), 154-66.
HAINES, BRIGID, 'Subjectivity (Un)bound: Libuše Moníková and Herta Müller', in Keith Bullivant, Geoffrey Giles, and Walter Pape (eds.), *Germany and Eastern Europe: Cultural Identities and Cultural Differences*, Yearbook of European Studies, 13 (Amsterdam: Rodopi, 1999), 327-44.
—— 'The Alien Gaze: The Traces of Trauma in Herta Müller's Berlin Novel *Traveling on One Leg*', paper given at EPOCC (Centre for Interdisciplinary Research in European/Post-colonial Cultures) conference on 'Migrations and Minorities', 26 May 2000, Manchester University.
—— '"The Unforgettable Forgotten": The Traces of Trauma in Herta Müller's *Reisende auf einem Bein*', *German Life and Letters*, 55/3 (2002), 266-81.
—— (ed.), *Herta Müller* (Cardiff: University of Wales Press, 1998).
HARNISCH, ANTJE, '"Ausländerin im Ausland": Herta Müllers *Reisende auf einem Bein*', *Monatshefte*, 89/4 (1997), 507-20.
HEINZ, FRANZ, 'Kosmos und Banater Provinz. Herta Müller und der unliterarische Streit über ein literarisches Debüt', in Anton Schwob (ed.), *Beiträge zur deutschen Literatur in Rumänien seit 1918* (Munich: Verlag des Südostdeutschen Kulturwerks, 1985), 103-12.
HINCK, WALTER, 'Das mitgebrachte Land. Zur Verleihung des Kleist-Preises 1994 an Herta Müller', *Sinn und Form*, 47 (1995), 141-6; also in *Kleist-Jahrbuch* (1995), 6-13.
HINTERMEIER, HANNES, 'Überleben war eben alles', *Konturen*, 3 (1992), 75-6.

JANSSEN-ZIMMERMAN, ANTJE, '"Überall, wo man den Tod gesehen hat, ist man ein bißchen wie zuhaus." Schreiben nach Auschwitz— Zu einer Erzählung Herta Müllers', *Literatur für Leser*, 4 (1991), 237–49.

KEGELMANN, RENÉ, *'An den Grenzen des Nichts, dieser Sprache...': Zur Situation rumäniendeutscher Literatur der achtziger Jahre in der Bundesrepublik Deutschland* (Bielefeld: Aisthesis, 1995).

KÖHNEN, RALPH (ed.), *Der Druck der Erfahrung treibt die Sprache in die Dichtung: Bildlichkeit in Texten Herta Müllers* (Frankfurt am Main: Peter Lang, 1997).

KRAUSS, HANNES, 'Jäger-Schnipsel. Herta Müllers Roman *Der Fuchs war damals schon der Jäger*', *Freitag*, 2 Oct. 1992, p. 27.

—— 'Fremde Blicke. Zur Prosa von Herta Müller und Richard Wagner', in Walter Delabar, Werner Jung, and Ingrid Pergande (eds.), *Neue Generation — Neues Erzählen. Deutsche Prosa-Literatur der achtziger Jahre* (Opladen: Westdeutscher Verlag, 1993), 69–76.

KUBLITZ-KRAMER, MARIA, 'Die Freiheiten der Straße: Zu Herta Müllers *Reisende auf einem Bein*', *Frauen in der Literaturwissenschaft Rundbrief*, 41 (1994), 5–8.

MOHR, PETER, 'Barfüssiger Februar. Roman', *Neue deutsche Hefte*, 35 (1988), 150–1.

OTTMERS, CLEMENS, 'Schreiben und Leben. Herta Müller, *Der Teufel sitzt im Spiegel. Wie Wahrnehmung sich erfindet*', in Paul Michael Lützeler (ed.), *Poetik der Autoren. Beiträge zur deutschsprachigen Gegenwartsliteratur* (Frankfurt am Main: Fischer, 1994), 279–94.

PREDOIU, GRAZZIELLA, *Faszination und Provokation bei Herta Müller* (Frankfurt am Main: Peter Lang, 2001).

REICHRATH, EMMERICH (ed.), *Reflexe II. Aufsätze, Rezensionen und Interviews zur deutschen Literatur in Rumänien* (Cluj-Napoca: Dacia Verlag, 1984).

SCHULLER, ANNEMARIE, 'Ihre Mittel: Arm und reich zugleich [Zur Prosa von Herta Müller]', *Karpatenrundschau*, 14 June 1985, pp. 4–5.

SCHWOB, ANTON (ed.), *Beiträge zur deutschen Literatur in Rumänien seit 1918* (Munich: Verlag des Südostdeutschen Kulturwerks, 1985).

SEILER, HELLMUT, 'Sachlich, aber phantasievoll [Zu Herta Müllers Prosaband *Niederungen*, Kriterion Verlag, Bukarest]', *Karpatenrundschau*, 12 Nov. 1982, pp. 4–5.

SOLMS, WILHELM (ed.), *Nachruf auf die rumäniendeutsche Literatur* (Marburg: Hitzeroth, 1990).

Text + Kritik, 155 (*Herta Müller*), ed. Heinz Ludwig Arnold (2002).

VON TÖRNE, DOROTHEA, 'Todesnetze, verbotene Früchte. Herta Müller entwirft in *Herztier* ein surreales Panorama der Diktatur', *Wochenpost*, 11 Aug. 1994, p. 23.

WINKLER, WILLI, 'Um den Preis einer Vorsilbe, Ausreiseantrag. Herta Müllers neue Erzählung aus einem Dorf in Rumänien', *Lesezeichen*, 7/12 (1986), 21-2.

Secondary literature on Libuše Moníková

ALMS, BARBARA, 'Fremdheit als ästhetisches Prinzip. Zu den deutschsprachigen Romanen der Tschechin Libuše Moníková', *Stint*, 3/6 (1989), 138-51.

BRAUNBECK, HELGA G., 'The Body of the Nation: The Texts of Libuše Moníková', *Monatshefte*, 89/4 (1997), 489-506.

CRAMER, SIBYLLE, 'Vaucansons Ente, das Rentier Foma Fomitsch, der Fahrradausweis des Josef K.: *Die Fassade* von Libuše Moníková—ein europäischer Roman', *Süddeutsche Zeitung*, 19/20 Sept. 1987, p. 164.

—— 'Lobrede auf Libuše Moníková' (Laudatio zur Verleihung des Adalbert-von-Chamisso-Preises), *Akzente*, 38/3 (1991), 229-35.

—— 'Triumphbogen für ein Opfer der europäischen Geschichte: Libuše Moníkovás Versuch, ein tschechisches Nationalepos zu formen: *Treibeis*', *Süddeutsche Zeitung*, 30 Sept. 1992, p. 8.

DELIUS, FRIEDRICH CHRISTIAN, 'Rede auf die Fürstin Libuše: Zum Tode von Libuše Moníková', *Deutsche Akademie für Sprache und Dichtung* (Jahrbuch 1998), 183-8.

DEUNELER, IRIS, 'Verzettelt und vertan: Zu Libuše Moníkovás Roman *Die Fassade*', *Der Tagesspiegel*, 7 Oct. 1987, Literaturblatt p. 10

FINGERHUT, KARLHEINZ, '"Ich taste nach Verhärtungen": Libuše Moníková, *Pavane für eine verstorbene Infantin*', *Diskussion Deutsch*, 26 (1995), 236-8.

GROSS, SABINE, 'Einleitung: Sprache, Ort, Heimat', *Monatshefte*, 89/4 (1997), 441-51.

HAINES, BRIGID, '"New Places from Which to Write Histories of Peoples": Power and the Personal in the Novels of Libuše Moníková', *German Life and Letters*, 49/4 (1996), 501-12.

—— 'Subjectivity (Un)bound: Libuše Moníková and Herta Müller', in Keith Bullivant, Geoffrey Giles, and Walter Pape (eds.), *Germany and Eastern Europe: Cultural Identities and Cultural Differences* (Amsterdam: Rodopi, 1999), 327-44.

—— and MARVEN, LYN (eds.), *Libuše Moníková: In memoriam* (Amsterdam: Rodopi, forthcoming 2005).

HEISSENBÜTTEL, HELMUT, 'Inwendige Traurigkeit: Libuše Moníkovás *Pavane für eine verstorbene Infantin*', *Frankfurter Rundschau*, 10 Mar. 1984, p. ZB4.

JÄHNER, HARALD, 'Dreizehn Fenster: Libuše Moníkovás Ausblicke', *Frankfurter Allgemeine Zeitung*, 21 Nov. 1994, p. 5.

JANKOWSKY, KAREN, 'Remembering Eastern Europe: Libuše Moníková', *Women in German Yearbook*, 12 (1996), 203–15.

―― 'Between "Inner Bohemia" and "Outer Siberia": Libuše Moníková Destabilizes Notions of Nation and Gender', in Karen Jankowsky and Carla Love (eds.), *Other Germanies: Questioning Identity in Women's Literature and Art* (Albany, NY: State University of New York Press, 1997), 119–46.

KRECHEL, URSULA, 'Blicke ins Zentrum der Macht. Libuše Moníkovás Erzählung *Eine Schädigung*', *Lesezeichen*, 3 (1981), 25.

―― 'Die Flucht der Fürstin in die Literatur. Libuše Moníkovás zweite Erzählung: *Pavane für eine verstorbene Infantin*', *Lesezeichen*, 7 (1983), 19.

KUBLITZ-KRAMER, MARIA, *Frauen auf Straßen: Topographie des Begehrens in Erzähltexten von Gegenwartsautorinnen* (Munich: Fink, 1995).

Literaturmagazin, 44 (1999) (*Prag-Berlin: Libuše Moníková*).

LITTLER, MARGARET, 'Beyond Alienation: The City in the Novels of Herta Müller and Libuše Moníková', in Brigid Haines (ed.), *Herta Müller* (Cardiff: University of Wales Press, 1998), 36–56.

MANSBRÜGGE, ANTJE, *Autorkategorie und Gedächtnis: Lektüren zu Libuše Moníková* (Würzburg: Königshausen & Neumann, 2002).

MARVEN, LYN, 'Women in Wheelchairs: Space, Performance and Hysteria in Libuše Moníková's *Pavane für eine verstorbene Infantin* and Ines Eck's *Steppenwolfidyllen*', *German Life and Letters*, 53/4 (2000), 511–28.

PIZER, JOHN, 'The Disintegration of Libussa', *Germanic Review*, 73/2 (1998), 145–60.

RADISCH, IRIS, 'Ein freier Mensch: Zum Tod der Schriftstellerin Libuše Moníková', *Die Zeit*, 22 Jan. 1998, p. 46.

ROSENSTRAUCH, HAZEL, 'Libuše Moníková *Die Fassade*', *L80*, 44 (1987), 158–60.

SCHWIDTAL, MICHAEL, 'Kunst im Zeichen der Diktatur: Libuše Moníkovás Roman *Der Taumel*', *Neue deutsche Literatur*, 48/4 (2000), 107–16.

TRUMPENER, KATIE, 'Is Female to Nation as Nature is to Culture? Božena Němcová, Libuše Moníková, and the Female Folkloric', in Karen Jankowsky and Carla Love (eds.), *Other Germanies: Questioning Identity in Women's Literature and Art* (Albany, NY: State University of New York Press, 1997), 99–118.

VEDDER, ULRIKE, '"Mit schiefem Mund auch 'Heimat"'—Heimat und Nation in Libuše Moníkovás Texten', *Monatshefte*, 89/4 (1997), 477–88.

―― '"Ist es überhaupt noch mein Prag?" Sprache der Erinnerung in der Literatur Libuše Moníkovás', in Helga Abret and

Ilse Nagelschmidt (eds.), *Zwischen Distanz und Nähe: Eine Autorinnengeneration in den 80er Jahren* (Bern: Peter Lang, 1998), 7-27.

―― 'Die Intensität des Polarsommers: Zu Libuše Moníkovás Roman Treibeis', *Frauen in der Literaturwissenschaft Rundbrief*, 41 (1994) ('Osteuropa'), 15-17.

Secondary literature on Kerstin Hensel

BAUME, BRITA, ' "Mein Thema war nie die DDR" (Hensel). Zur Literatur junger Autorinnen der DDR vor und nach 1989', in Helga Grubitzsch, Eva Kaufmann, and Hannelore Scholz (eds.), *'Ich will meine Trauer nicht leugnen und nicht meine Hoffnung': Veränderungen kultureller Selbstwahrnehmungen von ostdeutschen und osteuropäischen Frauen nach 1989* (Bochum: D. Winckler, 1994), 57-69.

BAUREITHEL, ULRIKE, 'Risse im Beton: Kerstin Hensel gräbt nach den Überresten der DDR', *Der Tagesspiegel*, 13 Oct. 1999 (source: *Tagesspiegel* web archive, **www2.tagesspiegel.de/archiv/1999/10/12/ ak-ku-li-sa-15264.html**).

BRANDT, MARION, 'Turnvater Unser: Zur Sportthematik in ausgewählten literarischen Texten', in Helga Grubitzsch, Eva Kaufmann, and Hannelore Scholz (eds.), *'Ich will meine Trauer nicht leugnen und nicht meine Hoffnung'* (Bochum: D. Winckler, 1994), 81-93.

COSENTINO, CHRISTINE, ' "Die Gegensätze Übergänge": Ostdeutsche Autoren Anfang der neunziger Jahre', *Germanic Review*, 69 (1994), 146-55.

DAHLKE, BIRGIT, ' "Im Brunnen vor dem Tore": Autorinnen in inoffiziellen Zeitschriften der DDR 1979-90', in Walter Delabar, Werner Jung, and Ingrid Pergande (eds.), *Neue Generation — Neues Erzählen. Deutsche Prosa-Literatur der achtziger Jahre* (Opladen: Westdeutscher Verlag, 1993), 177-93.

―― *Papierboot: Autorinnen aus der DDR — inoffiziell publiziert* (Würzburg: Königshausen & Neumann, 1997).

―― 'Traumtanz mit Klumpfüßen', *Neue deutsche Literatur*, 48/1 (2000), 180-2.

―― and LINKLATER, BETH (eds.), *Kerstin Hensel* (Cardiff: University of Wales Press, 2002).

FRANKE, KONRAD, 'Prosa probieren. Das erzählerische Debüt der Lyrikerin Kerstin Hensel', *Süddeutsche Zeitung*, 14 Nov. 1989, Literaturbeilage p. 48.

―― 'Stoff aus Stinopel', *Süddeutsche Zeitung*, 30 Apr.-2 May 1993, p. iv.

HINCK, WALTER, 'Simplizissima unter der Brücke: Kerstin Hensels Schelmenerzählung *Tanz am Kanal*', *Frankfurter Allgemeine Zeitung*, 2 Nov. 1994, p. 36.

KAUFMANN, EVA, 'Kerstin Hensel, *Hallimasch*: Erzählungen', in Siegfried Rönisch (ed.), *DDR-Literatur '89 im Gespräch* (Berlin: Aufbau, 1990), 230–40.

―――― 'Violine Statt Dackel', *Neue deutsche Literatur*, 1 (1995), 176–9.

KUBLITZ-KRAMER, MARIA, 'Literatur von Frauen der neunziger Jahre', *Der Deutschunterricht*, 51/4 (1999), 46–58.

LANGE, SIGRID, 'Topographische Irritationen: Frauenliteratur nach dem Ende der DDR', *Colloquia Germanica*, 27 (1994), 255–73.

LEHMANN, HORST H., 'Absurdität unseres Lebens', *Neues Deutschland*, 13 Nov. 1991, Kritik und Lektüre p. 14.

MADEA, ANDRZEJ, 'Das ES gegen das ICH: Neue Texte von Kerstin Hensel und Gabriele Kachold', *Freitag*, 21 Dec. 1990, p. 21.

MEYER-GOSAU, FRAUKE, 'Aus den Wahnwelten der Normalität: Über Brigitte Kronauer, Elfriede Jelinek und Kerstin Hensel', in Heinz Ludwig Arnold (ed.), *Vom gegenwärtigen Zustand der deutschen Literatur* (Munich: text + kritik, 1992), 26–37.

PÜSCHEL, URSULA, 'Ohne eine Spur Angst oder Hoffnung', *Neue deutsche Literatur*, 8 (1993), 129–34.

SALZWEDEL, JOHANNES, 'Ein Leben für den Grottenolm. Kerstin Hensel zeigt sich sehr weltläufig', *Frankfurter Allgemeine Zeitung*, 22 Nov. 1991, p. 34.

SCHMIDT, CLAUDIA, 'Grenzüberschreitung', *Unsere Zeit*, 28 Dec. 1989, p. 6.

SCHMIDT, KATHRIN, 'Frühkindliche Infektion mit Gedrucktem: Ein konservatives Stück Text. Kerstin Hensels neuer Roman "Gipshut"', *Freitag*, 8 Oct. 1999 (source: *Freitag* web archive, **www.freitag.de/ 1999/41/99411091.htm**).

SIEBENEICHER, STEFAN, 'Atemstöße und Lebensläufe: Sieben Rezensogramme', *Neue deutsche Literatur*, 4 (1997), 145.

VOGEL, URSULA, 'Polyphoner Sirenengesang', *Neue deutsche Literatur*, 6 (1992) 130–2.

OTHER SOURCES

ADAMOWICZ, ELZA, *Surrealist Collage in Text and Image: Dissecting the Exquisite Corpse* (Cambridge: Cambridge University Press, 1998).

ADELSON, LESLIE, *Making Bodies, Making History: Feminism and German Identity* (Lincoln: University of Nebraska Press, 1993).

ARNOLD, HEINZ LUDWIG (ed.), *Bestandsaufnahme Gegenwartsliteratur* (Munich: text + kritik, 1988).

ATKINS, ROBERT, and KANE, MARTIN (eds.), *German Monitor: Retrospect and Review: Aspects of the Literature of the GDR 1976–1990* (Amsterdam: Rodopi, 1997).

ATTIAS, REINA, and GOODWIN, JEAN (eds.), *Splintered Reflections: Images of the Body in Trauma* (New York: Basic Books, 1999).

BACHMANN, INGEBORG, *Das dreißigste Jahr* (Munich: dtv, 1966).

―― *Der Fall Franza* [with *Requiem für Fanny Goldmann*] (Munich: dtv, 1981).

―― *'Todesarten'-Projekt*, ed. Monika Albrecht and Dirk Göttsche (Munich: Piper, 1995).

BAKHTIN, MIKHAIL, *The Dialogic Imagination*, trans. Caryl Emerson and Michael Holquist (Austin: University of Texas Press, 1981).

―― *Rabelais and his World*, trans. Hélène Iswolsky (Bloomington: Indiana University Press, 1984).

BAMMER, ANGELIKA (ed.), *Displacements: Cultural Identities in Question* (Bloomington: Indiana University Press, 1994).

BARTHES, ROLAND, 'L'Effet du réel', *Communications*, 11 (1968), 84–9.

BATHRICK, DAVID, *The Powers of Speech: The Politics of Culture in the GDR* (Lincoln: University of Nebraska Press, 1995).

BEATLES, THE, *Sergeant Pepper's Lonely Hearts Club Band* (1967).

BEVAN, DAVID (ed.), *Literary Gastronomy* (Amsterdam: Rodopi, 1988).

BLACKSHINE-BELAY, CAROL AISHA (ed.), *The German Mosaic: Cultural and Linguistic Diversity in Society* (Westport, Conn.: Greenwood Press, 1994).

BOOTH, WAYNE C., *A Rhetoric of Irony* (Chicago: University of Chicago Press, 1975).

BORGES, JORGE LUIS, *El Aleph* (Madrid: Alianze/Emecé, 1971).

BRAIDOTTI, ROSI, *Nomadic Subjects: Embodiment and Sexual Difference in Contemporary Feminist Theory* (New York: Columbia University Press, 1994).

BRANDES, UTE, *Zitat und Montage in der neueren DDR-Prosa* (Frankfurt am Main: Peter Lang, 1984).

―― (ed.), *Zwischen gestern und morgen: Schriftstellerinnen der DDR aus amerikanischer Sicht* (Schöneiche bei Berlin: Peter Lang, 1992).

BRONFEN, ELISABETH, 'Exil in der Literatur: Zwischen Metapher und Realität', *arcadia*, 28/2 (1993), 167–83.

―― *The Knotted Subject: Hysteria and its Discontents* (Princeton: Princeton University Press, 1998).

―― 'Mourning becomes Hysteria: Zum Verhältnis von Trauerarbeit zur Sprache der Hysterie', in Gisela Ecker with Maria Kublitz-Kramer (eds.), *Trauer tragen – Trauer zeigen: Inszenierungen der Geschlechter* (Munich: Fink, 1999), 31–55.

BRONFEN, ELISABETH ERDLE, BIRGIT R., and WEIGEL, SIGRID (eds.). *Trauma: Zwischen Psychoanalyse und kulturellem Deutungsmuster* (Cologne: Böhlau, 1999).

BROOKE-ROSE, CHRISTINE, *A Rhetoric of the Unreal: Studies in Narrative & Structure, Especially of the Fantastic* (Cambridge: Cambridge University Press, 1981).

—— *Stories, Theories and Things* (Cambridge: Cambridge University Press, 1991).

BROOKS, PETER, *Reading for the Plot: Design and Intention in Narrative* (1984; Cambridge, Mass.: Harvard University Press, 1992).

BULLIVANT, KEITH, GILES, GEOFFREY, and PAPE, WALTER (eds.), *Germany and Eastern Europe: Cultural Identities and Cultural Differences*, Yearbook of European Studies, 13 (Amsterdam: Rodopi, 1999).

BUTLER, JUDITH, *Bodies that Matter: On the Discursive Limits of 'Sex'* (New York: Routledge, 1993).

—— *Gender Trouble: Feminism and the Subversion of Identity*, 10th Anniversary edn. (New York: Routledge, 1999).

CAMUS, ALBERT, *Le Mythe de Sisyphe* (Paris: Gallimard, 1942).

CARUTH, CATHY, *Unclaimed Experience: Trauma, Narrative, and History* (Baltimore: Johns Hopkins University Press, 1996).

—— (ed. and introds.), *Trauma: Explorations in Memory* (Baltimore: Johns Hopkins University Press, 1995).

CHIELLINO, CARMINE (ed.), *Interkulturelle Literatur: Ein Handbuch* (Stuttgart: J. B. Metzler, 2000).

CIXOUS, HÉLÈNE, with CLÉMENT, CATHERINE, *La Jeune Née* (Paris: Union Générale des Éditions, 1975).

CURRIE, MARK, *Postmodern Narrative Theory* (Basingstoke: Macmillan, 1998).

CURTI, LIDIA, *Female Stories, Female Bodies: Narrative, Identity and Representation* (Basingstoke: Macmillan, 1998).

DALMOLIN, ELIANE, *Cutting the Body: Representing Woman in Baudelaire's Poetry, Truffaut's Cinema, and Freud's Psychoanalysis* (Ann Arbor: University of Michigan Press, 2000).

DELETANT, DENNIS, *Ceaușescu and the Securitate: Coercion and Dissent in Romania, 1965–1989* (London: C. Hurst & Co., 1995).

DEMETZ, PETER, *Prague in Black and Gold: The History of a City* (London: Penguin, 1997).

Diacritics, 28/4 (1998) (*Trauma and Psychoanalysis*).

ECKER, GISELA (ed.), *Kein Land in Sicht: Heimat — weiblich* (Munich: Fink, 1997).

—— with KUBLITZ-KRAMER, MARIA (eds.), *Trauer tragen — Trauer zeigen: Inszenierungen der Geschlechter* (Munich: Fink, 1999).

EIGLER, FRIEDERIKE, and PFEIFFER, PETER C. (eds.), *Cultural Transformations in the New Germany: American and German Perspectives* (Columbia, Mo.: Camden House, 1993).
Elizabeth, dir. Shekhar Kapur (Universal, 1998).
ELLMANN, MAUD (ed.), *Psychoanalytic Literary Criticism* (Harlow: Longman, 1994).
EMMERICH, WOLFGANG, *Die andere deutsche Literatur* (Opladen: Westdeutscher Verlag, 1994).
―― *Kleine Literaturgeschichte der DDR, Erweiterte Ausgabe* (Leipzig: Kiepenheuer, 1996).
ERB, ANDREAS (ed.), *Baustelle Gegenwartsliteratur: Die neunziger Jahre* (Opladen: Westdeutscher Verlag, 1998).
FELMAN, SHOSHANA, *Le Scandale du corps parlant: Don Juan avec Austin ou la séduction en deux langues* (Paris: Seuil, 1980).
FOWLER, ROGER, *Linguistics and the Novel* (London: Methuen, 1977).
FULBROOK, MARY, *Anatomy of a Dictatorship: Inside the GDR 1949–1989* (Oxford: Oxford University Press, 1995).
FUNK, NANETTE, and MUELLER, MAGDA (eds.), *Gender Politics and Post-Communism: Reflections from Eastern Europe and the Former Soviet Union* (New York: Routledge, 1993).
FURST, LILIAN (ed.), *Realism* (London: Longman, 1992).
Genders, 22 (1995) (*Postcommunism and the Body Politic*).
GENETTE, GÉRARD, *Figures II* (Paris: Seuil, 1969).
GILBERT, SANDRA M., and GUBAR, SUSAN, *The Madwoman in the Attic: The Woman Writer and the Nineteenth-Century Literary Imagination* (New Haven: Yale University Press, 1979).
GRIMM, BRÜDER, *Kinder- und Hausmärchen, Jubiläumsausgabe* (Stuttgart: Philipp Reclam, 1980, 1984), vols. i and ii.
GRUBITZSCH, HELGA, KAUFMANN, EVA, and SCHOLZ, HANNELORE (eds.), *'Ich will meine Trauer nicht leugnen und nicht meine Hoffnung': Veränderungen kultureller Selbstwahrnehmungen von ostdeutschen und osteuropäischen Frauen nach 1989* (Bochum: D. Winckler, 1994).
HAASE, DONALD (ed.), *The Reception of Grimms' Fairy Tales: Responses, Reactions, Revisions* (Detroit: Wayne State University Press, 1993).
HAINES, BRIGID, and LITTLER, MARGARET, *Contemporary German Women's Writing: Changing the Subject* (Oxford: Oxford University Press, 2004).
HEIDSIECK, ARNOLD, *Das Groteske und das Absurde im modernen Drama* (Stuttgart: Kohlhammer, 1969).
HERMAN, JOST, and SILBERMAN, MARC (eds.), *Contentious Memories: Looking Back at the GDR* (New York: Peter Lang, 1998).

HERMINGHOUSE, PATRICIA, and MUELLER, MAGDA (eds.), *Gender and Germanness: Cultural Productions of Nation* (Providence, RI: Berghahn, 1997).
HOOPER, JOHN, 'East German Drugs Pushers Escape Jail', *Guardian*, 19 July 2000 (source: www.guardian.co.uk/international/story/0,3604,344746,00.html).
HUTCHEON, LINDA, *A Theory of Parody: The Teachings of Twentieth-Century Art Forms* (London: Methuen, 1985).
—— *The Politics of Postmodernism* (London: Routledge, 1989).
—— *Irony's Edge: The Theory and Politics of Irony* (London: Routledge, 1994).
IRIGARAY, LUCE, *Ce sexe qui n'en est pas un* (Paris: Minuit, 1977).
JACOBUS, MARY, 'Madonna: Like a Virgin; or, Freud, Kristeva and the Case of the Missing Mother', *Oxford Literary Review*, 8/1–2 (1986), 35–50.
JANKOWSKY, KAREN, and LOVE, CARLA (eds.), *Other Germanies: Questioning Identity in Women's Literature and Art* (Albany, NY: State University of New York Press, 1997).
KAFKA, FRANZ, *Sämtliche Erzählungen* (Frankfurt am Main: Fischer, 1970).
—— *Das Schloß*, ed. Malcolm Pasley (Frankfurt am Main: S. Fischer, 1981).
—— *Der Proceß*, ed. Malcolm Pasley (Frankfurt am Main: Fischer, 1993).
KAUFMAN, ELEANOR, 'Falling from the Sky: Trauma in Perec's *W* and Caruth's *Unclaimed Experience*', *Diacritics*, 28/4 (1998), 44–53.
KAYSER, WOLFGANG, *Das Groteske: Seine Gestaltung in Malerei und Dichtung* (Oldenburg: Gerhard Stalling, 1957).
KRISTEVA, JULIA, *Pouvoirs de l'horreur* (Paris: Seuil, 1980).
LIESSMAN, KONRAD PAUL, '"Ekel! Ekel! Ekel!—Wehe mir!" Eine kleine Philosophie des Abscheus', *Kursbuch*, 129 (1997), 101–10.
LINKLATER, BETH V., *'Und immer zügelloser wird die Lust': Constructions of Sexuality in East German Literatures* (Bern: Peter Lang, 1998).
LIPSCOMB, HARRY S., and HOFF, HEBBEL E., 'Saint Uncumber or La Vierge Barbue', *Bulletin of the History of Medicine*, 37 (1963), 523–7.
LÜTZELER, PAUL MICHAEL (ed.), *Poetik der Autoren. Beiträge zur deutschsprachigen Gegenwartsliteratur* (Frankfurt am Main: Fischer, 1994).
—— (ed.), *Schreiben zwischen den Kulturen: Beiträge zur deutschsprachigen Gegenwartsliteratur* (Frankfurt am Main: Fischer Taschenbuch, 1996).
MARTIN, BIDDY, *Woman and Modernity: The (Life)Styles of Lou Andreas-Salomé* (Ithaca, NY: Cornell University Press, 1991).

MAZZOLENI, DONNA, 'The City and the Imaginary', *New Formations*, 11 (1990), 91–104.
MAZZONI, CRISTINA, *Saint Hysteria: Neurosis, Mysticism and Gender in European Culture* (Ithaca, NY: Cornell University Press, 1996).
MOI, TORIL, *Sexual Textual Politics* (London: Routledge, 1985).
MOLINA, TIRSO DE, *El burlador de Sevilla* (1630).
Monatshefte, 89/4 (1997) (volume devoted to Müller and Moníková).
MORGNER, IRMTRAUD, *Leben und Abenteuer der Trobadora Beatriz nach Zeugnissen ihrer Spielfrau Laura: Roman in dreizehn Büchern und sieben Intermezzos* (1974; Munich: dtv, 1994).
—— *Amanda: Ein Hexenroman* (1983; Hamburg: Luchterhand, 1992).
MOZART, WOLFGANG AMADEUS, with DA PONTE, LORENZO, *Il dissoluto punito, ossia Il Don Giovanni* (1787).
MUDRY, ANNA, *Gute Nacht, du Schöne: Autorinnen blicken zurück* (Frankfurt am Main: Luchterhand, 1991).
MUECKE, D. C., *The Compass of Irony* (London: Methuen, 1969).
NÄGELE, RAINER, 'Trauer, Tropen und Phantasmen: Ver-rückte Geschichten aus der DDR', in P. V. Hohendahl and P. Herminghouse (eds.), *Literatur der DDR in den siebziger Jahren* (Frankfurt am Main: Suhrkamp, 1983), 193–223.
PARKES, STUART, PREECE, JULIAN, and WILLIAMS, ARTHUR (eds.), *Contemporary German Writers, their Aesthetics and their Language* (Bern: Peter Lang, 1996).
PAUL, GEORGINA, 'Towards *The Politics of Narration*. Narrative Theory and GDR Prose Literature', in Robert Atkins and Martin Kane (eds.), *Retrospect and Review: Aspects of the Literature of the GDR 1976–1990*, German Monitor, 40 (Amsterdam: Rodopi, 1997), 62–74.
PIETZCKER, CARL, 'Das Groteske', *Deutsche Vierteljahrsschrift*, 45 (1971), 197–211.
PLETT, HEINRICH F. (ed.), *Intertextuality*, Research in Text Theory/ Untersuchungen zur Texttheorie, 15 (Berlin: de Gruyter, 1991).
RADY, MARTYN, *Romania in Turmoil: A Contemporary History* (London: IB Tauris & Co., 1992).
REMMLER, KAREN, 'Sheltering Battered Bodies in Language: Imprisonment Once More?', in Angelika Bammer (ed.), *Displacements: Cultural Identities in Question* (Bloomington: Indiana University Press, 1994), 216–32.
RICHIE, ALEXANDRA, *Faust's Metropolis: A History of Berlin* (London: HarperCollins, 1998).
RIORDAN, JAMES (ed.), *Sport under Communism: The USSR, Czechoslovakia, the GDR, China, Cuba* (London: C. Hurst & Co., 1978).

RIORDAN, JAMES, and KRÜGER, ARND (eds.), *The International Politics of Sport in the Twentieth Century* (London: E & FN Spon, 1999).

ROBERTS, KATHERINE, 'The Wandering Womb: Classical Medical Theory and the Formation of Female Characters in *Hamlet*', *Classical and Modern Literature: A Quarterly*, 15/3 (1995), 223–32.

RÖNISCH, SIEGFRIED (ed.), *DDR-Literatur '89 im Gespräch* (Berlin: Aufbau, 1990).

SANDFORD, JOHN (ed.), *Encyclopedia of Contemporary German Culture* (London: Routledge, 1999).

SCARRY, ELAINE, *The Body in Pain: The Making and Unmaking of the World* (New York: Oxford University Press, 1985).

SCHMIDT, KATHRIN, *Die Gunnar-Lennefsen-Expedition* (Cologne: Kiepenheuer & Witsch, 1998).

SCHMIDT, RICARDA, 'Im Schatten der Titanin: Minor GDR Women Writers—Justly Neglected, Unrecognised or Repressed?', *German Monitor*, 29 (1993), 151–62.

SCHULZ, GENIA, 'Kein Chorgesang. Neue Schreibweisen bei Autorinnen (aus) der DDR', in Heinz Ludwig Arnold (ed.), *Bestandsaufnahme Gegenwartsliteratur* (Munich: text + kritik, 1988).

SEYHAN, AZADE, *Writing outside the Nation* (Princeton: Princeton University Press, 2001).

SHOWALTER, ELAINE (ed.), *The New Feminist Criticism: Essays on Women, Literature and Theory* (London: Virago Press, 1986).

SMEED, J. W., *Don Juan: Variations on a Theme* (London: Routledge, 1990).

SONTAG, SUSAN, *Illness as Metaphor* (New York: Farrar, Straus and Giroux, 1978).

STEPHAN, INGE, WEIGEL, SIGRID, and WILHELMS, KERSTIN (eds.), *'Wen kümmert's, wer spricht': Zur Literatur und Kulturgeschichte von Frauen aus Ost und West* (Cologne: Böhlau, 1991).

STROWICK, ELISABETH, 'Hinken, zur Atopie der Metapher', *Frauen in der Literaturwissenschaft Rundbrief*, 45 (1995), 33–8.

THOMSON, PHILIP, *The Grotesque* (London: Methuen, 1972).

TODOROV, TZVETAN, *Introduction à la littérature fantastique* (Paris: Seuil, 1970).

—— *Genres du discours* (Paris: Seuil, 1978).

VENSKE, REGULA, *Das Verschwinden des Mannes in der weiblichen Schreibmaschine: Männerbilder in der Literatur von Frauen* (Hamburg: Luchterhand, 1991).

VICE, SUE (ed.), *Psychoanalytic Criticism: A Reader* (Cambridge: Polity Press, 1996).

VON BORMANN, ALEXANDER, 'Das Groteske in der deutschen Gegenwartslyrik', *Études germaniques*, 43 (1988), 142–57.

BIBLIOGRAPHY

WAHLIN, CLAES (ed.), *Perspectives on Narratology* (Frankfurt am Main: Peter Lang, 1996).

WALKER, SUSAN, and HIGGS, PETER (eds.), *Cleopatra of Egypt: From History to Myth* (London: British Museum Press, 2001).

WEEDON, CHRIS, *Feminist Practice and Poststructuralist Theory* (Oxford: Basil Blackwell, 1987).

—— (ed.), *Postwar Women's Writing in German* (Oxford: Berghahn, 1997).

WEIGEL, SIGRID, *Topographien der Geschlechter* (Reinbek: Rowohlt, 1990).

—— *Bilder des kulturellen Gedächtnisses. Beiträge zur Gegenwartsliteratur* (Dülmen-Hiddingsel: tende, 1994).

—— *Die Stimme der Medusa*, 2nd edn. (Dülmen-Hiddingsel: tende, 1995).

—— *Entstellte Ähnlichkeit: Walter Benjamins theoretische Schreibweise* (Frankfurt am Main: Fischer Taschenbuch, 1997).

—— (ed.), *Die verborgene Frau* (Berlin: Argument Verlag, 1983).

WESTRUP, Sir JACK, and HARRISON, F. Ll., *Collins Encyclopedia of Music*, rev. Conrad Wilson (1959; London: Chancellor Press, 1976).

ZIPES, JACK, *The Brothers Grimm: From Enchanted Forests to the Modern World* (London: Routledge, 1988).

INDEX

1989 15, 51, 73, 181, 186, 233, 240
abject, the 28, 33, 35, 49, 249
abortion 18, 20, 72
agency 23, 57, 68, 79, 80, 81, 82, 178
alienation 45, 46, 47, 49, 54, 59,
    70–9, 84, 143, 148, 151, 152,
    183, 244
allegory 9, 24, 29, 41, 51, 87, 115, 119,
    125, 134, 181, 233, 234
alter ego 57, 87, 144, 147, 175, 216
Andersen, Hans Christian 230–1
android 130, 135–6, 137, 138
anger 74, 86
animals 62, 63, 99, 100, 194, 195, 197,
    206–7
appetite 41, 204–5, 206, 208, 209–10
associative links 89–91, 98
authenticity 9, 15, 16, 36, 39, 41, 42,
    121, 122, 128, 130, 131, 133,
    143, 148, 151, 153, 154–5, 157,
    171, 173–4, 246
autobiography 12, 42, 57, 111, 121,
    176–7

Bachmann, Ingeborg 40, 41, 112,
    140
    Anrufung des großen Bären 171 n. 82
    Der Fall Franza 40, 117–18, 123, 127,
        140, 170–1
    'Undine geht' 195, 197, 218, 228,
        234–5, 236, 237, 239
Bakhtin, Michael 49, 158, 162, 182,
    188, 190, 191, 201, 203, 210,
    229, 235, 236, 241, 242
Banat, the 11, 37, 56, 65, 84, 110
Barthes, Roland 160, 172 n. 84
Beatles, the 162
beauty 21, 27, 41, 138, 147, 183,
    194
Beethoven 159, 161
Berlin 68, 69, 73, 251
binary structures 32, 63, 150, 196
birth 20, 25, 189, 191, 192–3, 197, 251
bodily fluids 34–5, 182, 190–2, 249
body 7–8, 9–10, 15, 38, 39, 44, 45,
    46, 48, 49, 53, 60, 61–83,
    106–8, 110, 115, 116, 117, 118,
    121, 122–56, 180, 182–3,
    188–217, 241, 242, 244, 246,
    248–9
    artificial 132, 133, 135, 137–8, 140,
        141
    as beyond control 189–90, 192,
        193, 204, 212
    body image 144–6, 189–204; *see
        also* alienation; beauty;
        femininity; fragmentation;
        splitting; strength
    body parts 47, 57, 58, 63, 66, 71,
        78, 79, 86, 103, 106–7, 182,
        202–3, 249; *see also individual
        entries*
    body shape 32, 45, 49, 108, 144, 182
    boundaries of 21–2, 33–5, 45, 49,
        54, 55, 56, 57, 61, 62–70, 80,
        99, 134, 152, 182–3, 188, 189,
        190–2, 202, 204, 205, 232, 246
    damaged 122, 123–9, 132, 134, 190,
        195, 199
    disproportionate 197, 201
    interior of 20, 33, 35, 36, 56, 59,
        133, 138
    and language 27–36, 55, 58, 82,
        117, 186, 204, 214–16
    in literature 27–8, 29–30, 122, 127,
        128
    as metaphor 29, 34, 123, 124
    state appropriation of 1, 16–27
    as suffering 9, 10, 32, 122
    borders 19, 49, 67, 80, 81
    see also boundaries
Borges, Jorge Luis 126, 136, 161, 164
boundaries 22, 31, 33–5, 45, 51, 52,
    59, 63, 69, 73, 80–1, 83,
    84–95, 99, 109, 110, 219, 229,
    243, 244, 246
Bronfen, Elisabeth 8, 46, 47, 116, 117,
    118, 125, 247
Butler, Judith 27, 28, 32–4, 35, 46,
    117, 133, 134, 149, 177, 189,
    242

capital letters 102, 215, 235, 245
Caruth, Cathy 43, 44, 45, 56, 119,
    250

276 INDEX

causality 74, 80, 97, 218
Ceauşescu, Nicolae 12, 19, 51, 53, 56,
    62, 65, 67, 79, 83, 89, 100, 110,
    245
Ceauşescu, Elena 36-7
Celan, Paul 26 n. 49, 112
chance 94, 104, 135
choreography 24, 115, 148, 155-6
city 66, 68, 69, 155-6
Cixous, Hélène 196
Cleopatra 130, 138, 143
clothes 71, 85, 132, 137, 145, 146-7,
    249
code 93, 95
collage 12, 53, 95, 103-9, 110-11,
    245, 249
complicity 37-8, 39, 42, 47, 50, 57,
    83, 85-6, 103, 113, 147, 230
condensation of images 92, 93,
    94-5
contemporary literature 1-8, 9-10,
    239, 247, 252
contingency 69, 93, 95, 103, 173, 184
    see also chance
Czech literature 164
Czechoslovakia 1, 13, 17, 22-4, 38, 51,
    118, 119, 124, 125, 156, 172,
    250
    1968 invasion by Warsaw Pact
        troops 118, 119, 125, 179

dance 134, 155, 156
    see also choreography
death 19, 23, 43, 53, 63, 67, 71, 74,
    77, 80-1, 82-3, 87, 88, 92, 94,
    97, 105, 129, 131, 132, 134, 135,
    138, 139, 140, 156, 161, 166,
    191, 205, 208, 219, 226, 230
desire 31, 61, 116, 191, 198, 204, 207,
    208, 210-12, 214-17, 219-20,
    221
detail 59, 70, 97, 102, 107, 156,
    175, 176, 209, 221, 223,
    224
dictatorship 8, 12, 56, 96, 112
    see also Ceauşescu, Nicolae
différance 5, 58
    see also difference
difference 4, 5, 6, 51, 109, 124, 167,
    219, 221, 222
disability 126, 128-9, 166
'discours' 54, 83, 84, 87, 88, 89, 91,
    92, 94, 102, 103, 104, 109, 113,
    158, 159, 161, 163, 165, 167,
    185, 189, 193, 197, 200, 200,
    208, 217, 220, 244, 252
disgust 48, 49, 74, 191
disruption of expectations 16, 48, 49,
    159, 182, 185, 218, 224, 225,
    234, 235, 241
dissociation 45, 47, 57, 61, 69, 71, 77,
    83, 84, 88, 103, 108, 111, 130,
    135, 141, 252
Don Juan 41, 210-11, 213-14, 217,
    220, 228
doubles 35, 54, 56, 72-3, 151, 154-5
    see also alter ego; splitting
dreams 44, 90, 98, 102 n. 72, 130,
    139, 176, 213

Eastern Bloc 1, 2, 4, 8, 9, 10, 11,
    16-27, 36, 43, 244, 252
eating 67, 90, 204-10
    see also food
emotion 57, 74-6, 99, 131, 135, 180,
    252
    see also anger; fear; love
epilepsy 39, 178-9, 250
ethnicity 39, 118
exaggeration 31, 127, 144, 147, 181,
    197, 209, 211, 218, 220, 243
exile 8, 43, 51, 104, 105, 115, 118-20,
    121, 125, 144, 149, 175, 245
eye 57, 79, 98

face 66, 71, 72, 86-7, 91, 190
fairy tales 169, 188, 199, 206 n. 48,
    228, 229-34
fantastic, the 88, 91, 243, 252
fashion, *see* clothes
father 56, 74, 85-6
fear 48, 57, 71, 74, 75-6, 102, 195,
    197
femininity 38, 40, 124, 132-3, 137,
    140, 142, 143, 144-8, 151, 152,
    153, 194-9
feminism 7, 9, 36-42
feminist theory 7, 9, 10, 27-36, 37,
    113, 157-8
fetishism 128
fictionality 84, 87, 111, 117, 177, 185,
    200, 217, 243
film 154-5, 158, 165
fingers 72, 76-7, 79
food 25, 183, 205-6, 207, 209

INDEX

foreign languages 4, 43, 51, 52, 115, 119, 121, 136, 157–8, 167–73
Czech 2, 13, 119, 158, 168, 170, 172–3
English 131 n. 31, 138, 162, 164 n. 68, 168, 169–70
German 4, 8, 13, 119, 158, 164, 168, 170, 172–3
Russian 150, 162, 164, 169, 170
fragmentation 46, 52, 54, 55, 56, 59, 61, 67, 71, 77–9, 81, 83, 84, 95–103, 106, 109, 110, 111, 244, 245, 247
Freud 116, 117, 163, 203, 219
friendships 38, 53, 57

gaps 47, 51, 117, 119, 121, 136, 140
  in memory 44, 116; *see also* memory
  in narrative 44, 95, 98–100, 121
  psychic 46, 116, 178
  in text 31, 54, 60, 84, 95, 100, 125, 156, 244
GDR 1, 8, 14, 17, 24–6, 51, 181, 186, 187, 205, 226, 227, 233, 234, 240, 241–3, 251
GDR literature 1–7, 42, 181, 185, 186, 233–4, 238, 243
gender 9, 16, 19, 25, 26, 28, 32–3, 37, 41, 42, 46, 115, 118, 121, 122, 130, 132, 133, 134, 137, 140, 143–53, 174, 178, 183, 194, 200, 211, 241, 245, 249
  grammatical 144, 145, 148–9
genitive formulations 93
Germany 5, 7, 73, 186, 237, 240
gestures 31, 32, 33, 73, 215
grammar 96, 127, 150
  grammatical subject/object 63, 72, 73 n. 35, 84, 86
  see also gender, grammatical
Greenland 135, 171–2
Grimm, the Brothers 112, 229–30, 231–3
grotesque, the 4, 10, 16, 18, 26–7, 31, 35, 36, 42, 43, 51–2, 67, 76, 108, 189, 190, 191, 192, 193, 194, 195, 197, 198, 201, 203, 204, 205, 206, 210–11, 213–14, 218–19, 220, 222, 226, 229, 231, 232, 235, 236, 238, 240–3, 244, 246–7, 248–50
  and language 186, 200, 201, 203–4
  and social criticism 181, 184, 187, 206, 210–11, 220, 241, 242–3
  theory of 48–50, 180–8
  and trauma, *see* trauma and the grotesque;
  see also disruption of expectations; exaggeration; hybrid forms; etc.

hands 76, 137, 194
Hatshepsut 122, 130, 139, 140–1, 143, 153
Hensel, Kerstin xi, 1, 4, 9, 10, 14, 17, 18, 19, 24–7, 32, 35, 36, 40–2, 43, 50, 51, 52, 99, 113, 180–243, 244, 246–7, 248, 250–2
  reception of work 14, 16, 180, 236–7
  Angestaut 210–11, 212, 213, 214, 237
  Auditorium panopticum 14, 25–6, 41, 188, 191, 194, 197–9, 200–4, 209–10, 211, 215–16, 228, 229, 234, 236–40
  Gipshut 14, 51, 193–4, 220, 227, 228, 241–2, 251
  Hallimasch xi, 14, 25, 26, 41, 180, 183, 185, 186, 189–90, 1, 192–3, 193, 194–5, 197, 204–6, 207, 208, 210, 211, 212, 213–14, 215–17, 220–3, 225, 226, 227, 230, 232–3, 240, 241, 242, 248
  Im Schlauch 14, 41, 51, 220, 225, 226–7
  Im Spinnhaus 14, 208, 242, 251–2
  Neunerlei 14, 186, 194, 207, 208–9, 211, 212–13, 214, 220, 223–5, 226, 227, 229, 230–1, 233, 241
  Tanz am Kanal 14, 18, 24, 42, 51, 191, 216, 241, 250–1
  Ulrike und Kühleborn 14, 194, 195–7, 228, 229, 234–6, 237, 241
  'Das Licht von Zauche' 199–200, 229
  'Die Kette der Ricke' 206–7
  'Ein Hausmärchen' 230, 231–2, 233
heterosexuality 144, 149–50

INDEX

'histoire' 54, 83, 84, 87, 88, 89, 91, 92, 95, 103, 104, 109, 113, 115, 123, 158, 161, 163, 165, 167, 170, 184, 189, 197, 217, 244, 252
history 8, 9, 10, 13, 15, 45, 49, 118, 120, 131, 137, 140, 141, 157, 164, 178, 181, 237, 240, 245, 252
homosexuality 146, 149
horror 48, 63, 70, 182, 185, 191, 192, 208, 226–7
humans as objects 21, 23, 26, 49, 108, 184
humour 40, 67, 163, 167, 169, 175, 185, 189, 191, 192, 194, 209, 249–50
see also laughter
hybrid forms 183, 186, 195, 196–7, 229, 235, 238, 241, 246, 249
hysteria 4, 10, 15, 18, 24, 27, 30, 35, 40, 43, 51, 52, 115, 123, 124, 125, 126, 128, 129–30, 137 n. 38, 138, 140, 141, 153, 156–8, 159, 162, 166, 167, 168, 170, 174–5, 177, 184, 212, 215, 220, 228, 244, 245–6, 247, 248
in feminist theory 27, 31–32, 40, 121–122, 123–124, 157–158; *see also* Irigaray
and melancholy 125
theory of 46–8, 49, 50, 116–22, 167
and trauma, *see* trauma, and hysteria; *see also* imitation; mimicry; performance; etc.

identity 5, 45, 46, 53, 61, 63, 64, 68, 73, 76, 79, 81, 115, 117, 118, 120, 122, 126, 135, 136, 157, 174, 185, 210, 238, 245–6, 252
ethnic 118 n. 10
gender 33, 41, 115, 118, 130, 133, 137, 138, 143, 146, 148, 151, 178, 245; see also gender
national 5, 15, 118, 120, 125, 130, 143, 144, 149, 175, 178, 245; *see also* nationality
as performed 33, 123, 133, 153–4; *see also* performance
imitation 33, 40, 115, 117, 123, 129, 166–7, 176, 229, 236, 237, 246
see also mimicry

incest 180, 221, 222
incongruity 67, 99, 108, 109, 168, 169, 171, 187, 194, 231, 235
intercultural literature 1–2, 5, 6, 8 *see also* literatures by immigrant or ethnic German writers
interrogation 19, 37, 53, 54, 57, 61, 70, 78–9, 81–2, 83, 84, 97, 162
intertextuality 39, 43, 52, 112–13, 115, 117, 121, 128, 129, 136, 142, 157, 158–67, 174, 175–6, 177, 229–40, 246
theory of 159, 160, 161, 162
Irigaray, Luce 28, 29–32, 47, 113, 122, 123–4, 127, 147, 170, 245
irony 38, 41, 42, 50, 52, 151, 180, 185, 193–4, 199, 200, 216, 217, 229, 241, 246
theory of 186–8
italics 160, 161, 162, 168, 215

Janáček 130, 131, 161
The Makropulos Case 130, 139, 155, 162, 176
juxtaposition 109

Kafka, Franz 40, 112, 129, 131, 144, 157, 160–1, 162, 165, 245
Das Schloß 40, 112 n. 95, 129, 131 n. 31, 135, 161, 166–7
Der Proceß 160–1, 162, 165–6
'Das Stadtwappen' 173
'Der Bau' 128, 165
'Ein Landarzt' 128
'Körper-Sprache' 28, 29–31, 39, 45, 115, 124, 127, 128, 214, 252
Kristeva, Julia 28, 29, 34–5, 189, 214, 238, 249
Kümmernus 130, 136–7

Lacan, Jacques 56, 215, 219
landscape 64, 66, 67, 201–2
language acquisition 28, 34–5, 45, 55–6, 58
laughter 32, 48, 49, 79, 147, 182, 189–90, 249–50, 251
layout of text 100, 101–2
Libuše (founder of Prague) 122, 128, 130, 131, 132, 133 n. 33, 139, 141, 143, 153, 168 n. 77
Lilith 41, 207, 215–16, 228

INDEX

limp 115, 117, 123–6, 127, 129, 175, 245
literatures by immigrant or ethnic German writers 1–8
love 38, 63, 64–5, 139, 194

madness 183, 212–13
make-up 72, 147, 154
marginalization 6, 34, 37, 38, 41, 47–8, 117, 123, 126, 196
margins 34, 35, 124, 180
 see also boundaries
masculinity 145, 148, 149, 152, 189, 195, 196, 197
Mazzoleni, Donna 68, 69 n. 28
memory 44, 46, 60, 99, 104, 116, 117, 126, 135–6
menstruation 141–2, 191
merging of self and world 56, 58, 59, 61, 62–70, 83, 99, 192, 201–2, 244
 see also body, boundaries of
metaphor 26, 64, 68, 75, 80, 89, 93, 94, 95, 96, 103, 104, 107, 111, 124, 131, 144, 186, 200, 201, 202, 241, 243, 246
metonymy 57, 76, 79, 107
mimicry 10, 31–2, 40, 46, 47, 52, 61, 73, 75, 83, 113–14, 115, 119, 121, 122, 123–4, 127, 129, 137, 142, 147, 153–4, 174, 221, 245
 see also imitation; parody
minority literature
 see also literatures by immigrant or ethnic German writers 1
mirrors 56, 62–3, 84–8, 92, 108, 134, 147
Moníková, Libuše 1, 2, 4, 5, 7, 9, 10, 13, 17, 18, 19, 21, 22–4, 30, 32, 35, 36, 38–40, 42, 43, 50, 51, 52, 113, 115–79, 217–18, 244, 245–6, 247, 248, 250, 252
 autobiographical aspects of work 143, 144, 175, 176–7, 246
 reception of works 2, 4, 5, 13, 14–15
 use of German 4, 5, 13, 119, 165, 167, 168, 170, 173, 174
 Die Fassade: M.N.O.P.Q. 13, 39, 40 n. 88, 122, 146, 148–51, 156–7, 159, 161, 162, 163–4, 168–71, 174, 175, 176, 177

Der Taumel 13, 18, 39, 51, 162, 175, 178–9, 246, 250
Eine Schädigung 13, 40, 115, 119, 122, 123, 125, 141–2, 143, 144–5, 146–8, 151, 152, 153–4, 162–3, 165, 174, 177, 178, 179, 250
Pavane für eine verstorbene Infantin 13, 35, 39, 40, 113, 115, 117–18, 119, 121, 122, 123–9, 130, 131–5, 136, 138–9, 141, 142, 143, 145, 146, 153, 156, 158, 159, 160–1, 162, 163, 164, 165, 166–7, 168, 173, 174, 175, 176, 177, 245, 251
Prager Fenster 4–5 n. 8, 13, 23–4, 38, 40 n. 88, 118, 177
Schloß, Aleph, Wunschtorte 13, 40, 126, 158, 161, 163 n. 67, 165, 167, 177
Treibeis 13, 39, 115, 117 n. 6, 118, 119–20, 121, 122, 128 n. 28, 130, 135–9, 141, 142, 143, 145, 146, 153, 156, 161, 162, 163, 164, 165–6, 171–2, 173, 174, 175, 177, 178 n. 94, 248, 250
Unter Menschenfressern 13, 167 n. 76, 177
Verklärte Nacht 13, 22–3, 35, 40, 51, 115, 118, 120, 121, 122, 127 n. 27, 130, 139–41, 142, 143, 144, 145–6, 151–2, 153, 155–6, 159, 161–2, 163, 165, 172–3, 174, 175, 176, 177, 178
montage 102, 235, 237, 238–9
Morgner, Irmtraud 41, 218, 228, 236–40
mother 37, 38, 56, 63, 85, 98, 100, 121 n. 17, 150, 152
Müller, Herta x, 1, 2, 3, 4, 5, 7, 8, 9, 10, 11–12, 17, 18, 19, 20–1, 22, 30, 35, 36–8, 42, 43, 50, 51, 52, 53–114, 181, 204, 217–18, 235, 244–5, 247, 248–50, 252
 poetological writing 53, 57–61, 87, 89, 96, 98, 110; see also below *Der Teufel sitzt im Spiegel*
 reception of work 2–3, 4, 5, 11–12, 14–15, 53, 61
Barfüßiger Februar 12, 18, 22, 57, 72, 76–7, 86–7, 92, 98 n. 67, 101, 112

Müller, Herta (*cont.*)
Der Fremde Blick oder Das Leben ist ein Furz in der Laterne 12, 54, 70, 77 n. 42, 80, 102
Der Fuchs war damals schon der Jäger 3, 12, 19, 20, 57, 67, 71, 75, 78–9, 80, 81, 82, 88–9, 92–3, 96–7, 98 n. 67, 100, 101, 102, 112
Der König verneigt sich und tötet 21
Der Mensch ist ein großer Fasan auf der Welt 4 n. 8, 12, 20, 36, 37–8, 74, 80, 83, 85–6, 87, 89–90, 91, 98 n. 67, 100–1, 112
Der Teufel sitzt im Spiegel 12, 35, 57, 58–60, 61, 66, 70, 72, 77–8, 79, 80 n. 44, 84, 89, 92 n. 61, 96, 104, 110, 113, 114
Der Wächter nimmt seinen Kamm x, 12, 43, 54, 67, 74, 104, 105, 106, 107, 109, 110; see also collage
Drückender Tango x, 11, 54, 62, 65, 69, 71
Eine warme Kartoffel ist ein warmes Bett 12, 66
Herztier 12, 19, 20, 37, 38, 53, 56, 57, 66, 71, 74, 75, 76, 77, 78, 79, 80–3, 87–8, 93, 94–5, 97, 101, 102 n. 72, 107, 111–12
Heute wär ich mir lieber nicht begegnet 12, 38, 72, 77, 83, 97, 110, 111, 249–50
Hunger und Seide 5, 8, 12, 18, 19, 20–1, 76 n. 41, 102, 112
Im Haarknoten wohnt eine Dame x, 12, 54, 104, 105–6, 107, 108, 109, 110; see also collage
In der Falle 12,112, 113
Niederungen x, 11, 56, 61, 62, 63–5, 68, 83, 84–5, 88, 90, 97–100, 201, 248–9
Reisende auf einem Bein 3, 12, 53, 54, 56–7, 61–2, 63, 67–70, 71 n. 32, 72, 76, 77, 103, 111, 112, 113, 245, 247
'Das Haar auf der Schulter' 70
'Das Land am Nebentisch' 65, 77–8
multiculturalism 5
murder 18, 19, 24, 80 n. 47, 82, 83, 184, 208, 220, 222, 223–4
myth 40, 41, 121, 122, 129, 130, 132, 138, 139, 140, 142, 215, 236

names 125, 143–4, 150, 158, 159, 194, 196, 220, 234, 251
narrative 11, 44, 45, 42, 60, 61, 62, 74, 82, 83–103, 110, 111, 115, 117, 119, 120, 121, 155, 156–79, 180, 185, 186, 215, 216–17, 218–40, 244
see also gaps, in text; intertextuality; narrative perspective; parataxis; parody; plot; etc.
narrative perspective 37, 39, 42, 50, 59, 73, 83, 88, 94, 99, 100, 135, 142, 143, 147, 156, 159, 196, 200, 201, 215, 216, 217, 241, 251
nation, the 9, 18, 22, 134, 143, 144, 155
nationalism 26, 149, 168
nationality 8, 15, 39, 118–19, 120, 121, 124, 130, 131 n. 31, 149
naturalness 33, 121, 122, 130, 132, 135, 142
see also authenticity
nature 41, 62, 63–4, 65, 151, 194, 198–9, 201–2

objects 50, 56, 57, 69, 71, 72, 74, 75, 77, 80, 104
see also humans as objects
outsiders 13, 14, 31, 33–4, 36, 41, 51, 54, 72, 124, 126, 127, 146, 180, 195, 219, 242

pain 9, 23, 51, 55–6, 80, 82, 123–5, 131, 136, 141–2, 193, 251
Palach, Jan 18, 23, 82, 144
parataxis 44, 52, 54, 74, 81, 84, 96–8, 101, 105, 111, 156, 193, 245
parody 32, 33, 40, 41, 43, 113, 158, 159, 165–7, 174, 188, 191, 215, 218, 227, 228–40, 241, 246, 247, 248
theory of 166–7, 229, 236
patriarchy 31, 32, 36, 38, 40, 113, 122, 123, 127, 152, 157–8, 198, 246
performance 15, 32–3, 36, 46, 52, 115, 117, 118, 119, 120, 121, 123, 127, 128, 130, 143, 146, 148, 150, 152, 153–6, 157, 163, 166, 174, 245–6, 247
text as 52, 121, 130, 142, 153, 156, 157, 158, 170, 174, 175, 178, 216

INDEX   281

physicality 24, 28, 46, 53, 54, 58, 60,
    66, 84, 115, 122, 128, 143, 155,
    174, 190, 191, 193, 197, 199,
    246
plot 43, 74, 111, 180, 185, 204,
    217–28, 231, 242–3, 246
theory of 218–20, 227, 241
poetic function 55, 83, 101, 103
poetry 64, 76, 78, 81, 82, 94, 95, 96,
    100, 102, 105–6, 112
political literature 2, 3, 4, 12, 13, 22,
    44
politics 10, 22, 23, 46
postcards 74, 104, 105, 110
postmodern literature 11, 39, 46, 58,
    61, 73, 113, 129, 157, 161, 162,
    172, 185, 247–8
Prague 13, 130, 131, 136, 139, 155–6,
    172, 173, 178
Prague Spring 13, 51, 178
prosthetics 128, 132, 133–4, 137, 175,
    194
punctuation 74, 93, 121, 190, 216

quotation 52, 157, 158, 159–64, 166,
    176, 239
theory of 159
see also intertextuality

rape 24–5, 44, 48, 115, 122, 144,
    146–7, 148, 151, 179, 190, 200
    n.40, 250
Ravel 129, 131, 159
reader's involvement in text 50, 85,
    94, 95, 97, 100, 114, 165, 185,
    187, 217, 222, 229, 230, 238,
    239, 246
see also disruption of expectations
realism 11, 55, 59, 88, 89, 168, 169,
    185, 199, 221, 243
'récit' 84 n. 50, 88, 89, 167, 170
reflections, *see* mirrors
register 150, 200, 202, 235, 241
repression, political 1, 4, 8, 12, 19, 38,
    51, 53, 54, 65, 75–6, 79–83,
    102, 105, 111, 113, 181
repression, psychological 48, 50, 60,
    184, 205, 208, 211, 232–3
resistance to hegemonic structures
    (state/society) 22, 28, 32, 34,
    38, 43, 79, 124, 184, 189
see also writing as political
    opposition/social criticism

Riefenstahl, Leni 130, 139, 143
Romania 1, 11–12, 17, 19–22, 51, 53,
    54, 62, 65, 66, 67, 68, 69, 70,
    74, 77, 78, 80, 97, 105, 244,
    245
Romanian-German literature 2

Scarry, Elaine 55, 56, 60–1, 69, 80,
    82, 113
Schmidt, Arno 40, 163
Securitate (Romanian secret police) 11,
    18, 19, 20, 54, 70, 71, 76, 77,
    78, 79–83, 89, 93, 97, 100, 101,
    102, 105, 107
sex 20, 21, 37, 38, 41, 62, 85, 86, 94,
    131, 136, 144, 151, 152, 183,
    202–3, 204, 207, 208, 209–10,
    213, 214, 216–17
sexuality 9 n. 22, 19, 21, 25, 33, 34,
    37, 38, 74, 92, 116, 138, 180,
    190, 195, 196, 198, 206, 210–14
Shakespeare 117, 138, 162, 164
Sibyl of Cumae 134, 176
society 5, 32, 33, 34, 41, 47, 49, 50,
    124, 126–7, 134, 137, 145, 183,
    189, 191, 192, 198, 211, 225,
    232, 240
Spartakiada 22–3, 145–6, 155, 156,
    176
splitting 28, 45, 51, 55, 56, 58, 61, 69,
    71, 72–4, 84, 100, 110–11, 155,
    183, 244, 245
sport 18, 20–1, 22–3, 25–6, 193
strength 27, 183, 188, 196, 197
subjectivity 7, 9, 23, 24, 30, 31, 32, 47,
    58, 61, 114, 117, 143, 153, 190,
    204, 210, 212
suicide 23, 80 n. 47, 82, 97, 105, 184,
    251
symbols 63, 67, 69, 75, 76, 92, 93, 94,
    98, 102, 104, 140, 209, 211,
    220, 233
syntax 30–2, 35, 43, 60, 74, 96, 98,
    103, 105, 169, 186, 202, 204,
    215, 241, 244, 246

tense 45, 58, 75, 90–1, 98, 145, 156
theatricality 121, 127, 128, 147–8,
    150–1, 216
see also performance
topography 69, 122, 131, 144, 156, 213
torture 43, 53, 55–6, 61, 80, 81
see also interrogation

trauma 4, 8, 10, 15, 18, 22, 24, 30, 35, 38, 51, 53–61, 62, 63, 66, 67, 70, 71, 73, 76, 77, 79, 82, 83, 91, 93, 95, 99, 100, 103, 104, 106, 110–11, 112, 113, 114, 120, 126, 145, 147, 152, 178–9, 244–5, 246, 247–8, 249, 250–2
and exile 8, 51, 118, 119, 121, 125, 245, 247
and the grotesque 48, 49, 50, 181–2, 183, 184, 248, 249
historical 10, 118, 125, 247
and hysteria 46, 47, 48, 116, 117, 130, 156, 178–9, 245, 248
theory of 43–6, 55–61, 82, 103, 111
see also alienation; dissociation; fragmentation; splitting; etc.
trees 65, 75, 92–3
typography 95, 101–2, 105, 160, 235
see also capital letters; italics; punctuation

ugliness 41, 183, 188, 194–6
see also beauty
Uncumber, see Kümmernus
Undine, see Bachmann, 'Undine geht'
unreal, the 58, 60, 63, 74, 76, 84, 86–92, 103
urges ('Triebe') 183–4, 204, 208–9, 210, 214–17, 220
utopia 39, 93, 173

Velvet Revolution 51, 178
see also 1989
violence 19, 24, 40, 44, 53, 60, 63, 65, 68, 71, 76, 78, 80, 95, 98, 99–100, 105, 125, 180, 184, 204, 233
voice 9, 60, 73, 75 n. 38, 114, 150, 154, 226

war 41, 105, 139
Second World War 74, 85, 137, 205–6
Weigel, Sigrid 9, 16, 28, 29–30, 41, 112, 122, 159, 186, 214–15, 247
Wende 1, 3, 14, 51, 237
see also 1989
West German literature 9, 112
West Germany 11, 20–1, 80, 124
wheelchair 13, 115, 123, 124, 125, 126, 127–8, 129, 134, 156, 166, 176, 245
women's writing 6–7, 9, 29, 41–2, 122
writing, fictional images of 87–8, 112, 129, 139, 212–13, 216–17, 251
writing as political opposition/social criticism 3, 18, 22, 23, 24, 36, 38, 55, 65, 75, 77, 83, 93, 95, 100, 102–3, 111, 114, 146, 187, 193–4, 220, 223, 228, 233, 234, 237, 242–3
Woolf, Virginia 39, 128, 176